HUMAN ADJUSTMENT AND PERSONAL GROWTH: SEVEN PATHWAYS

FRANK J. BRUNO
San Bernardino Valley College

JOHN WILEY & SONS
New York   Santa Barbara
London   Sydney   Toronto

This book was printed and bound by Quinn & Boden, Inc.
It was set in Helvetica Light by Cherry Hill Composition.
The drawings were designed and executed by John Balbalis
with the assistance of the Wiley Illustration Department.
Penny Doskow supervised production.

The text and cover were designed by
Edward A. Butler.

Library of Congress Cataloging in Publication Data

Bruno, Frank Joe, 1930-
   Human adjustment and personal growth.

   Includes bibliographies and index.
   1. Adjustment (Psychology)   2. Self-actualization
(Psychology)   I. Title.

BF335.B74   155.2′5   76-54654
ISBN 0-471-11435-9

FOR JEANNE

PREFACE

TO THE INSTRUCTOR

It is possible to organize an adjustment-growth textbook in one of several ways.

1 A widely employed approach is to organize the book around what might be called "arenas of life." There are chapters devoted to the challenges of college, career, marriage, child-rearing, one's sexuality, and other domains of human concern. Advantages of this approach are that the book will be practical, relevant, and close to the problems of daily living. A drawback is the problem of redundancy. The same key principles are pertinent to various contexts, and must reappear in more than one setting. However, there may be no appropriate place to develop adequately such subjects as unconscious motivation, defense mechanisms, behavior modification, assertiveness training, emotional self-control, biofeedback, and the search for meaning in existence. The impact of these subjects is diluted when they are fragmented and spread throughout the text.

2 A second approach is to organize the text in terms of a principle orientation such as behavioral psychology or transactional analysis. By presenting a unified world view, systematic books often have a substantial impact on the thinking of the student. However, a difficulty with such textbooks is that many important concepts are simply left out. Also, their extreme bias may leave the student with the incorrect notion that there is one Royal Pathway toward greater adjustment and personal growth.

3 A third approach is to organize the book in such a way as to give primary attention to principles and concepts. Books so organized are eclectic, covering a wide spectrum of orientations toward adjustment and growth. The present book utilizes the third approach. For some time it has been my conviction that many of the principles and concepts of behavioral science may be construed as *psychological tools,* mental instruments by which we can more successfully cope with the challenges of human existence. Thus in the present book the emphasis is on these principles and concepts, including methods, management techniques, and coping devices by which persons effectively deal with the problems of day-to-day living. These psychological tools are illuminated by many examples drawn from all walks of human activity to provide a textbook with the breath of life in it. As such, *Human Adjustment and Personal Growth: Seven Pathways* is intended to be both academically sound as well as practical.

TO THE STUDENT

The psychology of adjustment and growth is a subject of universal interest, an exciting field of study with many dimensions and applications. A survey of a number of college catalogs reveals the following topics that tend to be stressed in adjustment-growth courses.

Personality dynamics
Defense mechanisms
Emotional self-control
Psychotherapy
Modifying habits
Mental health
Human potentialities
Human relations
Self-understanding
Conceptions of normality and abnormality
Applications of principles to daily living

The above list gives you a preview of some of the subjects discussed in the present book. All of the topics revolve around the core idea of leading a more gratifying and meaningful life—a unifying idea in this book.

Human Adjustment and Personal Growth: Seven Pathways has been designed to facilitate your study of its contents. Here are some of the text's principal features.

1   Seven principal pathways toward greater adjustment and growth are discussed. No one system is presented as having the Whole Truth. The book offers a wide spectrum of orientations, allowing you to use your own intelligence in making decisions about ideas that have the greatest personal value to you.

2   Each of the seven chapters devoted to a pathway contains a section titled *Critique*. Although the principal pathways are presented in generally favorable terms, the aim of the critiques is to help you strike a realistic balance between zealous acceptance or cynical rejection of a particular approach.

3   Each of the seven chapters devoted to a pathway contains a section titled *Implications for Growth and Adjustment*. These sections make explicit connections between general principles and applications of the principles to life itself.

4   Every chapter includes a *Summary and Self-test*. These are intended as *active* instructional devices, as opposed to the familiar passive summaries at the ends of chapters. You take the self-test and score it yourself after reading a chapter, thus allowing for feedback on your own learning processes.

5   Every chapter concludes with a set of *Discussion Questions.* The aim of these questions is to provoke you to re-examine your own assumptions about adjustment and growth, to stimulate your own thought processes.

6   Each important term is italicized and briefly defined the first time it appears. In addition, the principle or concept associated with the term is immediately clarified with a concrete example related to life. No term is allowed to stand in meaningless isolation without connections to reality.

7   All of the principal terms appear in the *Glossary* at the end of the book. In the glossary, a formal definition is given for the listed terms. A page number follows the definition.

8   There is an index at the end of the book, allowing for quick access to both subjects and persons.

In brief, an effort has been made to make *Human Adjustment and Personal Growth: Seven Pathways* a book that you will find to be both worth studying and enjoyable to use. I wish you success in your study of this exciting field of psychology.

OF SEX AND ENGLISH USAGE

Of late it has become increasingly obvious to thinking persons that words such as "mankind" and such phrases as "the rise of modern man" are unfair, ignoring the self-evident fact that approximately half of the human beings on this Earth are women. Consequently, in this book I have replaced "mankind" with "humankind," and have made similar modifications wherever possible. There remains the stubborn problem of the *generic he,* the widespread use of the pronoun "he" to indicate both sexes.

The generic "he," like the word "mankind," contains a certain amount of inequity toward females. I have dealt with this problem in various ways. I have frequently used plural pronouns instead of singular pronouns; for example, a sentence such as, "The self-actualizing person maximizes his potentialities, and he will not waste his life," becomes, "Self-actualizing pesrons maximize their potentialities, and they will not waste their lives." Also, examples in the book draw from the behavior of both sexes. In some instances, where I found it clumsy to use a plural pronoun, the generic "he" was retained in preference to the more cumbersome "he or she," or the alternative practice of randomly alternating *hes* and *shes* throughout the book.

ACKNOWLEDGMENTS

A number of people have helped me make this textbook become a reality. My thanks are expressed to my wife Jeanne for our many meaningful discussions about adjustment and growth, Ronald St. John, Jack K. Burton, Rochelle Sherwood, Janet Hearle, Deborah Herbert, Malcolm Easterlin, Anita Duncan, Ron Nelson, and Ed Butler, and to Pat Moore and Thelma Knea for typing the manuscript. I am also grateful to Bruce W. Benner of San Francisco State University, John Peters of Mesa College, Wayne Weiten of College of DuPage, and E. C. Holloway of Los Angeles Valley College for their careful reviews and valuable suggestions.

Frank J. Bruno

CONTENTS

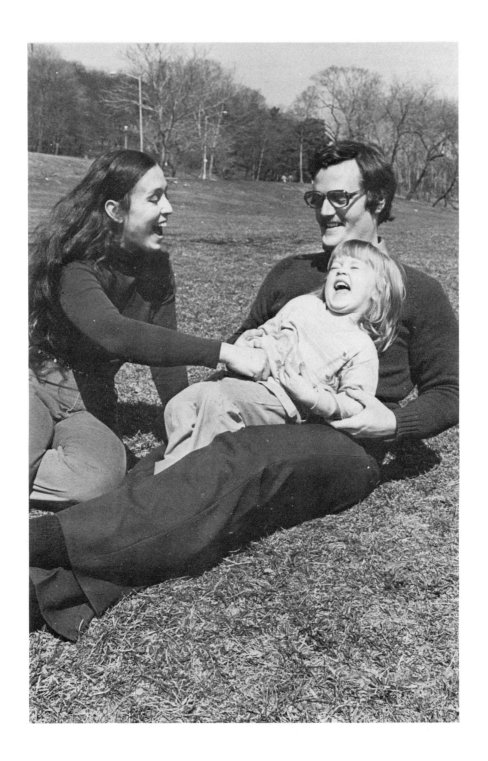

CHAPTER 1 PSYCHOLOGY, ADJUSTMENT, AND GROWTH

What do we mean when we use such words as *adjustment* and *growth*?

OVERVIEW

OUTLINE

I. Psychology and Human Beings
 A. The Study of the Soul   B. The Science of Behavior   C. Inner and Outer

II. Conceptions of Mental Illness
 A. Demonology   B. Neurosis   C. Psychosis   D. Character Disorders

III. Psychotherapy
 A. Roots of psychotherapy   B. Psychiatrists and Clinical Psychologists   C. Psychotherapy and Theories of Personality   D. Principal Modes of Psychotherapy

IV. Adjustment and Growth
 A. Adjustment   B. Personal Growth   C. Stability and Change

V. Concluding Remarks

VI. Summary and Self-test

VII. Discussion Questions

VIII. References

Do you consider yourself a well-adjusted person?

Are you making the most of your talents and potentialities as a human being?

Do you feel that you understand yourself?

Are there habits you want to break?

Are you living an authentic life?

Does life seem somewhat empty to you? Or does it seem to be filled with meaning?

The principal aims of this book are (1) to help you develop a deeper appreciation for the scope and implications of the preceding and related questions about human existence, (2) to point out ways you can find increasingly satisfactory answers to such questions, and (3) to establish some connection between abstract principles of adjustment and growth and the problems of your daily life. In brief, this book presents ideas that may contribute to a more rewarding life.

A concepts/principles book such as this one should be discriminated from the popular *how to* book that offers categorical advice about living. This book presents no formulas for successful living. No single philosophy or point of view is argued as the Truth. Instead, the book is designed to give you quite a bit of information about what outstanding psychologists have had to say about adjustment and growth. The author hopes that the content of the book will stimulate you to think for yourself. Effective living is your responsibility and no psychologist, guru, or self-proclaimed wise man can take over that responsibility for you.

As you already know, the title of the book is *Human Adjustment and Personal Growth: Seven Pathways*. Later in this chapter you will find a discussion concerning the distinction between the concepts of *adjustment* and *growth*. At this point, however, I want to stress the subtitle—*Seven Pathways*. In this book, seven general approaches to adjustment and growth are discussed. A chapter is devoted to each, and they are designated as follows:

1 Depth Psychology

2 Behavioral Psychology

3 Rational Analysis

4 Transactional Analysis

5 Psychotechnology

6 Existential-Humanistic Psychology

7 Transpersonal Psychology

The meaning and content of these approaches is, of course, the substance of this book. Therefore I will defer any discussion of the approaches them-selves until the appropriate chapters. For now, the primary point to be made is that the book is *eclectic*, that is, it does not see pathways toward adjustment and growth as mutually exclusive.

PSYCHOLOGY AND HUMAN BEINGS

Psychology has become the most popular course on college campuses. And in bookstores across the nation, best-sellers such as *How To Be Your Own Best Friend, I'm OK—You're OK, Games People Play*, and *The Primal Scream* fill the shelves. Why the interest in psychology? What do we expect to gain from its study?

I have frequently asked students in introductory psychology classes what they expect from a psychology course. There are, of course, those who give a cynical reply: "Three college units." Sincere students, however, tend to give replies such as these:

"I want to find out what makes people tick."

"I want to know why I do things."

"I'm not getting along very well with my boyfriend. I want to get some ideas about how we can communicate better."

"I think I'm neurotic, and I want to find out what I can do about it."

It would seem that most students with a real interest in psychology seek greater self-understanding or greater understanding of other persons. Of course, these two goals are not mutually exclusive and many students have an active interest in both.

Much of the implicit hope in the study of psychology is eloquently sum-marized in the following statement by a psychologist who has addressed much of his work to the lay public, Harry A. Overstreet:

Exactly as in the great humanistic religions of Lao-tse, Buddha, Isaiah, Jesus, so in Psychoanalysis, the aim is to free the individual from his various enslavements so that he is able "to see the truth, to love, to become free and responsible, and to be sensitive to the voice of his conscience." (p. 795)

It should be noted that in the quotation a reference is made to psycho-analysis, not psychology. The term *psychoanalysis* refers to a school of psychology fathered by Sigmund Freud, but it should not be used as a synonym for psychology. A general definition of psychology will be offered soon. For now it should be observed in passing that in the popular mind psychoanalysis and psychology are often equated.

In the 1940s one of the best-selling books on popular psychology was

Some people seek from psychology peace of mind.

Peace of Mind by Rabbi Joshua Loth Liebman. The book went through thirty printings in a relatively short time. More than a million copies of the book were printed in hardcover and paperback. What did Liebman offer? Here is an example:

As we observe the growing hordes of neurotics and little tyrants, self-mutilators and self-slayers, that trail about the world, we realize that a new, more honest, and more dynamic map of man's troubled soul must be drawn before we can hope to explore this most tangled of terrains. Only one crayon can draw such a detailed man—and this is the crayon of modern psychology.

. . . We learn to look upon our flaws and potentialities, and with searching fingers to probe out the causes of our failures, hates, and fears. We find out who we are! (pp. 7–8)

We find out who we are! What a promise! Perhaps those who write for Everyperson are too ambitious. Nonetheless, human beings seem to hunger for information that can help them live effective and meaningful lives. The popularity of modern psychology emanates from this hunger.

THE STUDY OF THE SOUL

The word *psychology* is a combination of two Greek words, *psyche* and *logos*. An informal translation of psychology into English is the "study of the soul." In much of classical philosophy, the soul and the body were thought to be distinct entities. Conscious awareness, personality, memory, and the mind itself were all associated with the soul, not the body. (The conscious mind, with its capacity for thought and reflection was believed to be an aspect of the soul.) The body was a thing or an object having no life without the soul. A useful metaphor for comprehending this point of view is to compare the human body with a toy mechanical man: Imagine a toy man that is activated by a battery; when the battery is in place the mechanical man walks, and when the battery is taken out the mechanical man does not walk. This was roughly the relationship between body and soul postulated by classical philosophy. The soul, like a battery, made the body move. (An animated cartoon is a *moving* cartoon; it is interesting to note that in several languages *anima* is the word for soul!)

Three giants of Western philosophy—Plato (427–347 B.C.), Saint Thomas Aquinas (1225–1274), and René Descartes (1596–1650)—did much to advance and establish the position that the soul is immortal, the body is mortal, and human existence arises from a combination of these two fundamentally different essences. *Dualism* is the word that is used to summarize the position that the body and soul are two distinct and different substances. The philosophy of dualism makes a science of psychology impossible. If the soul (and the mind) are members of a nonphysical realm, then precise explanation, prediction, and control of mental events is by definition impossible. This was a major theme in traditional philosophy and theology in the West.

THE SCIENCE OF BEHAVIOR

The twentieth century brought a fresh definition of psychology. The word "fresh" is used with a double meaning. First, it is used to indicate novelty or originality (e.g., "Fresh thinking was required for Charles Hard Townes to invent the laser and the maser"). Second, it is used to indicate brashness (e.g., "He got too fresh with me on our first date"). Thus a definition of psychology that was at once both novel and brash was the definition proposed by the father of behaviorism, John Broadus Watson, in the 1910s: *Psychology is the science of the behavior of organisms.* In one stroke Watson attempted to banish from psychology such traditional concepts as the human will and consciousness. Watson's attitude toward classical philosophy is well represented in these comments:

Before trying to understand the behaviorists' theory of thinking, won't the reader please pick up any introspective psychological text and read the chapter on thinking? Won't he then try to digest some of the pablum the philosophers have offered us on this all-important function? I have tried to understand it. I had to give it up. I believe the reader will give it up too.

. . . The behaviorist advances the view that what the psychologists have hitherto called thought is in short nothing but talking to ourselves. *(p. 176)*

Watson felt that traditional philosophical ideas applied to psychology led to circular arguments and meaningless debates. It was his desire to place psychology on a sound foundation of experiment and observation. He was an extremist, and his call for a hard science of objective psychology had an electric effect on many of his contemporaries. He was elected president of the American Psychological Association in 1915, and his call for a cutting away of philosophical deadwood has continued to reverberate to this day. The school of psychology called behaviorism has been a vigorous force in American psychology. Perhaps the most influential behaviorist of recent years has been B. F. Skinner. In the following quotation from his best-selling book *Beyond Freedom and Dignity*, it is evident that he is an intellectual heir to Watson:

Almost all our major problems involve human behavior, and they cannot be solved by physical and biological technology alone. What is needed is a technology of behavior, but we have been slow to develop the science from which such a technology might be drawn. One difficulty is that almost all of what is called behavioral science continues to trace behavior to states of mind, feelings, traits of character, human nature and so on. (p. 22)

The goals of psychology according to such thinkers as Watson and Skinner are to explain, predict, and control behavior. The traditional view of man as a creature with a mind and a will is dismissed as unscientific.

INNER AND OUTER
The follower of classical philosophical themes and the behaviorist live in different worlds. In spite of the impact of behaviorism, many sophisticated psychologists have returned to an emphasis on motifs suggested by Plato, Aquinas, and others. The rise of existential-humanistic psychology in the past decade or so is a case in point. This rise has been called a "third force" in psychology (the other two forces are psychoanalysis and behaviorism). Existential-humanistic psychology affirms the commonsense notion that we are conscious, that we make real choices, and that we are much more than creatures of habit. It asserts that for fully functioning persons, life is what they make it, not something that happens to them. The writings of Abraham Maslow, Carl Rogers, Viktor Frankl, and others (discussed in Chapter Seven) all have this common thread. For now, the

Existential-humanistic psychology affirms the common-sense notion that we are conscious, that we make real choices, and that we are much more than creatures of habit.

point to be made is that the Third Force in psychology represents a partial return to the subjective psychology of early philosophy.

It seems to me that we are not compelled to make a choice between subjective psychology and objective psychology. Although they do represent different worlds, they are equally valid worlds. The subjective psychologist is talking about the *inner world*, life as experienced. The objective psychologist is talking about the *outer world*, behavior as it presents itself to an observer. The sophisticated student of psychology does not take sides as if he is playing some child's game. There is no necessity to take sides. There is no decision to be made about which viewpoint represents Ultimate Truth. One can draw from both viewpoints those concepts that are meaningful and useful, and one can apply them in appropriate contexts.

Some years ago the dean of American psychologists, William James, made a distinction between those who possess tough-minded temperaments and those who possess tender-minded temperaments. Psychologists Heinz L. Ansbacher and Rowena R. Ansbacher write:

The objective psychologist is apt to be tough-minded, the subjective psychologist tender-minded, and hence we can extend our list by adding James's description of his antithesis.

THE TOUGH-MINDED	THE TENDER-MINDED
Empiricist (going by fact)	Rationalist (going by principles)
Sensationalistic	Intellectualistic
Materialistic	Idealistic
Pessimistic	Optimistic
Pluralistic (starting from parts, making of the whole a collection)	Monistic (starting from wholes, making much of the unity of things)
Irreligious	Religious
Hardheaded	Feeling
Fatalist	Free-willist
Skeptical	Dogmatical (pp. 5–6)

James points out that the individuals belonging to one category tend to have a low opinion of individuals belonging to the other category. This is unfortunate because we can learn a great deal under certain conditions from either point of view. As already indicated, I do not feel that a distinct choice must be made between the points of view.

In the pages that follow you will see both points of view underlying the specific ideas and concepts of different approaches to adjustment and personal growth. In many cases a theoretician or a school of psychology cannot be categorized easily as tough-minded or tender-minded, and we won't worry much about this difficulty. For example, Freud thought of himself as tough-minded. He saw psychoanalysis as an objective approach to the study of human behavior, with an emphais on natural science and cause and effect principles. Watson, however, thought of Freud as tender-minded and saw psychoanalysis as a soft psychology with a set of mushy, poorly defined concepts. Who was right? If one has read enough of psychoanalysis, behaviorism, and philosophy, it is possible to engage in hours of entertaining discussion about the question. But if one wishes to call a halt to circular argumentation, it is essential to note that the question cannot be answered in a definitive way. Much of Freudian theory is based on Freud's solid observation of his patients, and much of Freudian theory is based on his self-analysis and interpretation of his own dreams. Thus psychoanalysis represents an amalgamation of objective and subjective points of view.

The inner and the outer points of view have something to reveal to each other, and as we approach our study of adjustment and personal growth we will try to remember this point. In this book psychology will be approached as both a natural science (tough-minded) and a mental science (tender-minded). It is my hope that this unified orientation will provide you with a broad spectrum of useful psychological concepts.

CONCEPTIONS OF MENTAL ILLNESS

Consider the following tale told by the poet Edwin Arlington Robinson:

Whenever Richard Cory went down town,
We people on the pavement looked at him:
He was a gentleman from sole to crown,
Clean favored, and imperially slim.

And he was always quietly arrayed,
And he was always human when he talked;
But still he fluttered pulses when he said,
"Good-morning," and he glittered when he walked.

And he was rich—yes, richer than a king,
And admirably schooled in every grace:
In fine, we thought that he was everything
To make us wish that we were in his place.

So on we worked, and waited for the light,
And went without the meat, and cursed the bread;
And Richard Cory, one calm summer night,
Went home and put a bullet through his head.*

What was Richard Cory's problem? Was he neurotic? Psychotic? Alienated? Suffering from a character disorder? We cannot tell; the author purposely does not give us enough information. Arlington seems to say between the lines, "Don't be taken in by what you see on the surface. Another person's inner world cannot be judged by his behavior." On the surface Richard Cory seems well adjusted and content; below the surface, he is in a state of despair. A popular song of the 1940s conveyed a similar theme:

The crowd sees me out dancing,
Carefree and romancing,
Happy with my someone new.
I'm laughing on the outside,
Crying on the inside,
'Cause I'm still in love with you.†

It *is* difficult to understand other people. And we must be careful not to judge another's motives and feelings hastily. Nonetheless it seems to be a rather universal human enterprise. Therefore we might fruitfully consider

---

* "Richard Cory," *Selected Poems of Edwin Arlington Robinson.* Reprinted by permission of the Macmillan Co., New York.

† "Laughing on the Outside, Crying on the Inside." Copyright 1946 by Hansen Publications, New York. All rights reserved. Used by permission.

some of the ways human behavior has been and is being judged and categorized by mental health professionals.

DEMONOLOGY

The mental health professionals of primitive tribes were and are witch doctors and shamans. Depressed people, people who act oddly, and others who do not seem to fit in with the standard expectations of the group are believed to be possessed by some evil spirit. The tribe's witch doctor goes through a magic ritual designed to free the afflicted one of the demon. Interestingly enough, this approach often meets with success. Psychiatrist Jerome Frank, in *Persuasion and Healing*, argues that this may be primarily due to a *placebo effect*; that is, the expectation of cure restores the patient's capacity to hope for a better state of affairs. Frank suggests that under certain circumstances this may be sufficient to effect a ''cure'' of sorts.

The notion of demon possession as an explanation of pathological human states was also subscribed to by the church during the Dark Ages. Rites of exorcism performed by priests were common several centuries ago, but not so common today. That demonology retains a grip on the human imagination is revealed by the success of the motion picture *The Exorcist,* in which two Catholic priests deal with a demon that has invaded a child. In spite of the interest in exorcism generated by the film, most contemporary psychologists would reject any form of demonology as an adequate explanation for behavioral problems. The majority of psychologists would subscribe to a natural science point of view that puts the causes and effects of mental illness squarely in *this* world.

In the discussion that follows, three basic conceptions of behavioral pathology are presented: neurosis, psychosis, and character disorders. It should be stressed that these have become *traditional categories*; they are not necessarily ''real.'' As useful categories, they can be disputed. Indeed, there are those who dispute the utility of the concept of mental illness itself (e.g., psychiatrist Thomas Szasz, author of *The Myth of Mental Illness*). Alternate points of view to the traditional categories are discussed in later chapters. But to provide you with a backboard against which to bounce nontraditional ideas, it is rather important that you be familiar at least with the basic outline of the conventional classification scheme. It is also important to note that the following exposition gives minimal attention to the question of *why* a person has a problem and *how* he can be helped. These questions are also deferred for future chapters. For the present, let us content ourselves with a description of the traditional categories.

NEUROSIS

The concept of neurosis derives from medical practice. In pre-twentieth-century medicine, the neurotic person was believed to be suffering from an affliction of the nervous system (*neurosis* and *nerve* derive from the same root word). Freud's practice as a physician and his theories as a psychoanalyst were founded on his observations of neurotic persons: Persons were said to be suffering from *hysteria*, an inability to walk or talk or see or hear that was not caused by obvious organic nervous system damage. For a time it was believed that such people were suffering from "weak nerves" or something similar. Freud and others concluded that the basis of hysteria was *emotional conflicts.* Since Freud's day a concept has evolved that views the neurotic person not as one who suffers from a neurological impairment, but as one who suffers from personal problems (i.e., emotional conflicts) he seems unable to solve adequately.

Such people are seen as high-anxiety types (worrywarts) who think too hard about trivial things and feel that great disasters may be lurking around almost any corner. Such people tend to have *phobias*—irrational fears that their lives are endangered by events which seem trivial to the presumably normal person. Neurotic persons are often characterized as *compulsive*; they feel they should do this and they ought to do that. There is great guilt if these shoulds and oughts of life are not attended to. The traditional image of neurosis presents the sufferer as *feeling inferior*; other people seem to him to be better-looking, wiser, more competent, and so on. All-in-all we can conceptualize neurotic persons as persons who are *very troubled*; they are unhappy with themselves and with the conditions of their existence.

A vivid portrayal of the neurotic state of mind is given by Erica Jong in her novel *Fear of Flying.* The writer has received a request from an editor to see some of her poems. She wants to send the poems, but goes through all sorts of agonies in writing the editor a letter to accompany the poems. Her letters appear to her to range from too servile to too ego-tistical to too personal. She writes:

Finally, two years later, after many more attempts, I drafted a disgustingly submissive, meek, and apologetic letter to the editor in question, tore it up ten times before mailing, retyped it eleven times, retyped my poems fifteen times (they had to be letter perfect, one typo and I threw away the page— and I had never learned to type) and sent the damned manila envelope off to New York. By return mail, I received a really warm letter (which even my paranoia couldn't misinterpret), a notice of acceptance, and a check. How long do you suppose it would have taken me to get the next letter out if I had received a rejection slip?

This was the dazzlingly self-confident creature who began treatment (psycho-therapy) with Dr. Happe (a psychiatrist) in Heidelberg. . . . (pp. 168–169)

In the preceding quotation we can see the compulsivity, the high anxiety, the rigidity, the desire for an exalted status (published poet), the fear of failure, the inferiority feelings, and the lack of confidence that are the hallmarks of the neurotic individual. To repeat, a person may be conceptualized as neurotic if that person feels very troubled.

TABLE 1.1. Selected Kinds of Neurotic Reactions

ANXIETY REACTION
The anxiety reaction is characterized by chronic apprehension. The individual often feels that something terrible is going to happen, but he doesn't know what. It is as if a black cloud of fear and worry floats constantly over his head.

HYSTERICAL NEUROSIS
There are two kinds of hysterical neurosis: *conversion type* and *dissociative type.* In the conversion type, the individual converts anxiety into a bodily symptom such as blindness, deafness, or paralysis. In the dissociative type, the person may manifest such symptoms as amnesia or multiple personality.

PHOBIC REACTION
A phobic reaction is an irrational fear, a fear that the individual himself recognizes as groundless. The person may have an excessive fear of heights, the dark, open spaces, insects, and so forth.

OBSESSIVE-COMPULSIVE REACTION
The obsessive-compulsive reaction is characterized by a constant preoccupation with certain ideas. The individual may be preoccupied with the idea of death, loss of status, or loss of sexual ability. The individual finds partial relief from the anxiety associated with his obsessions by performing personal rituals designed to magically counteract the nagging ideas.

DEPRESSIVE NEUROSIS
The phrase *chronic dejection* aptly describes the individual suffering from a depressive neurosis. He has "the blahs," is discouraged and demoralized, and life barely seems worth living.

NEURASTHENIC REACTION
The neurasthenic reaction involves feelings of fatigue, lack of energy, and general weakness. The individual feels unable to cope with his problems: "Life is just too much." The complaints of weakness have little or no physical basis.

HYPOCHONDRIACAL REACTION
The hypochondriacal reaction is characterized by excessive worry over physical health. The individual jumps to conclusions. A skin blemish may produce an instant self-diagnosis of skin cancer, a pain in the chest is said to be a heart attack, and so forth.

PSYCHOSIS

When an individual takes leave of ordinary reality, he is said to be *psychotic*. (The nature of what we refer to as "reality" is discussed in Chapter Eight.) A psychotic reaction refers to a "splitting from reality." The most common kind of psychotic reaction, *schizophrenia*, literally means "split head." The most appropriate meaning we should attach to these terms is *not* "split personality," but "a head split from reality." The psychotic person is described by the phrase, "a mind that lost itself." About 25 percent of the persons admitted to mental hospitals are given the label schizophrenic. The mental health movement in the Untied States considers psychosis to be a prime problem, and many avenues are being explored in an effort to understand and treat various sorts of psychotic reactions.

A common characteristic of psychotic reactions is *delusions.* A delusion occurs when an individual perceives the world in a way that most of us would reject as "untrue." (This definition, like many definitions, has its problems; existential psychiatrists, for example, would be unhappy with it. Alternate points of view will be discussed in future chapters. For now, I can only repeat that in this chapter conventional and more or less traditional views are being explained.)

A good way of getting the feeling of what is meant by a delusion is to consider a perceptual experience that is common with normal persons. Consider optical illusions. Take a look at the Necker cube in Figure 1. If you stare at the figure, it will at first appear in one orientation, that is, one of the surfaces will seem to be in front of the other one. Continue staring at the figure. Suddenly it seems to reverse its orientation! Now the surface that was formerly forward seems to go through the surface that was in back, and the back surface moves to the forward position. You see all of this, but you do not mistake it for reality. You think of it as an illusion, which means that you make a distinction between appearance and reality.

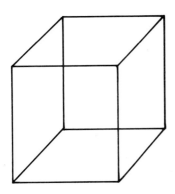

FIGURE 1. The Necker cube. This optical illusion can be perceived from two different orientations. How does an illusion differ from a delusion?

Let us say that you were to be upset by the reversals of the figure, however. You put your hand on the paper and say, "I'll stop this thing from moving back and forth!" If you were to do this, really believing in the actuality of the back-and-forth motion, you would be suffering from a delusion.

Psychotic delusions can affect almost any sense modality. A person may have visual or auditory delusional experiences. He may see things that are not there (visual hallucinations) or hear sounds that are not present (auditory hallucinations). He may think he is a famous character in history (delusions of reference). He may think he is being tortured or punished unfairly (delusions of persecution). All these delusions, and others, are fairly commonly experienced by individuals going through psychotic reactions.

In *The Quiet Furies*, by psychologist Elton B. McNeil, a case history of a schizophrenic patient is presented. Sam B. developed a preoccupation with such topics as the devil, sin, death, and reincarnation. He began to spend his time sitting around the house, gave up his job, and lost interest in ordinary affairs. His wife reported that he talked to himself and ignored her when she talked to him. His pajamas became his regular attire twenty-four hours a day. His wife was upset by such odd questions as, "Would God care if I didn't eat breakfast?" Then he was apprehended by the police at 3:00 A.M. while driving his car over eighty miles per hour through a town a moderate distance from his home. He said to the arresting officers that he was trying to "get up escape velocity for a trip to Mars." When McNeil visited Sam B. in the state hospital, Sam was "openly hallucinating and in an agitated state. He was wild, unshaven, disheveled, and incoherent." (p. 178) At one point during his hospital stay he developed the delusion that he was Robin Hood. This brief sketch of Sam B.'s symptoms provides a graphic illustration of the schizophrenic reaction.

Earlier I characterized the neurotic reaction with the words *very troubled*. The psychotic reaction can be characterized with the words *extremely disoriented*.

CHARACTER DISORDERS

The term *character disorder* is associated with an individual who, in conventional terms, exhibits irresponsible behavior (note that the term *personality disorder* is synonymous with character disorder). An illustration of one kind of character disorder is that of seriously delinquent adolescents. The psychiatrist William Glasser has had a substantial amount of experience counseling adolescent girls. In *Reality Therapy*, he sketches the background behavior of sixteen-year-old Jeri prior to treatment. Jeri

TABLE 1.2.   Selected Kinds of Psychotic Reactions

SCHIZOPHRENIA
Schizophrenia is the principal kind of psychotic reaction. It is a broad general class, and includes a number of subclasses. Examples of significant kinds of schizophrenic reactions are (1) *simple type,* (2) *hebephrenic type*, (3) *catatonic type*, and (4) *paranoid type*. The simple type of schizophrenia is characterized by a general disintegration of the personality. The individual is disoriented, presenting a portrait of confusion, emotional numbness, illogical thought, and irrational behavior. The hebephrenic type is characterized by regression to an infantile level of functioning. The individual becomes childish, acting like a preschooler or an infant. The catatonic type is characterized by withdrawal, inactivity, and sometimes by odd postures and poses. The paranoid type is characterized by feelings of grandeur or persecution.

AFFECTIVE DISORDERS
Affective psychotic reactions are mainly disturbances of mood. The two principal kinds of affective disorders are (1) *involutional melancholia* and (2) *manic-depressive reactions.* Involutional melancholia is characterized by depression and is associated with the later years of life—the involutional or "change of life" portion of the life cycle. Manic-depressive reactions are characterized by states of extreme elation or of great depression. In the circular type of manic-depressive reaction, the individual alternates between the two mood extremes.

PARANOIA
The chief characteristic of paranoia is an organized delusional system. The difference between paranoia and the paranoid type of schizophrenia is that in paranoia, the delusions fit logically together into a coherent whole. In the paranoid type of schizophrenia the delusions may be random, fleeting, and not associated with any particular pattern.

had been such a problem to her parents in Florida that she was sent to live with an uncle in San Francisco. She ran away from her uncle's home, made a living by shoplifting, teamed up with a group of older girls, and posed as being nineteen years of age. Jeri boasted to Glasser that one department store in San Francisco "must be out of the red now that she was locked up." Glasser writes, "Many of the things she stole she had no use for; much was wasted, thrown away, or given away. The act of stealing expensive furs, for example, was more important than the furs themselves." (p. 75)

It is easy to visualize all sorts of variations on the general theme of the individual who is wayward, who deviates from the norms of the social order. Sometimes such individuals are glorified and presented in a semiadmirable way. The fictional character Captain Nemo in Jules Verne's *Twenty Thousand Leagues under the Sea*, is such an example. Having become disenchanted with civilization, he builds a submarine with fantastic capacities and becomes a law unto himself. He personifies what we might call the *alienated man*, the man who feels no emotional ties with the traditional institutions of our world. At one point in the novel he says with passion, "I am not what you call a civilised man! I have done with society entirely, for reasons which I alone have the right of appreciating. I do not therefore obey its laws, and I desire you never allude to them before me again!" (He is speaking to the narrator of the novel.) Captain Nemo was an outlaw, and yet it has been claimed that he is the man Jules Verne would like to have been. Whether this claim is correct or not, it can hardly be doubted that such characters as Captain Nemo have a certain universal appeal.

The person with a character disorder is said to *act out*. He acts out the behavior patterns that are repressed and denied in the neurotic person. In a sense we can conceptualize the personality disorder as the logical opposite of the neurotic reaction. Whereas the neurotic person is anxious and inhibited, the individual with a character disorder is (perhaps superficially) fearless and willing to take action. I have suggested you think of the neurotic person as very troubled. In contrast, think of the person with a character disorder as *very troublesome.* He does not appear to experience much anxiety himself, but he certainly produces anxiety in others.

Individuals with personality disorders tend to be *impulsive.* They act without sufficient attention to the consequences of their actions. The future is held in little regard. The underlying motto is often, "Live today for tomorrow we may die." Neurotic persons tend to be compulsive instead of impulsive; compulsive persons live by oughts and shoulds. In response to "Live today for tomorrow we may die," they are inclined to give the response suggested by psychologist O. Hobort Mowrer: The trouble with the live today for tomorrow we may die philosophy is that we usually don't die tomorrow!

PSYCHOTHERAPY

The word *psychotherapy*, in its classical sense, means "a healing of the soul." In contemporary terms, psychotherapy refers to the efforts of trained professionals to offer help to those who suffer from some sort of psychological-emotional disturbance. The road to be taken by the therapist in his endeavor to offer assistance is not always an obvious one, however. In an old Charlie Chan film, the fictional detective commented, "Every day, when you are doing good deed, remember kindhearted ele-

TABLE 1.3. Selected Kinds of Character Disorders

ANTISOCIAL REACTION

Psychopathic personality and *sociopath* are sometimes used as alternates for the term *antisocial reaction*. Characteristics of the antisocial reaction include the following behavioral patterns: a willingness to manipulate and "con" others, with little regard for their feelings or well-being; a tendency to feel little anxiety about violations of moral codes; a superficial charm; a poor development of conventional conscience; a high likelihood of acting impulsively, with small regard for ultimate consequences; and a preoccupation with momentary pleasures. An example is a person who succeeds from time to time in the role of the Great Imposter; for limited periods he pulls off a caper as a physician, teacher, or other professional. On a lesser scale, psychopathic trends are sometimes evident in more or less "normal" persons when they are somewhat manipulative in their dealings with other people.

SEXUAL DEVIATIONS

Our society makes certain kinds of sexual behavior taboo and pinpoints some types of sexual behavior as criminal. These forms of sexual behavior are given a variety of labels, including (1) *exhibitionism*, the act of of exposing one's body (often the genitals) in public places; (2) *pedophilia*, sexually molesting a child; (3) *rape*, a hostile and aggressive sexual attack perpetrated against another's will and consent; (4) *voyeurism*, a preoccupation with attaining sexual gratification by looking at arousing stimuli (e.g., a nude member of the opposite sex or a couple engaged in coitus); and (5) *homosexuality*, a preference for sexual activity with members of the same sex. The inclusion of homosexuality as a sexual deviation has received considerable debate, and the American Psychiatric Association no longer lists homosexuality as a pathological category. Nonetheless, society at large continues to judge homosexual behavior harshly, and a great many states have laws against homosexual behavior. Perhaps the neutral term *sexual variation* instead of sexual deviation should be applied to homosexual behavior.

DYSSOCIAL REACTION

Criminals are sometimes members of a subculture that stresses and prizes violations of the norms of "straight" society. An individual who identifies with such a subculture may in a sense be "normal" in terms of his group. He may do things that ordinary people consider terrible and immoral; nonetheless, he cannot be considered neurotic or psychotic. An example is a child born into a family of professional criminals. As an adult, he conforms to family values and is a competent professional criminal. The novel and film *The Godfather* portrays the theme of loyalty to "the family" against the forces of the outside world.

CONDUCT DISORDERS

Two common types of conduct disorders are (1) *alcoholism*, an abusive use of alcohol to the point where it seriously interferes with daily living or produces organic damage; and (2) *drug addiction*, a dependence on such drugs as stimulants, sedatives, narcotics, or psychotherapeutics (antianxiety and antidepressant drugs).

phant who tried to help hen hatch chicks—he sat down on a little hen's eggs.'' Like the kindhearted elephant, a well-meaning psychotherapist often finds that good intentions are not enough; sometimes he fears that his intervention may do more harm than good. Eric Berne, the father of transactional analysis, pointed out that patients in psychotherapy often unconsciously play a game in which the therapist is cast in the role of ''fall guy'' or ''patsy.'' The client seeks to make a fool out of the therapist. He wants to be ''one up'' and prove he can outwit the therapist. Such clients perceive psychotherapy as a power struggle. Their real aim is not to get better, but to put the therapist down and demonstrate his incompetence. All of this can be quite subtle. On the surface, the patient may be ''trying to get better'' and ''making an effort'' and ''improving.'' When a patient wins such a power struggle, psychotherapy did not succeed in ameliorating the individual's long-term psychological-emotional problems.

In spite of the snares and pitfalls of psychotherapeutic efforts, a need and a demand for the services of therapists still remain. Increasing numbers of persons are turning to psychiatrists, clinical psychologists, and social workers for help with their personal problems. And our understanding of what constitutes effective psychotherapy is definitely advancing.

The psychiatrist Jerome Frank specifies three key features of psychotherapy: (1) The healer is trained and accepted by the patient and his social group; (2) the sufferer seeks relief from the healer; and (3) the contacts between the sufferer and the healer are structured and defined in terms of time and place (e.g., one hour a week of psychotherapy in the therapist's office). The aim of the therapy is, of course, to effect positive changes in ''the sufferer's feelings, attitudes, and behavior.''

The topic of psychotherapy is of substantial importance in the context of this book. Many of our notions about adjustment and personal growth have been derived directly from the experiences of psychotherapists with their clients. When one offers services as a psychotherapist, one often listens for many hours to the problems of another person. Under such circumstances, it is possible to know that someone rather well. Many facets of the human condition are explored. It would seem inevitable that therapists would begin to get some rather definite notions about what constitutes the good life. For these reasons, psychotherapy has been a rich source of hypotheses about the factors contributing to adjustment and personal growth. Many of the concepts in this book owe their existence to the conclusions of intelligent and observant psychotherapists. I hasten to add, however, that psychotherapy is not the sole source underlying the various pathways outlined in future chapters. Other sources are learning theory, philosophy, biopsychology, pharmacology, and both Western and Eastern religions.

ROOTS OF PSYCHOTHERAPY

The roots of psychotherapy extend beyond recorded history. Both anthropological studies of present-day primitive tribes and the excavations of archaeologists suggest that some form of psychotherapy has existed since the dawn of human existence. The shaman and the witch doctor play the role of psychotherapist among prescientific people, which reveals the first basic trend underlying psychotherapy: *the magical trend.* Contemporary psychotherapy springs partly from a centuries-old belief in magic. To this day, many persons who go to a psychotherapist are unconsciously seeking some sort of magic from the therapist—he will be Merlin the magician and make their woes vanish by an esoteric ritual.

The peripheral belief in magic contributes to what has been called the *placebo effect* in psychotherapy, that is, a temporary improvement in the client's symptoms caused by a momentary mobilization of his capacity to hope for the best. During the first few visits to a therapist, the client often feels that "everything's going to be OK now—I'm in good hands." But successful psychotherapy demands a contribution from the client. Psy-

Contemporary psychotherapy springs partly from humankind's centuries-old belief in magic.

chotherapy is a learning process, and the client can hardly expect beneficial results if he remains passive and psychologically inert. Some therapists might argue that the element of faith in magic is to some degree a necessary element in effective psychotherapy; however, few therapists would be willing to take the position that faith in magic is a sufficient condition for effective psychotherapy.

A second trend underlying psychotherapy is the *organic approach*, an approach that explains behavioral disturbances in terms of factors residing within the physical body. The organic approach also has a long history. For example, around 400 B.C. Hippocrates suggested that there are four basic kinds of personality types, which arise from varying amounts of body "humors" (fluids). A first type was said to be *sanguine* —a person who was optimistic and good-natured in temperament. An individual with ample amounts of blood fell into this category. A second personality type was described as *melancholic*—an individual with a tendency to be easily depressed. Such a person was presumably afflicted with excess amounts of black bile. A third type was called *choleric*—an individual who was easily excited to anger. This person was asserted to have just too much bile (no particular shade). The fourth type was the *phlegmatic* person—one who shows a considerable apathy toward life. Nothing is of much importance or interest to this person, and such an individual was thought to be overloaded with phlegm (mucus secretions of the nose and throat). You may laugh a bit at old Hippocrates, but his conclusions were based on the little information he could obtain. For example, is it not true that young men (optimistic and filled with great expectations) have a lot of red blood? And is it not true that someone dying of tuberculosis coughs up a lot of mucus and is rather uninterested in things that stimulate the attention of most people?

In any event, such thinkers as Hippocrates played a role in establishing the view that personality disturbances can arise from organic conditions. This view was crucial in the establishment of psychiatry. It was the principal assumption on which psychiatry as a medical specialty was originally built. The psychiatrist is a physician and his training is as a medical doctor. Mental illness is often seen as just that, an illness. Anxiety, depression, delusions, and so forth are symptoms of an underlying problem, which may very well have an organic basis. A convenient example is the condition known as hypoglycemia, which is a tendency toward chronic low blood sugar. Hypoglycemic individuals may exhibit symptoms that mimic neurosis, such as anxiety, nervous tension, inability to concentrate, and depression. Such individuals will not benefit from conventional psychotherapy; they need to be treated for low blood sugar. The point is that a so-called mental illness is not necessarily mental; it may have its source in an organic condition. Let me be quick, though, to correct what may be an erroneous impression: Although psychiatrists are trained as medical doctors, few of them think of mental illness in exclusively organic terms. They combine the organic approach with a third principal trend underlying psychotherapy, the *psychological approach.*

This approach explains disturbances of emotion or behavior in terms of *psychological concepts*, such as *motives, thought processes, wishes, fears, conditioned responses*, and *habits.* This third trend underlying psychotherapy owes a great deal to the work of Sigmund Freud. Although Freud was a medical doctor, he refused to see his patients' problems in strictly organic terms. As you will learn in the next chapter, he developed in detail a number of psychological concepts for dealing with neurotic reactions in the absence of apparent organic difficulty. The psychological trend continued with great vigor into contemporary times. Since the time of Freud, however, there has been a proliferation of theories and techniques associated with psychotherapy.

The History of Psychiatry, by psychiatrists Franz G. Alexander and Sheldon T. Selesnick, contains an outstanding discussion of the magical, the organic, and the psychological approaches. Commenting on the relationship of the organic approach to the psychological approach, they say:

Brain chemistry undoubtedly has a part in all mental processes, in all our strivings, learning, and ambitions, and also in our mental ailments. But brain chemistry cannot be isolated from man, from what is the core of his existence, his personality. Brain chemistry, indeed, can be altered by emotional stress, by anxiety, rage, fear, and hopelessness. (p. 34)

Once again we see the necessity of avoiding an either–or way of thinking. Psychotherapy can obtain something of value from both the organic and the psychological approaches, one approach does not cancel the other.

PSYCHIATRISTS AND CLINICAL PSYCHOLOGISTS

The two principal kinds of professionals who practice psychotherapy are psychiatrists and clinical psychologists. Psychiatrists are physicians, medical doctors who make the treatment of mental illness their specialty. A clinical psychologist has a master's degree or a doctorate in psychology; the clinical psychologist is *not* a medical doctor and may not prescribe drugs.

Although psychiatrists can and do practice psychotherapy, they also use various types of *somatic therapies*—therapies applied directly to the body for the purpose of alleviating the effects of mental illness. Some of the principal types of somatic therapy are (1) electroshock therapy, (2) chemotherapy, and (3) psychosurgery. *Electroshock therapy* involves inducing a convulsion similar to an epileptic seizure; the convulsion is induced by sending a small amount of electric current through the frontal lobes of the brain. A course of shock treatments may be prescribed for a person suffering from psychotic depression. *Chemotherapy* is based on the use of drugs as a form of treatment. Stimulants are sometimes used to improve a patient's mood; sedatives are often administered to calm mental patients. In the past decade there has been a great increase in the use of *psychotherapeutics*—drugs that have a specific effect on psychosis, anxiety, and depression. *Psychosurgery* is a broad term that includes lobotomy and electrical stimulation of the brain.

In a *lobotomy,* the patient's frontal lobes are severed from the rest of the brain. It has been suggested that the frontal lobes are the seat of the higher thought processes in man. Therefore the operation is indicated only in "hopeless" cases. The theory of lobotomy is simple: Anxiety and depression are the result of distorted thought processes; remove the organs of thought, and the anxiety and depression will be reduced in intensity. Interestingly, patients who have received lobotomies do not necessarily become "vegetables," as is commonly believed. Indeed, they can think; people think with more of their brain than the frontal lobes. Such patients do, however, seem to lose much of their capacity for planning ahead and for original thinking. There has been much controversy within the ranks of mental health professionals about whether lobotomy is ever appropriate. Some defend it as the most humane treatment when all else has failed; others contend that it is a form of barbarism.

Electrical stimulation of the brain (ESB) is a subtle form of psychosurgery. Electrode implants are placed deep within the paleocortex ("old brain"), and it is possible, by applying small amounts of electric current to tiny areas, to affect emotions and behavior. (ESB receives more adequate treatment in Chapter Six.)

The two principal functions of clinical psychologists are psychotherapy and *psychological testing.* Psychotherapy has already been defined, but nothing has been said yet about psychological testing. Psychological testing in a clinical setting is undertaken for two principal reasons: (1) It is useful for diagnosing a patient's condition and thus for suggesting appropriate lines of therapy. (2) If a patient is hospitalized, the information from psychological tests may be helpful in making a sound decision about whether the patient is ready for release. Two principal kinds of psychological tests are *intelligence tests* and *personality tests*.

One example of an intelligence test is the Wechsler Adult Intelligence Scale (WAIS). The WAIS not only yields a global IQ score, but it also provides scores on different dimensions of intelligence. A comparison of these scores can give an astute clinician information that discriminates functional from organic mental disorders. For example, a senile person undergoing organic deterioration of the brain would be likely to score poorly on a subtest of the WAIS called "comprehension." However, his score on the vocabulary subtest might, in comparison, be substantially better than that on the comprehension score. His basic vocabulary was learned many years ago, and it is deeply entrenched; to some extent, the individual is parroting what he has known for years. But the comprehension subtest measures the ability to think now, which is decreasing because of brain damage.

One example of a personality test is the Minnesota Multiphasic Personality Inventory (MMPI). The MMPI is designed to yield a set of scores revealing one's level of personal adjustment along different dimensions of adjustment. The principal ones measured by the MMPI are (1) *hypochondriasis,* a tendency to be overly occupied with one's health; (2) *depression*, a tendency toward feelings of dejection, being in a sad mood, frequently having "the blues"; (3) *hysteria*, a tendency toward converting emotional conflicts into a bodily symptom; (4) *psychopathic deviation*, a tendency to act out emotional conflicts and to develop antisocial patterns of behavior; (5) *masculinity-femininity*, an individual's tendency toward interests that are usually associated with either males or females; (6) *paranoia*, a tendency to mistrust other people excessively; (7) *psychasthenia*, a tendency to develop neurotic reactions; (8) *schizophrenia,* a tendency to become disconnected from conventional reality; and (9) *hypomania*, a tendency to "solve" emotional conflicts by excessive and often irrelevant activity.

The MMPI consists of 550 items that a subject responds to as "true," "false," or "cannot answer." A normal person will sometimes smile with amusement at some of the items; most of them deal with fears, complaints, physical symptoms, and so forth (e.g., "I am afraid when I look down from a high place"). Nonetheless, the results of an MMPI can be both revealing and useful.

I could go on to describe numerous kinds of other measuring instruments used by psychologists. To illustrate, *projective tests*, tests based on the assumption that an individual's response to an ambiguous stimulus (a stimulus that can be perceived in more than one way) reveals "projections" of his ego are commonly used by clinicians. One example of a projective test is the Thematic Apperception Test (TAT), which requires a subject to relate his reactions to a set of pictures portraying somewhat indefinable situations. Another example of a projective test is the Rorschach test, which asks a subject to reveal his perceptions of a set of basically meaningless inkblots.

My major purpose in this section is not to present an exhaustive review of diagnostic instruments, however. My main purpose has been to draw a distinction between the functions of a psychiatrist and of a clinical psychologist. In brief, both kinds of professionals practice psychotherapy. A psychiatrist is a medical doctor and may use drugs and somatic therapies along with psychotherapy. A fully qualified clinical psychologist holds a Ph.D. degree and often has extensive training in administering and interpreting psychological tests. The similarity of the roles of psychiatrist and psychologist is revealed by the fact that the dubious honor of being called a "shrink" can be bestowed on either.

PSYCHOTHERAPY AND THEORIES OF PERSONALITY

There is a close relationship between psychotherapy and theories about the human personality. Psychotherapists, as has been noted already, often develop in-depth relationships with their clients. They may grow to feel that they have gathered powerful insights into the human condition. It seems almost inevitable that intelligent and creative therapists would develop general conceptions about what motivates people, what upsets people, and how people learn. Those with a talent for writing and for organizing their observations have reflected on their learnings and pre-

The psychotherapist often develops an in-depth relationship with his clients.

sented them to the world at large. Such individuals as Sigmund Freud, Carl Jung, Alfred Adler, Karen Horney, Erich Fromm, Carl Rogers, Viktor Frankl, Abraham Maslow, Rollo May, and many, many others have formulated broad general conceptions of what it is to be a human being.

But no precise definition can be given to the terms *personality* or *personality theory*. The psychologist Gordon Allport once said, perhaps rather lightly, that "personality is what a man really is." This definition is a bit too circular for our purposes, however. At the risk of being a bit imprecise, I will attempt to define the concepts of both personality and personality theory.

Let us somewhat loosely define personality as *a more or less stable set of traits, habits, and motivational predispositions characteristic of a particular individual.* What we mean by personality is really a kind of consistency in behavior. If human behavior were not to some degree predictable, the concept of personality would not have arisen. Thus, if John has gotten into a number of fights in recent years, we may begin to think of his as "an aggressive character." We use the adjective "aggressive" to modify the noun "character" because we conceptualize him as "having" the trait of excessive aggression in his personality. Let us say that Jane has gotten a straight A average in college. We may see in her the motivational predisposition of "high need achievement." We thus say, "Jane is an ambitious person," and we have outlined a salient aspect of her personality. As you will see in Chapter Three, a critique of some value can be made of our conventional way of looking at human personality. Nonetheless, folk psychology—the psychology of daily usage—relies heavily on the common-sense approach to personality outlined in this paragraph.

Let us define a theory of personality as *a set of concepts designed to explain the behavior of the whole human organism.* The emphasis is on the word "whole." A theory of personality attempts to deal with the person as he actually lives in the world. The classical theories of personality are quite ambitious and often lay out, within one theory, explanations of human behavior and a philosophy of life. A distinction is sometimes made in psychology between molecular behavior and molar behavior.

Molecular behavior is "little" behavior and is thought of as such isolated phenomena as color perception, sensory thresholds, the effects of massed practice on learning, and so forth. Thus a theory may be limited in its scope to a rather restricted range of events. The Young-Helmholtz theory of color perception is an example of a classical theory that attempts to deal with molecular behavior.

Molar behavior is "big" behavior and is thought of as including such phenomena as how to raise children, communication between husband

and wife, overcoming personal problems, seeking meaning in life, and so forth. Theories of personality are designed to deal with these larger issues of human existence, and as such they play an important role in this book. They appear as an underlying motif in the chapters to come.

It would be an error to think that all theories of personality derive from the clinical tradition of psychotherapy. Another major source of personality theories in American psychology is the tradition of experimental psychology. Although experimental psychology is often conceptualized as limited in its interest to molecular behavior, this is a mistaken impression. Experimental psychologists can be as ambitious in their theorizing as psychotherapists, and individuals like Clark L. Hull, Edward C. Tolman, John Dollard, Neal Miller, and B. F. Skinner are often identified as personality theorists. Indeed, the formerly sharp distinction between psychotherapy and experimental psychology is blurring today because so many of the findings from experimental psychology are becoming effective tools of psychotherapy. Also, research psychologists in university settings seem to be increasingly willing to attempt direct psychotherapy derived from the experimental, as opposed to the clinical, approach.

PRINCIPAL MODES OF PSYCHOTHERAPY

Let us distinguish three principal modes of psychotherapy: (1) analytic therapies, (2) behavior therapies, and (3) existential therapies. Like so many attempts at categorization, the categories overlap and are to some degree arbitrary. They are set up because they allow us to discriminate some major themes in psychotherapy.

Analytic therapies stress the concept of *insight*. There is something about oneself that is not completely understood. The assumption is that an analysis or interpretation of one's motivational structure will help one "see into" the deeper roots of a psychological-emotional problem. This "seeing into," or development of insight, is presumed to remove psychic material from an inaccessible unconscious level to a more accessible conscious level. The process is what has been described as "consciousness raising."

As an illustration of how analytic therapy might work, consider a client who has chronic ulcers. At one point in the therapy the client might remark, "I'm beginning to see things in a new way. I thought I was a nice person—liked everybody. I always got good marks in school for 'gets along well with others.' But I'm beginning to see that I've got a lot of bottled-up anger. There are a lot of things I want to tell my wife, but I don't let myself. I haven't even been letting myself think these things! Gads! There's so much about myself that I don't know. I'm just beginning to understand some of these things for the first time. I think my ulcers are aggravated by anger directed inwardly when it should really be directed outwardly.'' The client and the therapist will discuss such observations and attempt to evaluate them. At times the therapist may offer interpretations: ''Do you think that maybe you were attracted to Mabel because she reminded you of your mother?'' The basic assumption is that there is an unconscious level to mental life; a secondary assumption is that exploring this unconscious level is useful in freeing a person from his inner struggles.

Behavior therapies tend to emphasize *action* instead of insight. The attitude tends to be tough-minded: ''Get off your duff and do something about your problems!'' (Such a statement would seldom be communicated to a client so bluntly; it is an implicit theme of the therapy, not an explicit directive.) The point of intervention is not the inner psychic struggle, but the observable behavior patterns. A behavior therapist will tend to be impatient with long-winded discussions about why this and why that; he tends to be much more concerned with the question of how. ''How is this undesirable behavior pattern maintained?'' is a much more fruitful question for the behavior therapist than ''Why did this undesirable behavior pattern come into existence?'' The following exchange illustrates the attitude of the behavior therapist:

Client. I don't know why I smoke so much. I guess I've just got a weak ego or something. No willpower—I can't quit no matter how hard I try.

Therapist. Do you take coffee breaks at work? Do you usually smoke when you're taking a coffee break? And do you usually have coffee at the break?

Client. Yeah, I take breaks and I usually have coffee.

Therapist. OK. Let's try this: Tomorrow, when break time comes, go to a different place than the usual place. Or maybe take a ten-minute walk around the block. Don't drink any coffee—you're probably being cued by the coffee to light up. You're also probably being cued by the familiar place and the conversation of friends and the fact that some of them light up. Just take a walk by yourself for a few days and see if you can break the pattern. Let's make a start somewhere.

Client. It's worth a try.

Existential therapies tend to emphasize the importance of making the most of one's life. Two broad themes can be identified. One deals with the question, ''What is my proper place in the scheme of things?'' The other deals with the question, ''What am I meant to be in terms of my talents and potentialities?'' In existential therapy, a great deal of emphasis is on the principle of *becoming*, a growth-oriented concept. The assumption is that individuals who refuse to grow and who fail to make the most of their possibilities as human beings will suffer from *existential guilt*, the feeling that they have wasted their lives. To the existential therapist, neurotic reactions and other human disturbances are the result of some kind of interference with the capacity of the individual to grow and to become the person he was meant to be. Existential therapies tend to reject the unconscious-conscious dichotomy of mental life made by the analytic therapies. The existential therapist regards the concept of an unconscious mental life as an abstraction and excess explanatory baggage. The emphasis is on the importance of human consciousness as a tool for self-mobilization and self-realization. What is analyzed in the existential approach to adjustment and growth is not the relationship of elements within the mind, but the relationship of the person to existence itself. We will return to these themes in Chapter Seven.

ADJUSTMENT AND GROWTH

This chapter began with the question, "Do you consider yourself a well-adjusted person?" The second question in the chapter was, "Are you making the most of your talents and potentialities as a human being?" The second question was intended to evoke your interest in a concept closely related to the concept of adjustment—the concept of personal growth. Although the concepts are closely related, they are not the same. Both are important, and it will be of value to examine their similarities and differences.

ADJUSTMENT

The *Dictionary of Behavioral Science* defines adjustment as follows:

> *Adjustment.* 1. A harmonious relationship with the environment involving the ability to satisfy most of one's needs and meet most of the demands, both physical and social, that are put upon one. 2. The variations and changes in behavior that are necessary to satisfy needs and meet demands so that one can establish a harmonious relationship with the environment.

The emphasis in the definition is on *harmony*. In practical terms, this means that you are adjusting if you eat when you are hungry, drink when you are thirsty, run when you are afraid, try to find shelter in a storm, seek relief from sexual tension, and avoid a disagreeable person. In all of these instances, you are coping with life in general; you are trying to survive.

This is the central theme of the concept of adjustment: A more or less harmonious relationship with the environment has been established when you find it relatively easy to survive on a day-to-day basis.

PERSONAL GROWTH

The term *personal growth* as used in this book is intended to be synonymous with the concept of self-actualization. The *Dictionary of Behavioral Science* defines self-actualization as follows:

> *Self-actualization.* 1. (K. Goldstein) Striving toward completeness; fulfillment of one's potentialities. 2. (A. Maslow) Developing and fulfilling one's innate, positive potentialities.

The emphasis in the definition is on *fulfillment.* Clearly, in some cases the striving to fulfill one's potentialities may upset standing adjustments in one's life. Therefore we must not be glib and try to pass over adjustment and growth as if they were equivalent concepts. This is particularly important in view of the increasing emphasis on the concept of self-actualization in recent years.

Why bother with self-actualization at all? It is clear that moving forward does entail running risks. The psychologist Abraham H. Maslow was probably the one person most responsible for calling popular attention to the need for self-actualization. In *Toward a Psychology of Being*, he has this to say:

Growth has not only rewards and pleasures but also many intrinsic pains and always will have. Each step forward is a step into the unfamiliar and is possibly dangerous. It also means giving up something familiar and good and satisfying. (p. 24)

So we see that there are risks in growth. However, Maslow argues, it is important that we concern ourselves with our need for self-actualization:

If this essential core (inner nature) of the person is frustrated, denied, or suppressed, sickness results. Sometimes in obvious forms, sometimes in subtle and devious forms, sometimes immediately, sometimes later. These psychological illnesses include many more than those listed by the American Psychiatric Association. For instance, the character disorders and disturbances are now far more important for the fate of the world than the classical neuroses or even psychoses. From this point of view, new kinds of illness are most dangerous, e.g., "the diminished or stunted person," i.e., the loss of any of the defining characteristics of humanness, or personhood, the failure to grow to one's potential, valuelessness, etc. (p. 181)

We now have the answer to our question: Why bother with self-actualization at all? The answer is that a person who does not try to make the most

For the person who is willing to run some of the risks inherent in a policy of personal growth, life is perceived as a challenge.

of his life runs the risk of falling into existential despair. There are risks in growth, as already noted. Less obviously, however, there are also risks in avoiding growth, refusing to act on one's talents, and rejecting opportunities when they present themselves. The person who clings like Linus to a psychological security blanket may someday regret his "safety first" policy. The eventual feeling that life has little meaning, that existence is empty, and that there is nothing really worth doing may turn out to be his "reward" for excessive caution. "Is this all there is?" asked a once popular song, reflecting the pervasiveness of what the psychiatrist Viktor Frankl has called the *existential vacuum*—a feeling of emptiness in existence. But for the person who is willing to run some of the risks inherent in a policy of personal growth, life is perceived as a challenge; the person has many constructive escapes from boredom and there is zest in living.

STABILITY AND CHANGE

Does a person have to make a choice between adjustment and self-actualization? Fortunately, for most of us the choice is not such a stark one. We must avoid categorical thinking, feeling that we have to choose one psychological box over another. The concept of adjustment represents stability in life; the concept of self-actualization represents change (and growth) in life. Consider as an analogy a tightrope walker. He must maintain his balance on the rope to move forward successfully. Maintaining his balance is analagous to the concept of adjustment; moving forward successfully is analagous to the concept of growth. For most of us, this image of an integral relationship between stability and change is a preferable one to the image of stability and change as antagonistic forces. If we can keep the image of the tightrope walker in mind, we can see the value of the traditional concept of adjustment as well as the value of the more recent concept of self-actualization.

CONCLUDING REMARKS

The economist Kenneth Boulding said, ''The world of today . . . is as different from the world in which I was born as that world was from Julius Caesar's. I was born in the middle of human history, to date, roughly. Almost as much has happened since I was born as happened before.'' Such a statement is, of course, impossible to evaluate with any precision. It does, however, serve a purpose in calling our attention to the fact that we do live in a rapidly changing world. The social critic Alvin Toffler coined the term *future shock* to indicate the stress reactions that can take place in people when change in a society is rapid.

In the three short decades between now and the twenty-first century, millions of ordinary, psychologically normal people will face an abrupt collision with the future. Citizens of the world's richest and most technologically advanced nations, many of them will find it increasingly painful to keep up with the incessant demand for change that characterizes our time. For them, the future will have arrived too soon. (p. 9)

As Toffler notes, many cannot adapt to changing times; others seem to thrive on change. If you must face change, certainly you would prefer to be among those who thrive on it. This book may not be able to show you how to thrive on change. (As noted in the opening pages, it is not a how-to book.) Nonetheless, it is my hope that some solid information is provided that will help you live a rewarding life in a painful-pleasurable world.

SUMMARY AND SELF-TEST

1 The textbook takes an eclectic point of view, that is, it does not see pathways toward adjustment and growth as mutually exclusive.
T   F

2 The term *psychoanalysis* may be used correctly as a synonym for psychology.
T   F

3 According to dualism, the body and the soul are two distinct and different substances.
T   F

4 Watson attempted to bring back into psychology such traditional concepts as the human will and consciousness.
T   F

5 B. F. Skinner is a Gestalt psychologist.
T   F

6 The author feels that we are compelled to make a choice between subjective psychology and objective psychology.
T   F

7 The objective psychologist is apt to be tender-minded and stresses the rationalist, feeling, and freewill approach to psychology.
T   F

8 The concept of the placebo effect suggests that the expectation of cure helps an afflicted person to improve.
T   F

9 Neurotic persons tend to be troublemakers, but not troubled.
T   F

10 There are two kinds of hysterical neurosis: (1) obsessive-compulsive reaction and (2) depressive neurosis.
T   F

11 When an individual takes leave of ordinary reality, he is said to be suffering from a character disorder.

T   F

12 A common characteristic of psychotic reactions is a tendency to suffer from delusions.

T   F

13 The chief characteristic of paranoia is a tendency to regress to an infantile level of functioning.

T   F

14 The fictional character Captain Nemo personifies the concept of the alienated man.

T   F

15 Individuals with character disorders tend to be impulsive, acting without sufficient attention to the consequences of their actions.

T   F

16 Sexual deviations are grouped with the psychotic reactions.

T   F

17 A basic trend underlying psychotherapy is the magical trend.

T   F

18 The approach to psychotherapy that explains disturbances of emotion or behavior in terms of symptoms of an illness and organic impairment is the psychological approach.

T   F

19 Electroshock therapy is a somatic therapy.

T   F

20 The Minnesota Multiphasic Personality Inventory (MMPI) is primarily an intelligence test.

T   F

21 The concept of personality arose because human behavior is almost completely unpredictable.

T   F

22 Molar behavior is "little" behavior.

T   F

23 The three principal modes of psychotherapy identified in the book are analytical therapies, behavior therapies, and existential therapies.

T   F

24   Behavior therapies stress the importance of the concept of insight.
T   F

25   The existential approach asserts that individuals who refuse to grow and who fail to make the most of their possibilities as human beings will suffer from existential guilt.
T   F

26   The concept of adjustment stresses the importance of a harmonious relationship with one's environment.
T   F

27   The concept of self-actualization stresses the importance of fulfilling one's potentialities.
T   F

28   The psychologist John Watson was probably the one person most responsible for calling popular attention to the need for self-actualization.
T   F

29   The psychiatrist Viktor Frankl refers to a feeling of emptiness in existence as the "existential vacuum."
T   F

30   Unfortunately, we are forced to make a stark choice between adjustment and self-actualization.
T   F

ANSWER KEY

1   *True.* The textbook takes an eclectic point of view. It does not see pathways toward adjustment and growth as mutually exclusive.

2   *False.* The term psychoanalysis is not a synonym for psychology.

3   *True.* According to dualism, the body and the soul are two distinct and different substances.

4   *False.* Watson attempted to cast out of psychology such traditional concepts as the human will and consciousness.

5   *False.* B. F. Skinner is a behaviorist.

6   *False.* The author does not feel that we are compelled to make a choice between subjective psychology and objective psychology.

7   *False.* The objective psychologist is apt to be tough-minded and rejects the rationalist, feeling, and freewill approach to psychology.

8   *True.* The concept of the placebo effect suggests that the expectation of cure helps an afflicted person to improve.

9   *False.* Neurotic persons tend to be troubled, suffering from internal conflicts.

10   *False.* The two kinds of hysterical neurosis are (1) conversion type and (2) dissociative type.

11   *False.* When an individual takes leave of ordinary reality, he is said to be suffering from a psychotic reaction.

12   *True.* A common characteristic of psychotic reactions is a tendency to suffer from delusions.

13   *False.* The chief characteristic of paranoia is an organized delusional system.

14   *True.* The fictional character Captain Nemo personifies the concept of the alienated man.

15   *True.* Individuals with character disorders tend to be impulsive, acting without sufficient attention to the consequences of their actions.

16   *False.* Sexual deviations are grouped with the character disorders.

17   *True.* A basic trend underlying psychotherapy is the magical trend.

18   *False.* The approach to psychotherapy that explains disturbances of emotion or behavior in terms of symptoms of an illness and organic impairment is the organic approach.

19   *True.* Electroshock therapy is a somatic therapy.

20   *False.* The Minnesota Multiphasic Personality Inventory (MMPI) is primarily a personality test, not an intelligence test.

21   *False.* The concept of personality arose because human behavior is, to a large degree, stable and predictable.

22   *False.* Molar behavior is "big" behavior.

23   *True.* The three principal modes of psychotherapy identified in the book are analytical therapies, behavior therapies, and existential therapies.

24   *False.* Behavior therapies tend to emphasize action.

25   *True.* The existential approach asserts that individuals who refuse to grow and who fail to make the most of their possibilities as human beings will suffer from existential guilt.

26   *True.* The concept of adjustment stresses the importance of a harmonious relationship with one's environment.

27   *True.* The concept of self-actualization stresses the importance of fulfilling one's potentialities.

28   *False.* The psychologist Abraham Maslow was probably the one person most responsible for calling popular attention to the need for self-actualization.

29   *True.* The psychiatrist Viktor Frankl refers to a feeling of emptiness in existence as the "existential vacuum."

30   *False.* Fortunately, for most of us a stark choice between adjustment and self-actualization is not demanded.

DISCUSSION QUESTIONS

PSYCHOLOGY AND HUMAN BEINGS

1 Have you recently read a popular book on psychology? What did you think of it? Was it of any personal value?

2 What is your opinion of dualism? Are the body and the soul (including the mind) two distinct and different substances?

3 Do you favor the tough-minded or the tender-minded orientation toward psychology?

CONCEPTIONS OF MENTAL ILLNESS

1 Can you give an example from your own experience of the placebo effect?

2 The traditional categories of behavioral pathology are neurosis, psychosis, and character disorders. Do you find anything to disagree with in this classification scheme?

3 Have you ever had any personal contact with a psychotic person? Under what circumstances?

4 Do you know someone you might think of as suffering from a character disorder? What does the person do that would suggest such a label is justified?

PSYCHOTHERAPY

1 Are you afraid of psychotherapy? Or would you go willingly to a therapist if you thought you were suffering from a psychological-emotional disturbance?

2 Do you tend to favor the medical-organic or the psychological approach to treating behavioral disorders?

3 In your own words, how does a psychiatrist differ from a clinical psychologist?

4 Think of someone you know well. If you were limited to three adjectives, what personality traits would you list as his or her dominant ones? Do you feel that the trait approach captures the core of an individual's personality?

5 As you were reading about analytical, behavior, and existential therapies, did one approach seem more valid to you than another? If so, why?

ADJUSTMENT AND GROWTH

1 Do you consider yourself a well adjusted person? Why do you answer as you do?

2 Do you feel that you are making the most of your talents and potentialities as a human being? Why do you answer as you do?

3 What does the phrase *personal growth* mean to you?

4 *Adjustment* is not the same as *self-actualization*. In what ways are the concepts similar and/or different?

REFERENCES

Alexander, F. F., and Selesnick, S. T. *The History of Psychiatry*. New York: New American Library, 1968.

Allport, G. As quoted in Hall, C. S., and Lindzey, G., *Theories of Personality*. New York: John Wiley and Sons, 1970.

Ansbacher, H. L., and Ansbacher, R. R. *The Individual Psychology of Alfred Adler*. New York: Harper & Row, 1964.

Berne, E. *Games People Play*. New York: Grove Press, 1964.

Boulding, K. As quoted in Toffler, A., *Future Shock*. New York: Bantam Books, 1971.

Frank, J. *Persuasion and Healing*. Baltimore: Johns Hopkins Press, 1961.

Glasser, W. *Reality Therapy*. New York: Harper & Row, 1965.

Harris, T. *I'm OK—You're OK*. New York: Harper & Row, 1967.

Janov, A. *The Primal Scream*. New York: G. P. Putnam's Sons, 1970.

Jong, E. *Fear of Flying*. New York: Holt, Rinehart & Winston, 1973.

Liebman, J. L. *Peace of Mind*. New York: Simon & Schuster, 1946.

McNeil, E. B. *The Quiet Furies*. Englewood Cliffs, N.J.: Prentice-Hall, 1967.

Maslow, A. H. *Toward a Psychology of Being*. New York: D. Van Nostrand Co., 1962.

Mowrer, O. H. As quoted in Glasser, W., *Reality Therapy*. New York: Harper & Row, 1965.

Newman, M., and Berkowitz, B. *How To Be Your Own Best Friend*. New York: Ballantine Books, 1971.

Overstreet, H. A. As quoted in *The Great Quotations*. New York: Pocket Books, 1967.

Skinner, B. F. *Beyond Freedom and Dignity*. New York: Alfred A. Knopf, 1971.

Szasz, T. *The Myth of Mental Illness*. New York: Harper & Row, 1961.

Toffler, A. *Future Shock.* New York: Bantam Books, 1971.

Verne, J. *Twenty Thousand Leagues Under the Sea.* New York: The World Publishing Co., 1946.

Watson, J. B. "What Is Thinking?" In *Good Reading in Psychology.* (Gazzaniga, M. S. and Lovejoy, E. P., Eds.) Englewood Cliffs, N.J.: Prentice-Hall, 1971.

Wolman, B. B., ed. *Dictionary of Behavioral Science.* New York: Van Nostrand Reinhold Co., 1973.

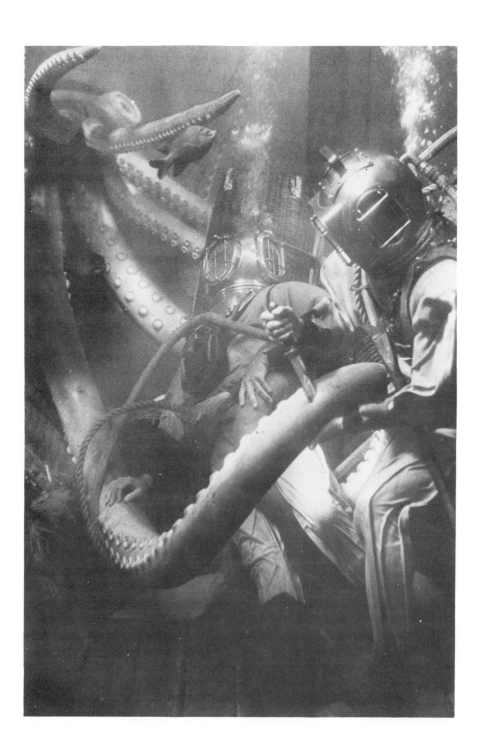

CHAPTER 2 DEPTH PSYCHOLOGY: EXPLORING UNCONSCIOUS LEVELS

Depth psychology asserts that, like inhabitants of an undersea world, many forces reside below the surface of the conscious mind. (Scene from the movie ''Reap the Wild Wind.'')

OVERVIEW

OUTLINE

TWO KEY QUESTIONS

What is depth psychology?
Depth psychology is the psychology of unconscious mental processes. It asserts that there is a "lower" level to the personality, a level below the threshold of consciousness, and that this level is the scene of action for forbidden motives, painful memories, and disturbing ideas. Depth psychology further asserts that these unconscious forces have a profound effect on an individual's emotions and behavior.

How do the principles of depth psychology relate to adjustment and growth?
Depth psychology views human problems as the result of lacks in self-understanding. A basic principle of depth psychology is that by gaining insight into one's own unconscious dynamics, the individual can attain freedom from their involuntary influence. The "normal" person is not under the excessive domination of invisible psychological agents. Adjustment and growth take place as a function of unlocking the secrets of the unconscious contents of the personality.

Sigmund Freud died in 1939. In his obituary, which the *New York Times* published on September 24, Freud is quoted as having said, "The mind is an iceberg—it floats with only one-seventh of its bulk above water." In this short sentence Freud revealed the heart of his approach to psychology. This is why Freud's psychology and its derivatives are classified under the general heading of *depth psychology*. Depth psychology may be defined as any psychological system that places great emphasis on the assumption that most of our mental life takes place below the threshold of conscious awareness. The iceberg is utilized as a striking metaphor to convey the importance of unconscious forces in human behavior.

Freud is seldom thought of as a poet. And yet in the same *New York Times* obituary, the following words are attributed to him:

The conscious mind may be compared to a fountain playing in the sun and falling back into the great subterranean pool of the subconscious from which it rises.

Here Freud uses a different metaphor, that of a fountain, to illustrate his view of the mind as an active and living entity. It is clear from the fountain illustration that he did not think of "the unconscious" as a place or thing. Freud has often been accused of *misplaced concreteness*, making a process an object. One can find in the writings of many Freudians

Freud said that the mind is an iceberg.

frequent references to the unconscious as if it were a territory or region. Such a notion was present in Freud's earlier writing, but his mature viewpoint was to think of the unconscious much more in terms of a process than of a thing. He preferred to use the word unconscious as an adjective; thus he spoke of unconscious motives, unconscious ideas, unconscious wishes, unconscious feelings, and so forth.

Before we go on, let me illustrate how the idea of unconscious factors in mental life can be used to explain human behavior. Assume that a man is away from home on a business trip. He spends a weekend away, and dashes off a postcard to his wife: "Having wonderful time, wish you were here." When he arrives home his wife is furious. She shows him the card. Much to his dismay he sees that he inadvertently left the *e* off the word "here." He finally convinces his wife that it was a meaningless error, that there was no time spent with another woman. He made the mistake because he was in a hurry and wrote the card rapidly. And in fact he was objectively innocent—there was no other woman. Freud, however, would have said that the error was not meaningless. It reveals the presence of an unconscious wish; unconsciously, the man wanted to be with another woman. But in terms of his particular self-concept, this was a forbidden wish. Therefore the wish was *repressed*, involuntarily shoved down by force to an unconscious level. The wish was not destroyed by repression; it made its existence known by causing the slip of the pen.

Perhaps you protest. The man was in a hurry. Are there no innocent errors that are just that—errors? Freud would reply that because the man was in a hurry proves nothing. It is precisely under such conditions that the censorship of unconscious elements becomes momentarily lax. They slip out and find some sort of route to a conscious level when one is off guard. As for innocent errors, Freud categorically denied them status. Freud adhered to the principle of *psychic determinism*, the assertion that all mental events have a cause.

It would be incorrect to think that Freud was responsible for introducing the concept of an unconscious mental life to the Western world. The history of unconscious functioning can be traced through many centuries. More than three hundred years before the birth of Christ, Plato said that the soul of man has two divisions. The first division is the rational soul. It is with the rational soul that we think, reflect, analyze, evaluate, do arithmetic, and make decisions. The second division is the irrational soul. The irrational soul is the source of our appetites, our desires. The irrational soul is outside of conscious control; it is a blind force that gives impetus to our lives. As you can see, the irrational soul operated as a basically unconscious agent. In the thirteenth century, the great Roman Catholic theologian Saint Thomas Aquinas said that one of the powers of the human soul is the *nutritive power,* which gives human beings the capacity to grow, mature, and reproduce. This bears a strong resemblance to Plato's irrational soul. Both concepts are prototypes for Freud's more fully articulated concept of the *id,* an unconscious aspect of the human personality that is the source of our basic biological drives. (More will be said about the id later.)

Toward the latter part of the seventeenth century, the philosopher Gottfried Wilhelm Leibnitz proposed the concept of *apperception.* In contemporary terms, apperception would be equivalent to our concept of *subliminal perception*, the ability to record an event without conscious awareness. In the 1950s an advertising agency reported a "brave new world" kind of experiment wtih subliminal perception. The words "Eat popcorn" or "Buy soda" were flashed on a movie screen so briefly (e.g., one-tenth of a second) that the presentation did not intrude on consciousness. The brief presentations were repeated a number of times. The agency reported that at intermission time popcorn and soda sales increased by a measurable degree. The validity of the experiment is in dispute, and it is likely that the impact of subliminal presentations, if they affect behavior at all, is slight. The experiment is cited because it provides a vivid example of what is meant by subliminal perception.

To take another example, if sexually taboo words are flashed on a screen, subjects tend to take longer to consciously recognize them than they take to consciously recognize neutral words. Now we get into a bit of a quandary! If conscious recognition time is delayed because of some sort of perceptual defense mechanism (which is strongly implied), wouldn't the subject have to unconsciously recognize the word before "deciding" not to consciously recognize it? Odd as it sounds, the answer seems to be yes, and we have another example of subliminal perception. Leibnitz also proposed the concept of the *limen,* or the threshold of consciousness. (You can see the presence of the word *limen* in the word *subliminal,* meaning below the threshold.) Although Leibnitz did not do experiments, the point is simply that his views antedate Freud and modern psychology by almost three hundred years.

Writing and thinking in the eighteenth century, a giant of German philosophy, Immanuel Kant, accepted the doctrine of apperception and expanded it. Kant said that the mind organizes experience for man through its power of apperception. Translated into contemporary language, this means that the world makes sense to us because we subconsciously organize it. We do not will it to be organized; it is not a voluntary process. It just seems to be quite proper and natural that event A precedes event B and that thing X stands in front of thing Y. We think nothing of it; the perception of a world neatly ordered in terms of time and space seems effortless. This is what Kant meant by apperception or subconscious perception. He thus asserted that an important mental process takes place below the threshold of consciousness. That this can happen is a central assumption in Freud's system. This is particularly important in that Freud was certainly familiar with the basic outlines of Kantian philosophy.

In the early part of the nineteenth century, another German philosopher, Johann Friedrich Herbart, spoke of the *apperceptive mass*, a mental reservoir consisting of all our ideas and all our past experiences. Moment-to-moment experiences exist only briefly at a conscious level, then they sink below the limen and become part of the apperceptive mass. According to Herbart, all meaning comes from our apperceptive mass. Thus the notion is important for educators. Suppose you tell a four-year-old child, "I'm going to teach you a little algebra. $X+3=5$. Think it over. What do you think X equals?" The odds are that you are not going to get a sensible answer because the child has not yet acquired the concept of number; this concept is not part of his apperceptive mass (or in popular terms, his subconscious mind). Suppose, however, that you pose the same problem to an eight-year-old child. He has not studied algebra, but the problem is meaningful to him because he does have the concept of number stored in his apperceptive mass. He may very well give the correct answer. Herbart asserted that we store a great deal of important information at an unconscious level. This view is important in the Freudian system.

More importantly, Herbart wrote that ideas have energy and that certain ideas are compatible and others are incompatible. Thus Herbart laid down the outline of another assumption in Freud's thought, the assumption that ideas can fight each other—that there can be mental conflicts. Assume that a man has been raised with idea A, "Thou shalt not kill." He has also been raised with idea B, "One should be a patriot and do battle for one's country." The ideas are incompatible, and we have an example of a mental conflict. Assume that the conflict is intense, that he holds tightly to both ideas. The "solution" to such a conflict may come from an unconscious idea: "If I were paralyzed nobody would expect me to fight." The man might develop a *conversion reaction*, a neurotic response in which a conflict is resolved by converting it into a bodily symptom. He loses his ability to walk. It is essential to note that basic psychoanalytic doctrine postulates that the unconscious idea is really just that—unconscious. It is repressed and its content does not pass above the threshold of consciousness.

In the preceding few pages, an attempt has been made to establish the view that Freud did not invent or discover the existence of unconscious levels of mental functioning. This point is not made to downgrade Freud. On the contrary, Freud himself was not unaware of the contributions to his thought of philosophers and other psychologists. He saw himself as building on a solid tradition of thought. His way of seeing human behavior was very much a part of what is called the *zeitgeist*, the mode of thinking of the times. Having noted this, we should also note that Freud was an original thinker. He modified existing concepts in ways that had an enormous impact on man's view of man.

PSYCHOANALYSIS: INSIGHTS ON THE COUCH

When the layman thinks of psychoanalysis, he probably visualizes the patient reclining on a couch with the psychoanalyst sitting out of the patient's vision. This stereotype has been perpetuated by countless cartoons. One cartoon may show a duck dressed up like a man, lying on the couch and saying, "I don't know, doc. Lately I've developed a tremendous craving for milk and quackers." Another may find the psychiatrist commenting coldly to a skinny little man, "I've discovered your problem, Mr. Jones. You aren't suffering from an inferiority complex. You *are* inferior!" And there is the story of the female patient who says to her psychoanalyst, "Love me! Love me madly! I want only you! You're the man of my dreams!" The analyst smiles and says, "My dear, you are merely experiencing the transference phenomenon. This isn't real love, only an illusion. And furthermore it would not be professional for me to respond to your invitation. You see the many degrees on my wall representing my years of training. Indeed, I shouldn't even be lying here on the couch with you!" So we see that cartoons and jokes about patients and their analysts reveal a certain theme of hostility toward both. The jokes are usually put-downs of either the patient or the therapist. The general public has mixed positive-negative feelings about psychoanalysis.

The stereotype of the reclining patient is not in fact so farfetched. Classical psychoanalysis does imply insights on the couch. Freud had his patients recline and look away from him. There are theoretical reasons for this, but in addition it seems that Freud was a bit shy and found it painful to be stared at all day. *Inside Psychotherapy*, edited by Adelaide Bry, is a book of interviews with various kinds of psychotherapists. One interviewee was psychoanalyst Van Buren O. Hammett, chairman of the Department of Psychiatry at Hahnemann Medical College in Philadelphia. In the following exchange, Miss Bry asks about the role of the couch in psychoanalysis:

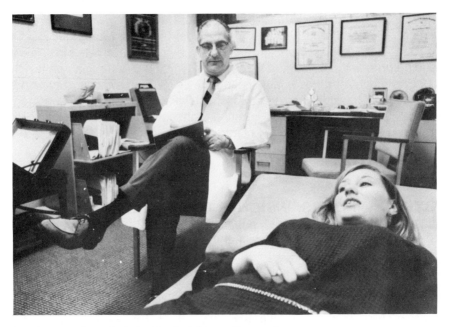

Classical psychoanalysis implies insights on the couch.

Adelaide Bry. Does the patient now and then lie down on the traditional couch, and do you sit behind him?

Dr. Hammett. Yes—there are advantages to that. One is purely practical: it's a little more comfortable for both the patient and the doctor. You know, unless people are very fond of one another, or unless they're fighting, it's easier not to have to watch one another all the time while talking.

Adelaide Bry. I never thought of that before.

Dr. Hammett. It's more relaxed to just talk without watching the other person's face to see how you're being received, and this, incidentally, is the main reason for asking the patient to lie down and not see the doctor: so that he won't watch the doctor's face and change his thoughts according to what he sees or thinks he sees in the way of reaction in the doctor's face. So we try to remove that distraction, and the way we do this is to have the patient lie down, looking at the ceiling. (p. 37)

Freud once said that the therapist should be the opaque mirror upon which patients can see themselves. The unobtrusive presence of the therapist is designed to facilitate the mirror function. There are other points of view, of course. Many contemporary psychotherapists prefer a face-to-face relationship with their clients.

WHO WAS SIGMUND FREUD?

Sigmund Freud was a man for all seasons. He was loved and hated, admired and despised. To some he was "the Master"; to others he was "that fool" or "that sex maniac" or, in his later years, "that dirty old man." He is widely regarded as one of the greatest thinkers of the twentieth century. He was a man with many friends and many enemies. Some of his early friends became disenchanted with Freud and fell away from his psychoanalytic circle; the two most prominent examples are Carl Jung and Alfred Adler. He was the most famous psychologist who ever lived, and yet he did not hold a university degree in psychology. He was a medical doctor, a specialist in neurology, and he developed his psychological theories from his work with neurotic patients. He never wanted to be a practitioner. As a young man he yearned for a university position as a researcher in physiology, but the low status of the Jews in Austria at the time made him unable to realize his dream of a career in pure science.

Freud was born in 1856 in the Austro-Hungarian Empire, and he died in London at the age of eighty-three. He spent most of his years as a practicing physician in Vienna, Austria. He was finally convinced to leave his beloved Vienna toward the end of his life, fleeing the anti-Semitism of the Nazis. His old age was marred by his flight to London and cancer of the

Sigmund Freud was the father of psychoanalysis.

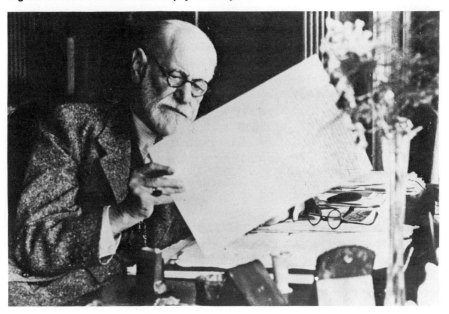

mouth; for several years he wore a painful prosthetic device that gave him an artificial palate. In spite of the pain and the great difficulties in speaking, he saw some patients until shortly before he died.

Freud was the first child of a "May-September" marriage. His mother was considerably younger than Freud's father; she was his second wife. Freud was born with a thick shock of black hair, the sign of a prophet among Jewish people. Freud's mother took this sign seriously and treated him throughout his development as a special person. His brothers and sisters referred to him as "the little genius." One of Freud's major theoretical conceptions is the Oedipus complex, which involves guilt over sexual attraction to the parent of the opposite sex. It seems clear enough now that some of the theory arises from his own romantic attachment to his mother. She was young when Freud was born, retained her beauty for many years, and always treated Freud like a crown prince. Indeed, Freud maintained a close relationship with her as long as she lived, visiting her at least once a week.

A major influence on Freud's thinking was the doctrine of *antivitalism*, as proposed by that giant of German physiology and physics, Hermann Ludwig Ferdinand von Helmholtz. The doctrine of antivitalism asserts that to explain the existence of life, it is not necessary to postulate the presence within living things of some special force, such as a soul or a "vital energy." Life is explained by the interaction of known electrochemical reactions. A major proponent of this point of view was the physiologist Ernest Brucke, and Freud was one of his most devoted students.

From his early years Freud thought of himself as a natural scientist, and he always sought cause-and-effect explanations. Thus we can see why he was so dedicated to the principle of psychic determinism; mental events are like any other events—they are caused and follow lawful principles. One of Freud's discoveries in Brucke's laboratory was the anesthetic properties of cocaine. A few drops in the eye made painless eye surgery possible. Freud published his findings, but somehow early fame passed him by. Another man publishing at the same time was credited with discovering the value of cocaine. This was one of Freud's greatest disappointments in life.

Turning from pure to applied science, Freud graduated from medical school at the age of twenty-five. He spent a period of time in postgraduate study in France with the famous neurologist Jean Martin Charcot. Charcot had great skill as a hypnotist and demonstrated to his students that some persons who seemed to have neurological problems were really *hysterics*. Such individuals had the symptoms of a neurological impairment. They were deaf, blind, or paralyzed. Under hypnosis, however, Charcot was able to relieve their symptoms temporarily, thus demonstrating that some sort of psychological, emotional, or personality disturbance was the real cause of their difficulties. Freud was impressed by Charcot and his demonstrations, and the idea grew in Freud that unconscious forces played a part in hysteria.

Another idea thrown out rather carelessly by Charcot impressed Freud— the idea that neuroses have a sexual origin. Freud was at a party at Charcot's home, and a discussion arose about a young married woman who suffered from neurotic reactions. There was reason to suspect her husband of either impotence or great sexual awkwardness. In *The Passions of the Mind,* a biographical novel about Freud by Irving Stone, an exchange at the party between Charcot and a colleague is dramatized:

"Are you suggesting, Monsieur Charcot, that the wife's illness could have been caused by the husband's condition?"

Charcot cried with great vitality: "But in this kind of case it's always a question of the genitals . . . always . . . always . . . always."

Sigmund was astonished. He watched Charcot wrap his arms around his stomach and jump up and down with insistence. (p. 188)

This incident is said to have had a great impact on Freud's thinking. The importance of frustrations and distortions in the sexual drive play an important part in the Freudian theory of neurosis.

As a young and struggling physician in Vienna, Freud was befriended by the successful Dr. Josef Breur. Breur sent Freud patients, discussed cases with him, and lent him money. Like Charcot, Breur also had an enormous impact on Freud's early theorizing. One of Breur's patients was a young woman named Bertha Pappenheim. When Freud and Breur subsequently wrote her case history, they protected her identity. (In the annals of psychoanalysis she is famous as "Anna O.") Bertha suffered from a variety of neurotic symptoms. Breur discovered that her symptoms could be greatly alleviated by encouraging her to talk freely under hypnosis. Breur called his treatment the "talking cure." Bertha herself nicknamed it "chimney sweeping." The things she revealed were filled with emotional content; she experienced distress and cried as she spoke. Breur and Freud worked together on the theory of why the talking cure worked and called the emotional release an *abreaction,* a relieving of painful emotional experiences. They theorized that the abreaction was essential for improvement; the pent-up feelings associated with key experiences had to be discharged.

Freud was anxious to publish the result of their research, but Breur was reluctant. There were certain problems. For one thing, Bertha's conflicts revolved around sexual feeling for her dead father. For another, during the treatment Bertha went through a phase in which she fell in love with

Breur. In straitlaced Vienna of the late nineteenth century, such an occurrence would be considered extremely shocking and unmentionable. Breur feared for his reputation; he wanted to keep his lucrative private practice thriving and not run risks. Freud, of course, had less to lose. He was not yet established and wanted to make a reputation. Also, he was more willing than Breur to shock the establishment. As it worked out, Freud was able to convince Breur that they should publish jointly *The Case of Anna O.* and other investigations. Breur, however, did not pursue his early leads, gradually withdrew from Freud, and detached himself from psychoanalysis. It is ironic that the man who introduced Freud to the talking cure and the effects of abreaction fell into relative obscurity.

Freud was a family man. He married Martha Bernays and fathered six children. One of his children, Anna, became a famous psychoanalyst in her own right. The Freud family spent many years in a large apartment, and Freud saw his patients in one of its rooms. Freud's sister-in-law lived with the family, and it has been claimed that Freud had an affair with her. In an interview with Theodor Reik, a psychoanalyst and one of Freud's closest friends, this was denied:

Reik. Freud talked about his work to his sister-in-law, whom I knew quite well. He made some trips with her. She was much younger than Mrs. Freud, and there were suspicions that he had an affair with her. Nothing of the kind. I don't believe it. Freud had a certain puritanical trend in his nature. (p. 48)

Freud worked in relative obscurity for many years. His ultimately influential book *The Interpretation of Dreams* was published in 1900, when Freud was forty-four years old. The first printing was small, and several years passed before all the copies sold. Freud continued writing and lecturing, however, and his ideas began to capture the imagination of many laymen and some professionals. By 1909 he had achieved sufficient fame to be invited to give a series of lectures at Clark University in Massachusetts. He traveled to the United States by ship with the psychiatrist Carl Jung, who had become an advocate of psychoanalysis. The lectures at Clark University are generally regarded as the key event marking the transition of psychoanalysis from a local Austrian phenomenon to a way of thinking that gained worldwide recognition.

Only one year later the International Psychoanalytic Association was founded, and Carl Jung was named its president, not Sigmund Freud! But, this was at Freud's request. He was still concerned about psychoanalysis being perceived as a strictly Jewish phenomenon. Jung was a Christian, Swedish, and the son of a clergyman; Freud felt that Jung's credentials were impeccable. It was one of Freud's major disappointments in life when, a few years later, Jung resigned as president of the association and detached himself from the Freudians. By now, however, the association had gathered strength and momentum. Psychoanalysis was on its way.

UNCONSCIOUS ASPECTS OF MENTAL LIFE

Alan M. is a high school English teacher. For three years he has been working on a novel and has been revising it for several months. It is complete, but he resists sending it to a publisher. His wife encourages him to submit the novel. She thinks it is excellent and that it will become a best-seller. Finally Alan gathers his courage and takes the novel to the post office. He sends it to a leading New York publisher. Much to his surprise, the package containing the novel appears at his home two days later! Alan can't help laughing when he sees that the mailing container is not addressed to the publisher, but to his own home address! He had inadvertently sent the book to himself. How would psychoanalysis explain the error? Freud would have said that Alan's ego was threatened by having to face the reality that the novel may be rejected. It is more pleasant to live in a world of fantasy and imagine oneself a best-selling author than to confront the realization that perhaps no publisher will actually want the manuscript. The act of mailing the novel sets the stage for the following unconscious thought: "I wish I didn't have to face this. I don't want to run the risk of having my work turned down." The mailing error is a response to the unconscious wish, and its purpose is to defend the ego against the potential harshness of the real world.

Freud used the word *unconscious* in two ways. First, it was used as a noun; the unconscious is a region of the mind. Second, it was used as an adjective; there are unconscious ideas, unconscious motives, and unconscious memories. Let's elaborate on these two usages.

In 1915 Freud published a paper called "The Unconscious." In this paper he presents the unconscious as a region of the mind. He postulated that the human mind is divided into a *system conscious* and a *system unconscious*. The system conscious functions on the basis of the *secondary process*, the mental process by which we are in contact wtih reality, think logically, and make rational decisions. The *system unconscious* functions on the basis of the *primary process*, the mental process by which ideas have nonrational connections. In the system unconscious, wishes, magic, and egocentricity reign supreme. Thus when a tobacco company tells you that "famous race driver George Wilson smokes Iron Man cigarettes," it is appealing to your system unconscious. The primary process happily associates, on a nonrational basis, a desirable human attribute, such as courage (race drivers are presumed to have this trait), and cigarettes.

The system unconscious is a kind of Alice-in-Wonderland region of the mind where A doesn't have to come before B, and where wishing *can* make it so.

The magical thinking of the system unconscious produces the following conclusion: "If I smoke Iron Man cigarettes I will be a person of courage." Of course the connections are absurd. But that is just the point. The system unconscious is a kind of Alice-in-Wonderland region of the mind where *A* doesn't have to come before *B* and where wishing can make it so.

Freud divided the system conscious into two subsystems, the *perceptual-conscious* and the *preconscious.* The perceptual-conscious refers to whatever you are aware of right now. Let us say you have a corn on your foot and, at the moment, you are painfully aware of how much it hurts. Then the idea "it hurts" and the pain associated with the idea are the content of consciousness; the idea and the feeling are "in" the region of the mind called the perceptual-conscious.

The preconscious refers to a region of the mind just below the conscious surface. Its contents consist of any ideas or feelings that can be made to enter the perceptual-conscious by an act of will. Let us say that someone is asked his date of birth. He answers, "February 4, 1940." The date was stored in the preconscious and was brought into the perceptual-conscious by a voluntary act of remembering. It will sink back into the preconscious region after a short residence in the perceptual-conscious. Thus the preconscious is a large storehouse of memories and useful information. It is parallel to what is called "the subconscious mind" in popular psychology. It is also identical to what Herbart and pre-Freudian thinkers called the apperceptive mass. Freud's description of the preconscious was not particularly original, nor did he claim that it was. It was merely included as part of the whole of his formal theorizing about the structure of the mind. The really important addition by Freud is his conception of the unconscious as a region of the mind *containing repressed ideas.*

To Freud, the content of the unconscious consisted of ideas and motives unacceptable to the conscious personality. He said that ideas in the unconscious are in a state of *repression*, a process by which a psychological force opposes certain ideas and shoves them down into the nether territory of the unconscious. This is why Freud's psychology is sometimes called a *dynamic psychology*—ideas within the mind push and shove each other about. They struggle with each other for survival. It is crucial to realize that the ideas in the unconscious are dynamically repressed, not merely forgotten. Sometimes this is spoken of as *motivated forgetting,* a kind of forgetting that takes place because it serves the needs of the conscious ego.

To illustrate, say that Mary R. considers herself, on a conscious level, a good wife and mother. Her ego demands that nothing intrude on this self-concept. She was raised in a strict family having a conservative set of moral values. The thought of divorce is unthinkable, something no decent woman would do. Further assume that her husband has an authoritarian personality; he is forever putting her in her place, telling her what to do, criticizing her character, and in general treating her like a child. A tremendous resentment toward her husband begins to grow within Mary. Although she may think, "I'd like to kill him," the thought is quickly repressed. It does not fit in with the thought, "I'm a loving wife." But the repressed idea does its dirty work in her life nonetheless. Perhaps Mary is an excellent cook. Perhaps her husband is overweight and suffers from hypertension, and his physician has told him to cut down on starchy foods and desserts. But Mary just can't help herself. She keeps cooking in the old ways, refusing to learn to make lighter meals. Indeed, she keeps right on experimenting with new desserts. Behind Mary's back one family friend remarks, "She is killing him with her oven." Mary is behaving in a destructive manner, but because she is repressing her hostility toward her husband, she is able to be destructive and live with herself.

"Very sick!" you say. Yes, and these are just the kinds of patterns in human behavior that are the concern of psychoanalysis—the "sickness" of everyday life. To Freud, the average person does not control his life fully with his conscious ego. Instead, he is "lived" by unknown and uncontrollable forces from the unconscious. Freud, however, was not without hope. The aim of psychoanalysis is to explore the unconscious and bring repressed ideas up to a conscious level. Then they are presumed to lose their destructive power.

THE STRUCTURE OF PERSONALITY

In 1923 Freud published a book called *The Ego and the Id.* This book is one of the central psychoanalytic documents, and it contains the outlines of Freud's theory of personality. It also contains a revision of his theory of the unconscious. The 1915 view described in the previous section was modified in an important way, to be described shortly.

Freud theorized that each of us has a basic component to our personality that is present at birth. He called this basic component the *id.* (In German the term "das Es" was used, which merely means "the it." Id is the Latin word for *it.* The term and its use were not Freud's invention. In *The Ego and the Id*, he credits the concept to a German physician, Georg Groddeck. Freud also notes that the term goes back to the philosopher Nietzsche.) According to Freud, the id never leaves us. It is our deepest self, our primal self. The id is the source of our basic biological drives: hunger, thirst, pain avoidance, temperature regulation, reflex action, sex, and aggression. The last two drives, sex and aggression, play an important part in psychoanalytic thinking. These are the two drives subject to the greatest amount of repression from civilization; more will be said about this point later.

The id has sometimes been called the Frankenstein monster within the personality. This is a correct analogy if we think of Frankenstein's monster as neither good nor bad, but devoid of morality. Thus if an adult human organism were pure id, he would stomp about and take whatever he wanted without regard for the rights of others. He wouldn't wait patiently in a school cafeteria line; he would shove others aside and grab his food without paying. If he saw an attractive female and craved sexual relations, he would knock her down and proceed to rape her. Obviously, the individual would not last long as a free person; he would be quickly apprehended and treated as a mental patient. Thus a human being must learn to control his id if he is to live and function in the world. The crucial characteristic of the id is captured if we say it is *pleasure-oriented.*

When a baby is born, its personality is pure id. With development, though, the infant learns that the world is often a frustrating place. Certain things cannot be obtained in an instant on demand. The infant must wait to have his diapers changed, to be fed, to be picked up. Later he will find that he can't obtain certain things directly; he has to make a detour. He has to learn to walk, to talk, to feed and dress himself, and so forth. Thus a part of the personality that may be called the *ego* is formed. The ego is the *I*, or the conscious center of the personality. Its aim is to try to meet the demands of the id within the constraints imposed by external reality. Assume that a preschooler sees some candy on a high shelf. From the id's point of view, there is nothing but the pure wish, "I want the candy." As far as the id is concerned, "Let's just fly right up there." Indeed, one might observe a young preschooler jumping up and down in frustration before the shelf, stretching for something that can't be reached. An older preschooler, however, might drag a chair to a spot below the candy, climb up on the chair, and solve the problem. Thus the ego has been brought into action in service of the id.

One of the functions of the ego is *reality-testing.* Human beings, whether adults or children, often want to see how far they can go without getting into trouble or hurting themselves. This can be particularly important in raising children. Sometimes when a child is being willful and unreasonable, he is trying to find out the practical boundaries of his allowable world. Parents who cannot resist the child's persistence and "cave in" against their better judgment do the child a disservice. The child may get a mistaken concept of what is safe or what is appropriate. In a famous passage from *The Ego and the Id*, Freud compared the id to a horse and the ego to its rider:

The functional importance of the ego is manifested in the fact that normally control over the approaches to motility devolves upon it. Thus in its relation to the id it is like a man on horseback, who has to hold in check the superior

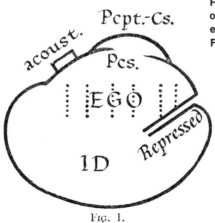

Fig. 1.

Freud said that the three sub-structures of the human personality are the id, the ego and the superego. (Drawing by Freud himself.)

strength of the horse; with this difference, that the rider tries to do so with his own strength while the ego uses borrowed forces. The analogy may be carried a little further. Often a rider, if he is not to be parted from his horse, is obliged to guide it where it wants to go; so in the same way the ego is in the habit of transforming the id's will into action as if it were its own. (p. 25)

Briefly, the ego is that part of the human personality which is *reality oriented*. It tries to accommodate the demands of the id by taking into account practical obstacles in the external world, the world outside the mind and body. In essence the ego says to the id, "Wait a bit, you impulsive child. I'll find a way to get you what you want." The ego exists in service of the id; it is its agent. Thus if a person's personality were only id and ego, he would be, in colloquial terms, a "con artist," a "wheeler-dealer," or "a guy who plays all the angles." In clinical terms the individual would be said to have a character disorder (not a neurosis), and a label such as "sociopath" or "psychopath" would be used. The cold-blooded person who seems to have no heart would fall into the general category we are describing. Of course, it is doubtful that there are pure types, people with only an id and an ego. We are exaggerating to make the point that human existence seems to demand some sort of value-morality principle.

This third demand is satisfied by the third major component of the human personality structure, which Freud called the *superego*. The superego is that aspect of the personality which orients itself toward abstract concepts of good and bad, right and wrong, decency and indecency. When a child is growing up it is not enough that he learn practical ways of satisfying his id's wishes. His parents also send him various messages that certain actions are shameful. Assume that a child has been told not to take cookies from the cookie jar. When mother is out of the room, the child ignores the prohibition and tries to steal the cookies. The ego is functioning in service of the id. It has made the child wait until mother is out of sight. But there is no superego yet. Nothing inside the child is saying, "It's wrong. Don't do it." This comes with development. The child is caught with his hand in the cookie jar when mother comes back into the kitchen. She says, "You naughty child! I told you not to take any cookies! You should be ashamed of yourself." Perhaps she spanks the child, or perhaps she sends him to his room. In either event her behavior is designed to make the child feel ashamed.

The word *shame* refers to what is felt when one is caught doing something that others judge to be wrong or bad. The person who is caught feels discredited and awkward. Assume that a particular child has been caught stealing cookies ten times and has experienced shame ten times. The eleventh time he looks at the cookie jar, starts to walk toward it, and begins to *anticipate* the feeling of shame. It is unpleasant and he is beginning to think twice about whether he should take the cookies. If his mother has been consistent in catching him and shaming him, he almost certainly feels the enterprise is doomed to failure. It is as if his mother is in his head, saying, "Don't take the cookie, Billy. If you do, you are a bad boy." The superego is forming. He is beginning to feel guilt for thinking about a forbidden action. Say that he overrides the voice of his budding superego and steals the cookies anyway. After the cookies are eaten, he is feeling bad—and it isn't from a stomachache; he is feeling bad because he feels guilty. Perhaps he even goes to his mother and blubbers, "I stole the cookies." He confesses crime to get relief from the nasty feeling of guilt that is poisoning his existence. Once he is punished and subsequently forgiven by mother, he no longer feels guilty. The word *guilt* refers to what is felt when one has internalized the standards of external agents and uses these standards to judge oneself. Shame and guilt are closely related. Shame is the result of external judgments; guilt is the result of internal judgments. Guilt feelings have their origin in earlier shame experiences.

We can see from the example of the child and the cookie jar a prototype of how a child develops a superego out of his ego. The ego must not only learn ways of accommodating itself to the practical limits of time and space; it must also learn ways of accommodating itself to the abstract values of its culture. For a human being to be accepted by his parents, his relatives, and his peers, he must hold approximately the same values they do. We call such a person *socialized*; a socialized person is a full-fledged member of his culture. If he happens to be a headhunter, then it is the right thing to do to hunt the heads of enemies of the tribe. If he lives in a communist country, then it is the right thing to do to be frugal and look down on people who want to own large amounts of real estate. If he is an American, then it is right to be ambitious and to own property.

The superego itself can be divided into two subagents. The first of these is designated the *ego ideal*. The ego ideal sets an individual's level of aspiration. It presents him with a mental picture of what he should do with his life, or what he might become. Freud felt that the ego ideal is created by the attitudes and beliefs of the person's parents. The cliché example would be the Jewish mother who "brainwashes" her son: "You were meant to be a doctor. I feel it in my soul. I feel it in my bones. You are such a bright, talented boy. Don't waste these things!" Such statements may form the ego ideal of becoming a doctor within the child. Thus we get the "my son the doctor" syndrome. Freud notes that he himself was an example of just such a self-fulfilling prophecy.

The second subagent of the superego is the *conscience*. The ego ideal is a plus factor; it says what ought to be strived for. The conscience is a negative factor; it says what ought not be done. The conscience sets up inhibitions, restraints within the individual against taking certain kinds of action. The voice of conscience says, "Stop! Don't do it! That's a sin! That's bad! That's nasty! That's dirty! That's immoral! You're no good if you do that!" A person with a strict superego that sets a high moral tone often finds it difficult to act with flexibility and spontaneity. His conscience is like a straitjacket. He is too inhibited; there are too many internal frustrations. As already noted, a superego is probably necessary for one to be what is termed a "socialized person." But it is probably better for both the individual and his society if the superego is more like a comfortable sport coat than a straitjacket.

It would be an error to think that only the conscience can act like a straitjacket. The positive side of the superego, the ego ideal, can also be too rigid, demanding too much of the person. Theodore I. Rubin, a practicing psychoanalyst, provides an example from his own analysis:

In psychoanalytic treatment, I learned a great deal about myself that I had no previous idea about at all. This included many emotional problems and confusions as well as much about human substance, too. But despite these quite valid and important insights, my depression and despair went on and on and I began to feel that I never really would get better. I became aware that I was, in fact, psychologically beating myself unmercifully. I realized that much of the beating came from a false, perfectionistic, impossibly exalted image of myself. I felt that in falling from this image I had descended to considerably less than a subhuman status. (p. 13)

He explains how he learned to stop berating himself, to simply let go and let be what would be, to relax and not make such a great effort to put his life together; he came out of his depression. Some of us have grand expectations based on an unrealistic ego ideal. The frustration that results from failing to attain our impossible dreams can result in depression if we are not wise enough to revise our standards to a more realistic level, as Rubin did. In psychoanalytic terms, the superego must be tempered by a strong, reality-oriented ego.

In the previous few pages, we have been describing Freud's final view of the structure of personality: The personality is made up of three substructures—the id, the ego, and the superego. There is no longer such a structure as the unconscious. In this final view of the human personality, Freud no longer spoke of the unconscious as a *place* in the mind. He now proposed that the word "unconscious" be used to refer to a *quality* of mental life. Thus unconscious wishes, unconscious ideas, unconscious memories may exist, but not wishes in *the* unconscious, ideas in *the* unconscious, memories in *the* unconscious. Instead, Freud proposed that repressed wishes, ideas, and memories become a part of the id. The id operates in terms of the magical, fantasy-oriented primary process. Thus repressed elements of mental life are subject to the same distortions, the same nonrational connections that Freud had spoken of for years.

In spite of Freud's suggestion, many contemporary psychoanalysts still speak of the unconscious as if it were a place in the mind. Apparently this usage has a certain attraction and utility. Freud's early theorizing is retained along with his conception of the id, ego, and superego. Thus we can say that the word "unconscious" in depth psychology has acquired two meanings: (1) It is used in a substantive sense to indicate a region of the mind; it is used as a noun when one speaks of the unconscious. (2) It is used in a dynamic sense to indicate a quality of mental life; it is used as an adjective when one speaks of unconscious wishes, ideas, and memories. Let us note again that Freud's final preference was for the second usage.

HUMAN DEVELOPMENT

Psychoanalysis stresses human development, the growth of the personality over time. It has already been noted, for example, how the ego grows out of the id as the id is faced with the problems of the external world. Now let us turn our attention to another aspect of human development, the maturation of the sexual drive. Freud felt this was a particularly important subject because he was convinced it had a great deal to do with basic character types in people. The theory I will describe is called a *psychosexual theory* because it has to do with the simultaneous development of the personality and the sexual drive. A central concept in the theory is *libido*, which Freud defined as "psychosexual energy." Psychosexual energy is the force that resides behind our mental life and our sexual life. It arises from the basic metabolism of the body. It is not, however, a measurable physical energy; libido is a *psychological* concept. As a concept, libido is a bit vague and escapes precise definition. If you can imagine a diffuse energy that is associated at once with both mental life and sexual life, you have a rough image of what Freud meant by libido.

Freud theorized that infants and children have a sexual life of sorts. Their sexual life is described as *pregenital*, a sexual life that takes its pleasures in ways that precede adult heterosexual relations. The development during the pregenital period is merely a forerunner of adult sexuality and bears only a small resemblance to it. When Freud said that infants and children have a sex life, this is what he meant: They go through developmental stages that build toward genital sexuality. But the character of childhood sexuality is more quickly understood if the word *sensual* is substituted for *sexual*. During the early years the child does seek and experience sensuous gratification, and these experiences play a formative role in adult sexual life. The sensuous gratification is received via the three principal *erotogenic*, or *erogenous, zones* of the body, zones that are particularly rich in nerve endings responsive to touch. These are the oral, the anal, and the genital areas.

During the first twelve to eighteen months of life, the libido is presumed to be concentrated in the oral area: This is the *oral stage*. The infant gets a great deal of gratification out of sucking and putting things in his mouth. The pleasure received from such activities is "sexual" in the broadest possible sense—the activities bring sensuous gratification by stimulating an erogenous zone. Parents can testify that it is often difficult to wean a child from the breast or the bottle; many parents complain of what they consider to be an inordinate amount of thumb-sucking in a child. All these behaviors are indicators of the gratification infants receive from oral stimulation.

During the next eighteen months to the third year of life, the libido moves out of the oral zone and concentrates itself in the anal zone: This is the *anal stage*. Now the infant gets his principal erotic gratification from sensations associated with this region. The voluntary control of the retention and expulsion of fecal matter is learned during the anal stage, and the acquisition of this kind of bodily self-control gives the child a great deal of pleasure. It may also be noted that during the toilet-training period, the child can "get back" at punitive parents. Not having a bowel movement at the right time or having one at the wrong time (or in the wrong place) are events that send some parents into states of great emotional agitation.

The time period from about the third year of life to the sixth year of life is designated as the *phallic stage*. Libido moves from the anal area and concentrates itself in the phallus. (The male phallus is the penis, and the female phallus is the clitoris.) The word *phallus* should not be confused with the term *external genitalia* (the external genitalia include phallus and other sexual structures). During the phallic stage, the child receives great bodily pleasure from masturbating. It should be noted that such masturbation is merely the prototype of adolescent masturbation. The child does not masturbate to orgasm; instead the phallus fills with blood and becomes firm for a time during autostimulation. When Freud first proposed the existence of childhood masturbation, he was scoffed at by many of his fellow physicians. Today we know that Freud was partly wrong and partly right. He thought that childhood masturbation was universal, but he apparently was incorrect about this. Contemporary studies suggest that about 60 percent of children engage in childhood masturbation. Freud was thus partly correct in that childhood masturbation does take place and is common.

The famous *Oedipus complex* comes into being during the phallic stage. The boy is said to develop a sexual yearning for his mother. In classical Freudian theory, this was thought to be a full-blown incest fantasy. The boy feels guilty about his forbidden wish, and he develops another fantasy —the fear that his father will somehow cut off his genital organs as punishment for wanting to have sex with his own mother. This leads to *castration anxiety.* Anxiety about castration is too high a price to pay for maintaining the incest fantasy, and the whole conflict is repressed to an unconscious level. The Oedipus conflict is psychologically useful to the boy in that it fosters an identification of the son with the father. It is a case of, "If you can't lick your enemies, join them." The son controls his castration anxiety by unconsciously associating his own ego with the ego of the father. Guilt about forbidden sexual impulses and the self-control of such guilt play a crucial role in the formation of the superego, the internal agent of social control. The socialized boy feels, at a conscious level, that the idea of sexual relations with his own mother is disgusting.

The things I have said about the boy can be applied to the girl. The girl has an incest fantasy about the father. She also experiences guilt and repression. The associated complex is sometimes called the *Electra complex.* The term "Oedipus complex" is often used to refer to either males or females, however.

The repression of sexual impulses during the sixth year of life leads to the fourth stage of psychosexual development, the *latency stage.* The latency stage lasts from about the sixth to the twelfth year of life. This time period is sometimes referred to as "the golden years of childhood." These are the elementary school years. During these prepubertal years there is much running, playing, and constructive activity. In our culture, boys tend to develop interests in such areas as scouting, model-building, baseball, and so forth. Girls tend to develop interests in such areas as dancing, sewing, cooking, and so forth. Avoiding the current debate over to what extent these sex-role patterns are innate or learned, the simple point is being made that the prepubertal child has no apparent interest in sex per se. His or her interest seems to turn outward toward the larger world. Children during this period show a tremendous intellectual vitality and interest in learning about their environment. To Freud, this was evidence of *sublimation*, a process in which direct sexual expression of libido is repressed and reappears in modified form as a general interest in the wider world.

The final stage of development is called the *genital stage.* This stage

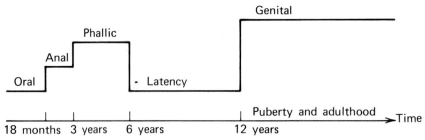

FIGURE 2.1   The five psychosexual stages proposed by Freud.

begins at approximately the twelfth or thirteenth year of life. The mature adult who has developed the capacity to work and to love is in the genital stage. It is the optimal stage of development, and not all adults can be said to have reached it. Genital sexuality implies more than self-oriented pleasure. The oral, anal, and phallic stages are *narcissistic*, the pleasures of sex being aimed solely at the self. The genital personality takes pleasure in giving pleasure. He or she cares about the sexual experience of the other person. More than this, the genital personality can care about others beyond the sexual domain.

The path of personality development is seldom smooth. *Emotional traumas*, painful psychological events, can cause the unfolding of the psychosexual stages to become distorted. (Also, overindulgence during a stage is sometimes postulated to produce distortions.) Freud spoke of *fixations*, meaning that the libido or part of the libido can get "stuck" at one of the infantile stages. Thus a person who was weaned too quickly or was punished for thumb-sucking as an infant may develop oral fixations, seeking unconsciously to return again and again to forbidden pleasures. Such an individual has an *oral character* and may be inordinately fond of such oral gratifications as talking, smoking, and eating. The oral mode may also be generalized. For example, the oral personality may be gullible—he is willing to "swallow anything." Or, he may be fond of saying sarcastic things—his words "bite" others and hurt them.

Emotional conflicts between parent and child over toilet-training may produce anal fixations. When these fixations are generalized and form part of an adult's life-style, the adult is said to have an anal character. Two basic kinds of anal characters are postulated. The *anal-expulsive character* is described as a disorderly and defiant person; he gets a great deal of satisfaction out of "making a mess." The person who actually enjoys being cruel to others would fall into this category. The *anal-retentive character* is described as a stingy and excessively orderly person; he gets a great deal of satisfaction out of "not giving" and "holding back.'' (Such a person may also have actual problems with constipation; he is forever taking laxatives in a vain attempt to unclog himself. A psychoanalyst would say that he needs to become emotionally unclogged first.) The famous miser Scrooge, in Dickens' *A Christmas Carol*, captures the image of the concept of the anal character.

Emotional conflicts taking place during the phallic stage of development may also produce fixations, and it is possible to postulate a *phallic character*. Such an individual might have unresolved conflicts over masturbation and incest wishes. The phallic character is unable to give others real love, only synthetic love; such persons exhibit behavior that has the appearance of caring but lacks the inner core of real concern. This is revealed by not meeting others' needs at crucial times and by discounting others' evaluations. Psychoanalytic theory hypothesizes that phallic fixations play a role in homosexuality.

It is, of course, absurd to speak of pure types. If the psychoanalytic conceptions have any value, that value resides in terms of dominant and minor themes in the human personality. It is far too constricting to say, ''Jim is obviously an anal-retentive character. He's so damn tight with his money!'' and thus act as if one has explained the whole person. But it may be of value to realize that Jim shows traits that may be partly, but not completely, grasped in terms of Freud's developmental theory.

DEFENSE MECHANISMS

One of the more useful concepts of psychoanalysis for explaining behavior is the concept of *ego defense*, a tendency of the ego to distort its perception of reality in favor of the fantasy-oriented wishes of the id. Briefly, the ego protects itself against ''the slings and arrows of outrageous fortune.'' It should be understood that the defense mechanisms to be described ''kick into action'' automatically. They are not willed; one does not say, ''Now I think I will use a defense mechanism and defend my ego.'' That is why they are called *mechanisms*; like the parts of a machine, they operate in fixed and predictable ways.

Repression. The most important defense mechanism is *repression*, a tendency of the ego to shove down anxiety-arousing information to unconscious levels of the personality structure. As we have already seen, Freud theorized that the Oedipus complex is ''solved'' for most individuals by repression. He also said that we have a general amnesia for many of the events of early childhood because we repress memories that are too painful.

A person who has the tendency to criticize others ''for their own good'' may in fact be doing so out of hostility. There is a wish to inflict pain on

FIGURE 2.2   The function of an ego defense mechanism. Like a shield, the defense mechanism protects the ego from the harsher aspects of reality.

others, but this is unacceptable to the ego. It is necessary to think, "I am a nice person." Thus the destructive wish is repressed and becomes an unconscious motive; the unconscious motive reappears in the guise of a critical do-gooder.

"But surely people cannot be so blind to themselves!" one may protest. "A hostile person must realize he is hostile." There is some validity to the protest. The person using the defense mechanism does in a sense know; however, repression implies that *he does not know that he knows.* If this sounds abstruse, the whole thing can be made much less complicated by saying, "Human beings have a tremendous capacity for kidding themselves."

Reaction formation.   What has just been described not only defines repression; it also captures the essence of a defense mechanism called *reaction formation.* This is a tendency for repressed motives to emerge on the conscious side as mirror opposites of their repressed cousins.

Regression.   The defense mechanism called *regression* is associated with the concept of fixation in one of the pregenital stages of development. The literal meaning of regress is "to go back." Under stress, persons have a tendency to go back to behavior patterns that brought comfort at an earlier age. A person with oral fixations, for example, may eat large quantities of food when frustrated. I know one woman who goes on eating binges when she has an argument with her husband and feels temporarily unloved. In general, we can speculate that the greater the stress, the greater the regression. There are numerous reports of prisoners of war who became so demoralized that they regressed to infantile levels. Under such conditions, formerly brave men have been known to urinate and soil themselves as if they were babies. There are reports of others who curled up into fetal positions and sucked their thumbs. On a more familiar level, almost any of us may cry like children if our frustration, pain, or anxiety is great enough.

Rationalization. Say that you are studying for an important examination. A friend calls and invites you to a party. You are in a state of conflict. You know realistically that if you don't study this evening you will probably turn in a poor performance on tomorrow's exam. On the other hand, you have a strong desire to go to the party (a certain member of the opposite sex to whom you are attracted is probably going to be a guest). Then the thought comes into your mind, "I've been studying too hard. I need to get out and relax a little, unwind a bit. It would do me good." You reply to your friend, "OK. I'll see you in a half hour," and you go to the party. What has happened? You have rationalized your behavior. The defense mechanism called *rationalization* is used when the real motive for one's behavior is unacceptable to the ego. The real motive is replaced with a cover motive. The cover motive makes it possible to behave in what seems to be good faith with one's conscience. In the above case, the real motive for going to the party was simply to have a good time. But this unadorned motive is unacceptable to the ego. "If that's your only reason for going, you should stay home and study," says a small voice within. The ego now becomes a cosmetic expert and "fixes up" the motive so it becomes prettier. "You're really going to relax and unwind. All work and no play makes Jack a dull boy." Now one is going to the party for a virtuous purpose.

Compensation. The defense mechanism known as *compensation* is used to defend against feelings of inferiority. The cliché example is, of course, the dictator who holds the power of life and death over millions of people. It turns out he is a short man, only five feet, four inches tall. His craving for power arises from an unconscious desire to be a big man and show others that at least psychologically, he "stands above them." Or take the case of Skinny Gertrude. She has big teeth, a flat chest, and the boys don't ask her out for dates. She is, however, a straight A student, a real "grind." She is compensating for her feelings of inferiority by trying to prove she is adequate in some area of life. Another example is provided by Happy Horace. He is fat and none of the girls in school will go out with him. Yet he is the star comedian of his class; he is always surrounded by an audience that is both laughing with him and laughing at him. Through the mechanism of compensation, he is making himself feel more worthwhile.

Human beings can be handicapped in many ways. If the handicap is not so severe that the individual is completely incapacitated by it, the handicap can sometimes be turned to a sort of advantage. Countless numbers of people with real or imagined deficiencies have used the mechanism of compensation to convince themselves and others that they have value as human beings.

Identification.   Happy Horace is not only a comedian. He is also a comic book fan. His favorite comic books are the ones about the adventures of such superheroes as Superman, Batman, and Captain Marvel. This interest reveals Horace's use of the defense mechanism called *identification.* When an individual uses identification, he unconsciously associates his ego with the ego of an admired person. As a consequence, he picks up feelings of competence or power by association. Many of us identify with movie stars, sports heroes, and other famous people. Our own deflated egos are pumped up and made to swell to greater size through the identification process.

Fantasy.   Closely related to the defense mechanism of identification is the defense mechanism of *fantasy.* When we fantasize, we usually use our imaginations to create mental pictures in which we visualize our fondest dreams coming true. The transient daydream is familiar to almost

An intense interest in the exploits of superheroes may reveal the existence of the defense mechanism called identification. (George Reeves as Superman in the TV series.)

everyone. In these daydreams, we may take revenge on someone who has wronged us; we may succeed in love with someone who in reality is not interested in us; we may see ourselves overcoming personal inadequacies; or we may find ourselves acting out forbidden sexual impulses. Perhaps you are familiar with James Thurber's *The Secret Life of Walter Mitty.* Mitty was a submissive husband who was constantly being pushed around by his wife. In his daydreams, however, he saw himself in various heroic roles. His fantasy life was extremely important to him. It was his method of maintaining self-respect and surviving the harshness of his real life.

Displacement.   The philosopher Aristotle is credited with the following statement: "Anybody can become angry—that is easy; but to be angry with the right person, and in the right degree, and at the right time, and for the right purpose, and in the right way—that is not within everybody's power and it is not easy." Aristotle's statement is pertinent to the defense mechanism known as *displacement.* Displacement takes place when an individual places on one person an emotional reaction that should properly be placed on another person. A husband who is angry with his boss may come home and pick a fight with his wife. We say, "He takes out his anger on her" or "She is the scapegoat for his aggressions." Assume that a college professor has just had a serious disagreement with a colleague. He may go into his next class and give students sarcastic answers when they ask questions. His punitive approach to teaching reveals his underlying anger.

Projection.   Projection is a defense mechanism in which a person actually perceives the external world in terms of his own personal emotional conflicts. He takes reality to be the equivalent of his own somewhat distorted conception of it. A particular man may be ambitious and overly willing to take advantage of others to foster his own financial success. Such a person may think, "You've really got to watch out for people nowadays. They all want to use you and manipulate you." Of course, it is he himself who is the wheeler-dealer and the manipulator. But such a self-image is threatening to the ego. He protects his ego by his perception that "they" are the ones with the reprehensible motives.

Although there are other defense mechanisms, the ones listed are perhaps sufficient to convey the general theme that human beings have many self-deceptive ways of maintaining self-esteem. The professional psychological consensus seems to be that when used in moderation, the defense mechanisms play a positive role in coping with life. They *are* crutches, though, and—like physical crutches—they should not be used when one can function without them. One of the values of knowing about the defense mechanisms is that such knowledge alerts us to their possible misuse.

TABLE 2.1. Selected Kinds of Defense Mechanisms

REPRESSION
Shoving down anxiety-arousing information to unconscious levels of the personality structure. Example: the unconsciously motivated forgetting of painful experiences.

REACTION FORMATION
Repressed motives tending to emerge on the conscious side as mirror opposites of their repressed cousins. Example: a person with a great deal of blocked hostility who, on the surface, is supersweet.

REGRESSION
Going back, under stress, to behavior patterns that brought comfort at an earlier age. Example: crying like a child when confronted with great frustration.

RATIONALIZATION
Replacing a real motive for behavior with a more acceptable cover motive. Example: denial by a student preparing for an exam that the real reason for going to a party is simply to have a good time; asserting instead that it is essential to go for the purposes of mental relaxation.

COMPENSATION
Defending against feelings of inferiority by taking action designed to enhance one's sense of self-esteem. Example: Skinny Gertrude counterbalancing the negative feelings arising from her lack of popularity by studying hard and earning high grades.

IDENTIFICATION
Associating one's ego with the ego of an admired person. Example: Horace, feeling that he is unattractive and incompetent, pumping up his own ego by vicariously experiencing the adventures of superheroes in comic books.

FANTASY
Using the imagination to create mental pictures in which a person visualizes his fondest dreams coming true. Example: having a daydream in which one succeeds in romance with someone who in reality is not responsive.

DISPLACEMENT
Placing on a second person (or animal or inanimate object) an emotional reaction that properly should have been placed on a first source. Example: a husband who is angry with his boss coming home and picking a fight with his wife.

PROJECTION
Perceiving the external world in terms of one's personal emotional conflicts. Example: a person with a great deal of stifled anger seeing others as hostile and dangerous.

THE MEANING OF DREAMS

Freud believed that dreams have meaning, that they are symbolical messages from the unconscious level and reveal the existence of unconscious wishes. Freud distinguished a minimum of two levels to every dream: the *manifest level* and the *latent level*. The manifest level refers to the actual content of the dream, the images the dreamer experiences. The latent level refers to what the dream is about, what the dream means. One could say that the manifest level is the superficial, or false, layer of the dream and that the latent level is the deep, or real, layer of the dream.

The reason the dream has two layers is that the latent level is unacceptable to the ego. It contains impulses that are disagreeable to the conscious self. Thus the latent material is distorted, by what Freud called the *dream work*, into a set of events that seem relatively innocent to the conscious mind. The purpose of symbolism in dreams is to act as a mask or cover for the real meaning of the dream. Freud further theorized that most dreams concern either sex or aggression. These, he proposed, are the two impulses most subject to repression in society.

One of Freud's patients, an unmarried adolescent girl, reported a dream in which she saw herself in the nude riding a horse through the forest. The girl was a virgin. Freud had her give associations to the images of the dream (the manifest content), and her associations revealed that the horse made her think of the male phallus. The up-and-down motion of the horse made her think of sexual intercourse. (Such associations do not necessarily occur in one step; there may be several links before the last link of the chain is reached.) Freud interpreted the dream as meaning that the girl wished to have sexual intercourse (the latent content). Because she was a "good" girl and unmarried, such a wish was unacceptable to her conscious ego. To maintain a positive self-image, it was necessary for her to have her fantasy of sexual intercourse in disguised form. Perhaps this all seems rather farfetched. But keep in mind that Freud was working in the climate of a prudish and Victorian society. Adolescent girls from the "better" families in 1910 in Vienna were not supposed to have "animal cravings." Under these conditions, one can appreciate that Freud's interpretation is not too unlikely.

Assume that a man dreams he is a knight in rusty armor, having a swordfight with another knight. With his sword, the first knight penetrates the armor of the second knight, and the second knight screams out—not in pain but in ecstasy! The Freudian interpretation of such a dream might be that the dreamer has a repressed wish for homosexual relations. He is wearing rusty armor because homosexuality is a "low" or "deteriorated" act. The sword is a symbol for the male phallus, and the penetration of the sword into the body represents penetration by the penis. That the second knight screams out in ecstasy reveals the fantasy-oriented quality of the dream. When a person is pierced by a sword he certainly does not experience ecstasy.

One can see that the Freudian conception of dreams is associated with the defense mechanism of fantasy. Dreams are more powerful fantasies than those we allow ourselves in a waking state. Like conscious fantasy, they are defensive; they maintain our self-esteem while allowing us to express conflicting emotions.

But what about dreams that contain little or no symbolism? Don't people have frank sexual dreams? Don't people often express their hostilities directly in dreams? The answer to these questions is yes. Thus one of the problems with the Freudian theory of dreams is that it makes a certain kind of dream, a heavily symbolized dream, a universal type. This is probably because Freud derived his data from patients. It is plausible to suppose that a neurotic person who has many repressed conflicts would find it necessary to dream in symbols to censor real meanings. A more normal person, however, might not have such a need; consequently, many of his dreams might be more explicit. That so many people do report symbolical dreams, however, suggests the generality of neurotic trends in human behavior.

THERAPY

The basic tool of traditional psychoanalytic therapy is *free association.* The patient reclines on a couch and is told to say aloud anything at all that comes to his mind. This is to be done without inhibition, without conscious censorship, and without regard to logical order. The instruction to free associate is called the *fundamental rule* of psychoanalysis. It is not particularly easy to consistently observe the fundamental rule, and most patients have to spend a period of time learning to free associate successfully. The reason the fundamental rule is difficult to learn is the tendency toward ego defense. Thus the psychoanalytic patient often offers *resistances*, blocks that thwart honest self-disclosure. For example, while free associating, a woman patient may have an image of her therapist sitting on the toilet while she is thinking, "He seems so kingly. But he sits on an ordinary 'throne' like anyone else." Perhaps she dismisses this as an unimportant image, not worthy of repeating to the therapist. But the dismissal itself is a defense against the awkward feeling that would come to her if she repeated her thoughts to the therapist. It is not until patients have come to trust their therapists and feel accepted by them that they are willing to free associate without reservation.

Freud saw free association as the major road to repressed material.

Remember that he believed in the principle of *psychic determinism*, the view that all mental acts have a meaning. Thus he believed that seemingly random associations actually have a common thread and that if this thread is followed to its end, one will discover the core element in a particular personal problem.

To illustrate, assume that a male patient is having a great deal of difficulty in his marital relationship. He feels his wife is a shrew and tries to dominate him. He is asked to free associate to the word "wife." " 'Wife' for some reason makes me think of words like 'kitchen,' 'sink,' 'bread,' 'knife,' and 'butter.' Now I'm seeing my own mother standing in the kitchen and she's chewing me out for something, like she always did. I'm thinking that she was a real put-down artist and I'm wondering why she always loved my brother Tommy more than she loved me. Now I'm thinking of a day in the park with my mother. The sun was shining and I was about six years old and we had a good time. For some reason I had her all to myself—no brothers or sisters around. But I don't remember many good times with her, and I never really learned how to talk with her. Now I'm seeing my Dad standing next to her—but he's an invisible man! Don't ask me how I can see him when he's invisible. Maybe he's not invisible—he's sort of transparent or something. She hits him and he shatters into a million pieces like glass."

A classical psychoanalytic approach would suggest that the patient's associations to his wife have led him back to his relationship with his mother and his perception of her relationship with his father. His present conflict with his own wife is probably a compulsive repetition of old problems that have never been resolved adequately. In psychoanalysis, he can work through some of these psychological leftovers and explore some new ways of interacting with a female.

The basic principle of growth in psychoanalysis is *insight,* which may be defined as "seeing into" the essence of a problem. It is the well-known "ah-hah!" phenomenon. We are trying to solve a problem—can't get it, can't get it—and then "click!" something happens and things fall into place. A patient in therapy may declare, "Now I see why I always had trouble with my officers in the Army and why I'm always on the outs with teachers, bosses, and even ministers. It all goes back to dear old dad and the way he treated me—like I was some kind of puppet or something. I had to strangle my rage and act like I loved it when he ordered me around. As an adult, I'm trying to prove to every 'father' I meet that I'm not a puppet—that I'm a living person!"

Early psychoanalytic work stressed the concept of *abreaction.* An abreaction takes place when a patient remembers an emotional trauma (with an emphasis on childhood memories) and "relives" the event *with feeling*. The patient thus discharges stored-up negative emotions and at the same time transfers the painful memory from an unconscious to a conscious level. The present day psychoanalyst does not reject the importance of abreaction, but feels that abreactions are not the key to long-term personal growth. The majority of contemporary analysts place greater emphasis on *ego analysis*, an approach that scrutinizes the patient's defense mechanisms, ways of relating to other people, and mode of adjusting to reality. The aim of ego analysis is to help the patient build *ego strength*. A person with a high level of ego strength is well oriented in time and space, knows the practical limits of his capacities, is able to make good working compromises between the fantasy-oriented demands of the id and the morality-oriented demands of the superego, and in general is able to cope effectively with life's challenges.

Another major concept in psychoanalytic therapy is the *transference relationship*. The theory of psychoanalytic therapy proposes that patients tend to transfer to the therapist feelings held in childhood toward their parents. In most cases the therapist becomes a "father figure." Thus one female patient may start to flirt with her therapist and another may, during free association, profess that she has fallen in love with him. To the traditional Freudian, such moves on the part of patients do not arise out of reality-oriented considerations. Instead they arise from the fantasy-oriented images of the primal self, the wishful id. It is the therapist's responsibility to recognize the existence of a transference relationship and to eventually interpret it to the patient.

It is also possible for him to use the relationship in a constructive way during the patient's psychoanalysis. The therapist does not allow the client to act on the transference feelings; this would be giving in to the fantasy-oriented id and would take the patient away from reality. The therapist may, however, rely on the transference to a certain extent as a means of energizing the therapy. As long as the patient sees the therapist as a parental figure, the possibility exists that the therapist has a greater impact on the patient than if he is seen as just another person. Up to a point, the emotional attachment of the patient to the therapist may have a place. It is crucial in a successful psychoanalysis, however, that the transference not go too far and that it be analyzed for what it is before the termination of therapy. When the transference relationship has been analyzed and accepted by the patient, the traditional psychoanalytic case is closed.

Not all schools of psychotherapy accept the use or the fostering of the transference relationship. Specifically, Adlerian therapy, transactional analysis, and client-centered therapy would all look down on the fostering of a transference relationship. These schools of psychotherapy would prefer an adult-adult relationship with the client. They would criticize classical psychoanalysis as encouraging a parent–child relationship and thus undermining the client's capacity for self-sufficiency. The classical analyst would answer that these criticisms are valid only if the transference is not analyzed and finally revealed for what it is. The responsible Freudian does not allow the patient to leave analysis with a therapist hang-up.

The most important assumption of psychoanalytic therapy is that psychological material which is available at a conscious level can be dealt with in a rational fashion. The work of therapy is seen much as a "dredging" operation in which repressed material is brought up from the darkness of the unconscious domain to the light of the conscious domain. Thus the principal orientation of psychoanalysis is as old as the ancient dictum, "Know thyself."

NEO-FREUDIANS

It is reported that the motion picture producer Samuel Goldwyn once said to author Garson Kanin, "I hear that you are a very clever genius." The exaltation implied by the statement's redundant quality can readily be applied to Freud. And yet, although Freud was "a very clever genius," few psychologists take the position that the whole story of psychology was told by Freud. There are those who completely reject the entire Freudian apparatus consisting of id, ego, superego, defense mechanisms, unconscious motivation, and so forth. Behavioral psychology (discussed in Chapter Three) disassociates itself completely from Freudian psychology; in many ways it tends to be actively hostile toward it.

Some other thinkers accept many of the general proposals of Freudian theory, but reject many of its specific conclusions. These thinkers are termed *neo-Freudians*, and the first thread that unifies them is a common agreement on the importance of the unconscious level of the human personality. The second unifying thread is an emphasis on cultural factors in development as opposed to Freud's emphasis on biological factors. The three neo-Freudians to be discussed in this section are Karen Horney, Harry Stack Sullivan, and Erich Fromm.

Karen Horney (1885–1952) felt that neurotic trends were common in human beings. The title of one of her books, *The Neurotic Personality of Our Time*, reveals this bias. She felt that neurotic trends stem from *basic anxiety*, a feeling that one is alone and helpless in a hostile world. Adults who suffer from basic anxiety generally have experienced, as children, a family life that failed to meet their psychological-emotional needs. They thus grow up as warped adults, blindly seeking unmet needs. The unmet needs produce neurotic personality trends, such as an excessive need for affection and approval, a great need for power, a need to restrict life within narrow borders, a need to exploit others, an inordinate need for personal admiration, or a need for perfection and unassailability.

Horney felt that such distortions in the human personality were not so much the result of defects in psychosexual development (as did Freud); rather, she felt they were much more the result of defects in *psychosocial development*, the development of the human personality that is based on a child's relationship to significant other persons in his life. For example, it is not too difficult to imagine how cold and rejecting parents or parents incapable of giving sound guidance might produce children who exhibit the neurotic trends described by Horney. Stressing the importance of cultural factors in contrast to biological factors as she did, we can understand why Horney rejected Freud's version of the Oedipus complex. To Horney, the child in the family does not have a blatant incest wish. The child wishes to have the status and power of the parent of the same sex. Thus a boy may have a guilt-ridden wish to displace the father from his proper station and take over his role. But the sexual drive plays little part in the conflict.

Harry Stack Sullivan (1892–1949) was a psychiatrist who did a great deal of work with schizophrenic patients. He placed much emphasis on the role played by *interpersonal processes* in human behavior, which refer to the psychological-emotional exchanges we have with other persons. As Horney noted, these are particularly important when we are growing up. But Sullivan is of particular importance to us in that he stresses the continuing importance of human relations *in the present*. He felt that the basic unit of analysis for understanding the person was not the person himself, but *his exchanges with other persons*. To Sullivan, a person is not disturbed in a vacuum. It is a question of *who* is involved in the person's disturbance. Let us not elaborate the point now. Sullivan is generally recognized as an important precursor to transactional analysis (Chapter Five), which views personal problems in terms of disturbed human relations; the importance of Sullivan's thesis will become evident when transactional analysis is discussed.

It may be of some value at this point, though, to introduce at least one other important idea of Sullivan's. He spoke of *dynamisms* in the human personality. A dynamism is similar to the more familiar concept of "habit" or "trait." But the concept of dynamism stresses the importance of habitual reactions to *other people*. Thus a dynamism may be thought of as a programmed response to persons falling within a given category. Susan might always find her heart melting if a man who is tall, dark, and handsome talks to her; Tom, a white man, may always feel hostile when he is talking to a black man; Clark may say, "I really groove on blondes"; Donald may find himself becoming angry whenever a salesman approaches him in a department store. These are all examples of dynamisms, and they are all unreflective responses—the person does not think through his behavior. Thus dynamisms tend to give human relations a mechanical quality that leaves much to be desired.

Erich Fromm was born in 1900 and studied psychoanalysis at the Psychoanalytic Institute in Berlin. In 1973 Fromm published *The Anatomy of Human Destructiveness*, a book that sets forth many of his ideas in their most developed form. *Alienation* is a major theme in Fromm's writings. To be alienated is to be an outsider. Of course, one cannot be alienated without reference to something or someone else. Alienation is always *alienation from*.

To Fromm, modern men and women exhibit excessive alienation from two important realms: (1) nature, and (2) other people. We of the Western world are alienated from nature because we do not see ourselves as part of nature; rather, we see ourselves as its conqueror. We use and abuse the earth for our vast technology and think ourselves masters of the world. We must learn to realize that we are really one with nature to guarantee our long-term survival on this planet. Fromm says we are alienated from

Erich Fromm says modern man is alienated from nature because he does not see himself as a part of nature.

other people in a consumer society because we have to use each other to ''make sales'' and ''get ahead.'' Thus people get trampled on and become mere things or objects within the waste-oriented culture. The forces described by Fromm tend to produce neurotic reactions in people and make it difficult for them to live deeply satisfying lives.

Fromm suggests that one of our most powerful needs, a need that is uniquely human, is our need for *relatedness*. The need for relatedness is the need to care for others and feel cared for in return. Personal growth, in Fromm's view, would imply the capacity to overcome alienation and find relatedness. His ideas are closely related to existential-humanistic psychology (Chapter Seven).

ANALYTICAL PSYCHOLOGY: DIGGING DEEPER

In *Memories, Dreams, Reflections*, the psychiatrist Carl Jung comments:

Among the so-called neurotics of our day there are a good many who in other ages would not have been neurotic—that is, divided against themselves. If they had lived in a period and in a milieu in which man was still linked by myth with the world of his ancestors, and thus with nature truly experienced and not merely seen from outside, they would have been spared this division within themselves. (pp. 143–144)

This statement captures the central theme of Jung's *analytical psychology*, an approach that asserts there is a deeper and more primitive layer of the mind than the unconscious level postulated by Freud. We return to this point of view in the pages that follow. It requires augmentation for it to acquire greater meaning. For the present, let us identify Carl Jung as a person.

WHO WAS CARL JUNG?

Carl Jung was a Swiss psychiatrist who was born in 1875 and died in 1961. His childhood years were characterized by an interest in the same kinds of subjects that make up the body of analytical psychology: myth, magic, religion—the subjective and ''unscientific'' domain of human existence. From his early years, Jung had an interest in finding the meeting ground between the rational and the irrational worlds. Jung's father was a Swiss Reform pastor, and he seems to have been a man who had a cold-blooded approach to religion. Jung could not accept his father's rather technical approach to God, and much of Jung's search as a man was for a deep and meaningful relationship with the Universe.

For a time Jung was a student of Freud. As you already know from the previous section, Jung was the first president of the International Psycho-

Carl Jung was one of the principal founders of depth psychology.

analytic Association. Perhaps too much has been made out of the Freud–Jung relationship, however. Jung was a psychiatrist before he met Freud, had already done important word-association experiments, and had formulated theories about mental complexes. The work done after his break with Freud is original and independent of Freudian influence; it would be unfair to Jung to see him as always standing in Freud's shadow. In proper perspective, we would have to say that Freud was the father of depth psychology. But Jung was one of its principal founders and is generally considered to have been a giant of the field.

Carl Jung was a scientist. Carl Jung was a mystic. If these two statements strike you as contradictory, Jung would have commented that your thinking takes arbitrary categories too seriously. It is perfectly possible for a man to be at once both a scientist and a mystic. Much of Jung's work was devoted to showing how superficial opposites could be united to form a meaningful whole. Thus it is possible to say of Jung that he was a scientist-mystic.

THE COLLECTIVE UNCONSCIOUS

Jung accepted the Freudian unconscious. He agreed that there was a layer of the personality which consisted of repressed ideas. Jung designated this layer the *personal unconscious*. But Jung also said that there is a deeper layer to the human personality—the *collective unconscious.* The collective unconscious is impersonal—we all have the same collective unconscious. Its contents are the residual memories of the human race. These memories are based on more or less similar experiences had by all peoples in all times and places since the dawn of human existence. These oft-repeated experiences have somehow made a deep and permanent impression on the human mind. These enduring patterns Jung termed *archetypes* (pronounced "ar-ke-types").

By postulating the existence of archetypes, Jung was in essence saying that the human mind is much more than a blank slate at birth. We have inborn behavioral predispositions. Archetypes are for humans what instincts are for animals. Like an instinct, the archetype guides behavior and tells us what to do in certain circumstances. A particular set of circumstances will cause us to "plug into" a particular archetype. Once we are in the grips of the archetype, our behavior becomes robotlike; the archetype takes over, and for a period of time determines the course of events. The archetypes make up the inner core of human nature, and it was Jung's view that we need to know our archetypes if we do not wish to be controlled blindly by them.

Jung felt that Western men and women are alienated from their deepest nature, that they do not have a creative contact with the archetypes. As a consequence, they place too much trust on conscious reason and are "sitting ducks" when an emotion-arousing set of circumstances activates an archetype. A familiar example is provided by the rise to power of a dictator in a country beset by economic woes. A figure comes forth who promises to cure everything. He rants and raves and presents "solutions" to the country's great crises. The emotional state of the populace is such that an archetype is activated. This archetype could be called the Rescuer or the Hero or the Saviour. The dictator quickly becomes a demigod. He acquires all the attributes of the age-old archetypes. He will lead the people out of the wilderness of their problems, he will defeat enemies both inside and outside the country, and he will have at his disposal great powers. The dictator's success is based on the ancient wish of a group of people to follow a leader who is all-knowing and all-wise. If, for a time, a dictator is perceived as an archetypal figure, he has it made.

The archetypes can also operate at an individual level. Say that Tom falls in love with Julie. He is on cloud nine, head over heels in love with her. She is Miss Perfect, everything he ever wanted in a woman. When he thinks of their future together he can visualize only bliss and unadulterated happiness. Somehow Julie has enabled Tom to plug into the archetype represented by such familiar symbols as Cinderella, Snow White, and Miss America. Note that Cinderella, Snow White, and Miss America are not themselves archetypes. They are *symbols*, figures presented at a conscious level that stand for the underlying archetype. In this case the underlying archetype might be called the Beautiful One. In the grips of the archetype of the Beautiful One, Tom has obviously taken leave of his senses. His behavior has become robotlike, programmed by the attributes of the archetype.

Before we proceed, let us discuss the plausibility of the existence of archetypes. Many psychologists have rejected the Jungian archetypes and the collective unconscious because the two seem to demand the acceptance of an outmoded evolutionary theory, *Lamarckian inheritance* —the doctrine that experiences affecting the individual can be directly transmitted through the germ plasm to that individual's children. To illustrate, assume that a man is a weight lifter and builds up powerful muscles. Lamarckian inheritance would say that this man will have children with powerful muscles. Modern biologists are convinced that the evolutionary process does not work in such a crude and obvious way. It is more likely that changes in a species over time are determined by the processes of *mutation* (spontaneous changes in genetic structure) and *natural selection* (survival of the fittest). Thus it seems absurd to many individuals who know something about modern biology and contemporary evolutionary theory that there can be "racial memories" in the form of archetypes.

Jung did not, however, pin the existence of the archetypes on the doctrine of Lamarckian inheritance. The way the archetypes arose was not the central issue for him. He felt that their presence was documented amply by the way human beings behave and, in particular, by the themes that reappear in myth and folklore. If modern biology cannot explain how archetypes come to be, this was a problem for modern biology, not a problem for Jungian theory.

Perhaps a compromise position is possible. First, if we think of the archetypes not as specific memories, but as *patterns*, it is possible to see how the human brain and nervous system might have certain kinds of predispositions; these predispositions could easily fit within the framework of mutation and natural selection. Second, we must realize that an archetype is a concept, an abstraction that is utilized to explain sets of events. As such, concepts are neither true nor false. It is a basic error to argue over the reality of concepts. They are like tools; they are either useful or useless. If they are useful, they should be retained. If they are useless, they should be discarded. A number of psychologists and other thinkers have found the Jungian archetypes to have a degree of utility in certain contexts; thus one might agree that for some behaviors they have both explanatory and predictive power. One may use the concept of the archetype as a working hypothesis without asserting that it represents the Truth.

KINDS OF ARCHETYPES

Archetypes may be classified as falling into three broad categories: (1) personifications, (2) processes of the world, and (3) systems of the self.

Personifications. Examples of personifications are the Hero, the Wise Old Man, the Earth Mother, the Evil One, and the Beautiful One. The same personifications appear and reappear in myth, folklore, fairy tales, novels, plays, motion pictures, television dramas, and comic books. Consider the Wise Old Man. The archetype suggests a kindly soul with great vision and magical (or at least semimagical) powers. Specific symbolizations of the Wise Old Man are Merlin the Magician (King Arthur's ''godparent''), Shazam (the ancient one who gave Billy Batson the power to turn into Captain Marvel), and Marcus Welby, M.D. An obvious example of the Earth Mother is Mother Nature; a somewhat less obvious example is Betty Crocker. Sentimental songs about mother and the kind of mother portrayed in Mother's Day cards are stimuli that evoke the archetype of the Earth Mother—a *good* mother who will stroke us and nurse us for as long as we wish. Satan, Dr. No in the James Bond series, the intelligent alien from Planet X who seeks to destroy the Earth, the mad professor who confronts Superman, and the bad guy in a Western saga all symbolize the archetype of the Evil One.

Processes of the world. It was Jung's contention that aeons of experience with processes of nature also gave rise to certain kinds of archetypes in humankind. These are the archetypes that represent processes of the world; examples are Rebirth, Sunrise and Sunset, and the Circle. Specific symbolizations of the archetype of Rebirth can take many forms and may sometimes seem quite remote from the archetype. A relatively risky one-week trip down a river with straits and rapids may symbolize, for some people, a death and rebirth of the spirit. They come out of such an adventure feeling they have a new lease on life. Jung said that for modern man such returns to nature may well connect with the ancient archetypes of Birth and Death in the broadest sense. Actual birth is itself a ''water trip'' down a narrow passageway; the river trip provides an obvious parallel for the collective unconscious.

Another symbol for the archetype of Rebirth would be skydiving. As the person plunges toward earth, a feeling of death may close in; when the parachute flowers overhead, the sense of being reborn takes over. It could be argued that from a Jungian standpoint, the exhiliration of such sports as skydiving arise from the activation of the archetype of Rebirth. More obvious and familiar examples of symbols for Rebirth than the ones already given are the Phoenix rising from the ashes, Igor Stravinsky's *Rites of Spring*, pagan festivals marking the beginning of new seasons, and the Resurrection.

Many familiar symbols portray the archetype of Sunrise and Sunset. The Japanese flag uses the symbol of the rising sun. Many Americans worship at Easter Sunday sunrise services. The Pueblo Indians in New Mexico believe in Father Sun; their religion requires that they pray and thus help the Father across the sky each day to save the world from darkness. In the musical play *Fiddler on the Roof*, the central character, Tevye, and his wife, Golde, sing:

Is this the little girl I carried?
Is this the little boy at play?
I don't remember growing older,
When did they?

Sunrise, Sunset,
Sunrise, Sunset
Swiftly flow the days;
Seedlings turn overnight to sunflow'rs,
*Blossoming even as we gaze.**

The tendency of many processes of nature to bring into existence circular and spherical structures gives rise to the archetype of the Circle. An example of such a process is the tendency of a soap bubble to form a sphere. The planets, including Earth itself, and the sun are spheres (note also that the planets travel in more or less circular orbits). There is magic in the circular form. In alchemy and magic, the circle is used for casting spells. On an everyday level, the wedding band is a circle symbolizing wholeness and unity—aspects of the archetype of the circle. The following poem by Edwin Markham invokes the power of the circle:

He drew a circle that shut me out,
Heretic, rebel, thing to flout.

But love and I had the wit to win,
We drew a circle that took him in.†

Would it not seem odd to you if the poem used the phrase, ". . . a square that shut me out"? The square does not connect with the collective unconscious. Jung was fond of pointing out the universal appearance of *mandalas,* circular figures—often elaborate—divided into four quadrants. Indeed, mandala is a Sanskrit word meaning a circle and has the specific connotation of a magic circle. The mandala tends to appear in cultures greatly separated by space and time. It was Jung's contention that these were spontaneous appearances, not appearances arising from communication between cultures. Although the possibility of cultural transmission can always be advanced, Jung felt that this interpretation of the mandala (and other symbols representing archetypes) was farfetched. He felt it was much more plausible and had much more meaning to think in terms of intrinsic processes in all people. In any event, one can find many examples of the mandala in different cultures. The ground plans of many temples in the East are based on the mandala, and the mandala appears in the form of pictures in Eastern temples. On the American continent, the mandala was used by the Plains Indians. In *Black Elk Speaks,* the life story of a holy man of the Oglala Sioux, is the following passage:

You have noticed that everything an Indian does is in a circle, and that is because the Power of the World always works in circles, and everything tries to be round. In the old days when we were a strong and happy people, all our power came to us from the sacred hoop of the nation, and so long as the hoop was unbroken, the people flourished. The flowering tree was the living center of the hoop, and the circle of the four quarters nourished it. The east gave peace and light, the south gave warmth, the west gave rain, and the north with its cold and mighty wind gave strength and endurance. . . . Birds make their nests in circles, for theirs is the same religion as ours. (pp. 39–40)

The sacred hoop of the Sioux, with its four quadrants, was clearly a mandala.

Systems of the self. The third broad category of archetypes refers to systems of the self, such as the Anima and Animus, the Persona, the Shadow, and the Self. The Anima and the Animus refer, respectively, to the female and the male personalities in all of us. The Anima is nurturing, tender, and intuitive; the Animus is aggressive, tough, and practical. In the female the Anima is dominant and the Animus is recessive, and in the male the Animus is dominant and the Anima is recessive. But every individual, regardless of objective sex, has both archetypes. One of life's principal tasks is to acknowledge the existence of both archetypes and bring their opposing tendencies together for a meaningful synthesis. Say that one woman has acknowledged only her Anima. She takes care of her home, loves her husband and children, and is a good cook. But she goes to pieces in the face of adversity, hates to leave her home for more than a few hours at a time, will not learn to drive a car, blushes when she hears an off-color joke, and never takes the sexual initiative with her husband. By not acknowledging her Animus, she falls far short of being a whole person. On the other hand, let us say that another woman has psychologically "become a man." Her Animus reigns supreme, and her Anima is denied. Here we have the stereotype of the militant feminist who curses like a deckhand, speaks frequently of "male pigs," and complains of universal sexism. If she is married, she is the dominant one in the marriage; her husband is a meek and passive fellow who tries to make his behavior conform to her wishes.

The male may be subject to the same imbalances in the relationship between his Anima and Animus. The male who tries to completely repress his Anima tends to be an extroverted go-getter. He rejects shows of emotion and attempts to remain stolid in the face of adversity. In the business world, he thinks in terms of dog-eat-dog and conceptualizes success in terms of a battlefield. If he is married, he refuses to do any of the things around the home that are usually the wife's task. He won't change the baby's diapers, wash dishes, vacuum, or dust. This would be true even if his wife were fatigued or clearly operating under a time pressure. He distinguishes between women's work and men's work, and never the twain shall meet. He will, in all likelihood, be handy with tools; carpentry, painting, and yard maintenance are all perceived as masculine tasks, and these do not threaten his self-image as a real man's man. His relationship with his children will entail difficulties revolving around his tendency to be authoritarian with them; it will be difficult for such a man to develop emotional closeness with his children. He is of the old school, in which the father must have an exalted status in the household.

Now imagine a different situation. Another man has a dominant Anima and a recessive Animus. Such a man will speak softly, have difficulty asserting himself, and may display female mannerisms in his walk and speech. He will hate to do any kind of rough or dirty work. The idea of getting into a fight and getting cut or bruised is abhorrent. His interests will be in the fine arts—music, painting, sculpture, and literature. He will be looked down on as a sissy and a fool by the man with a highly dominant Animus. Our society appears to have much less tolerance for the femalelike man than for the malelike woman. Although both types receive their share of hostility, the femalelike man receives more, probably because traditional male roles have tended to receive more status than traditional female roles. Thus the woman who mimics male behavior seems to take a psychological step up; however, the male who mimics female behavior seems to take a psychological step down.

The Persona is the public self, the social role an individual has chosen to play. The mask worn by a Greek actor was called a *persona*, and it designated the actor's role in the drama. Thus one's Persona is thought to be one's mask. The Persona (1) defines how a person is to act in certain situations and (2) provides a disguise for real thoughts and feelings. Thus the Persona acts like a "skin" between the inner self and the outer world. As such, the Persona is as necessary as the physical skin that covers the human body. It is a protection, and without it the ego would be naked in the world. Thus it is clear that Jung did not believe it was possible to be absolutely authentic and a "transparent self" in all one's human relations. On the other hand, he did feel that trouble arises for the individual when he makes the mistake of identifying his ego with his Persona. Such an individual thinks that his inner being is identical with his social role, and this is a mistake. For example, the judge who continues to play the part of powerful magistrate with his wife, with his children, and with his friends fails to recognize that the sober demeanor of the professional judge is a role that fits nicely in the courtroom and is, of course, expected in that setting. When he is with his family, however, a different role should be played. When people are unable to be flexible, we often have an inner reaction toward them such as, "Oh, come off it" or "I wish he would get off his high horse."

The minister's wife who is all smiles and kindness we take to be a "wonderful person with a heart of gold." We forget that this is her social role. Any other behavior might strike us as deviant or odd. If she departs too sharply from the behaviors defined by the role, members of the congregation are apt to gossip and say, "She's gone crazy!" In *Two Essays on Analytical Psychology*, Jung writes:

Society expects, and indeed must expect, every individual to play the part assigned to him as perfectly as possible, so that a man who is a parson . . . must at all times . . . play the role of parson in a flawless manner. Society demands this as a kind of surety: each must stand at his post, here a cobbler, there a poet. No man is expected to be both . . . that would be "odd." Such a man would be "different" from other people, not quite reliable. In the academic world he would be a dilettante, in politics an "unpredictable" quantity, in religion a free-thinker—in short, he would always be suspected of unreliability and incompetence, because society is persuaded that only the cobbler who is not a poet can supply workmanlike shoes. (p. 48)

In Jung's statement, one can detect a note of frustration with conventional society. Social roles are necessary, but they should not act like straitjackets that inhibit the growth of the whole person. Unfortunately, the social roles do just that for many persons.

A poignant example of how the inner self can rebel against the public mask is provided in the autobiography of Edward G. Robinson. Robinson was an actor who made many motion pictures in which he starred as a

The Persona is the public self, the social role the individual has chosen to play. The inner self may be very different from the public self. (Edward G. Robinson and Humphrey Bogart in a scene from "Bullets or Ballots.")

tough guy. During World War II, he volunteered to entertain troops. But what was he to do? He was not a singer or a stand-up comic. He tells his story as follows:

Well, I'd been forewarned. What they wanted was not Edward G. Robinson, but Little Caesar. Accordingly, I had worked out, before I left, with the help of Jack Benny, whole idiotic routines, inevitably beginning with "Hey, youse guys," and including "Buy your beer from me or else." I even took along a felt hat and a trench coat, and it didn't work very well until I remembered whole speeches from The Racket, *a play in which I'd appeared. When I played them—and thank God, I was working as an actor with lines engraved on my consciousness—I was a smash. A sweaty, shivering, shaking, heart-throbbing smash—but a smash.*

I remember the opening of one of my earlier speeches at an Air Force base in the north of England. I began by saying: "I am happy to be here, the most privileged moment of my life to see the men who are defeating Hitler." I have never laid so big a bomb in my life. I could sense the audience despising me. So that crazy actor instinct took over, and to stop the buzz of their boos and

Bronx cheers, I ad-libbed, "Pipe down, you mugs, or I'll let you have it. Whaddaya hear from the mob?" There was an instant burst of high laughter and applause. What they didn't know was that I wasn't laughing; I was crying. (pp. 229–230)

The Shadow is the animal side of the human personality. (The archetype of the Shadow is similar to Freud's concept of the id.) The Shadow is a kind of inferior being within each person. Robert Louis Stevenson's novel *Dr. Jekyll and Mr. Hyde* captures well the archetype of the Shadow. Mr. Hyde is everything that Dr. Jekyll is not. Dr. Jekyll is decent, kind, altruistic, law abiding, and so forth; Mr. Hyde is immoral, cruel, selfish, and cares nothing for the law. The perennial fascination of Stevenson's novel may be that many of us see an undiscovered self reflected in the behavior of Mr. Hyde. He is a monster, but we are nonetheless intrigued. A popular radio series of the 1940s was called *The Shadow*. It was about an invisible detective. The show opened with a mocking laugh, and the Shadow said, "Who knows what evil lurks in the hearts of men? The Shadow knows!" And then the mocking laugh was repeated. This captures rather accurately what Jung had in mind with his concept of the Shadow. One wonders if the author of the series was familiar with Jungian theory. (Jung's views were presented and well known long before the 1940s). Or

The story of Dr. Jekyll and Mr. Hyde captures well the archetype of the shadow. (Spencer Tracy in a scene from the movie.)

perhaps the author chose the image of the Shadow for the same reason that Jung chose it: There is a self that resides in the darkness.

It was Jung's view that denial is not the proper way to handle the Shadow. Many persons are horrified by the Shadow when they get a glimpse of it, and they quickly repress it into the unconscious. Jung felt that the Shadow should be acknowledged, even welcomed, and integrated into the whole personality. When this is done the Shadow becomes a source of creativity, and there is no risk of being taken over and destroyed by the Shadow. On the other hand, if the Shadow is completely blocked in its expression, it will find ways of kicking up and creating trouble. There are many possibilities: nightmares, chronic anxiety, episodes of irrationality, and so forth. Over and over in Jung we find the point of view expressed that opposites should be united to form a higher whole.

The archetype of the Self represents the whole person. Let us defer our consideration of the Self for a few pages. We will return to this archetype in the discussion under the heading "The Individuation Process."

TYPES OF PERSONS

The idea that there are different types of persons is centuries old. You will recall from Chapter One that more than two thousand years ago Hippocrates designated four different kinds of personality types. Jung also designated personality types, and he felt that such a classification scheme could be of value in understanding ourselves and other people.

The most well-known dichotomy from Jungian theory is the distinction between the extrovert and the introvert. This distinction has become part of popular psychology and is familiar to millions of people from articles in magazines and newspapers. Unfortunately, popularizations of Jung's work do not do justice to the richness and complexity of his thought. His approach to personality types was not based so much on a static classification scheme as it was on a recognition of dominant and recessive processes in the individual. To clarify, Jung postulated that the human personality takes an orientation toward the world that is either outgoing or ingoing. The basic orientation is called the individual's *attitude*.

If an individual has an extroverted attitude, he tends to have a dominant interest in the outside world as opposed to the inner world of thought and the mind. It is cliché to suppose that all extroverts are talkative and popular. In many instances this may be the case. A practical person who likes to make his living with his hands, enjoys using tools, and takes satisfaction in completing a physical task, however, would also be an extroverted type. Practical inventors, such as Thomas Alva Edison or Alexander Graham Bell, would thus also be considered extroverted types. On the other hand, the introverted type tends to be interested in philosophical discourse, abstract issues, and such subjects as mathematics. Theoreticians such as the philosopher Immanuel Kant and the physicist Albert Einstein could be considered introverted types.

Jung felt that the basic attitude is built into the individual. It is innate, not learned. It is true that family life and the environment can modify the basic attitude, but nonetheless the foundation remains. This point of view has been repugnant to American psychology, which has leaned heavily on the Lockean tradition of the *tabula rasa*. (The British philosopher John Locke taught that the mind at birth is a *tabula rasa*, or blank slate containing no inborn ideas.) In the past decade, however, there has been a partial return to accepting the idea of inborn differences in personality traits. Research evidence suggests that some infants are more stolid than others. Such findings bear a partial resemblance to Jung's notion of inborn types.

In addition to the attitudes of extroversion and introversion, Jung postulated *psychological functions*—processes by which the conscious mind orients itself toward the outer world and the inner world. Jung designated four functions: *thinking, feeling, sensation,* and *intuition.* He arranged these into two sets of opposed pairs: thinking versus feeling and sensation versus intuition. Thinking and feeling are called the "rational functions" because they are used primarily to evaluate ideas. When an individual attempts to make an evaluation of an idea in terms of other ideas, he will use logic and abstract concepts; he may be said to be using the thinking function. Say that another individual evaluates the same idea in terms of the pleasant or unpleasant feelings the idea evokes within him; such a person would be using the feeling function.

Sensation and intuition are called the "irrational functions"; the designation irrational is merely meant to imply that these functions have little to do with conventional thought processes. Sensation and intuition both refer to *knowing about.* Assume that one individual is convinced that all we can know about the world is what we see, taste, touch, smell, or hear. His philosophical position corresponds to what is called *empiricism,* the doctrine that all man's knowledge comes in through the sense organs. Such an individual takes the position, "I'm from Missouri. You've got to show me." On the other hand, say that another individual is intrigued by meditation and the teachings of the mystics. Such a person might be convinced that through the power of intuition, one could be aware of all sorts of things not available through the sense organs. A belief in the possibility of *psi* phenomena, such as extrasensory perception and telepathy, would give status to the intuitive function.

Jung contended that all of us use the complete set of attitudes and func-

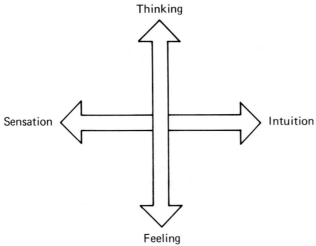

FIGURE 2.3 Jung designated four psychological functions arranged into two sets of opposed pairs.

tions, that no one is either a pure extrovert or a pure introvert and no one is either a pure thinking type or a pure feeling type. Nonetheless, there is a tendency within persons to develop habitual modes of preference. Thus Jung would contend that there are types, even though the types are far from pure. The problem for the individual arises when he has become too lopsided in his dependence on one of the attitudes or functions. Adjustment and growth would imply bringing the opposing pairs into better harmony. One should, for example, recognize that thinking and feeling are only superficially opposed. They both have their place and purpose in the well-balanced personality.

DREAM ANALYSIS
Like Freud, Jung believed that dreams have meaning. And also like Freud, Jung agreed that dreams are messages from unconscious levels of the personality. Unlike Freud, however, Jung did not believe that the aim of the symbols in a dream is to act as a disguise or cover for the real meaning of the dream. On the contrary, the symbol appears in the dream because the symbol is rich in connotative meaning. When someone seems dense and cannot grasp an explanation, we sometimes say, "Do you want me to draw you a picture?" The implication is that a picture has the capacity to make things obvious. Thus to Jung, a dream is an attempt on the part of the deeper self to send important clarifying messages to the

conscious self. A dream is a projection of "motion pictures" into the conscious mind from the unconscious mind. The pictures aim to *inform,* not conceal or distort.

Because Jung accepted the personal unconscious of Freud, it was also acceptable to Jung that some dreams had to do with personal conflicts, repressed desires, sexual problems, and aggressive themes. Jung felt, however, that some dreams also emanated from the collective unconscious. Such dreams contain an archetypal content—they speak the "wisdom of the ages." These dreams seem to glow in the mind and are long remembered in consciousness as somehow being of great importance. These "glowing" dreams Jung referred to as *numinous* dreams. One example is a dream which sends a warning to the dreamer that he has taken a wrong path in life, which will lead to possible disaster. Another numinous dream may have a positive motif; it may show the dreamer what he might be able to do with his life if he were to act on his highest aspirations and best talents.

One of my students had a numinous dream in which a kindly magician turned him from a snake into an angel. The magician, the snake, and the angel are all symbols for familiar archetypes. A Jungian interpretation of the dream would suggest that the dreamer is trying to go from a "lower" to a "higher" status in life; it also suggests that he feels he has the potential to make such a transformation. Like Cinderella, however, he is waiting for someone else to do the job for him. But I hasten to add that such an interpretation is risky without knowing quite a bit about the dreamer's circumstances in life and without having heard a *series* of dreams from the dreamer. Jung emphasized the importance of collecting a series of dreams and searching out common patterns in dreams over a time span.

Freud's method of dream analysis called for the dreamer to free associate to the elements of the dream. Jung rejected this approach. He felt that random associations to the content of a dream led one away from the dream message itself. Of course, free associations do lead somewhere; Jung contended that they always lead one back to the same set of predictable Freudian concepts. The dreamer is led to the Oedipus or Electra complex, infantile oral or anal trauma, and so forth. Thus, following the Freudian method, the unique meaning of the dream for the individual is destroyed. He finds himself at the end of his dream-analysis journey in the same place as all other dreamers. Thus he has got nowhere. He might as well read a textbook on Freudian theory as analyze his own dream.

Instead of free association, Jung used a method that may be called *amplification*, which requires that the individual use his creative imagination and elaborate and augment the symbols in a dream. This may be done in a variety of ways: by daydreaming and consciously fantasizing, by taking up oils and painting a picture, by writing a story that augments the dream symbols, and so forth. Jung felt that in this way one is drawn into the inner meaning of the dream and properly identifies with it.

THE INDIVIDUATION PROCESS

The phrase *individuation process* was used by Jung to indicate a process of psychological growth within the person, a tendency to become whole within oneself. In his later years, he said that the process of individuation had to become the central concept in his particular approach to psychology. Many people live in a state of self-alienation, divided within themselves. The Animus in a man may be at war with his Anima; or the Anima in a woman may be at war with her Animus. There is a tendency to attach too much importance to the conscious ego and think that is the whole personality; troubled persons try to handle the Shadow and other archetypes that represent their deepest human nature by the brute method of repression. Such inner tactics only aggravate the state of self-alienation.

To overcome self-alienation and attain psychological wholeness, Jung felt that the task of the individual was to become acquainted with the contents of his personal and collective unconscious. Jung felt that this was a slow process of personal maturation, not something that could happen overnight. The emphasis is on *process*, not instant awakening. The individuation process is thus a natural process, an inherent tendency in people—not something reserved for people in psychotherapy.

The task of individuation is to overcome the arbitrary polarity of opposites within the personality. The Anima must make peace with the Animus. The emotional content of the archetypes of the collective unconscious must be acknowledged at a conscious level. In particular, the ego is no longer taken to be the center of the personality. Jung argued that the ego is a false center; it is the center of a self-alienated personality. In this kind of troubled personality, the Shadow is an undiscovered self. In the individuated personality, the ego and the Shadow have overcome their age-old enmity and have learned to live at peace with one another. Thus a new center emerges, and this center is none other than the Self. The Self is the real person, the person that one was always meant to be. An individuated person is thus relaxed and spontaneous and free to live a rewarding life because he is truly himself.

In *Two Essays on Analytical Psychology*, Jung writes:

Individuation means becoming a single, homogeneous being, and, insofar as "individuality" embraces our innermost, last, and incomparable uniqueness, it also implies becoming one's own self. We could therefore translate individuation as "coming to selfhood" or "self-realization." (p. 171)

It is important to stress that because individuation refers to a process, there is almost always room for more growth in the individual. It is probably better to speak of persons who are well along the path of individuation than it is to speak of a completely individuated person. As long as a person is alive, regions of the self to be explored remain.

PRIMAL THERAPY: REMEMBERING PAIN

In 1970 a book titled *The Primal Scream*, by Arthur Janov, became a bestseller. It was widely read by interested laymen, and it had a great impact on college campuses. Something about the book seemed to strike a responsive chord in many readers. On the whole, the book's ideas have not been dealt with kindly by the psychological community. But, in spite of the rejection of primal therapy by the majority of clinicians, the interest in primal theory continues. For example, monthly issues of *Psychology Today* often contain classified advertisements for primal therapy. Because primal therapy is very much alive and has a substantial following, it would seem important to consider it objectively and give it a rational evaluation. The subject is included in this chapter because primal therapy is basically a variant of depth psychology. This statement will be clarified later.

The father of primal therapy, Arthur Janov, holds a Ph.D. degree in psychology and is a licensed clinical psychologist. He was a conventional therapist for seventeen years and now practices primal therapy in Beverly Hills. His patients have come to him from all walks of life, but he has acquired additional fame because a number of his patients have been show business celebrities (e.g., Dyan Cannon, actress and ex-wife of Cary Grant, and John Lennon of Beatles fame underwent primal therapy). A limited number of therapists have studied with Janov, and they have in some cases branched out on their own. These therapists independently offer modified versions of Janov's primal therapy, and they practice in some of the nation's larger cities.

In 1971 Janov published *The Anatomy of Mental Illness*, in which he presented a physiological model for primal therapy and discussed the characteristics of postprimal patients. In 1972 *The Primal Revolution: Toward a Real World* appeared; the book reflects on some of the larger implications of primal theory for society.

PRIMAL THEORY

Primal theory conceives of neurosis as a common condition that affects untold numbers of people. The basic explanation of neurosis is presented by Janov in *The Primal Scream* as follows: "Neurosis is a disease of feeling. At its core is the suppression of feeling and its transmutation into a wide range of neurotic behavior'' (p. 20). He contends that neurosis begins in childhood:

We all are creatures of need. We are born needing, and the vast majority of us die after a lifetime of struggle with many of our needs unfulfilled. These needs are not excessive—to be fed, kept warm and dry, to grow and develop at our own pace, to be held and caressed, and to be stimulated. These Primal needs are the central reality of the infant. The neurotic process begins when these needs go unmet for any length of time. (p. 22)

Janov contends that in childhood one can experience many *minor primal scenes*, transient experiences in which the parents may fail to meet the child's primal needs. For example, a parent may ridicule a child who is having difficulty in learning something. Another child might sustain a great deal of emotional rejection from his parents. Still another child is driven to perform; he must get good grades or learn a musical instrument so that his parents can experience pride. In these examples, the child's primal needs are ignored.

Between the ages of five and seven, the child with a history of minor primal scenes will experience the *major primal scene*. There is only one major primal scene, and it need not be particularly traumatic in and of

According to primal theory, the real self is the original self. (Artist George Segal with one of his sculptures.)

itself. It *is* a culmination, however, and the child generalizes from it that his primal needs will not be met by his parents *unless he earns their approval on their terms.* In essence, this means that the child who experiences a major primal scene realizes that his parents will not accept him for himself. Love and affection become conditional. This realization produces the *split* in the child. The split refers to a division within the child between his real self and a manufactured unreal self. The *real self* is the original self; it represents the child's primal needs and the kind of person the child would be if it were not for parental manipulation. The *unreal self* is the self that is "up front," a facade erected by the child so he will have at least some of his primal needs met by his parents. The unreal self strives to have the primal needs of the real self met. But most of the striving is in the direction of symbolic satisfactions—things that stand for the primal needs but are not the primal needs in fact.

Thus the neurotic person is forever chasing psychological rainbows. The neurotic businessman who compulsively strives for status and power is really a little child inside who is crying out for affection and understanding. His compulsive striving is a nonverbal way of saying, "Please look at me. Please love me. I am important." But he was taught that primal needs are not met merely by asking. The unreal self lives by the fantasy that if he struggles hard enough, *someone*—his parents, his wife, his children, his peers—will give him the love and understanding he seeks. Janov declares that such people live by illusions. They construct false values and philosophies in the vain hope that their need-feeling will be met.

FIGURE 2.4 Primal theory says that the self is split into a real self and an unreal self by realizations associated with the primal scene.

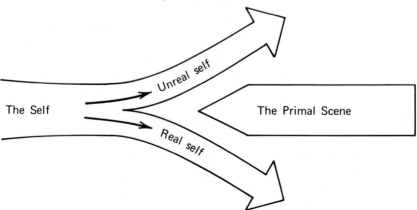

Janov is not the first psychologist to make the distinction between the real self and the unreal self. Karen Horney made such a distinction. Jung's notion of the error of identifying one's self with one's Persona is similar conceptually to the distinction between the real self and the unreal self. In 1960, more than ten years before the publication of *The Primal Scream,* the Scottish psychiatrist R. D. Laing published a book called *The Divided Self.* Laing's formulation is a precursor of Janov's formulation. Nonetheless, Janov writes about the inner split with great clarity and power; his examples touch the heart and make the reader feel the intensity of the child's struggle.

THE TREATMENT

Janov sees neurosis as a disease of repression. There is a *pain block* that arises in the child and remains in the neurotic adult. This pain block is a barrier between primal needs and symbolic striving, between the real self and the unreal self. This is why primal theory can be categorized as a kind of depth psychology. The real needs and the real self are repressed and shoved down into the unconscious area. Janov notes that he has in a sense returned to early Freudian theory. Freud spoke of the need for abreaction in psychotherapy, a release of bottled-up emotion; this emphasis was stronger in Freud's first formulations.

Primal therapy thus consists of helping the patient to "remember pain." The patient is encouraged, with the help of various techniques, to recall primal scenes. The patient connects with his feelings, but does not attempt to block them as he did as a child. Instead he "goes with" the feeling and may curl up on the floor in a pain convulsion or let out a scream of pain. Such an experience is called a *primal*, an intense reliving and release of the pain associated with primal scenes. After the primal is over, the patient feels drained and relaxed. He also feels he has moved in the direction of closing the split between his real self and his unreal self. Janov contends that a series of appropriate primals will cure the neurotic patient.

You might be wondering why primal therapy has not won wide acceptance by mainstream psychologists. There are several bases for objection to primal therapy. First, primal therapy is presented as *the* cure for neurosis, not *a* cure. Most psychologists might agree that primal therapy would be suitable for certain patients having certain kinds of problems: They would not agree that it is the treatment of choice for all neurotic reactions.

Second, primal theory is a unicausal explanation of neurosis; suppression of feeling is at the core of all neurosis. The mainstream psychologist would contend that there are probably several explanations for neurosis. The notion that suppression of feeling is the main factor in some neurotic reactions is a rather useful notion, however.

Third, in *The Primal Scream* Janov systematically analyzes current psychotherapies and finds them lacking in contrast to primal therapy. Understandably, men and women who have placed their professional chips with one school of psychotherapy are not going to take kindly to a man who says they are on the wrong track. If Janov had made the milder claim that he had some innovations which might be of interest to psychotherapists, he would have had a warmer reception.

Fourth, primal therapy is intense. In its original form, the patient is seen every day for three weeks. This is followed by group sessions. Some psychologists feel that primal therapy tries to dig too deep too fast. They fear that a rapid, high-pressure psychotherapy may be more than a patient can handle and in the long run may do more psychological harm than good. Based on Janov's writings, it appears that this is a false fear. Nonetheless, the reservation about intense therapy continues; much more data are needed before consensus can be reached concerning the merits of intense therapy versus a slow-paced approach. For now, mainstream psychotherapists prefer to think of personal growth as a gradual process of self-discovery, not an abrupt transformation by a psychological quantum leap.

In spite of the objections, I do not feel that primal theory and primal therapy deserve categorical rejection. Janov's writings can be approached as inputs for your own thought processes. As such, they provide much food for thought and can stimulate a substantial amount of reflection. Janov has something to say, and he says it with passion and power. As long as you appreciate that no one author has all the answers, you may use any author's views as stimuli for your own personal growth processes.

CRITIQUE

To illustrate the kinds of attacks that can be made on depth psychology, here is a quotation from *Doctor Freud* by biographer Emil Ludwig:

The constant restatement of Freud's themes, the growing acceptance of them by bandwagon-climbers, both professional and lay, does not prove his theories. Not one general thesis advanced by Freud is actually proven in the scientific sense to this day—as any honest psychoanalyst would be the first to admit. But today his teachings operate to undermine effort, especially among young people—to excuse weakness often masquerading as passivity—and to make ignorant folk contemptuous of the cultural treasures accumulated by Mankind down the ages. Seducing all manner of men from the simplest to the most enlightened. Freud's opium endangers our generation. (p. 35)

It is possible to throw all sorts of critical stones at depth psychology. It is far from being an unassailable citadel. On the contrary, it is really quite easy to find numerous weak spots in what at first seems to be a formidable fortress of theory. It is not my purpose, however, to attack and "destroy" depth psychology or any other model for adjustment and growth. The aim of the "Critique" sections in this chapter and in Chapters Three through Eight is to help you gain the broadest possible perspective on the psychologies discussed in this book; each Critique may be thought of as an outline that is filled in by the content of the other chapters. You should look at each school of thought with the proverbial grain of salt. A bit of doubt will help restrain you from getting carried away and giving all your credence to a particular way of thinking.

The following are some of the difficulties with depth psychology:

1 The concepts of depth psychology are "mushy." Freud, Jung, and the other depth psychologists tend to use large global concepts such as the id, the ego, the superego, the Shadow, the Self, the collective unconscious, the real self, and so forth. These concepts are not well-anchored in antecedent and consequent events. It is difficult to point a finger at exactly what events in a person's life history modify these large global agents within the person. It is also difficult to specify precisely what behaviors are being "caused" by the inner agents. Harsh critics would argue that the inner agents of the depth psychologists really represent nothing more than a new demonology. Everything is explained by word magic, by reference to all sorts of wonderful and powerful forces within the human personality. To such critics, the problem of depth psychology is not that it does not explain enough; on the contrary, it explains too much.

2 The conclusions of depth psychology are based on clinical data, not on the experimental method. In a proper experiment, various conditions must be met. Subjects should be randomly assigned to a control condition and to an experimental condition. Data should be objectively gathered, with an effort to protect against biases of perception. Quantitative data are preferred to allow for a statistical analysis. The giants of depth psychology—Freud and Jung—did none of these things. They observed patients, their own patients, in private practice. Their sample was not randomly selected, there were no control observations, and no statistical analysis was made. Thus the principal method of depth psychology, the clinical method, is a weak method that does not meet the rigorous demands of hard science. As a consequence, the "discoveries" of depth psychology are not really discoveries; they are interesting hypotheses that require further verification.

3 Depth psychology tends to perpetuate dualistic thinking. Plato, some thinkers contend, made the error of arbitrarily dividing the whole person into a mind and a body as if these two aspects of the individual were separate realities. Freud makes the same error when he divides the personality into two realms, conscious and unconscious, and proceeds to treat these two domains as distinct entities. Jung perpetuates the same kind of error when he speaks of the collective unconscious mind and the conscious mind. Janov also utilizes a dualistic model of personality when he writes about the unreal self and the real self. A softer criticism would be that the error of the depth psychologists is not so much that they use dualistic models, but that they act as if they were working with discovered realities instead of useful abstractions. The distinction between the unconscious and the conscious may be used as a convenient tool for self-exploration, but it should be recognized that the tool is manufactured by the mind of man. It should, of course, be noted that the aim of depth psychology is to overcome arbitrary opposites within the human personality. Thus in the long run, depth psychology also rejects dualism.

4   Existential thinkers charge that depth psychology is not a humanism. It is modeled too much after the natural sciences in that it places great stress on cause and effect. You will recall that Freud was a strict determinist: Nothing happens in the mind that is not caused. This, claim existential authors, is not the fabric of our experience. We experience ourselves much of the time as self-moving agents. Our inner reality is not determinism; our inner reality reveals a world where choices are made and there is responsibility for action. Interestingly, you would not find the same charge leveled by behavioral psychologists. They would contend that depth psychology fails because it is not sufficiently rigorous and does not come up to the ideals of natural science. Thus depth psychology is caught between existential thinkers who claim it is too much of a natural science and behavioral psychologists who claim it is not enough of a natural science.

5   Humanistic psychologists contend that depth psychology places too much emphasis on man's animal nature. Freud's id, Jung's Shadow, and Janov's primal needs are all representations of basic biological drives. The depth psychologist makes the set of inborn biological drives the foundation of the human personality. Good manners, ordinary politeness, and so forth represent a thin veneer of civilization—the superego, the Persona, or the unreal self—depending on the theorist. Ask yourself this question: Do you believe that biological drives are the only inborn drives? We shall return to this question in Chapter Seven, where we discuss existential-humanistic psychology.

6   In connection with the criticism that depth psychology overemphasizes our animal nature, it can be argued that Freud in particular made too much of sex and aggression. Although it may be reasonably contended that civilization subjects these drives to a substantial amount of repression and modification, it can hardly be contended that they are the only important themes in human existence. Freud's error was that he made the sexual and aggressive motifs universal explanations of neurotic reactions. This was one of Jung's basic criticisms of Freudian theory. There are other great drives in life. Alfred Adler proposes an inborn will to power in human beings. Viktor Frankl speaks of the will to meaning. Abraham Maslow postulates an inborn urge toward self-actualization. And Jung himself postulates an innate striving toward psychological wholeness (the individuation process). The frustration of any of these impulses can be associated with neurotic reactions. But we should continue to recognize that the frustration of sexual and aggressive drives remains one of the common factors behind neurotic reactions.

7 Classical psychoanalytic therapy is slow and expensive. A fully qualified psychiatrist of Freudian persuasion charges his patients in the vicinity of fifty dollars per session. If you paid the therapist only one visit per week (and many patients go two or three times per week), it would cost about two hundred dollars a month to see a psychoanalyst. A full-scale psychoanalysis takes three to five years; thus the cost of a complete psychoanalysis ranges from seven thousand to twelve thousand dollars! Psychoanalysis is hardly the treatment of choice for the majority of persons with personal problems. Thus the value of psychoanalysis resides not in its capacity to treat a limited number of persons, but in whatever light it can shed on the human condition and in whatever ideas can be adapted from it by eclectic psychotherapists.

It would be possible to go on at much greater length regarding the various problems with depth psychology. But by now you certainly catch the trend the criticisms would take, and there is no point in belaboring the obvious. In spite of the many competent criticisms leveled against it, the edifice of depth psychology remains. Granted, it stands with a few large holes and many small holes in it. But it stands all the same. We would be rash and somewhat foolish if we declared, "Oh, depth psychology is just a lot of mumbo jumbo about the unconscious and sex. Freud was a dirty old man, and Jung was a mystic. Let's get to more scientific matters if we want to understand ourselves." My position is that we have a great deal to learn from depth psychology; its concepts are psychological tools that can help us in our daily adjustment and personal growth.

IMPLICATIONS FOR ADJUSTMENT AND GROWTH

Well, what's in depth psychology for you? Are there any applications you can make that will help you improve your adjustment or contribute to your personal growth? The aim of this section and corresponding sections in Chapters Three through Eight is not to make you into a do-it-yourself psychotherapist. Certain kinds of approaches to the self should be re-served for professional settings. Powerful techniques that produce strong emotional reactions should be used only in a setting where there is a competent and qualified therapist or counselor available. On the other hand, there are applications of depth psychology that can be made by the individual. These self-applications are conservative because they imply remaining at a completely conscious level and retaining all one's mental faculties. They represent logical adaptations from the theory and practice of depth psychology. As you read over the following applications, be selective and judicious. Respond only as the material applies to you. In no case take the point being made as categorical advice. Keep in mind the trite but valid saying, "One man's meat is another man's poison." You are an individual, and a valuable idea for one person may be worthless for you. Bearing in mind these reservations, the following are some of the ways depth psychology can contribute to your adjustment and growth:

1   Many persons find that extensive reading of the works of Freud, Jung, and other depth psychologists is a mind-expanding activity. (The same claim can, of course, be made for reading in general.) The writings of the depth psychologists have been quite popular, and you will have no trouble finding a large supply of readable books in inexpensive paperback for-mats. If depth psychology speaks strongly to you, you will gain from your reading a broader perspective on life and a different perception of the human condition. It is expected that these larger orientations will be life enhancing and contribute to more effective living.

2   Most of us are curious about our motivations. We like to have an answer to the question, "Why do I do the things I do?" The subject of motivation is the particular forte of depth psychology, and a knowledge of depth psychology makes the individual feel that he is not a mystery to himself. If one accepts the doctrine of unconscious motivation, much that was previously opaque about one's behavior becomes transparent. The person has the feeling that he has insight into the deeper sources of his actions. No one likes to feel that he is pushed and pulled by invisible and nameless psychological forces. Depth psychology shines a spotlight on these forces and gives them names.

3   A knowledge of depth psychology tends to make us more tolerant of the behavior of others. The person who sees behavior in largely determi-nistic terms and who explains the behavior of others in terms of childhood experiences, unconscious motives, and ego defense mechanisms will not tend to be a blaming person. He may think, "Oh, what fools we mortals be." But he will not think, "When a person suffers it's his own fault. Any-one who wants to can use his willpower to help himself if he really wants to." The student of depth psychology recognizes that this is somewhat like shouting to a man sinking in quicksand, "Quick! Reach down to your bootstraps and tug! You can pull yourself out!"

4   A practical advantage of learning about depth psychology is that you become a more aware member of the advertising audience. It is common knowledge that advertising agencies employ psychologists to assist in making a pitch more effective. Some of these psychologists do motivational research based on depth psychology principles. Advertisements are often designed to appeal to unconscious motives for sex, security, status, and so forth. *The Hidden Persuaders* by Vance Packard details how your submerged urges are the target of many sales promotions. The impressario P. T. Barnum once said, "A sucker is born every minute." You take yourself out of the sucker class if you know how advertisers make appeals to your unconscious motives.

5   Some persons find it useful to keep a journal of thoughts and feelings. Frequent entries in such journals set up a reflection process that may help produce insights into unconscious motives. A temporal distance of several hours or several days may often unmask the prior action of an unconscious motive. If this is noted in writing, commented on, and integrated into one's conscious thought processes, somewhat less chance exists that the same old motive will operate against one on subsequent occasions.

6   You may feel you can learn something from your dreams. If so, you may find it helpful to keep a notebook of your dreams. Record as much of a dream as you can remember immediately after awakening. The remembered content of dreams tends to be quickly lost and quickly distorted with the passage of time. Can you really interpret your dreams? You will recall that Freud thought dreams were meant to conceal unconscious wishes, and he attempted to interpret his dreams. You will also recall that Jung felt that dreams are meant to reveal, that they are messages from the unconscious to the conscious ego. The unconscious chooses the dream symbols because of their great meaning, not because of their disguise value. If you accept the Jungian view, there is no reason why you would not be able to draw at least some meaning from your dreams. If this general line of self-investigation appeals to you, I refer you to the original writings of Freud and Jung. In addition, you would probably find *The Meaning of Dreams*, by Calvin S. Hall, a useful book. He subscribes to the dream series method of Jung and gives many clues to what various kinds of dreams seem to be saying to the dreamer. Also, *Dream Power*, by Ann Farraday, presents a broad spectrum of approaches to dream meanings.

7   A technique known as *divergent writing* is used by some individuals for bringing forth unconscious content. Our daily thinking is usually *convergent*; we try to think in "a straight line" and maintain a logical flow of

associations. Divergent writing is similar to Freud's concept of free association. When a person uses divergent writing, he adopts a sort of Alice-
in-Wonderland mental stance and just lets associations reveal themselves
without particular rhyme or reason. Here is an example of divergent writing
turned in by a student: .

*The man from Mars is an alien and so are many many many of my butterflies on the
rocket. And so? And so? Well, if the primal episodes of Pinocchio are to really
go waltzing with Walt Disney then there are eclipses of the moon and the sun
that should be marinated in oil at sunrise. Songs that I sing are songs that I sing
for you and only you my beloved.*

It seems like nonsense, of course. And it is. But it is the nonsense of the
unconscious. The "chatter" of the unconscious has been allowed to
reveal itself. Now one can, from a convergent thinking posture, ask, "Why
this particular nonsense? Why this particular chatter? Are unconscious
motives or emotional conflicts that seem important in terms of my life
revealed in the content of the divergent writing?"

You would be ill advised to plunge ahead with dream interpretation or the
divergent writing technique if all you know about depth psychology is
what you have read in this book. Such techniques are better reserved for
individuals who have a comprehensive grasp of depth psychology principles. Also, all intensive attempts at self-exploration are better undertaken under the guidance of a competent professional person. The
methods discussed in this section are meant to be illustrations of the
ways depth psychology can contribute to adjustment and growth, but
they are not blanket recommendations for all readers.

Depth psychology assumes that you have an unconscious mental life.
The ancient dictum "Know thyself" captures the essence of what depth
psychology is all about. This dictum is augmented and presented with
particular impact in "The Stranger in the Pumpkin," by the poet John
Ciardi:

The stranger in the pumpkin said:
"It's all dark inside your head
What a dullard you must be!
Without light how can you see?
Don't you know that heads should shine
From deep inside themselves—like mine?
Well, don't stand there in a pout
With that dark dome sticking out—
It makes me sick to look at it!
Go and get your candle lit!"*

Go and get your candle lit! That is what depth psychology tells you to do.

We started this chapter with Freud's statement that the mind is an iceberg, floating with only one-seventh of its bulk above the water. Extending Freud's metaphor, depth psychology attempts to give us a radar capable of revealing the hidden outline of the iceberg. Such information may make it possible for us to steer clear of hidden dangers that interfere with living a full and rich life.

SUMMARY AND SELF-TEST

1 A quotation attributed to Freud is, "The mind is an iceberg—it floats with only one-seventh of its bulk above water."
T   **F**

2 Freud rejected the principle of psychic determinism.
T   **F**

3 The doctrine of antivitalism asserts that life can be explained by the interaction of known electrochemical reactions.
T   **F**

4 Hysterics display the symptoms of neurological impairment, but they are not neurologically impaired.
T   **F**

5 A technical term for emotional repression is *abreaction.*
T   **F**

6 The *primary process* refers to an unconscious mental process by which ideas have nonrational connections.
T   **F**

7 The concept of repression is sometimes referred to as "motivated forgetting."
T   **F**

8 According to Freud, the basic component of the personality present at birth is called the *ego.*
T   **F**

9 One of the functions of the id is reality-testing.
T   **F**

10 One of the subagents of the superego is the conscience.
T   **F**

11 Freud said that the first psychosexual stage is the anal stage.
T   **F**

12   Freud said that the final stage of psychosexual development is the genital stage.
T   F

13   The concept of "ego defense" asserts that the human ego has a tendency to distort its perception of reality in favor of the fantasy-oriented wishes of the id.
T   F

14   *Repression* is a tendency of the id to push up anxiety-arousing information to conscious levels of the superego.
T   F

15   The defense mechanism called "rationalization" is used when the real motive for one's behavior is unacceptable to the ego.
T   F

16   The concept of "regression" suggests that a person unconsciously identifies his ego with the ego of an admired person.
T   F

17   A general theme of the ego defense mechanisms is that human beings have many self-deceptive ways of maintaining self-esteem.
T   F

18   Freud distinguished a minimum of three levels to every dream: the manifest level, the explicit level, and the latent level.
T   F

19   The basic tool of traditional psychoanalytic therapy is free association.
T   F

20   *Insight* in psychoanalysis may be defined as "the reformulation of two field-Gestalten into a single field-Gestalten."
T   F

21   A thread that unifies neo-Freudians is a common agreement on the importance of the unconscious level of the human personality.
T   F

22   According to Karen Horney, basic anxiety is a feeling that one is alone and helpless in a hostile world.
T   F

23   Harry Stack Sullivan said that the study of interpersonal processes in human behavior will not help us understand the behavior of disturbed persons.
T   F

24   According to Erich Fromm, individuals in modern society exhibit excessive alienation from two important realms: (1) nature and (2) other people.
T   F

25   It is completely incorrect to say of Carl Jung that he was a scientist-mystic.
T   F

26   According to Jung, archetypes are enduring patterns stored in the collective unconscious.
T   F

27   Rebirth, Sunrise and Sunset, and the Circle are archetypes of the Self.
T   F

28   The archetypes of the Anima and the Animus refer, respectively, to the female and the male personalities in all of us.
T   F

29   The Persona refers to the private self, the introverted, latent role an individual has chosen to play.
T   F

30   According to Jung, the Shadow should be managed by denial and repression.
T   F

31   Jung designated only two psychological functions: thinking and intuition.
T   F

32   According to Jung, the aim of a dream is to inform, not to conceal or distort.
T   F

33   Jung's phrase "the individuation process" refers to a tendency within the person to become whole.
T   F

34   According to Janov, the major primal scene splits the neurotic person into two selves: a real self and an unreal self.
T   F

35   Primal therapy consists of various ways of helping the neurotic person to repress, block, and forget pain.
T   F

ANSWER KEY

1 *True.* A quotation attributed to Freud is, "The mind is an iceberg—it floats with only one-seventh of its bulk above water."

2 *False.* Freud accepted the principle of psychic determinism.

3 *True.* The doctrine of antivitalism asserts that life can be explained by the interaction of known electrochemical reactions.

4 *True.* Hysterics display the symptoms of neurological impairment, but they are not neurologically impaired.

5 *False.* An *abreaction* is a release of painful emotional experience.

6 *True.* The *primary process* refers to an unconscious mental process by which ideas have nonrational connections.

7 *True.* The concept of repression is sometimes referred to as "motivated forgetting."

8 *False.* According to Freud, the basic component of the personality present at birth is called the *id*.

9 *False.* Reality-testing is a function of the ego.

10 *True.* One of the subagents of the superego is the conscience.

11 *False.* Freud said that the first psychosexual stage is the oral stage.

12 *True.* Freud said that the final stage of psychosexual development is the genital stage.

13 *True.* The concept of "ego defense" asserts that the human ego has a tendency to distort its perception of reality in favor of the fantasy-oriented wishes of the id.

14 *False. Repression* may be defined as a process by which a psychological force opposes certain ideas and shoves them down into the unconscious level of the personality.

15 *True.* The defense mechanism called "rationalization" is used when the real motive for one's behavior is unacceptable to the ego.

16 *False.* "Regression" refers to the tendency of a person under stress to go back to behavior patterns that brought comfort at an earlier age.

17 *True.* A general theme of the ego defense mechanisms is that human beings have many self-deceptive ways of maintaining self-esteem.

18 *False.* Freud distinguished a minimum of two levels to every dream: the manifest level and the latent level.

19 *True.* The basic tool of traditional psychoanalytic therapy is free association.

20 *False. Insight* in psychoanalysis may be defined as "seeing into" the essence of a problem.

21 *True.* A thread that unifies neo-Freudians is a common agreement on the importance of the unconscious level of the human personality.

22 *True.* According to Karen Horney, basic anxiety is a feeling that one is alone and helpless in a hostile world.

23 *False.* Harry Stack Sullivan asserted that the study of interpersonal processes in human behavior is useful in helping us to understand the behavior of disturbed persons.

24 *True.* According to Erich Fromm, individuals in modern society exhibit excessive alienation from two important realms: (1) nature and (2) other people.

25 *False.* It is correct to say of Carl Jung that he was a scientist-mystic.

26 *True.* According to Jung, archetypes are enduring patterns stored in the collective unconscious.

27 *False.* Rebirth, Sunrise and Sunset, and the Circle are archetypes that represent processes of the world.

28 *True.* The archetypes of the Anima and the Animus refer, respectively, to the female and the male personalities in all of us.

29 *False.* The Persona refers to the public self, the social role an individual has chosen to play.

30 *False.* According to Jung, the Shadow should be acknowledged and integrated into the whole personality.

31 *False.* Jung designated four psychological functions: thinking, feeling, sensation, and intuition.

32 *True.* According to Jung, the aim of a dream is to inform, not to conceal or distort.

33 *True.* Jung's phrase "the individuation process" refers to a tendency within the person to become whole.

34 *True.* According to Janov, the major primal scene splits the neurotic person into two selves: a real self and an unreal self.

35 *False.* Primal therapy consists of helping the patient to "remember pain."

DISCUSSION QUESTIONS

PSYCHOANALYSIS: INSIGHTS ON THE COUCH

1 Do you find yourself in agreement with the principle of psychic determinism? What problems do you see with it?

2 From the greater objectivity of the present, can you look back in time and see how you have sometimes made decisions on the basis of unconscious motives? Or do you feel that all your decisions have been consciously motivated?

3 What are some of the ways advertisers appeal to unconscious motives?

4 What is your ego ideal? What do you aspire to achieve in life?

5 Do you know a person with an eating, drinking, or smoking problem? Does Freud's concept of oral fixation make sense to you? Or would you tend to explain the troubled person's behavior in some other way?

6 Do you agree that you sometimes use ego defense mechanisms? If so, can you think of any examples from your own experience?

7 Remembering a recent dream, does it seem to you that the dream has a latent level of obscure meaning? Or do you feel that the dream makes sense in its own terms?

ANALYTICAL PSYCHOLOGY: DIGGING DEEPER

1 How do you evaluate Jung's concept of the collective unconcious? How do the concepts of the collective unconscious and the personal unconscious appear to be similar? In what ways do they differ?

2 Think of a favorite myth, fairy tale, novel, play, or motion picture. What archetype is represented by the central character? What archetypes are represented by some of the other characters?

3 Do you know a man who seems to have a stronger Anima (female personality) than Animus? Do you know a woman who seems to have a stronger Animus (male personality) than Anima?

4 Do you feel that you have a Persona, or public self, that is in a sense a mask you wear?

5 In your contacts with other persons, do you feel it is valid to infer from their behavior that they have a Shadow personality—an inferior inner being which they often hide, even from themselves?

6 Using Jung's system, would you say that you display a personality type? What is it?

7 Have you had a series of dreams having a common pattern?

PRIMAL THERAPY: REMEMBERING PAIN

1 Do you agree with primal theory that neurosis is a common condition that affects untold numbers of people? Do many of the people you know seem neurotic to you? Or is there a tendency to exaggerate the prevalence of neurosis?

2 How does Janov's concept of minor primal scenes and a major primal scene square with your own childhood experiences?

3 Do you agree with the primal theory view that many persons are split into a real self and an unreal self?

REFERENCES

Bennet, E. A. *What Jung Really Said.* New York: Schocken Books, 1966.

Bry, A. (ed.) *Inside Psychotherapy.* New York: New American Library, 1972.

Faraday, A. *Dream Power.* New York: Berkley Medallion Books, 1973.

Fordham, F. *An Introduction to Jung's Psychology.* Baltimore: Penguin Books, 1966.

Freud, S. *The Ego and the Id.* London: Hogarth Press, 1923.

————. *The Interpretation of Dreams.* London: Hogarth Press, 1900.

————. "The Unconscious," in *A History of the Psycho-Analytic Movement, Papers on Metapsychology and Other Works.* London: Hogarth Press, 1915.

Fromm, E. *The Anatomy of Human Destructiveness.* New York: Holt, Rinehart & Winston, 1972.

Hall, C. S. *The Meaning of Dreams.* New York: McGraw-Hill Book Co., 1966.

Hall, C. S., and Nordby, V. J. *A Primer of Jungian Psychology.* New York: New American Library, 1973.

Horney, K. *The Neurotic Personality of Our Time.* New York: W. W. Norton & Co., 1937.

Janov, A. *The Anatomy of Mental Illness.* New York: G. P. Putnam's Sons, 1971.

————. *The Primal Revolution: Toward a Real World.* New York: Simon & Schuster, 1972.

————. *The Primal Scream,* New York: G. P. Putnam's Sons, 1970.

Jung, C. G. *Memories, Dreams, Reflections.* New York: Holt, Rinehart & Winston, 1972.

———. *Two Essays on Analytical Psychology.* Princeton, N.J.: Princeton University Press, 1953.

Laing, R. D. *The Divided Self.* London: Tavistock Publications, 1960.

Ludwig, E. *Doctor Freud.* New York: Manor Books, 1973.

Markham, E. "Outwitted," as quoted in C. W. Cooper, *Preface to Poetry.* New York: Harcourt Brace, 1943.

Neihardt, J. G. *Black Elk Speaks, Being the Life Story of a Holy Man of the Oglala Sioux.* Lincoln: University of Nebraska Press, 1961. NYT-56 (1939).

Reik, T. As quoted in E. P. Freeman, "Theodor Reik, A Conversation." *Psychology Today,* Vol. 5 (April, 1972), pp. 47–50.

Robinson, E. G. (with L. Spigelgass). *All My Yesterdays.* New York: Hawthorn Books, 1973.

Rubin, T. I. *Compassion and Self-Hate.* New York: David McKay Co., 1975.

Stone, I. *The Passions of the Mind.* New York: Doubleday & Co., 1971.

Sullivan, H. S. *The Interpersonal Theory of Psychiatry.* W. W. Norton & Co., 1953.

CHAPTER 3
BEHAVIORAL PSYCHOLOGY: NEW HABITS FOR OLD HABITS

The subject matter of behavioral psychology is behavior itself, not the mind.

OVERVIEW

OUTLINE

I. Desensitization: Fighting Fears with Fantasy
   A. Classical Conditioning   B. Aversive Conditioning   C. Systematic Desensitization   D. Implosive Therapy

II. Behavior Modification: Shaping Actions
   A. Instrumental Conditioning   B. B. F. Skinner and Operant Conditioning   C. Kinds of Reinforcers   D. Applications of Behavior Modification

III. Self-Modification of Behavior: Becoming Your Own Pygmalion
   A. Cue Management   B. Reinforcement Management   C. Classical Habit-Breaking Methods

IV. Assertiveness Training: The Worm Turns
   A. What Is Assertiveness Training?   B. Assertiveness Skills

V. Critique

VI. Implications for Adjustment and Growth

VII. Summary and Self-test

VIII. Discussion Questions

IX. References

TWO KEY QUESTIONS

What is behavioral psychology?
Behavioral psychology is an approach that emphasizes the *learning process.* It calls attention to such concepts as *habits* and *conditioned responses.* The subject matter of behavioral psychology is *behavior itself,* not the mind (the subject matter of classical psychology). Thus behavioral psychology tends to downgrade such concepts as the ego, unconscious motives, and defense mechanisms—the stock-in-trade of depth psychology.

How do the principles of behavioral psychology relate to adjustment and growth?
Behavioral psychology sees human problems as the result of *learned error tendencies.* Just as they were learned, they can be unlearned. This point of view can be applied with equal facility to overt behavior (e.g., chronic nail-biting) or to covert behavior (e.g., excessive anxiety). Thus for the behavioral psychologist, the prime pathway toward adjustment and growth is learning new and more effective ways to behave.

Adjustment and growth through the self-modification of behavior is an increasingly dominant theme of behavioral psychology. But the idea is far from new. Consider this poem written more than sixty years ago by John Boyle O'Reilly:

How shall I a habit break?
As you did that habit make.
As you gathered, you must lose;
As you yielded, now refuse.
Thread by thread the strands we twist
Till they bind us, neck and wrist.
Thread by thread the patient hand
Must untwine, ere free we stand.
As we builded, stone by stone,
We must toil, unhelped, alone,
*Till the wall is overthrown.**

A contemporary behavioral psychologist would be able to agree with only parts of O'Reilly's poem. He might agree with the "Thread by thread" image, which could be taken as a metaphor for the hypothesis that a *set* of related conditioned responses taken together make up a larger habit. Implicit in the poem, however, is the traditional concept of *willpower*; the idea of resolution is crucial to O'Reilly's method. The behavioral psychologist would reject this approach to habit breaking. Indeed, the very idea of "breaking" habits is poor language usage to the behavioral psychologist. He would much prefer to speak of modifying behavior or unlearning habits. The advantages of this second approach over the breaking approach will become evident as we progress in this chapter.

O'Reilly's poem does at least reveal that the concept of habit has been around for much longer than the past few years. The role of habits in human behavior is important. Many people feel that they are slaves to undesirable habits, but they do not know how to free themselves and find a more independent existence.

Of course, habits are not all bad. We need them to function smoothly, to do countless everyday things with a minimum of conscious thought. If a professional pianist had to think consciously of where to put each finger, he would be unable to give any attention to his interpretation of the music. The simultaneously desirable and undesirable aspects of habits is well expressed by author Colin Wilson in *New Pathways in Psychology:*

We need habits in order to function smoothly. (Pianist Van Cliburn at a recording session.)

I am writing this on an electric typewriter. When I learned to type, I had to do it painfully and with much nervous wear and tear. But at a certain stage, a miracle occurred, and this complicated operation was "learned" by a useful robot whom I concealed in my subconscious mind. Now I only have to think about what I want to say: my robot secretary does the typing. He is really very useful. He also drives the car for me, speaks French (not very well), and occasionally gives lectures in American universities.

He has one enormous disadvantage. If I discover a new symphony that moves me deeply, or a poem or a painting, this bloody robot promptly insists on getting in on the act. And when I listen to the symphony for the third time, he begins to listen to it automatically, and I lose all pleasure. He is most annoying when I am tired, because then he tends to take over most of my functions without even asking me. I have even caught him making love to my wife. (p. 4)

Wilson's "robot" is a powerful metaphor for conveying that in many ways everyone's life becomes routinized and much behavior becomes semi-automatic. If this is the case, and if it is unavoidable, the question of interest becomes: How may we keep our advantageous habits and rid ourselves of (or modify) our disadvantageous ones? The balance of this chapter concerns itself with answers to this question.

DESENSITIZATION: FIGHTING FEARS WITH FANTASY

One of the principal symptoms of neurosis is *chronic anxiety*, which may be defined as a perpetual state of alarm. The person with chronic anxiety is afraid of his own shadow, a worrywart. He feels that something terrible is going to happen—but he isn't quite sure what. A dark cloud seems to hang over his head. The most prescribed drug in the United States today is Valium, a tranquilizer designed to help individuals cope with unwanted emotional reactions such as chronic anxiety. We begin to realize the great frequency with which unwanted emotional reactions occur when we consider that about 44 million prescriptions for Valium are written each year! And Librium, also used to treat anxiety, is prescribed about 7 million times per year.

Thus more than 50 million prescriptions per year are written to specifically modify the moods of human beings. One survey estimated that approximately one-third of adults took some kind of tranquilizer or mood-modifying drug in 1970. There is reason to believe that the usage of such drugs has continued to increase since 1970. Is there a better way to cope with negative emotional reactions? Behavioral psychologists think so, and the method called *systematic desensitization* is the treatment they specify. Desensitization is a method by which an individual *learns to respond differently* to anxiety-arousing and fear-arousing stimuli.

CLASSICAL CONDITIONING

Before we deal specifically with the method known as systematic desensitization, it would be of some advantage to examine its theoretical basis. One of the principal roots of desensitization is in the work of the Russian physiologist Ivan Pavlov, who made most of his great discoveries about animal conditioning in the early part of this century. He earned a Nobel Prize in 1904 for his work on the functions of the digestive glands, prior to his interest in conditioned reflexes.

It is said that Pavlov's interest in the phenomena of conditioning began when he made a chance observation. He noticed that his experimental dogs salivated when they heard the footsteps in the corridor of the man who was about to feed them. They did not salivate when they heard unfamiliar footsteps. In ordinary parlance, we might say that the animals were using the footsteps as a cue and were anticipating being fed. Pavlov found it fascinating that an auditory stimulus could produce a reaction in the salivary glands, and he termed the saliva produced in response to the footsteps "psychic secretion." He decided that it was a phenomenon worthy of investigation.

To make an orderly study of psychic secretions, Pavlov placed a typical experimental dog in a restraining harness. Meat powder was placed in the dog's mouth, and the dog quite naturally salivated to the meat powder. In this instance the meat powder is referred to as an *unconditioned stimulus*, a stimulus to which an unlearned response potential exists in the organism. It is assumed that this unlearned response potential is inborn and that it forms the foundation on which learned responses can be built. The salivary response to the meat powder is termed an *unconditioned response* or an unlearned response.

Now suppose that a dog is in its harness and it has already been established that the dog responds properly to meat powder. What would happen if we provided the dog with a signal that meat powder would be presented soon? Almost everyone has heard of "Pavlov's bell," an auditory stimulus presented before the presentation of meat powder. In actuality, Pavlov used a simple tone as the auditory stimulus. With a tone generator he could control precisely the pitch, the amplitude, and the duration of the auditory stimulus. Such considerations became quite important as Pavlov's research progressed.

Assume that the tone is sounded and a few moments later meat powder is placed in the dog's mouth. Assume that this is done many times. These would be considered *training trials*, associated presentations of the tone and the meat powder. After a number of training trials, the dog is ready for a *test trial*, a presentation of the tone alone without meat powder. If the dog salivates to the tone alone, the tone has become a *conditioned stimulus*, or a stimulus to which there is a learned response. The learned response itself (salivation to the sound of the tone) is termed a *conditioned response*. Although the response to the meat powder is the production of saliva, and the response to the tone is also the production of saliva, the unconditioned response and the conditioned response *should not be considered as identities*. This point will become clearer and its importance will emerge when we discuss aversive conditioning. For now, note that the saliva given to the meat powder is greater in quantity and more viscous than the saliva given to the tone.

A number of phenomena of classical conditioning studied by Pavlov merit consideration. Each of these bears a distinct relationship to the systematic desensitization approach to be discussed later. One of the most important phenomena of classical conditioning is *extinction*, which takes place when an organism ceases to respond to the conditioned stimulus. Say that at some point the experimenter decides that salivating to the bell is a "bad habit." How would he "cure" the dog of his affliction? The easiest and most reliable method of extinguishing a conditioned response, if the experimenter has total control, is merely to pre-

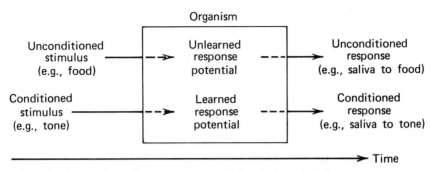

FIGURE 3.1   A schematic representation of classical conditioning

sent the conditioned stimulus over and over again without the backup of the unconditioned stimulus. In other words, the dog hears the tone many times without getting fed. In time, salivating to the tone will stop. Thus we can see that extinction is essentially the *unlearning* of a response pattern, not a forgetting of the response pattern.

Assume that a dog has been through a successful series of extinction trials, he no longer salivates to the tone. Allow him a break, or rest period, of several days. Now bring him back into the laboratory and expose him to the tone. What happens? He salivates. This kind of response pattern is called *spontaneous recovery*—the reappearance after a rest period of a conditioned response previously extinguished. Spontaneous recovery is often explained by psychologists by postulating a two-factor theory of extinction. During extinction trials, some actual unlearning takes place. Thus the first factor in extinction is the intended one, unlearning. But if extinction trials are too close to each other in time (i.e., if trials are not sufficiently spaced), a second factor such as fatigue or boredom tends to build up in the animal. This fatigue or boredom factor artificially suppresses the extinction response. It is an artifact of the experimental setup, and it creates the illusion that more extinction has taken place than is actually the case. It is further postulated that fatigue or boredom dissipates spontaneously between trials, and thus a rest period allows for the reappearance of the conditioned response.

The phenomenon of spontaneous recovery is particularly important to remember in connection with human habit modification. You may think you have kicked a habit and later are dismayed to find that the habit has abruptly returned. As with animals, human beings often have to go through the process of habit extinction several times before extinction is complete.

Say we are working with a dog that has a strong conditioned response to a tone. No attempt has been made to extinguish the response; on the contrary, we are interested in variations that can occur when a strong and well-established conditioned response exists in an animal. Say we raise the pitch of the tone slightly. The animal has received all his conditioning trials on a tone of a standard pitch, but he is now confronted with a slight variation in the stimulus. What will happen? He will salivate to the changed tone, *but not as much as to the original tone.* This phenomenon is called *stimulus generalization.* It can be demonstrated that if the tone is raised or lowered from an original standard tone, the animal will show progressive decrements in magnitude of his conditioned response on either side of the standard tone. If this is graphed, the resultant function on a graph is called a *stimulus generalization gradient.*

In brief, the phenomenon of stimulus generalization tells us that the experimental animal can detect similarities and differences. We may thus define stimulus generalization as the capacity of an organism to respond to stimuli that are similar to an original conditioned stimulus by exhibiting a fractional component of the original conditioned response. As you will see, this principle plays an important role in systematic desensitization with human beings.

Assume that a dog has been trained to salivate to a conditioned stimulus. The question now arises: Could the conditioned stimulus serve as the foundation stimulus for a conditioning chain? To be explicit, say that the dog is shown a circle projected on a screen. This presentation is followed quickly by the sounding of the tone. He receives many such pairings of the circle and the bell. Obviously, if we do too much of this, he will extinguish his response to the tone. So from time to time it is necessary to pair the tone with food. *At no time is the circle paired with food*, however. The circle is associated with the tone, which is associated with food. Assuming that the animal has had repeated pairings of the circle with the tone, will the animal salivate on a test trial when he is presented with the circle and no tone? He certainly will, and this reaction is known as *higher-order conditioning.*

In brief, higher-order conditioning may be defined as a learned response to a second conditioned stimulus in which the learning is reinforced by a first conditioned stimulus, *not* by an unconditioned stimulus.

Dogs are not capable of building long higher-order conditioning chains. Human beings, however, are capable of doing so, presumably because of their neocortex, or "new brain." Pavlov considered the extensive use of language in human beings an example of a higher-order conditioning chain. We are capable of giving emotional reactions to words almost as if they were physically present entities. This is evident in the polygraph test, in which pulse rate, galvanic skin response, and other autonomic indicators change

We are capable of giving emotional responses to words almost as if they were physical things.

as a response to questions posed by the examiner. It is also implicit in the bit of children's folklore that proclaims, "Sticks and stones may break my bones, but words will never hurt me." It is precisely because words can inflict psychological hurt that we feel it necessary to set up a "countervoodoo." Pavlov considered words a "second signaling system" in man. Words are obviously the main tool used in every form of verbal psychotherapy, and they are used in systematic desensitization to evoke mental images in place of actual stimuli.

Say that a dog has been conditioned to salivate to the sight of a circle projected on a screen. Further assume that the animal has been trained to inhibit his salivation when a narrow ellipse is projected on the screen. What will happen when the projected circle is elongated just a bit? The dog will salivate because of stimulus generalization. What will happen if the narrow ellipse is thickened just a bit? The dog will inhibit his salivation, also because of stimulus generalizaton. What will happen if we show the dog a figure that resides between the circle and the ellipse? Here we have a paradoxical situation. Two stimulus generalization gradients cross, and the animal doesn't know what to do. The stimulus seems to say, "Salivate—don't salivate."

If the animal receives many presentations of such a stimulus, he will cease to be a willing experimental subject. He will snap at his trainer, froth at the mouth, urinate when the confusing stimulus is shown, and so forth. The animal is "mad," or has "gone crazy." Pavlov termed this response pattern *experimental neurosis* and considered it a model that provides a partial explanation for human disturbances. In recent years, such thinkers as Gregory Bateson and R. D. Laing have postulated the psychological "double bind" as an important factor in psychotic reactions. Note that Pavlov's disturbed dogs were placed in a double bind in which a reasonable choice could not be made.

AVERSIVE CONDITIONING

Aversive conditioning is readily conceptualized as a special case of classical conditioning that takes place when the unconditioned stimulus is "unpleasant" or "punitive." At a behavioral level, an aversive stimulus is one that an animal tends to escape from. An example of aversive conditioning is provided by an experiment conducted by Notterman, Schoenfeld, and Bersh (1952). The subjects were human beings. A typical subject sat quietly in a chair for ninety minutes while his heart rate was monitored by an electrocardiograph to establish a heart-rate baseline. Then the subject received a moderate and brief electric shock to his hand. As a response, the heart rate increased. In this case, electric shock is the unconditioned stimulus and heart-rate increase is the unconditioned response.

After it was established that there was an unconditioned response to shock, the subject heard a tone just prior to being shocked. The tone and shock were paired eleven times, and then a test trial was held in which the tone alone was presented. There was a heart-rate response to the tone alone. You will recall that the heart rate speeded up after the shock. In this experiment, the tone is the conditioned stimulus and the heart-rate reduction is the conditioned response. The findings of this experiment illustrate why a conditioned response should not be thought of as identical to an unconditioned response. There are similarities, of course. Both responses have something to do with heart rate. Thus we can say that there are similarities and differences between conditioned and unconditioned responses to paired stimuli, but the responses are not identities. Also, the experiment provides a clear-cut case of the relative ease with which a human being can be conditioned.

Aversion therapy applies the principles of aversive conditioning to psychotherapy. In aversion therapy, the cues that trigger an undesirable behavior pattern are paired with some noxious stimulus. After a sufficient number of pairings, the cue creates anxiety or some other kind of negative emotional reaction (e.g., nausea), and the subject may opt for a different kind of behavior than his familiar and unwanted one. In *Behavior Control*, psychologist Perry London notes:

Conditioned avoidance can also be used to reduce the pleasure of behavior patterns that patients wish to get rid of. To free a man of homosexual desires, for example, the electric shock is connected with pictures of nude males. Each time the patient is aroused by a picture, he is shocked, till eventually the pleasure of the picture is destroyed by coupling it with pain. The resulting "unlust" generalizes to real-life situations where he faces homosexual stimulation. (p. 75)

Antabuse therapy, a form of aversion therapy, is an increasingly popular means of treating alcoholic patients. When a patient is taking antabuse, he feels no ill effects from the antabuse itself. If he takes a drink, however, the mixture of alcohol and antabuse in the body releases a toxin into the blood. The toxin produces dramatic reactions: nausea, vomiting, dizziness, hyperventilation, an increase in blood pressure, flushing of the skin, and an increase in heart rate. If the patient has experienced one or several such untoward reactions, the mere sight of a drink is likely to make him anxious and slightly nauseous.

Aversion therapy is used with all kinds of behavior problems, ranging from homosexuality and alcoholism to smoking and overeating. Is aversion therapy ethical? Many object to aversion therapy on the grounds that therapists have no right to shock people or determine what is "right" behavior. If a homosexual wants to be a homosexual, it is certainly an intrusion on his existence to insist that he undergo aversion therapy. But if a homosexual is distressed by his behavior, seeks therapy, feels willing to undergo aversion therapy as a matter of choice, there is no ethical issue. But, it could be argued, even the homosexual who seeks therapy voluntarily has been pressured into it by the generally negative view that society takes of homosexual behavior. Thus the gay liberationist would say that even self-referred homosexual patients are victims of an unfree world.

In the case of patients who overeat, there would certainly seem to be no ethical objection to aversion therapy if they are willing subjects. Even in this area of treatment, though, there are those who decry the efforts of psychotherapists—a small but vocal group of overweight persons who might be called "fat liberationists." They argue that "fat is beautiful" and that some people are born to be fat. Again, they see the larger society as a watchdog that unfairly imposes arbitrary standards of appearance and conduct.

As you can see, there are no easy answers to questions about what kind of therapy is appropriate and who it is appropriate for. The debate continues. In the case of aversion therapy, the debate is brought to a head because there is a general loathing in a democratic society to use punitive means to control behavior. For one thing, such means may have undesirable side effects, such as anxiety and suppressed anger. These side effects may occur even when the aversion therapy is chosen voluntarily. Also, it is not farfetched to imagine that such side effects may be complicating factors in stress-induced illnesses. Thus substantial care must be exercised in the application of aversion therapy.

Aversion therapy seems to point toward a "brave new world" in which human beings are reduced to robots. Such fears are in all probability greatly exaggerated. Nonetheless, if aversion therapy is to be used, a minimum safeguard should continue to be the consent and cooperation of the patient.

SYSTEMATIC DESENSITIZATION

The father of systematic desensitization is generally acknowledged to be Joseph Wolpe. His already classic book *Psychotherapy by Reciprocal Inhibition*, published in 1958, describes how a behavioral psychologist can approach personal problems along avenues not traveled by traditional psychotherapists. Wolpe was greatly impressed by the writings of Pavlov and was influenced strongly by the learning theorist Clark L. Hull's *Principles of Behavior* (1943). Wolpe's work represents imaginative adaptations of the principles espoused by Pavlov and Hull, however. Thus it should be considered as significant and original in its own right.

The first principle underlying systematic desensitization is easily grasped. Imagine yourself at a swimming pool. You stick a toe into the water and withdraw it. "It's too cold to get into!" you declare. A companion who is already in the water calls out, "Nonsense. Just jump in! The water's fine!" You get up your courage and take the plunge. In a few minutes, you are happily splashing around and the water is just right. What has happened? You have gotten used to the water, you have adapted. The word *desensitization* could be used: You have desensitized to the low temperature, and it is no longer capable of evoking a response. This familiar behavioral phenomenon is the foundation stone of Wolpe's systematic desensitization method.

Let's apply the method to a personal problem. Suppose a client has a fear of flying. Further suppose that this is a great inconvenience to him. He is employed by a corporation and will be promoted to an important position if he demonstrates a willingness to travel around the country on short trips when required to do so. He is highly motivated to earn the promotion and thus has a strong incentive to overcome his phobia. Fur-

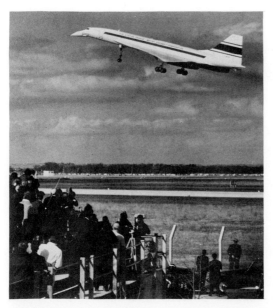

Systematic desensitization can be used to help a person overcome a fear of flying.

ther assume that he does not appear to be grossly maladjusted otherwise. Such an individual would probably make an optimal candidate for
systematic desensitization of his flying phobia.

Countless numbers of people have a phobia of flying, but they have no
strong and evident incentive to overcome it. Such individuals would not
present themselves for therapy. Again, behavior therapy is not designed
to "cure" everybody of everything. It is a question of the person being
distressed by a behavior pattern or an emotional reaction that is the
necessary condition for effective psychotherapy. The necessary condition is not the same as the *sufficient condition.* If it were, all people who
are unhappy with themselves could cure themselves by just wishing to
be cured. It is because the sufficient conditions for effective psychotherapy are open to question that there are so many modes of psychotherapy in existence. In any event, assuming that our man who has
a fear of flying meets the conditions we have set forth, therapy can
proceed.

A first step would be to have the client make a list of fear-producing
situations. He is then asked to rank-order the list, placing the least fearful situation first and the most fearful situation last. A typical list might
look like this:

1   Reading an aviation magazine.

2   Seeing a movie about flying.

3   Building a model airplane.

4   Having coffee in an airport coffee shop.

5   Talking to a ticket clerk about taking a trip.

6   Watching airplanes take off and land.

7   Having a stewardess take me on a tour of a parked airplane.

8   Talking to the captain of a jet airliner and having him show me the control room.

9   Sitting in one of the seats, fastening the safety belt—with the assurance that the plane will not take off.

10   Being in the plane while it taxis from one spot to another.

11   Being in the plane when it takes off.

12   Looking out the window while flying.

The desensitization therapist then trains the client to deeply relax his muscles. Once the client is capable of deep relaxation, the first and least offensive stimulus situation is described by the therapist in such a way as to induce vivid mental images. If the client indicates anxiety, the therapist stops describing situations from the list. Instead, he again induces deep relaxation. This procedure is repeated over and over again until the client is able to tolerate without anxiety presentations that suggest actual flight in an airplane. Of course, the entire desensitization procedure generally requires a number of sessions; from ten to fifteen sessions tend to be typical.

The term *reciprocal inhibition* is used by Wolpe to indicate the importance of relaxation to his form of treatment. If a person is deeply relaxed, he is not anxious. Thus relaxation is a behavioral response that is antagonistic to anxiety. If fearful stimuli—real or imagined—can be produced when a client is in a state of relaxation, the relaxation response will "fight" the anxiety response. This antagonism between the two responses will weaken the association between the fearful stimulus and the involuntary anxiety reaction. In the same way that water is used to fight fire, Wolpe uses relaxation to fight anxiety. This is what is meant by reciprocal inhibition.

Wolpe also cites Hull's principle of *reactive inhibition* and gives it a major role in explaining the effects of systematic desensitization. You will recall that the principle of reactive inhibition was already introduced in connection with classical conditioning. Hull theorized that it is a temporary fatiguelike process and that it acts to "hold back" a response. In view of the contention that reactive inhibition spontaneously dissipates between trials, however, deconditioning is seldom complete in one session. That is why there is a spontaneous recovery of symptoms from one treatment to the next and why a number of sessions are required before extinction of a symptom is complete.

But the real importance of reactive inhibition in desensitization is as follows: Although reactive inhibition dissipates with rest, it leaves a permanent residual called *conditioned inhibition*—a learned tendency to not respond. According to Hull, it accounts for permanent extinction effects. Thus, drawing on Hullian learning theory, Wolpe theorized that every time a stimulus is used to produce anxiety without actual pain or injury, a small but permanent tendency builds up to not respond to that stimulus with the usual anxiety. In brief, systematic desensitization is an extinction procedure. In the same way that Pavlov's dogs unlearned salivary responses to tones, human subjects unlearn anxiety responses to fearful stimuli.

The importance of the concept of stimulus generalization is also evident in systematic desensitization. This is what the word "systematic" refers to. Stimuli are picked that are far down the line on the stimulus generalization gradient, stimuli that evoke a "weak" anxiety response. As these anxiety responses are extinguished, the subject is moved closer and closer to the central conditioned stimulus.

Also take note of the tremendous importance of higher-order conditioning in systematic desensitization. The therapist uses words—not actual stimuli—to produce anxiety responses. It is because of the capacity of human beings to respond to symbols with strong emotional reactions that systematic desensitization is possible as a form of verbal psychotherapy. Our capacity to give emotional responses to symbols is an example of higher-order conditioning. Would systematic desensitization be more effective if actual stimuli were used? For example, if the man with the fear of flying were instructed to actually go to an airport coffee shop, talk to a ticket agent, take a tour of a parked airplane, and so forth—would this be preferable to an office procedure? Many experiments have been designed to answer this question. The answer seems to be that fantasy induction is as effective—perhaps more effective— than actual stimulus exposure. There are apparently at least two reasons for this. First, in an office setting, the patient can be relaxed when his anxiety level gets too high. The principle of reciprocal inhibition can be readily used. In actual situations, all sorts of irrelevant stimuli may also produce anxiety and little or no deconditioning will take place. Second, a much greater range of stimuli can be produced in fantasy than is practical in reality. Limitations of time and money make it difficult to expose the client to all the situations that can be generated readily by the fantasy method.

Systematic desensitization is appropriate for a large range of neurotic reactions and symptoms. It is particularly useful for individuals who suffer from chronic anxiety. Such persons often suffer from untoward psychosomatic reactions: hypertension, ulcers, muscle spasms, hyperventilation, tachycardia (excessively rapid beating of the heart), overfrequency of urination, and so forth. It can be useful to identify the stimuli associated with these reactions and then put the client through the systematic desensitization procedure.

A problem arises when the anxiety is said to be "free floating." Persons with free-floating anxiety seem to walk about with a dark cloud over their heads. Nothing in particular seems to be the source of their anxiety. The behavior therapist views free-floating anxiety as understandable in terms of stimulus generalization. The individual with free-floating anxiety has generalized his original fears to almost anything and everything. The therapist can help the client define a few stimuli or situations that invoke anxiety. The desensitization procedure can be applied to these first, and then other stimuli can be dealt with. By this procedure, free-floating anxiety will decrease gradually.

In this section, systematic desensitization has been associated with the treatment of anxiety and phobic reactions. But, can systematic desensitization be used to treat other negative emotional conditions? For example, can it be used to help persons who suffer from chronic anger or chronic depression? The answer is a qualified yes. We have to assume that the individual's anger or depression is perceived by himself as out of proportion to his life circumstances. We also have to assume that the potential client is sufficiently distressed by his anger or depression to be motivated to cooperate with the therapist. Given these assumptions, desensitization therapy can be applied to anger and depression.

To illustrate, relaxation is not antagonistic only to anxiety; it is also antagonistic to anger. Thus the client with chronic anger can be desensitized by alternating relaxation techniques with descriptions of situations that produce unreasonable anger. To illustrate further, happiness is antagonistic to depression. Using relaxation techniques and descriptions of memories and events that arouse feelings of serenity and happiness, the therapist can induce an emotional state that is antagonistic to depression. This positive emotional state can be alternated with descriptions of situations that generate unwarranted depression. Thus a gradual desensitization to the kinds of stimuli and situations that produce out-of-proportion depression takes place.

IMPLOSIVE THERAPY

From what you have just read, you are aware that systematic desensitization is a careful, step-by-step procedure. In particular, the anxiety of the client is never permitted to mount to high levels. Is there a more rapid and effective way to desensitize people? Would clients be able to tolerate vivid descriptions of horrible scenes that produce an "implosion" of anxiety? The researcher and therapist Thomas G. Stampfl thinks so. He has done a considerable amount of work with *implosive therapy,* a form of therapy designed to bring a client's anxiety to a maximal level. Like Wolpe, Stampfl constructs a hierarchy of fearful situations with the client. Unlike Wolpe, Stampfl may present descriptions of high-anxiety items before the client has completely extinguished his anxiety response to low-key items. Basically, Stampfl believes that clients, in the safety of the office, can tolerate high levels of anxiety. After all, they basically know they are safe. On one level is the vivid fantasy. On a second level is the conscious awareness that the whole thing is imaginary. Stampfl feels that the client can push things ahead at a somewhat more rapid pace than is conventional with systematic desensitization.

It is also the convention in systematic desensitization that the worst does not happen in the fantasy. The airplane takes off and lands successfully. After all, we want to cure the client of his fear of flying, not make him more fearful. Thus it would seem that word pictures portraying positive outcomes would be the commonsense way of proceeding in therapy. But Stampfl believes that extinction of anxiety occurs because of repeated presentations of anxiety-arousing stimuli in a safe environment. This being the case, it would make sense to produce super-anxiety-arousing stimuli. Logically, they would have greater extinction power. To illustrate, an implosive therapist might present a client who has a fear of flying with the following fantasy-inducing description:

Well, at last you're flying. The plane is aloft, and you are thinking, "Hey, this isn't so bad after all. What was I afraid of all those years?" Then suddenly there is a sharp jolt, and you look out the window. One of the jet motors has ripped off and there is a gaping hole in the wing. The rest of the passengers now realize what has happened, and panic is spreading fast. People are screaming. The stewardess is at the microphone begging people to remain calm, but no one is listening to her. Suddenly there is an explosion, and the whole left wing is on fire! The fire is spreading to the passenger compartment, and you will all be burned to death or suffocate in a few minutes. The plane begins to spin crazily and nose-dives toward Earth. You see the ground rushing up at supersonic speed. Now the fire has reached the people. You see the stewardess holding onto a seat to keep from falling, and her clothes are on fire. The flames are searing her face, burning her flesh. You think, "She was so pretty." Then you realize the flames have reached you. You feel a wetness on your legs and realize that you have unconsciously urinated out of terror. You try to scream, but your panic is so complete that you are paralyzed. There is nothing you can do to help yourself. You are completely helpless, and you face certain disaster as the plane continues on its reckless course to destruction.

Such a description hardly seems calculated to help a person overcome a fear of flying. But the contrary seems to be the case. With repeated exposures to scenes of horror and disaster, the scenes lose their power to evoke anxiety. The first few times clients force themselves to go along with such scenes, they do experience the implosion of anxiety: their pulses race, their hands grow damp, their mouths go dry, they feel faint, and so forth. Within a number of sessions, however, they build up a tolerance for the portrayal of doom and become able to face their fears with equanimity.

It somehow seems difficult to accept that fantasy techniques could have potent deconditioning effects. But, it should be remembered, phobic clients are responding more to their own fantasies than to real situations. It is their own imaginings that give them trouble. Otherwise, their responses would not be considered out of proportion or inappropriate. On the eve of World War II, Franklin Delano Roosevelt declared, "We have nothing to fear but fear itself." Similarly, it could be said that persons with chronic anxiety fear fear itself. Systematic desensitization and implosive therapy turn the tendency to ruminate about fears on its head, and by this method anxiety is made to defeat itself.

BEHAVIOR MODIFICATION: SHAPING ACTIONS

The following statement is credited to the Chinese sage Confucius: "Life is really simple, but men insist on making it complicated." This statement could almost be the slogan of the behavior modifiers.

In *About Behaviorism*, the foremost contemporary spokesman for behavioral psychology, B. F. Skinner, observes:

In the traditional mentalistic view . . . a person is a member of the human species who behaves as he does because of many internal characteristics or possessions, among them sensations, habits, intelligence, opinions, dreams, personalities, moods, decisions, fantasies, skills, percepts, thoughts, virtues, intentions, abilities, instincts, daydreams, incentives, acts of will, joy, compassion, perceptual defenses, beliefs, complexes, expectancies, urges, choice, drives, ideas, responsibilities, elation, memories, needs, wisdom, wants, a death instinct, a sense of duty, sublimation, impulses, capacities, purposes, wishes, an id, repressed fears, a sense of shame, extraversion, images, knowledge, interests, information, a superego, propositions, experiences, attitudes, conflicts, meanings, reaction formations, a will to live, consciousness, anxiety, depression, fear, reason, libido, psychic energy, reminiscences, inhibitions, and mental illnesses.

. . . No one has ever directly modified any of the mental *activities or traits listed above. . . . When a devotee of mentalism confesses that "we have not learned much about these problems in somewhat over two thousand years of reflective thought," we may ask why reflective thought has not sooner come under suspicion. Behavior modification, although still in its infancy, has been successful, whereas mentalistic approaches continue to fail. (pp. 207–209)*

And what does the behavior modifier offer in place of the worn-out mentalistic baggage? He offers the laws of conditioning and the principle of reinforcement. The principle of reinforcement notes that actions are shaped by their consequences. For example, if, when two-year-old Billy whines and screams, mother comes running to him, and if he seems to be whining and screaming more and more these days, we may infer that her behavior is augmenting the frequency of his whines and screams. Or suppose that a quiet young man begins to date a lively young woman. Whenever he speaks, she brightens and makes eye contact with him. On dates, he finds himself becoming increasingly talkative; eye contact is reinforcing talking behavior. Note that the behaviorist studiously avoids explanations that refer to the inner world of the organism. The behaviorist would not say, "The young man enjoys her attention, and he decides to do more talking." What the young man "enjoys" and "decides" are irrelevant and part of the mentalistic domain.

The principle of reinforcement leads to the concept of a *reinforcer.* We can see from the prior examples that a reinforcer is a stimulus that increases the probability that a certain class of behavior will occur. If mother-comes-running tends to increase the probability that Billy will whine and scream, mother-comes-running is a reinforcer. If eye contact from a young lady tends to increase the probability that a young man will talk, eye contact is a reinforcer. Technical distinctions between kinds of reinforcers will be reserved for a later section of this chapter.

INSTRUMENTAL CONDITIONING

Earlier in this chapter, classical conditioning was defined and discussed at some length. We are now ready to explore a different kind of conditioning, *instrumental conditioning*, which takes place when an organism learns that certain actions will produce certain results. A common example from experimental psychology is the rat who is taught to run a maze for food. Running the maze correctly is an instrumental action for the rat; it is a way of obtaining food. Correct maze-running can be thought of as a conditioned response. Note that in instrumental conditioning, the conditioned response *has an effect*. This is not the case in classical conditioning. If the dog does or does not salivate, he receives his food (the reinforcer). In instrumental conditioning, however, if the organism does not exhibit the conditioned response, no reinforcement is forthcoming. This is an important difference between classical and instrumental conditioning, and it has practical implications.

The distinction suggests that classical conditioning is more appropriate for understanding how we learn emotional responses (e.g., changes in heart rate, skin moisture, and blood pressure) and that instrumental conditioning is more appropriate for understanding how we acquire overt behavioral patterns (e.g., tying a shoelace, steering a car, speaking, walking, and writing). The distinction is to some extent a distinction between *passive* and *active* modes of behavior. The emotional response is passive in that it seems to have no particular effect on one's immediate world; in classical philosophy and traditional psychology, it is thought of as *involuntary*. The overt behavioral pattern, in contrast, is traditionally thought of as *voluntary*; it would seem to be only common sense that a person moves his body about by using his mind and his

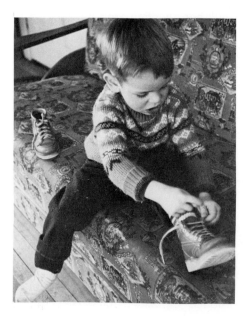

The principles of instrumental conditioning help us to understand how overt behavioral patterns are acquired.

will. Not so, says the behavioral psychologist. The mind and the will are useless concepts. A person moves his body about because of what he has learned and the ways in which that learning has been reinforced. In brief, *all* behavior is conditioned.

One of the first psychologists to study instrumental conditioning in substantial detail was Edward L. Thorndike (1874–1949), who is justly famous for his research into trial-and-error learning. Imagine that you are a visitor at Thorndike's psychological laboratory at Teachers College of Columbia University in the early 1900s. Thorndike places before you a puzzle-box for cats. The apparatus contains a string leading to a door via a pulley arrangement. If the cat pulls the string in the right place, the door will spring open and the cat may escape from the confines of the box to a bowl of waiting food. Thorndike places a cat in the box, the cat immediately reaches out and claws the string in the right place, escapes, and starts eating. The whole process is complete in minutes. "Pretty smart cat," you say. "He knows what's going on! He understood the way the string is connected to the door. I guess that shows you cats are pretty clever and can figure things out."

Thorndike would disagree with your analysis. He would point out that the cat you saw was a cat who had been placed in the puzzle-box many times. The first time the cat was placed in the puzzle-box, it made many random movements, most of them irrelevant to the problem. It clawed the string as one of its random actions, and it escaped more by chance than by intelligence. But each time the cat was placed in the box some learning took place. Little by little—with many ups and downs in its learning curve—the cat became quite adept at escaping. When the cat was placed before you, it appeared to have intelligence, insight, and thought power—attributes you gave the cat. Pavlov, Thorndike, and other behaviorists have disdainfully referred to explanations of animal behavior in terms of human consciousness as *anthropomorphism* (i.e., having the form or structure of man).

Thorndike theorized that responses in the cat's repertoire that were successful were "stamped in" the cat's nervous system. Those that were unsuccessful were "stamped out." What agent or force accounts for the stamping in and stamping out processes? Basically, Thorndike believed, organisms operate on the basis of *hedonism*, the view that pleasure and pain are the main factors in motivation. This is the same view of human motivation that was postulated by Aristotle more than two thousand years ago. Thus if an action leads to a state of *satisfaction*, it is preserved by the organism. Thorndike called this principle the *law of effect*. This law was the precursor to the contemporary principle of reinforcement. The important difference between Thorndike and such contemporary behavioral psychologists as B. F. Skinner is this: The contemporary behavioral psychologist does not speculate that the organism feels "satisfaction" when it receives a positive reinforcer. From a formal point of view, the inner world of the organism's experience is off limits for the behaviorist. He is interested in the functional relations between reinforcers and actions, not the thoughts, feelings, and perceptions of the subject.

Behaviorism has been a vigorous movement within American psychology. Thorndike was really the dean of American behaviorism, although he was not a self-labeled behaviorist. We might refer to him as an objective psychologist; he made no issue of swinging the sword that divides experience from behavior. John B. Watson (1878–1958), as you already know, is considered the father of behaviorism. In the 1910s he created such a stir among psychologists that he was elected president of the American Psychological Association. His most important thesis was that *behavior cannot be explained by making references to consciousness*. He placed great stress on conditioning and the unimportance of instincts.

Three important figures in the history of American behaviorism are Clark L. Hull, Edward C. Tolman, and Edwin R. Guthrie. Clark L. Hull (1884–1952) was the giant of learning theory in the United States for at least two decades. His great emphasis was on the importance of two theoretical constructs: *drive* and *habit*. The spring that energizes the behavior of an organism is its inherited set of biological drives. Habits are learned by their association with reduced drives. For example, if a hungry rat learns to turn right in a maze to obtain food, and if a reduction in the intensity of the hunger drive is the result, the animal learns to associate the response of turning right (the habit) with drive reduction (less hunger). Thus Hull's theory of behavior and learning is often called a *drive-reduction theory*.

Edward C. Tolman (1886–1959) was the gadfly of the behavoristic movement. Although he considered himself a behavorist, he labeled his approach "purposive behaviorism" (which tends to suggest that organisms are conscious and that there is some sort of meaning to their actions). Many of his experiments were designed deliberately to embarrass the Hullians. For example, Tolman hypothesized that learning can take place without drive reduction. He and his students conducted a series of experiments in which nonhungry rats were permitted to wander through mazes without food as bait. The rats actively explored the mazes. Subsequently, the rats were placed in the mazes in a state of hunger, and food was placed in a goal-box. Within a few trials, the rats ran the maze with a minimum of errors. When the exploration group's performance was compared with the performance of a group that did not have the exploration experience, it was clear that the rats had been learning the maze while they were randomly exploring it. Tolman referred to this phenomenon as *latent learning*, learning that takes place without reinforcement and lays dormant until it is ready to be used.

Assuming that the human learning process is in some ways similar to the rat learning process, the doctrine of latent learning suggests that we are making connections and storing information almost all of the time—even when there is no explicit reinforcer involved. The parlor game "trivia," in which a person is asked all sorts of random questions, provides an illustration: What is Superman's secret identity? Who was the male star in *Gone with the Wind*? Name the three men who traveled with Dorothy in the *Wizard of Oz*. Usually we can answer many such questions, which suggests the tremendous scope of the learning process.

Edwin R. Guthrie (1886–1959) stressed the importance of *contiguity* in learning. Things that are contiguous are adjacent to each other; they are touching or in contact. Thus if two stimuli are presented to an organism at the same time, the stimuli are "touching" in time and space and they tend to be associated. Familiar examples are the associations we make between thunder and lightning, bread and butter, parent and child, wind and rain, ham and eggs, wife and husband, car and road, and saw and wood. Similarly, if a stimulus is followed closely in time by a response, the stimulus and response become associated—thus forming habit patterns. Familiar examples are the associations we make between seeing a red light and stepping on the brake, hearing a buzzer go on and turning off the oven, hearing a bell and picking up the telephone receiver, and being touched on the back of the shoulder and turning in the direction of the touch.

Guthrie's emphasis on the importance of contiguity in learning was based on a rich tradition of philosophical observation. We have already observed that Aristotle wrote of the importance of the principle of hedonism; he also noted the importance of contiguity in the learning process. In the 1600s and 1700s, the British philosophers John Locke, George Berkeley, and David Hume made the association of ideas a cornerstone of their thinking. Guthrie's contribution resided in his ability to demonstrate the implications, generality, and power of the principle of contiguity. In particular, he developed a number of practical suggestions that are useful when a person is trying to extinguish an unwanted habit pattern. We will return to these suggestions in the section titled "Self-Modification of Behavior."

B. F. SKINNER AND OPERANT CONDITIONING

Who is B. F. Skinner? (The "B. F." stands for Burrhus Frederic, but these names do not appear on his book covers.) Skinner was born in 1904 in Susquehanna, Pennsylvania. Skinner's ambition in college was to be a writer and novelist. In a sense, this ambition has never left him. He has written one novel, *Walden II*, a utopian tale based on his views of human behavior. He has also written and published a number of books that explicate his basic psychological position. Skinner has demonstrated a substantial amount of inventive productivity. He designed a special crib for one of his infants, called the "air-crib." The air-crib provides a controlled environment for an infant: The temperature is just right, there are no unwanted drafts, the air circulates properly, and so forth. The infant can stay in the crib without blankets or diapers, thus allowing freedom of movement and eliminating diaper rash.

In World War II Skinner developed a guided missile system using a trio of pigeons pecking simultaneously at a visual target. The pigeons were reliable "pilots," and the system worked beautifully. The Pentagon did

B. F. Skinner is well-known for his research on instrumental conditioning.

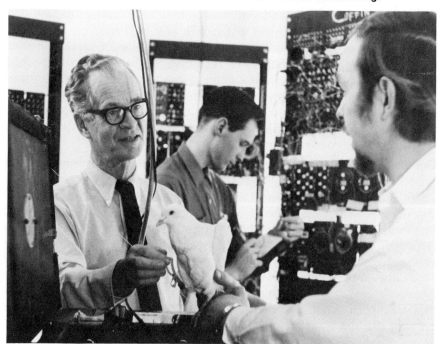

not share Skinner's visionary power, however, and the system was never made operational.

One of Skinner's inventions that has become operational is the widely used teaching machine. The teaching machine, through a learning program, presents material to the student in step-by-step fashion. The student is required to make responses. If the student makes the correct response, he is reinforced by being presented with the next frame. If the student makes an incorrect response, the program's forward motion is delayed until the correct response is made. The material is presented in such a way that the student will make a minimum of errors and a maximum of correct responses. In traditional terms we would say that the student is thus made to feel good about himself, the many small successes improve his self-image, he develops a feeling of competence as a student, and so forth. Skinner avoids such explanations. The important thing is what happens on an observable level. If the material is presented in a certain way, and if the student becomes a more effective learner as a consequence, that is all that is important. No hypothetical explanations in terms of inner processes are necessary.

Skinner is widely considered to be the arch-behaviorist of the twentieth century. His admirers call him the "Newton of psychology." But his detractors feel he has a cold-blooded and mechanical view of man and claim that his view of human beings as creatures who lack a conscious mind or an inner autonomy is degrading and destructive.

Skinner's most important invention is the *instrumental conditioning apparatus*, informally referred to as the "Skinner box." The basic version of the Skinner box was built in the 1930s for conditioning experiments with rats. The box is nothing more than a simple cubicle with a lever sticking out of one wall. Below the lever is a food cup. Outside the box is a food bin loaded with pellets. When the lever is pressed, a pellet is released through a tube into the food cup. A food-deprived rat will usually learn to press the lever at a fairly high rate. (Note that Skinner refers to the rat as food deprived, not hungry; he does this to stay as much as possible at the objective level of discourse.)

The Behavior of Organisms was published in 1938, and it sets forth Skinner's first experiments and his basic behavioral system. Skinner refers to his brand of conditioning as *operant* to suggest that the instrumental behavior of the organism *operates on the environment to produce a change in its environment*. The environment shapes the behavior of the organism, and the organism in turn shapes its immediate environment. The word *operant* is used the same way the word *operator* is used in mathematics. A plus sign, for example, is an operator because it can transform the independent numbers two and three into a five. Similarly, all organisms learn to use various kinds of operants to transform their local worlds. Henceforth the terms *instrumental conditioning* and *operant conditioning* will be used interchangeably. When a rat presses a lever to obtain food, the behavior can be called either an *operant* or an *instrumental act.*

Skinner was largely responsible for the distinction made between classical conditioning and instrumental conditioning. In *The Behavior of Organisms*, he designated Pavlov's kind of conditioning as *respondent behavior*, behavior in which a stimulus produces a response. He noted that this kind of behavior is *elicited* by a known stimulus. The kind of conditioning studied in the Skinner box, operant behavior, is *emitted* by the organism, and the stimulus for the behavior is unknown. For this reason operant behavior has been traditionally thought of as mysterious, incomprehensible, and under the influence of free will. Skinner contended that the traditional point of view merely represented a case of murky thinking and that, indeed, operant behavior could be conceptualized as being controlled by stimuli. This brings us to one of the most important concepts in operant conditioning, the discriminative stimulus.

A *discriminative stimulus* is a stimulus which provides an organism with information that an operant act is presently paying off or not paying off. To illustrate, say that a rat in a Skinner box has been trained to press the lever for pellets of food. Now let us place a small light in the box. When the light is on, lever-pressing brings pellets. When the light is off, lever-pressing is a useless activity—no pellets are forthcoming. Soon the rat will press the lever when the light is on and ignore the lever when the light is off. The light has become a discriminative stimulus, and it "controls" the behavior of the rat. The experimenter can use the light in the same way that a puppeteer uses a string to control a puppet. Viewed from outside the box, it is clear that the rat lacks autonomy over his own behavior. The experimenter turns the light on, and the rat presses the lever. The experimenter turns the light off, and the rat ceases.

Similarly, Skinner feels that there are many discriminative stimuli which control human behavior, countless cues that set the stage for operant acts. If the cues are present, the behavior takes place. If the cues are absent, the behavior is also absent. One of the most obvious examples would be a high school in which the students are conditioned to go to class when the bell rings. A less obvious example would be provided by "body language," in which a girl's way of sitting next to a boy says, "It's OK to kiss me." The bell and the girl's way of sitting are discriminative stimuli that set the stage for certain kinds of operant actions. The discriminative stimulus in operant conditioning is the equivalent to the conditioned stimulus in classical conditioning.

A girl's way of sitting next to a boy provides a discriminative stimulus, setting the stage for certain kinds of behavior.

KINDS OF REINFORCERS

It has already been noted that a reinforcer is a stimulus that increases the probability of occurrence of a certain class of behavior. If a pellet of food increases the likelihood that a rat will press a lever, then a pellet of food is a reinforcer for that rat. If a nickel or a dime increases the likelihood that little Billy will hang up his clothes, then a coin is a reinforcer for little Billy. If the words from a husband, "Great meal, honey," increase the likelihood that his wife will try to maintain and even improve the quality of her cooking, then that particular phrase is a reinforcer for that wife. A distinction of some value is made between a *reward* and a *reinforcer*. A reward is defined subjectively; it is what the giver thinks is of value to the organism. Rewards often backfire and have effects opposed to those intended by the giver. A reinforcer, in contrast, by definition cannot backfire. It is defined objectively and is *discovered* in an empirical way by observing the organism's responses to various kinds of stimuli. This distinction can be useful to beleaguered parents who feel that "nothing works." It is quite possible that they are trying to use inappropriate reinforcers based on what would be reinforcing to them, not what is reinforcing to the child.

A *positive reinforcer* is different from a *negative reinforcer*. A positive reinforcer *follows* an instrumental action. The instrumental action is a means of obtaining the positive reinforcer. The examples already given of pressing a lever to obtain food, hanging up clothes to obtain a coin, and so forth fit the concept of positive reinforcement. A negative reinforcer *precedes* an instrumental action, and the instrumental action is a means of avoiding or escaping from the negative reinforcer. Say that a rat is placed in a box which is marked off into two areas. Area A contains an electrified floor and is painted black. Area B is a safe area and is painted white. Whenever the rat wanders into the black area A, he is shocked. He scurries about and escapes into the safe, white area B. If the experimenter places the rat in the box directly on area A, the rat will run to area B. If the experimenter places the rat in the box directly on area B, the rat will avoid area A. In this illustration, shock is a negative reinforcer because it strengthens the likelihood of escape from and avoidance of area A. Escape and avoidance are both operants, or instrumental acts, designed to eliminate shock from the rat's environment.

What has just been described is called *avoidance conditioning*, in which an organism learns on cue to avoid contact with a particular kind of stimulus. The cue or discriminative stimulus in this case is the brightness dimension; a black stimulus says, "Run." Avoidance conditioning is similar to the earlier described aversive conditioning. Avoidance conditioning is instrumental in nature, however; the organism is active and can do something about the situation. In aversive conditioning, the organism is passive and helpless.

One of the interesting features of avoidance conditioning is that it is slow to extinguish. If the shock grid is disconnected from its power source, this will bring about extinction slowly—if at all. The rat has learned to avoid shock. It does not sit around and wait to see if the experimenter has suddenly decided to become kindly. A formal Skinnerian analysis of avoidance conditioning would preclude using such a word as *anxiety* to explain the rat's behavior; the radical behaviorist considers this a mentalism. Nonetheless, one could say that the rat runs away from the black stimulus because he feels anxiety. Why does he feel anxiety? Because he associates the black stimulus with *pain.*

Indeed, this is precisely the position of the learning theorists John Dollard and Neal Miller. In *Personality and Psychotherapy* (1950), they contend that many neurotic reactions in human beings may be thought of as conditioned avoidance responses. In view of the observation that chronic anxiety is often associated with neurosis, Dollard and Miller's contention seems tenable. Thinking of neurotic reactions in this manner also helps us to understand why they persist year after year. The neurotic individual's anxiety is functional; it is an alarm reaction that helps him avoid psychological pain. Like the rat, he is not about to find out if certain stimuli are no longer hurting. He is going to get out of a situation while the getting out is good. That certain stimuli, persons, and situations have long ago lost their pain-inducing power is something the neurotic person finds difficult to learn.

Negative reinforcement and punishment are easily confused because both utilize aversive stimuli. But there is an important difference between them. As already noted, a negative reinforcer *precedes* an instrumental action. In the case of punishment, the aversive stimulus *follows* the instrumental action. If a rat presses a lever, and receives an electric shock for his efforts, the shock is a punitive stimulus. The behavioral effects of negative reinforcement are quite different. As we have seen, behavior learned to escape from or avoid negative reinforcers is quite slow to extinguish. On the other hand, it is difficult to use punishment as a tool to extinguish a well-established instrumental response. Say that a rat has been reinforced with pellets of food many times for lever-pressing. We know we can bring about eventual extinction of the instrumental responses by the simple principle of nonreinforcement. If the lever stops paying off, the rat will in time stop pressing it at a high rate.

Can we speed up the extinction procedure by punishment? W. K. Estes (1944) made an in-depth study of this question and concluded that punishment temporarily suppresses a well-established operant but does not extinguish it. In the end, the organism must be allowed to emit its quota of nonreinforced operants before the operant is fully extinguished. Applications to human behavior are clear. Skinnerians assume that the laws of learning for rats, pigeons, and human beings are similar. Thus, generalizing the experimental studies of punishment to human behavior,

FIGURE 3.2 A schematic representation of the differences among positive reinforcers, negative reinforcers, and punishment.

we would infer that punishment will not bring about long-term extinction of well-established instrumental behavior in human beings.

A substantial amount of evidence seems to support the "soft-on-punishment" view. Parents who try to punish their children for such "bad habits" as thumb-sucking, stealing money, talking back to mom and dad, and so forth usually find that the punishment has a temporary effect. The behavior goes underground, the child becomes resentful, and usually the unwanted behavior bursts forth again stronger than ever. Similarly, penal institutions that attempt to "shape up" prisoners by various punitive measures more often than not find that the measures bring about superficial conformity for a time. But in the long run, there may be great discontent, riots, and little real behavioral change in the prisoners.

Do not conclude from the preceding paragraph that aversive stimuli and negative reinforcement have no place in the training of organisms. On the contrary, if the negative stimulus precedes the action, and if the action can reduce the intensity of the negative stimulus, then the organism will learn. To give a rough analogy, say that a teenage boy has just received his driver's license. His father can say, "Son, you don't have unlimited use of the car. Driving is a right that has to be earned. You have to earn the money for the gas and oil you use, and you have to pay your pro-rata share of the insurance. Before you can start driving the family car around, I want you to make a down payment on your share of the insurance." This hard-line approach is analogous to the principle of negative reinforcement. The teenager can do something about his negative condition. His instrumental actions will bring about a reduction in "car-use-deprivation."

Contrast this first case with another family in which, upon receipt of a driver's license, the teenage son begins to drive the car about at his own discretion. Say that he gets into a minor accident and badly dents a fender. Now the father gets angry and decides to punish his son. "You're grounded for two weeks. Hand over your driver's license until you can learn to be responsible. I want to teach you a lesson." This procedure will make the teenager resentful and is of questionable instructional value. Training via negative reinforcement appears to have substantial advantages over training via punishment.

It is not always easy to tell what will be a reinforcer for a particular organism. A major contribution to solving the problem of discovering effective reinforcers has been made by David Premack (1959). Premack has noted that behavior can be used to reinforce behavior. If behavior A is a high probability behavior, and if behavior B is a low probability behavior, then behavior A can be used to reinforce behavior B. Say that eight-year-old Susan has a low probability of doing her homework on her own. On the other hand, left to her own devices, there is a high probability that she will roller skate. She need not be allowed free behavior in which she is eventually punished for not studying. Using Premack's principle, her parents would insist that she do her homework first, then roller skate. Thus studying behavior is reinforced by its association with a positive reinforcer, being allowed to roller skate.

One of the interesting aspects of reinforcement is the effect different schedules of reinforcement have on extinction. Let us distinguish *continuous reinforcement* from *partial reinforcement*. Continuous reinforcement suggests a one-to-one relationship between the instrumental response and the reinforcer. If a rat presses a lever once, he receives one pellet for his efforts. Partial reinforcement suggests any situation in which there are more instrumental responses performed than reinforcers obtained. If a rat has to press a lever three times in a row to obtain one pellet of food, this would be one kind of partial reinforcement. Assume that rat A has learned to lever-press at a high rate under conditions of continuous reinforcement. Rat B has also learned to lever-press at about the same high rate under conditions of partial reinforcement. Now let us stop reinforcing both rats for lever-pressing. Which rat will have the faster rate of extinction? The answer is the rat that received continuous reinforcement, rat A. Organisms that learn instrumental responses under conditions of partial reinforcement show greater resistance to extinction than organisms trained under conditions of continuous reinforcement. This phenomenon is called the *partial reinforcement effect.*

When first noted, the partial reinforcement effect gave learning theorists quite a pause. For example, Hull's principle that habit strength is a direct function of reinforced trials was discarded. The partial reinforcement effect revealed that an organism with *less total reinforcement* than another organism could have a stronger habit than the greatly reinforced organism. Many theories have been proposed to account for the partial reinforcement effect. For example, there is the *unit-response hypothesis*: Perhaps the organism perceives a *set* of instrumental responses as a unit or, psychologically, one response. Another example is the *frustration hypothesis*: Perhaps an organism that receives partial reinforcement builds up more tolerance to frustration and thus has more resistance to extinction—is willing to perform longer without reinforcement. Still another example is the *expectancy hypothesis*: The organism that expects to get reinforced every time for an instrumental response will not persist if reinforcement is not forthcoming. An organism trained under conditions of partial reinforcement does not expect to be steadily reinforced and thus continues to produce operants even when there is no reinforcement. One more example is the *discrimination hypothesis*: Perhaps an organism which has been trained under continuous reinforcement can more readily discriminate that a nonreinforcement condition now exists than can an organism trained under conditions of partial reinforcement. To the organism trained under continuous reinforcement, the switch to nonreinforcement is like the change from black to white. To the organism trained under partial reinforcement, the switch to nonreinforcement is like the change from one shade of gray to another shade of gray; it has trouble telling the two shades of gray apart.

The multiplicity of theories offered to explain one isolated phenomenon in learning theory has been noted here to illustrate how many different theoretical constructions it is possible to offer to account for one behavioral phenomenon. For this reason Skinner and the radical behaviorists have no patience with any theory that proposes to explain behavior by processes that go on within the organism. Skinner has little interest in the various theories of partial reinforcement. As far as he is concerned, it is far more fruitful to study the functional relationships between behavior and reinforcement than it is to speculate on the why of such relationships. From a formal point of view, he takes the position that we are quite well off if we think of organisms as stuffed with cotton; then we don't have to bother with elaborate explanations of hypothetical inner processes.

In any event, the partial reinforcement effect has profound implications for behavior modification. Say that a parent wants to train a preschooler to wash his hands before dinner. Should the parent praise, give attention to, or otherwise reinforce the desired instrumental response (handwashing) every single time? This might be useful to get the desired behavior started. But in the long run the behavior will be much more likely to remain a permanent part of the child's repertoire if it is acquired under conditions of partial reinforcement. Keep in mind that classical philosophers and Western tradition have for centuries looked on instrumental behavior as springing from some deep and inaccessible source within the organism. Skinner turned this orthodox view on its head. One of the powerful arguments used to support the view that instrumental behavior is indeed a form of conditioning is the fact that most of the phenomena of classical conditioning, such as extinction, stimulus generalization, and higher-order conditioning, have operant parallels. Working from the premise that instrumental behavior can be understood in conditioning terms, it is possible to make a number of applications to practical situations.

Applications of Behavior Modification

Behavior modification has blossomed in the past decade. It has made tremendous inroads into child-rearing practices, education, industry, and counseling. A number of books for parents explain how to use the techniques of operant conditioning in raising children. One such book is *How To Make Johnny Want To Obey* by psychologist Stephen Beltz. The faith of the behavioral psychologist is revealed in the title of the book and in the following quotations:

The approach used in this volume represents an attempt to adopt the technology of Behavior Modification for use by parents and teachers as a general system of Behavior Management and Motivation. (p. iii)

This is a book about how to motivate children. It doesn't attempt to tell you what to teach Johnny or what Johnny should do. It tells you how to get him to do what you, the parent, want him to do. (p. v)

Another book with a behavioral approach, *Successful Parenthood* by psychologist Wesley Becker and coauthor Janis Becker, defends the right of parents to use behavior modification with their children:

Adults who take a scientifically-based approach to the care of children are often attacked for not caring about children by those who call themselves "child-oriented," or "humanistically-oriented." An attitude exists that to use scientific knowledge is incompatible with being a "good" human being. It can be argued, however, that effective care and caring can only exist when parents know ahead of time how their actions will affect their children; that is, when parents know enough about the learning process to anticipate the effects of their behavior on their children. (p. 1)

One of the main uses of behavior modification in the classroom is the management of unruly children. To illustrate, Lloyd Homme, a consulting behavioral psychologist, was called in to help a teacher manage a difficult group of children. He observed that there was a great deal of spontaneous running and screaming and decided to make use of Premack's principle. Time out to run and scream could be earned by sitting still and paying attention. He shaped and augmented attentive behavior gradually in this manner. In *Behavior Mod* by Philip J. Hilts, Homme is quoted as saying, "We were in control to the extent that we were able to teach everything in about one month that we could discover was ordinarily taught in the first grade."

Behavior modification can be applied in many ways in industry. It can be used to help workers maintain production schedules, to increase the number of calls made by salesmen, to improve the effectiveness of supervisors, to reduce the number of errors made by long-distance telephone operators, and so forth. Some of the largest corporations, such as General Motors, Bell Telephone, major airlines, and so forth, have used some version of behavior modification. As you already know, techniques derived from behavioral psychology can be used to treat various kinds of neurotic reactions. In addition, applications can be made to psychotic reactions. A substantial amount of research and experimentation has been done on a range of behavior modification techniques in mental hospitals. In *Behavioral Therapy* by psychologists Halmuth H. Schaefer and Patrick L. Martin, many examples of instrumental conditioning applied to the problems of psychotic persons are given. For example, one patient suffered from the delusion that people were trying to kill her. This is itself a too subjective statement for the behavioral psychologist. Instead, the statement should read: The patient often asked, "Why are you trying to kill me?" Now the therapist's task becomes to change her behavior, to reduce the frequency with which she asks the delusional question. Schaefer and Martin describe their approach in the quote that follows. It should be noted that prior to treatment it was established that, for this patient, *social interaction* was a strong reinforcer.

After baseline observation, nursing personnel concluded that the attention her questions brought controlled her reference to delusions. An extinction schedule was arranged in which talking did not bring attention when it contained refer-ence to her delusions. All nursing personnel were instructed to terminate social interaction as soon as the patient asked a "crazy" question. They were to act as if the patient weren't there and, on subsequent contacts, were not to answer questions as to why they had ignored her or in any way to discuss the delu-sion. However, especially close attention was to be given and tokens awarded whenever a "good conversation" occurred. (p. 142)

Schaefer and Martin note that their conditioning procedure brought about a substantial decline in delusional references when the patient was interacting with nursing personnel. She continued talking about her delu-sion with other patients and with people she met when she was off the ward however. Nonetheless, point out Schaefer and Martin, a substantial amount of behavioral control was achieved and the patient did learn an important discrimination between those who would listen and those who would not listen. The question naturally arises: Was she *really* less delu-sional? To the behaviorist, the question is wrong. It reintroduces what they feel to be an arbitrary distinction between the illness and the behav-ior. The illness *is* the patient's odd behavior. Or better yet, the behavior therapist feels we should discard the concept of mental illness and replace it with a concept such as "odd" or "difficult" behavior.

SELF-MODIFICATION OF BEHAVIOR: BECOMING YOUR OWN PYGMALION

The ancient tale of Pygmalion has fascinated mankind for centuries. In its oldest form, Pygmalion was a sculptor of Cyprus who fell in love with the statue of a lovely female that he had created. He prayed to Venus, asking the goddess to give life to the inert stone. The statue came to life and Pygmalion married her. The George Bernard Shaw play *Pygmalion* and its musical version *My Fair Lady* use the Pygmalion theme. The crude Eliza Doolittle is transformed into a charming young woman by Professor Higgins and his training methods.

The Pygmalion theme fits nicely with the concept of behavior modification. The sculptor shapes the stone. Professor Higgins shapes the person. In a corresponding fashion, the behavior modifier looks on the organism's behavior as a "clay" to be shaped by the control of cues (discriminative stimuli) and reinforcers. Skinner himself uses the term *shaping* when he "molds" behavior in the desired direction by reinforcing successive approximations of the desired behavior.

The question arises: Can you become your own Pygmalion? Can you, by applying behavior modification techniques to yourself, eliminate unwanted behavior patterns and augment desirable behavior patterns? The answer seems to be yes, within limits. Assuming a strong incentive to make a behavioral change, and assuming a basic knowledge of behavioral principles, there are times when a person can succeed in extinguishing a bad habit or acquiring a good habit by his own efforts.

There is a bit of a paradox in the behavioral psychologist's use of the word "self" in the phrase *self-modification of behavior.* If the organism has no mind and no world of inner experience, how can it have a self? The self is usually thought of as an inner agent, the person within. This concept does not square well with radical behaviorism. Also, the concept of self-modification of behavior seems to imply that an organism can be subject and object at the same time. The person can be both Skinner and the rat in the box! Absurd as this may seem, we do in fact seem to have some such capacity. Orthodox psychology uses such terms as *reflection, introspection, insight*, and so forth to deal with this peculiar human talent.

The behavior modifier sidesteps the issues by avoiding loaded words having to do with consciousness. Nonetheless, it seems to some thinkers that buried in the concept of self-modification of behavior is the old and venerated idea of human consciousness. They contend that only a self-conscious organism can be capable of self-modification of behavior. Whatever the case, the behavioral psychologists have much to offer in the way of practical suggestions. If we do not concern ourselves with philosophical niceties for the moment, it is possible to rally around the flag of behaviorism and follow it into some interesting psychological territories.

CUE MANAGEMENT

Cue management refers to the control of discriminative stimuli. You will recall that discriminative stimuli set the stage for operant behavior. They inform the organism that a situation is presently reinforcing or nonreinforcing. In the case of humans, there are many situations and persons that cue behavior. Numerous examples can be provided. For example, one alcoholic may drink only when he is alone in his apartment. The empty apartment has become the discriminative stimulus that sets the stage for drinking behavior. Another alcoholic may drink only when he is in a crowded bar with his friends. The crowded bar has become the discriminative stimulus for his instrumental behavior. A third alcoholic may have a drinking buddy. The presence of this second individual is required for the excessive consumption of alcohol to take place. All these individuals might be able to develop practical strategies for managing the cues that set drinking behavior in motion. The first person might find a roommate, the second person might avoid crowded bars, the third person might break off his relationship with his drinking buddy. In operant terms, such cue management would be likely to reduce the rate of responding (frequency of drinking), and some progress would be made with the alcohol problem.

Say that John has a smoking problem. He smokes over two packages of cigarettes a day. Further assume that he has a strong incentive to cut down: His physician has informed him that he is suffering from hypertension. Applying the principle of cue management, John can make a

The principles of behavior psychology can be used to modify habits.

list of the situations that cue off smoking behavior. A partial list might look something like this:

1 Getting up in the morning. The first thing I do—before I even get my pajamas off—is have a cigarette while sitting on the edge of the bed.

2 Coffee breaks. I take at least two a day and smoke with the other fellows.

3 Bowling. Whenever I go bowling, I smoke like a fiend.

4 After a meal. I usually stay in the chair at the table and relax with a cigarette and a cup of coffee.

Obviously, there would be more items on the list. Taking only these items, however, John might now ask himself this question: "How can I eliminate, avoid, or suppress these cues?" There are many possibilities. He could get out of the bed on the nonhabitual side, take off his pajamas immediately, and go brush his teeth each morning—thus avoiding the situation that sets the stage for his first cigarette. He might take a short walk during coffee breaks instead of socializing. He might avoid the bowling alley for a few weeks; or he could play fewer games when he does bowl; or he could go less often; or he might take up a different sport. He should avoid staying in the chair after a meal is over. As soon as he is done eating, he could rise and engage himself in some other activity. John would be ill advised to attempt to manage all these cues at once. His best plan would be to make a list of cues relevant to smoking behavior and to work on retructuring one or two at a time.

A common problem among college students is difficulty with studying. The behavioral psychologist Israel Goldiamond worked with a young lady who had study problems. She complained of feeling sleepy when she was at her desk. His first recommendation was that she replace a forty-watt bulb with a better one. His second recommendation was that she turn her desk away from her bed. Goldiamond further suggested that if the girl wanted to write a letter during her study time, she should leave the desk and write the letter in the kitchen. If she wanted to read a comic book, she should leave her desk and read it in the kitchen. If she wanted to daydream, she should get up from the desk and do the daydreaming elsewhere. When at her desk, she was to do her schoolwork. In a rather amusing exchange between Goldiamond and the young lady, the difference between the traditional view of human freedom and the view of the behaviorist is revealed:

This girl had previously had a course in behavioral analysis and said, "I know what you're up to. You want that desk to assume stimulus control over me. I'm not going to let any piece of wood run my life for me."

"On the contrary," I said, "you want that desk to run you. It is you who decided when to put yourself under the control of your desk. It is like having a

sharpened knife in a drawer. You decide when to use it; but when you want it, it is ready."

The first week the plan was carried out, the young lady spent only ten minutes at her desk. But she studied for that ten minutes. Eventually she reported that she spent three hours a day at the desk for four straight weeks; she had never done this previously.

The principle of cue management can be generalized to the self-modification of almost any behavioral problem. For another illustration, Goldiamond worked with a young man who overate. Goldiamond notes that food is seldom the cue that sets off eating behavior. In our society food is usually in a cupboard, a refrigerator, a box, and so forth. Television watching, time of day, being with friends, restaurant signs, and other stimuli tend to assume stimulus control over our behavior. Goldiamond advised the young man to find ways of making food, and only food, control his eating behavior. The client was advised not to fight the urge to eat, to eat whenever he wanted to. But he was to give food his complete attention when he ate; he was to put the food on a plate, turn off the television set, and not study or read while eating. Thus television and other cues would lose their power to start sequences of behavior leading to eating. Goldiamond reports that the young man stopped eating between meals within one week. "You've taken the fun out of it," he commented to Goldiamond. Goldiamond saw the young man about three months after he had stopped coming to therapy. The young man had lost quite a bit of weight, and he told Goldiamond that he no longer needed a therapist to help him deal with his problems. He felt in charge of himself.

REINFORCEMENT MANAGEMENT

In the self-modification of behavior, *reinforcement management* is fully as important as cue management. Unwanted behavior patterns can be eliminated or their frequency of occurrence reduced by the method of nonreinforcement. Correspondingly, desirable behavior patterns can be amplified by reinforcement. This is the basic approach used to extinguish and/or build habits in lower organisms, and the approach can be generalized readily to human behavior. Self-application of the principle of reinforcement management for unwanted behaviors involves asking yourself, "What is the payoff for this bad habit? What am I getting out of it? How can I get the same reinforcement value in a more constructive way?" Similarly, for wanted behaviors, you ask yourself, "How can I arrange things so that this desirable behavior will be strengthened by some kind of payoff? What can I make it earn that I really want?"

Let us return to John, the person with the smoking problem. John can ask himself these questions: "What is reinforcing my smoking behavior? What am I getting out of it?" An incomplete list of responses to the question might look like this:

1 Oral gratification. I like to put things in my mouth.

2 Gives me something to do—keeps my hands busy. I often get restless and a bit bored when I socialize.

3 Smoking helps me unwind when I'm tense. It seems to relax me.

Now John has to ask himself how he can obtain approximately the same reinforcement value out of his behavior without smoking. There are a number of possibilities. To illustrate, John could obtain oral gratification by eating, talking, drinking, or chewing his nails whenever he feels like smoking. He could carry with him at all times a package of gum or a roll of mints; these could be used as oral substitutes for cigarettes. John could keep his hands busy in a variety of ways other than lighting cigarettes. Greek men, for example, carry "worry beads" that they take out and manipulate when they get a bit restless. In our society, worry beads are not the fashion with men. But other, rather similar, behaviors might be more or less acceptable. For example, one can fold a small piece of paper into various forms, twist and untwist a paper-clip, or doodle. This may all sound a bit silly, but if you will actually observe human beings talking to each other in such places as coffee shops and snack bars, you will note many such behaviors taking place. They generally tend to take place without any particular planning, but the person who is trying to avoid smoking a cigarette can use these "busy-hand" behaviors deliberately. Finally, John can seek other ways to induce relaxation. He might decide to take a hot bath every day on arriving home from work. Or he could become interested in meditation (more will be said about that in Chapter Eight).

The main point is that roughly the same reinforcement value can be obtained by a variety of instrumental responses. In Skinnerian terms, a person doesn't have to keep pressing the same old lever to get the same old pellet.

Let us return to Goldiamond's young lady with the study problem. She has a behavior pattern that requires a positive reinforcement procedure, not an extinction procedure. How can she reinforce studying at her desk? It might seem offhand that the good grades she would get for organized study habits would be sufficient reinforcers to maintain the desired behavior. For some people this might be so. For many students, however, the grade is too remote a goal. A more immediate reinforcer is required. For such students, Premack's principle can be useful.

Goldiamond's client might ascertain that studying is a low-probability behavior and that television watching is a high-probability behavior. Now she could decide to make television watching contingent on studying. For example, she could "reward" a half hour of study with a half hour of "guilt-free" television viewing. It is important when such an arrangement is made to have the recreational activity *follow* the "responsible" activity. The instrumental behavior should be seen as the way in which the payoff was earned. This will have the effect of strengthening the instrumental behavior, in this case the likelihood of staying at a desk and studying. Almost anything she wants to do or wants to buy can be used to reinforce study behavior. If, for example, there is a magazine she wants to buy, she might make the purchase of the magazine contingent on remaining at her desk for a specified time period.

There is a close relationship between the concept of *feedback* and reinforcement. Feedback takes place when performance information is returned to a system or an organism. A guided missile can be kept on a correct course by the feedback principle. A radar system can be used to let the missile know if it is on-target or off-target. Positive feedback says to the missile, "Yes, you're on-target." Negative feedback says to the missile, "No, you're off-target." Constant corrections based on the positive and negative feedback keep the missile heading in the right direction.

Similarly, feedback is important in the behavior of organisms. In the psychology of human learning, a phrase used to communicate the feedback principle is *knowledge of results.* It is difficult to learn anything if you cannot know the results of what you are doing. If, for example, you tried to learn to shoot a bow and arrow with your eyes blindfolded, it is doubtful that you would ever develop much accuracy. For human beings, it seems that feedback or knowledge of results is reinforcing; we seek it when we are learning. In the self-modification of behavior, this tendency can be turned to an advantage.

Behavior modifiers often advise their clients to keep an accurate record of the behavior they are trying to change. John, the smoker, could keep a daily tally of the number of cigarettes he smokes. The girl with the study problem could keep a daily record of the amount of time spent at her desk. The young man with an eating problem could record everything he eats. This kind of record-keeping has the effect of giving the person a high-quality feedback. It lets him know how he's doing, and it helps him to keep his bearings.

Anything that can augment the feedback can be helpful. For this reason a number of behavior therapists are having their clients use behavior-counters. The behavior-counter is similar to a golf stroke-counter. It is usually worn on the wrist, counts up to ninety-nine, and can be reset at the wearer's convenience. The behavior-counter lends itself particularly well to behaviors that can be counted easily, such as cigarette smoking. I have used the behavior-counter on an exploratory basis with several overweight clients and have had mixed success. Clients were told to count each mouthful of food or beverage having caloric value. One obese young man started using the behavior-counter with great enthusiasm, became hostile to the whole idea within a few days, and discontinued using it. A young woman used it with great success while simultaneously using other behavioral strategies and lost twenty pounds. The young man was more than one hundred pounds overweight, and the young woman was only about twenty-five pounds overweight. A depth psychologist would probably be willing to speculate that superobese persons have more unconscious resistance to behavior modification techniques than those with a less severe problem. Thus we see that although the principle of feedback is important in learning, the way it can be used in the self-modification of behavior depends to a large extent on individual differences.

CLASSICAL HABIT-BREAKING METHODS

In his book *The Psychology of Learning* (1935), the behaviorist E. R. Guthrie formulated several methods for breaking undesirable habits. They have worn well with time and can be used to improve the likelihood of a self-modification program's success. Guthrie's basic rule of habit-breaking is to "find cues that initiate the action . . . and practice another response to those cues."

As a practical example of what Guthrie means, let us return to the subject of child guidance. Say that Nancy comes into the house every day, takes off her coat, and tosses it on the sofa. Her mother sees the coat, becomes irritated, and tells Nancy to hang up her coat. This has been going on for some time and is a well-established behavioral sequence. Nancy's mother feels exasperated. "Why can't that child learn?" Guthrie points out that the child has learned, and she has learned well. An obedient child, she has learned to get her coat and hang it up when her mother tells her to do so. She has not, of course, learned to enter the front door and hang up her coat. *But she has not been cued to do so by her mother.*

Guthrie suggests that to eliminate the undesirable behavior pattern, the child should be cued differently. When the child errs and throws her coat on the sofa, she should be told to put her coat back on, go outside, and close the door behind her. Now she should open the door, come in, take off her coat, and hang it up. In this manner the correct cue becomes associated with the correct behavior. The front door is the cue for entering. The behavior of entering is the cue for taking off the coat. Behavior or a response can be a cue for a next response; there is a chain of cues and responses here in which responses to cues become cues themselves. Taking off the coat is the cue for hanging it up, and so forth. Guthrie's concept is valuable not only in child training; it is also useful when we decide to train ourselves (i.e., embark on an attempt at self-modification of behavior).

The following, then, are several of Guthrie's methods of eliminating undesirable habits:

The method of incompatible responses. The object of this method is to make responses to the habit's cues that are antagonistic to the habit, that make it difficult to perform the habit. As an example, say that a girl has a nail-biting problem. One cue for nail-biting is television watching; another cue is identified as "being restless" or "being bored." The girl could decide to keep a nail file handy and file her nails whenever she is cued to bite them. The act of filing the nails is incompatible with the act of biting the nails. The more desirable act becomes a new habit attached to the old cues.

As another example, say that a mother comes to the conclusion that she has developed a bad habit of screaming at her children when they are disorderly. She also decides that the children are insensitive to her loud voice; they turn a deaf ear. She may, using the method of incompatible responses, decide to write short messages on slips of paper and hand them to the children instead of screaming at them. It is just possible that such an approach may be more attention getting than the screaming and will also be helpful in extinguishing the habit.

Exhaustion of an undesirable response. Using this method, the individual performs the undesirable response over and over again until the conditioned cues no longer have any power to elicit the response. It then becomes possible to learn new and more desirable responses to the cues that controlled the habit. An intuitive understanding of the exhaustion method is displayed by the father who lets his school-age son smoke cigarettes until he "turns green." Similarly, a person with a smoking problem may double or triple his cigarette consumption for several days until the thought of a cigarette makes him ill. At this point he may feel like making the break.

Persons suffering from various kinds of tics often find the exhaustion method helpful. Say that Herbert has a disconcerting tic—some of his face and neck muscles contract involuntarily. This is particularly embarrassing in social situations. Using the method of exhaustion, he might spend two ten-minute sessions per day in front of the mirror in his bathroom consciously contracting the muscles involved in the tic. This procedure will tend to have the short-run effect of producing some fatigue in the muscles used in the tic, thus reducing the likelihood of the tic's spontaneous occurrence. As a long-run habit-breaking method, it seems that some kind of voluntary control over the muscles is gained, which also reduces the spontaneous appearance of the tic.

An irritating spelling error can also be corrected by the use of exhaustion. Say that Betty tends to misspell the word *recommend*. She spells it r-e-c-c-o-m-e-n-d. She has looked it up many times, each time checking to see if it has one *c* and two *m*'s or two *c*'s and one *m*. Using the method of exhaustion, she could write the word *incorrectly* thirty or or fifty times! When she comes to the word again, she will not make the error involuntarily.

Guthrie's method of exhaustion is almost identical to the method called *negative practice* proposed by Knight Dunlap. Dunlap, a psychologist who did a great deal of research on human learning, published a book in 1932 called *Habits: Their Making and Unmaking.* He notes that for some forms of learning, "the occurrence of a response lessens the probability that on the recurrence of the same stimulus-pattern, the same response will recur" (p. 78). The exhaustion method and/or negative practice can be useful when one is trying to rid oneself of an unwanted error pattern.

Cue toleration. The cue toleration method, proposed by Guthrie in 1935, is similar to Wolpe's much more recent method of systematic desensitization. One difference is that in the cue toleration method, the actual stimuli are used in contrast to imaginary stimuli. A second difference is that in the cue toleration method as proposed by Guthrie, untoward emotional reactions are slightly aroused. To illustrate the cue toleration method, Guthrie gives the example of the way the U.S. Army prefers to break horses. First a light blanket is placed on the horse's back. When the animal is completely adapted to carrying a light blanket, a second blanket is added. After further adaptation, a light sack of grain is added; then a heavier sack of grain is added. This graduation procedure continues until the horse can tolerate the weight of a saddle. At no point is the horse aroused to anger, allowed to buck, and so forth. The whole procedure is painless and reliable. It is slow and requires patience, however.

The cue toleration method can be applied in the self-modification of human behavior in many ways. For example, the author knows a man who reduced a long-standing fear of dogs by buying a Doberman pinscher puppy and raising it to adulthood. He wasn't afraid of the puppy, and as the puppy grew up he still wasn't afraid of it. The whole process was so gradual that his fear was never aroused. Was he less afraid of dogs in general? Yes, the procedure resulted in generalization. He is somewhat more afraid of dogs than the hypothetical average person, but he is much less afraid of dogs than he once was.

A person with a smoking problem may say, "I can't stand to be with friends who smoke and not smoke myself." The presence of smoking friends is a cue that has become conditioned to the smoking response. Such a person might ask himself, "Can I stand to wait one minute before I light up?" If the answer is yes, this much delay can be self-imposed at first. The self-imposed delay can be extended after one week to two minutes. Week by week the delay can be continued until the person may eventually be able to tolerate a whole fifteen-minute coffee break in the company of others.

Similarly, a person with an eating problem may find ways to impose small delays on eating in the presence of conditioned cues. For example, an overweight homemaker may report a problem with eating between meals, particularly when she is alone in the house. I have sometimes suggested to such women that a three-minute egg timer can be used to impose a delay between whatever cues them to eat and the eating response itself. First she learns to tolerate a three-minute delay. This in itself is a success experience. It shows her that some degree of self-modification of behavior is possible; the case is not hopeless. With practice, the delay can be increased to the point where the conditioned cues no longer evoke the response. At this point the habit is broken or, in somewhat more precise language, extinguished.

As you can tell from the preceding material, there are many ways the self-modification of behavior can be accomplished successfully. It is one of the capacities of the human organism that a person can sometimes be his own Pygmalion.

ASSERTIVENESS TRAINING: THE WORM TURNS

The phrase "the worm turns" tends to evoke the following scenario: Harriet Shrew is married to Casper Milquetoast. It is Saturday morning. Casper wants to watch a ball game, have a beer, and relax after a hard week at the office. Harriet has a list of chores for him.

Harriet. I want you to mow the lawn and wash the windows today, Casper.

Casper. Yes, dear.

Harriet. And after that, I want you to clean the oven.

Casper. Yes, dear.

Harriet. And after that . . .

Suddenly a low moan escapes from Casper's lips.

Harriet. What's wrong dear?

Casper begins to shout and scream a list of obscenities at Harriet.

Harriet (shocked). Casper, this isn't like you! What's happened?

Casper (triumphantly). Sometimes the worm turns!

Terry Paulson of the Fuller Graduate School of Psychology in California wrote an assertiveness training syllabus for his students. He opens the syllabus with this quotation from the musical play about Charlie Brown and the Peanuts gang:

"You're a good man, Charlie Brown!
  You're the kind of reminder we need.
  You have the humility, nobility, and
  a sense of honor that is very rare indeed.
You are kind to animals and every little bird.
  With a heart of gold, you believe what
  you're told, every single solitary word.
You bravely face adversity;
  You're cheerful through the day;
  You're thoughtful, brave, and courteous.
You're a good man, Charlie Brown!
You're a prince, and a prince could be a king.
  With a heart such as yours you could open any door—
  If only you weren't so wishy-washy!*

WHAT IS ASSERTIVENESS TRAINING?

The term *assertiveness training* is used to refer to a program of learning designed to increase a person's competence in dealing with other human beings. Courses in assertiveness training are becoming increasingly popular and are being offered at various colleges, universities, and counseling centers throughout the country. The emphasis in assertiveness training is on *skills* and on putting these skills into action. There is a minimum of emphasis on the analytic concept of insight. Thus asser-

---

* Clark Gesner, *You're A Good Man Charlie Brown.* Copyright 1965, 1966, 1967 by Jeremy Music, Inc., 15 West 44th St., New York, N.Y. and reprinted by its permission.

tiveness training has come to be classified as a variant of behavioral psychology. As such, it can also be thought of as another approach to the self-modification of behavior.

The theory of assertiveness training is based on the hypothesis that many persons suffer from anxiety, depression, and similar unhappy reactions because they are unable to stand up for their rights. Such persons tend toward the neurotic direction. Their problem is that they are *oversocialized*. The distinction between the undersocialized and the oversocialized person is presented clearly in *Sense and Nonsense in Psychology* by H. J. Eysenck, a British experimental psychologist. Eysenck contends that the undersocialized person, a person with little respect for the law and the rights of others, tends to develop problems referred to as character disorders (see Chapter One). The oversocialized person, on the other hand, is too concerned with the letter of the law and what he conceives to be the rights of others. He is too inhibited, too correct, too shy, too timid, too vigilant, and so forth. The antidote for such a person involves recommendations that release his inhibitions and encourage him to become somewhat more spontaneous in what he does. As you can see, Casper Milquetoast and Charlie Brown fit within the category of the oversocialized person.

Eysenck ties undersocialization and oversocialization to innate characteristics of the person. He notes that some people are more conditionable than others. Those that are least conditionable are those having a propensity toward extraversion; the most conditionable ones are those having a propensity toward introversion. Although there does indeed seem to be increasing evidence that traits of temperament are to some degree intrinsic to the individual, we should not forget the tremendous importance of the whole socialization process. If parents are passive, emotionally uninvolved, and/or psychologically absent, it is possible that this may be a source of undersocialization. If parents are authoritarian, place great stress on being polite and doing the right thing, and make children purchase affection via their demeanor, this can be a major route toward oversocialization.

This, of course, is an environmental theory. There is no inherent incompatibility between a genetic theory and an environmental theory. It is easy to imagine how a "born introvert" could be raised in a family that reinforces "being proper." Such a person might be over-oversocialized and, as a consequence, have a double-loading in the neurotic direction. In any event, the faith of the behavioral psychologist is that some degree of learning and unlearning can take place in adulthood. The oversocialized person can engage in a program of systematic assertiveness training and overcome many of his personal problems.

An important distinction should be made between assertiveness and aggression. The two are easily confused, and the oversocialized person —in an effort to become more assertive—may be in danger of becoming too aggressive. It is helpful to imagine a passive-aggressive continuum. The left end of the continuum represents passivity in human relations; the right end of the continuum represents aggression in human relations; and the middle of the continuum represents assertiveness in human relations. The person who habitually gives the passive response in his dealings with other people is variously classified as a "dishrag," a "jellyfish," a "spineless wonder," a "self-sacrificing martyr," and so forth. The person who habitually gives the aggressive response in his dealings with other people is variously classified as "a dirty dog," "a rat," "a hostile person," "a put-down artist," a "stinker," and so forth. The assertive response is, on the other hand, "just right." It seeks the middle ground between passivity and aggression and permits the person to stand up for himself without putting other individuals down.

In *Don't Say Yes When You Want To Say No*, Herbert Fensterheim, a New York City behavior therapist, and Jean Baer, his wife and coauthor, clarify the distinction between assertiveness and aggression. Here is one example from their book:

Madge and Rose work as secretaries in a two-girl insurance office. Three times a week, Madge leaves early to see her psychiatrist. Rose has to answer the phone and finish the day's work. She doesn't really mind the extra labor; she does have an increasing feeling that the situation is unfair.

Unassertive: Not wanting to interfere with Madge's psychiatric sessions, Rose keeps quiet. Tension mounts. Rose decides she should look for another job.

Aggressive: Rose fights with Madge and says things like "I'm tired of doing your work" . . . "This office isn't a nice place anymore because you take advantage of me" . . . "Better stop seeing the doctor, or I'll tell the boss about you."

Assertive: Rose brings the subject up for discussion with "We have a problem. What can we do about it?" They discuss possible solutions, such as Madge coming in earlier and doing work ahead, or trying to change her analytic time to an evening hour. (pp. 30–31)

As you can see, the assertive response is a graded response, the happy medium between passivity and aggression. As such, it should bring optimal results in human relations.

A guide to assertive behavior titled *Your Perfect Right* by Robert E. Alberti and Michael L. Emmons contains a chart (p. 11) that summarizes the relationship between different behavior patterns and one's feelings. The chart is presented in Table 3.1.

TABLE 3.1 The Relationship Between Behavior Patterns and Feelings*

	NON-ASSERTIVE BEHAVIOR	AGGRESSIVE BEHAVIOR	ASSERTIVE BEHAVIOR
As Actor	Self-denying	Self-enhancing at the expense of another	Self-enhancing
	Inhibited	Expressive	Expressive
	Hurt, anxious	Depreciates others	Feels good about self
	Allows others to choose for him	Chooses for others	Chooses for self
	Does not achieve desired goal	Achieves desired goal by hurting others	May achieve desired goal
As Acted Upon	Guilty or angry	Self-denying	Self-enhancing
	Depreciates actor	Hurt, defensive, humiliated	Expressive
	Achieves desired goal at actor's expense	Does not achieve desired goal	May achieve desired goal

* Robert E. Alberti and Michael L. Emmons, *Your Perfect Right.* Copyright 1970, 1975. Reprinted by permission of publisher, Impact, Box 1094, San Luis Oluspo, Calif.

ASSERTIVENESS SKILLS

It is the conviction of behavior therapists who offer assertiveness training that inhibited persons can acquire assertiveness skills and put them into action *before* they feel the self-confidence of the already assertive person. The working hypothesis is that feelings can follow from actions. The commonsense view that feelings always precede actions is disputed by behavior therapists. They cite the James-Lange hypothesis, formulated around the turn of the century by William James and the Danish physiologist Carl Lange. These two thinkers noted that common sense tells us that when we see a bear we run because we are afraid. They also note that we feel fear because we run, however. The act of running stirs up our nervous system. The runner's heart pounds, his respirations increase, and all these sensations augment the feeling of fear. Actions feed back to the organism information that changes the moment-to-moment feeling. Consequently, behavior therapists argue, a passive person need not wait until he has acquired insight into the roots of his passivity before starting to assert himself. On the contrary, he can rid himself of his chronic passivity by consciously learning and practicing assertive skills. Some of the assertiveness skills frequently discussed by behavior therapists are as follows:

Feeling talk. Feeling talk is one of the oldest of the systematic assertiveness skills. It was first identified and discussed by Andrew Salter, therapist and hostile critic of psychoanalysis, in his book *Conditioned Reflex Therapy.* He argues that the neurotic person suffers from excessive inhibition—he "holds back" too much. He needs to express feelings and act more decisively. As one technique for reducing inhibition, Salter recommends that the timid person more openly express feelings. He should state feelings of dislike, approval, relief, impatience, discomfort, appreciation, curiosity, skepticism, amazement, anticipation, confidence, contentment, regret, love, anguish, annoyance, and surprise. A few examples of feeling talk given by Salter are:

"I don't like this pie."

"That shade of green is perfect for you."

"You did a marvelous job, Miss Jones."

"You're looking fine!"

"Today is Friday. I thought it would never get here."

Feeling talk is one of the systematic assertive skills.

"I cried when he came home safely."

"You can't do this to me!"

"Excuse me, but I was here first."

"My feet hurt."

"You don't expect me to believe that, do you?"

"Say it again. I like it." (p. 98)

In connection with feeling talk, Salter also suggests the associated technique of the *deliberate* use of the word *I* with great frequency. "I am angry about . . ." "I saw that movie and . . ." "I wish I could . . ." "I think . . ." The fear expressed by the inhibited person when he hears about the techniques of feeling talk and the conscious use of the word *I* is that he will either lose self-control or be thought of as conceited. Salter argues that these are false fears. Feeling talk and the more frequent use of the word *I* are skills designed to counterbalance the excessive inhibition of the oversocialized person.

Broken record. Broken record is an assertiveness skill that involves calm repetition of one's position. It can be used in a negative sense or in a positive sense—for saying no to an unreasonable request or for asserting one's own wishes. One of the concepts which goes with broken record is that the user should not be sidetracked into explanations of his position. He simply repeats his position over and over again. The argument is that his feelings about the matter are legitimate simply because he has them, not because they can be demonstrated to be rational.

An example of the negative use of broken record can be given in connection with dealing with a salesman:

Salesman. This is the finest life insurance policy ever offered by the Galaxy Insurance Company.

Prospect. I'm sorry, I don't want any insurance.

Salesman. But don't you want to protect your wife and children in the case of your death?

Prospect. Maybe I wasn't clear. I don't want any insurance today.

Salesman. Let me ask you a question. How much insurance do you have now? Do you have a group policy where you work?

Prospect. As I said, I really don't want any insurance today.

Salesman (getting frustrated). Are you aware of the new changes in the social security laws? May I explain the law changes to you? You will find the information of value even if you don't buy insurance.

Prospect. No thanks. Let me repeat, I just don't want to buy any insurance.

Salesman. OK. I guess you don't want to buy any insurance today.

Prospect. That's right.

To illustrate the positive use of broken record, imagine a situation in which a wife wants to see a particular movie and the husband is showing no interest. Keep in mind that she has determined already in her mind that it is fair and proper that he take her. Last week she went to see a science-fiction movie he wanted to see. Now she feels it's her turn to see a love story. Also, note that broken record is not manipulative. She is being honest about her feeling, asserting herself, not playing the angles, and not trying to trick her husband:

Wife. I want to go see *Jane Eyre Remarries.*

Husband. I'm tired tonight.

Wife. That's OK. We can tomorrow night or the night after that. It's playing until Wednesday.

Husband. Why do you want to see that corny movie?

Wife. I just want to see it. That's all.

Husband. Yeah. But it stars Judy Morningstar. She can't act her way out of a paper bag.

Wife. Honey, I just want to see it. That's all.

Husband. Don't you think you'd rather go see *Frankenstein Lands on the Planet of the Apes?*

Wife. No, I want to see *Jane Eyre Remarries.*

Husband. I hear it got terrible reviews.

Wife. I don't care. I want to see it.

Husband. You really want to see it, huh?

Wife. Yes. I want to see it.

Husband. Well, OK. When do you want to go?

Wife. Tonight if you're not too tired. I really want to see it.

Husband. Well, OK. I guess I'm not too tired.

Wife. Thanks, honey.

Fogging. In *When I Say No, I Feel Guilty* by Manuel J. Smith, the following definition is given of the assertiveness skill called "fogging":

A skill that teaches acceptance of manipulative criticism by calmly acknowledging to your critic the probability that there may be some truth in what he says, yet allows you to remain your own judge of what you do. Clinical effect after practice: Allows you to receive criticism comfortably without becoming anxious or defensive, while giving no reward to those using manipulative criticism. (p. 301)

Fogging is particularly useful when dealing with a nagging person. Parents, husbands, wives, relatives, and others in positions of great or small authority may fall into patterns of criticizing behavior. Smith gives the following example of a daughter using the fogging technique with a critical mother:

Mother. Sally, you know how important looking good is to a young girl who wants to meet a nice man and get married. If you keep staying out late so often and don't get enough sleep, you won't look good. You don't want that to happen, do you?

Sally. You're right, Mom. What you say makes sense, so when I feel the need I'll get in early enough. (p. 98)

Smith notes that Sally can augment the assertion by adding at various times such statements as, "But I wouldn't stay up so late worrying about me if I were you" or "But I'm not worried about it."

In his assertiveness training syllabus, Paulson notes that fogging is useful in that it makes the person under critical attack a small target. The essence of the skill resides in agreeing without making a behavioral promise. Paulson suggests that the fogger use placating and nondefensive statements. Examples he gives are as follows:

"You're absolutely right. I should never do that."

"That's a good point."

"I really should try to be more serious."

"I can't understand why I have been so insensitive."

"I really should do that." (p. 7)

Feeling talk, broken record, and fogging are just three of the assertiveness skills taught by behavior therapists. If you are interested in learning more about systematic assertiveness skills, the books cited in this section are good starting places. All the skills, however, revolve around the central point made at the beginning of our discussion of assertiveness training: The thesis is that, in Salter's language, many people suffer from a "well-bred" neurosis. They are too inhibited, hold back feelings, and are oversocialized. Behavior therapists contend that the conscious practice of assertive behavior is a specific corrective remedy for the creampuffs of the world.

CRITIQUE

In spite of its success and popularity, behavioral psychology is far from problem-free. There is something about the behavioral approach that seems to make certain kinds of people start "frothing at the mouth" and making noises like mad dogs. The tender-minded person who has great hopes for humanity tends to detest the kind of psychologist who explains human behavior by drawing parallels with salivating dogs, lever-pressing rats, and pecking pigeons. Those who are hostile to behavioral psychology have presented a number of challenges to its authority. Let us examine some of these challenges.

1   Behavioral psychology grossly oversimplifies the nature of human existence. In *The Ghost in the Machine*, Arthur Koestler, a well-known author and social philosopher, writes:

Behaviourism is indeed a kind of flat-earth view of the mind. Or to change the metaphor: it has replaced the anthropomorphic fallacy—ascribing to animals human faculties and sentiments—with the opposite fallacy: denying man faculties not found in lower animals; it has substituted for the erstwhile anthropomorphic view of the rat, a ratomorphic view of man. . . . Its declared aim, "to predict and to control human activity as physical scientists control and manipulate other natural phenomena," sounds as nasty as it is naive. Werner Heisenberg, one of the greatest living physical scientists, has laconically declared: "Nature is unpredictable"; it seems rather absurd to deny the living organism even that degree of unpredictability which quantum physics accord to inanimate nature. (p. 17)

Behaviorists would reply that one aim of science is to simplify complex phenomena. It could also be argued that even if total prediction and control of behavior is impractical, partial prediction and control is a realistic goal.

2   Behavioral psychology in general and radical behaviorism in particular deny the existence of free will. Thinkers in theological, existential, and humanistic traditions take behaviorists to task for their position on free will. It is argued by the more tender-minded thinkers that to deny free will is absurd. We experience ourselves as free; a primary datum of human existence is our inner awareness of the capacity to make decisions and choices. This criticism of behaviorism is implicit in Koestler's reference to the physicist Heisenberg. Heisenberg's principle of indeterminacy in physics is often cited as evidence in favor of the existence of a free will in man. Sophisticated behavioral psychologists respond to their critics by saying that they are not making statements about Ultimate Reality; they do not pretend to be metaphysicians. They are talking about the here and the now, what can be measured and observed. Under these conditions, they feel that the predictability of human behavior is an excellent *working hypothesis*. In terms of the modification of behavior, it is possible to get more mileage out of a conditioning approach than a free-will approach.

3   Behaviorism denies the existence of consciousness. This seems like some sort of joke. We all know we are conscious. Critics of behaviorism assert that behaviorists must be idiots or malicious villains to try to take away from human beings so precious a possession as consciousness. Advocates of behaviorism could again talk about the working hypothesis versus Ultimate Reality. They would point out that behaviorists feel it is more fruitful from a scientific point of view to do research and sometimes therapy *as if* the organism were not self-aware. Acknowledging the consciousness of the organism takes behavioral scientists in the wrong direction. It takes them away from the functional analysis of behavior in terms of the physical and social environment. Instead, they end up in the head, heart, or soul of the individual—making the person himself the prime cause of his behavior. To behaviorists, this is a serious error and a major problem with explanations of behavior in terms of such familiar concepts as free will and consciousness. For these reasons, radical behaviorists adopt the formal position that the organism is not conscious.

4 Behaviorists are quick to charge other schools of psychology with sloppy thinking. Behaviorists themselves, however, tend to be sloppy when they start counseling others. Their elegant ideas are often left behind when it comes to doing practical work with troubled clients. For example, Wolpe draws from Pavlovian and Hullian theory for his concept of desensitization. But Pavlov and Hull worked with actual stimuli; Wolpe works with imaginary stimuli. There seems to be a world of difference. Indeed, doesn't the use of imaginary stimuli and fantasy imply that the subject is conscious? "I'm confused!" cries out the beginning student. To clarify the situation, let us note that there are behaviorists and then there are behaviorists. In other words, behaviorism is not itself a unitary and completely consistent approach. It is true that radical behaviorists would not speak of imaginary stimuli and/or fantasy images. But as the behavioral approach has matured, many behaviorists, particularly behavior therapists, have tended to seek a middle ground. Thus we might speak of a large group of therapists who are soft behaviorists, not radical behaviorists. The mellow group find it useful, particularly when talking to clients, to use familiar mentalistic concepts.

5 The concept of reinforcement is said to be circular. The hostile critic makes a mockery of the behaviorists' view of reinforcement. "Why does the organism do what it does? Because it is reinforced for doing it. When is a stimulus designated a reinforcer? When the organism does what it does to get it!" Ergo, declares the critic, reinforcement is an empty concept. This charge is more clever than accurate. Anyone who has seen the concept of reinforcement applied in an experimental laboratory or in practical settings with troubled children or disturbed mental patients can hardly deny that reinforcement is a powerful concept. Its application has observable effects. Actually, the problem of circularity seems to be a pseudoproblem arising from the unfortunate way reinforcement is usually defined: any stimulus that increases the probability of a response. The definition seems to make behavior fold back upon itself. If, instead, we keep in mind that "a response" really means a *response category*—such as pressing a lever—we break out of the circularity. The reinforcer follows act 1; this increases the probability not of act 1, *but of act 2.*

It should also be noted that Premack's principle of using a more probable behavior to reinforce a less probable one has done much to undermine the charge that reinforcement is a circular concept. Premack's formulation does not define a reinforcer in terms of its effects, but in terms of behavioral relationships. This is a substantial advance and a contribution to the theory of reinforcement.

6 Behaviorism has no larger vision of man. This charge is basically accurate. Behavioral psychology sees the human being as an organism to be conditioned, not as a person seeking to lead a life of meaning. There is no concept of a "higher" destiny for the individual. The traditional glorification of man in myth and fable as a hero and as a creature with a higher purpose is implicitly rejected by the behaviorist. If you find the behaviorists' restricted view of human existence distasteful, you can still take out of behavioral psychology those elements that you find useful. In my view, there is much of value in behavioral psychology even if one does not completely agree with the basic premises. We are free to abstract from the behavioral system whatever we find of worth. Rejecting everything behaviorists have to say because one is a humanist is like "throwing the baby away with the bathwater."

7 Behaviorists treat the symptom, not the cause, of a psychological problem. This complaint charges behaviorists with superficiality. Say that a person has a phobia and the intensity of his phobia is reduced with systematic desensitization. The depth psychologist protests, "But you have done nothing about the underlying reasons for his phobia. The question of *why* he had an irrational fear goes unanswered. The basic conflict that produced the phobia remains and is likely to produce a phobia of something else." The behaviorist answers, "I make no arbitrary distinction between underlying causes and behavior. The maladaptive behavior *is* the problem, not some invisible and hypothetical unconscious conflict. The notion of the behavior being one thing and the underlying problem something else is based on the medical model, which distinguishes between symptoms of the illness and the illness itself. This approach is a poor metaphor for behavioral disorders, which are often the result of faulty conditioning histories."

8   Aversive therapy, one kind of behavior therapy, is said to dehumanize the client. The individual is shocked, receives Antabuse, or is in some other way made to feel uncomfortable for his undesirable behavior. "You can't rehumanize a person by treating him like an animal," says an opponent of behavior therapy. The behavior therapist answers, "On the whole, these individuals seek the therapy themselves. We don't impose it on them." This point was discussed at some length earlier in the chapter.

9   The parent who raises a child by using behavior modification techniques is not an authentic parent. He is manipulating the child and using bribes to control behavior. Behaviorists answer that all parents use some form of manipulation in raising children. It is only a question of what methods have the greatest effectiveness. Furthermore, an important distinction is made between a bribe and a reinforcer. A bribe is usually given to get a child to *stop* an undesirable behavior; thus a bribe is a form of blackmail and teaches a child to become a blackmail artist. As such, behaviorists are against bribes. A reinforcer, on the other hand, is given to get a child to *maintain* or *augment* desirable behavior. Thus reinforcers have long-run beneficial consequences in socializing the child.

10   Assertiveness training will make a person selfish and egocentric. Behavior therapists answer that this charge is based on a misunderstanding of the difference between assertiveness and aggression. Assertive behavior is an optimal response between passivity and aggression. Assertiveness training teaches that a person has a right, within broad limits, to live his life in his own way. It is interesting that this same doctrine is in the best tradition of existential-humanistic psychology, and yet behaviorism and existential-humanistic psychology are usually presented as opposing views. It seems that, starting from quite different theoretical starting points, they have—at least in this one area—arrived at the same end point. This is encouraging. In any event, the complaint that assertiveness training makes a person selfish and egocentric seems to have little merit. The idea is to bring persons out a bit and help them overcome neurotic inhibition, not to make them vain and self-centered.

It is possible to fire a number of gunshots at behavioral psychology. But for every shot fired, the behaviorists have an answering salvo. When the smoke of battle clears, we see that neither the behaviorists nor their detractors have won the field. Each side commands a goodly portion of the terrain. Behavioral psychology was, is, and will be for some time to come a dominant influence in American psychology.

IMPLICATIONS FOR ADJUSTMENT AND GROWTH

In what ways can behavioral psychology contribute to the adjustment and growth of the individual? Let us review some of the major possibilities:

1 One of the great values of behavioral psychology is its emphasis on the learning process. This emphasis brings to our attention the simple fact that we were not born able to talk, do arithmetic, drive a car, or perform countless other important functions of human existence. Most complex human behavior is learned, which suggests that much of our self-destructive behavior is also learned; so-called bad habits are made, not inborn. In this position there is hope. What was learned can be unlearned. This is the essence of the extinction principle. And it is a useful point to remember. It is a good antidote to such well-worn clichés as, "You can't teach an old dog new tricks." Behaviorists see the human organism as a creature with great plasticity.

2 Behavioral psychology emphasizes the specific as opposed to the global. For example, it transforms a problem with smoking into a set of problems with smoking. The monster is chopped up into bits and pieces, each of which can be attacked with relative ease. Self-modification of behavior requires that a person not moan and groan in generalities, but "zero in" on the particular cues and reinforcers which maintain the undesirable behavior.

3 The emphasis that behavioral psychology places on the *how to* as opposed to the *why* is refreshing and useful. Classical schools of psychology (e.g., psychoanalysis) have traditionally placed great emphasis on why the individual is the way he is. It has often been tacitly assumed that self-understanding and insight are sufficient to bring about new adjustments and/or personal growth. Behaviorists have lost faith in this position. They feel that too much emphasis on the why of behavior leads the individual into a morass. Behavioral psychology is a brass-tacks approach that orients the individual to ways of actually implementing behavioral change.

4 Knowledge of the desensitization principle may sometimes help us face threatening situations with greater equanimity. Say that Bill is supposed to take a public speaking class for his major. He has never heard of desensitization and thinks to himself, "I'm not going to take public speaking. No way. I can't stand to talk in front of people. I've got to think of a way to get out of taking the class or change my major." Assume that Tom understands the principle of desensitization. Faced with the need to take a public speaking class, he reflects, "I know I'll have a hard time at first. But it will probably work like desensitization in behavior therapy. I'll be less anxious each time I give a talk, and taking the class will probably help me get over my fear." This lucid recognition of the desensitization principle may provide us with a bit of cold comfort when faced with anxiety-arousing situations.

5   A knowledge of the basic principles of conditioning can be helpful to parents. The work of the Skinnerians on instrumental conditioning suggests the great power of positive reinforcement and opens up for many parents the possibility of constructive training with a minimum of punishment. In my view, conditioning principles are relevant at any stage of human development. They seem, however, to have a maximum value for parents when their children are quite young. Parents will find that a knowledge of behavioral psychology is particularly useful for helping children learn basic skills and basic manners.

6   If persons develop a good grasp of fundamental laws of learning, and if they have a strong motivation to make some kind of a behavioral change, the self-modification of behavior is possible. It is possible to unlearn bad habits. I would like to note at this point that the familiar term *bad habit* is usually unexamined. *Bad* and *good* are moralistic terms. One man's bad habit is another man's good habit. It would be more neutral and more realistic to speak of wanted habits and unwanted habits. In any event, a substantial amount of research supports the possibility of the self-modification of behavior. If you are interested in pursuing this line of thinking, you might look into *Toward a Self-Managed Life Style* by Robert L. Williams and James D. Long. They note:

Self-management has emerged as an important dimension of behavior modification; it could make quite an impact on society as a whole. The tone of self-management is consistent with our society's ethic of self-responsibility. We are held responsible for our behavior because we are assumed to be in control of that behavior. Thus, any orientation that increases the possibility of self-control ought to be highly acceptable. (p. 12)

7   The basic model on which assertiveness training is built is helpful. Everyone deals with other people. It is valuable to have the image of the assertive response in human relations as a graded response between passivity and aggression. The concept of constructive assertive behavior lends itself to daily applications.

8   A sound understanding of behavioral psychology can be used to improve human relations. Behaviorists note that with or without intention we shape and reinforce the behavior of each other. We modify the behavior of those close to us with our praise and our attention. By his responses to her cooking, a husband can modify his wife's cooking behavior. By her responses to his lovemaking, a wife can modify her husband's lovemaking behavior. It is prudent to realize that behavior does not take place in a vacuum. We live in a social environment. Our social interactions provide numerous reinforcers; these reinforcers in turn have a substantial effect on our behavior patterns.

A Spanish proverb observes, "Habits are at first cobwebs, then cables." Behavioral psychology takes the optimistic viewpoint that the cables making up unwanted habits can be unwound strand by strand. Continuing the metaphor, behavioral psychology also asserts that we can, strand by strand, build the strong cables of wanted habits in ourselves and in our children. It is evident that the basic principles of learning have many direct applications to the human condition.

SUMMARY AND SELF-TEST

1 The behavioral psychologist accepts the validity of the willpower approach to habit modification.
T   F

2 Systematic desensitization is a method by which the individual learns to respond differently to anxiety-arousing and fear-arousing stimuli.
T   F

3 An unconditioned stimulus is a stimulus that evokes a learned response.
T   F

4 The unconditioned response and the conditioned response should be thought of as identities.
T   F

5 The phenomenon of stimulus generalization refers primarily to the ability of organisms to detect similarities.
T   F

6 Pavlov said that it is impossible to produce experimental neuroses in dogs.
T   F

7 In aversion therapy, the cues that trigger an undesirable behavior pattern are paired with a pleasant stimulus.
T   F

8 The principle of reciprocal inhibition takes advantage of the antagonism of relaxation and anxiety.
T   F

9 Implosive therapy presents anxiety-arousing stimuli at a much more conservative rate than does systematic desensitization.
T   F

10 Behaviorists are strong believers in the importance of mental life as a source of explanations for human behavior.
T   F

11 Instrumental conditioning takes place when an organism learns that certain actions will produce certain results.
T   F

12 Thorndike said that if an action leads to a state of satisfaction, it is preserved by the organism; he called this principle the "law of effect."
T   F

13 Clark L. Hull's theory of behavior and learning is often called a "drive-reduction theory."
T   F

14 If two stimuli are presented to an organism at the same time, they are said to be discontiguous.
T   F

15 Operant conditioning refers to changes or modifications an organism makes in its internal environment, not its external world.
T   F

16 A discriminative stimulus provides an organism with information that an operant act is presently paying off or not paying off.
T   F

17 A reinforcer is a stimulus that increases the probability of occurrence of a certain class of behavior.
T   F

18 A negative reinforcer always follows an instrumental action.
T   F

19 Avoidance conditioning is clearly not instrumental in nature.
T   F

20 In the case of punishment, an aversive stimulus follows an instrumental action.
T   F

21 Organisms that learn instrumental responses under conditions of partial reinforcement show greater resistance to extinction than organisms trained under conditions of continuous reinforcement.
T   F

22 Behaviorists say that behavior modification should not be used by parents; it is too cold-blooded an approach for a loving home.
T   F

23 The behavior therapist feels that we should discard the concept of mental illness and replace it with a concept such as "odd" or "difficult" behavior.

T   F

24 Cue management is one of the behavioral techniques available in the self-modification of behavior.

T   F

25 Reinforcement management is not one of the techniques available in the self-modification of behavior; it is impossible for people to self-control their own reinforcements.

T   F

26 The method of incompatible responses is a classical habit-breaking method.

T   F

27 Say that a person reduces a long-standing fear of dogs by buying a puppy and raising it to adulthood. He is using the classical habit-breaking method known as "exhaustion of an undesirable response" or "negative practice."

T   F

28 Assertiveness training refers to a program of learning designed to increase a person's competence in dealing with other human beings.

T   F

29 The concept of an assertive response is synonymous with the concept of an aggressive response.

T   F

30 The assertiveness skill known as "broken record" requires that its user firmly explain his position from a rational point of view to another person.

T   F

ANSWER KEY

1 *False.* The behavioral psychologist rejects the validity of the willpower approach to habit modification.

2 *True.* Systematic desensitization is a method by which the individual learns to respond differently to anxiety-arousing and fear-arousing stimuli.

3 *False.* An unconditioned stimulus is a stimulus that evokes an unlearned response.

4 *False.* The unconditioned response and the conditioned response should not be thought of as identities.

5 *True.* The phenomenon of stimulus generalization refers primarily to the ability of organisms to detect similarities.

6 *False.* Pavlov produced experimental neuroses in dogs.

7 *False.* In aversion therapy, the cues that trigger an undesirable behavior pattern are paired with a noxious stimulus.

8 *True.* The principle of reciprocal inhibition takes advantage of the antagonism of relaxation and anxiety.

9 *False.* Implosive therapy presents anxiety-arousing stimuli at a much less conservative rate than does systematic desensitization.

10 *False.* Behaviorists discount the concept of mental life as a source of explanations for human behavior.

11 *True.* Instrumental conditioning takes place when an organism learns that certain actions will produce certain results.

12 *True.* Thorndike said that if an action leads to a state of satisfaction, it is preserved by the organism; he called this principle the "law of effect."

13 *True.* Clark L. Hull's theory of behavior and learning is often called a "drive-reduction theory."

14 *False.* If two stimuli are presented to an organism at the same time, they are said to be contiguous.

15 *False.* Operant conditioning refers to changes or modifications an organism makes in its external world, not its internal environment.

16 *True.* A discriminative stimulus provides an organism with information that an operant act is presently paying off or not paying off.

17 *True.* A reinforcer is a stimulus that increases the probability of occurrence of a certain class of behavior.

18 *False.* A negative reinforcer always precedes an instrumental action.

19 *False.* Avoidance conditioning is instrumental in nature.

20 *True.* In the case of punishment, an aversive stimulus follows an instrumental action.

21 *True.* Organisms that learn instrumental responses under conditions of partial reinforcement show greater resistance to extinction than organisms trained under conditions of continuous reinforcement.

22 *False.* Behaviorists tend to recommend the use of behavior modification by parents.

23 *True.* The behavior therapist feels that we should discard the concept of mental illness and replace it with a concept such as "odd" or "difficult" behavior.

24 *True.* Cue management is one of the behavioral techniques available in the self-modification of behavior.

25 *False.* Reinforcement management is one of the techniques available in the self-modification of behavior; behaviorists feel it is possible for people to self-control their own reinforcements.

26   *True.* The method of incompatible responses is a classical habit-breaking method.

27   *False.* If a person reduces a long-standing fear of dogs by buying a puppy and raising it to adulthood, he is using the classical habit-breaking method known as "cue toleration."

28   *True.* Assertiveness training refers to a program of learning designed to increase a person's competence in dealing with other human beings.

29   *False.* The concept of an assertive response is different from the concept of an aggressive response.

30   *False.* "Broken record" is an assertiveness skill that involves calm repetition of one's position without explaining one's feelings about the matter.

DISCUSSION QUESTIONS

DESENSITIZATION: FIGHTING FEARS WITH FANTASY

1 Can you think of an example that shows the existence of classical conditioning within yourself?

2 Do you feel that aversion therapy is appropriate with certain kinds of behavioral problems, such as alcoholism, smoking, and overeating? Would you object to someone you love undergoing aversion therapy? Would you submit to it voluntarily?

3 Have you ever got over a fear through a process of informal desensitization? Can you give an example?

4 Do you agree with the logic of implosive therapy?

BEHAVIOR MODIFICATION: SHAPING ACTIONS

1 Do you have a bad habit you want to break? What is it?

2 Do you agree with the behavior modifier that the laws of conditioning and the principle of reinforcement are more potent concepts for changing behavior than mentalistic concepts such as images, wishes, and will?

3 What is your personal reaction to the point of view of B. F. Skinner?

4 Are you clear on the similarities and differences among a positive reinforcer, a negative reinforcer, and punishment?

5 What are your feelings about the use of behavior modification by parents?

SELF-MODIFICATION OF BEHAVIOR: BECOMING YOUR OWN PYGMALION

1 What are some of the ways a behavioral problem such as heavy smoking or overeating might be controlled by cue management?

2 If you have a bad habit, can you think of some ways it might be broken or modified by reinforcement management?

3 If you have a bad habit, can you see any ways that you might apply the classical habit-breaking methods to yourself?

ASSERTIVENESS TRAINING: THE WORM TURNS

1 Do you see yourself as basically an unassertive, aggressive, or assertive person? Think of a close friend. How would you rate that person on assertiveness?

2   Do you find yourself in agreement with the general philosophy underlying assertiveness training? Is it the optimal response between being unassertive or aggressive?

3   Do you believe that assertiveness skills can be learned through conscious practice? Or is one's basic personality always the source of behavior?

REFERENCES

Alberti, R. E., and Emmons, M. L. *Your Perfect Right*. San Luis Obispo, Calif.: Impact, 1970.

Becker, W. C., and Becker, J. W. *Successful Parenthood*. Chicago: Follett Publishing Co., 1974.

Beltz, S. *How To Make Johnny Want To Obey*. Englewood Cliffs, N.J.: Prentice-Hall, 1971.

Dollard, J., and Miller, N. *Personality and Psychotherapy*. New York: McGraw-Hill Book Co., 1950.

Dunlap, K. *Habits: Their Making and Unmaking*. New York: Liveright, 1932.

Estes, W. K. "Experimental Study of Punishment." *Psychological Monographs*, 57 (1944), 1–40.

Eysenck, H. J. *Sense and Nonsense in Psychology*. Baltimore: Penguin Books, 1957.

Fensterheim, H., and Baer, J. *Don't Say Yes When You Want To Say No*. New York: David McKay, 1975.

Goldiamond, I. "Self-control Procedures in Personal Behavior Problems." Reprinted in Gazzaniga, M. S., and Lovejoy, E. P., eds., *Good Reading in Psychology*. Englewood Cliffs, N.J.: Prentice-Hall, 1971.

Guthrie, E. R. *The Psychology of Learning*. New York: Harper & Row, 1935.

Hilts, P. J. *Behavior Mod*. New York: Harper's Magazine Press, 1974.

Homme, L. *How to Use Contingency Contracting in the Classroom*. Champaign, Ill.: Research Press, 1970.

Hull, C. L. *Principles of Behavior*. New York: Appleton-Century-Crofts, 1943.

Koestler, A. *The Ghost in the Machine*. New York: Macmillan, 1967.

London, P. *Behavior Control*. New York: Harper & Row, 1969.

Notterman, J., Schoenfeld, W. N., and Bersh, P. J. "Conditioned Heart Rate Response in Human Beings During Experimental Anxiety." *Journal of Comparative and Physiological Psychology*, 45 (1952), 1–8.

O'Reilly, J. B. "How Shall I Habit Break?" in A. L. Alexander, comp., *Poems that Touch the Heart*. New York: Doubleday, 1941.

Paulson, T. *Assertion Training Syllabus.* Pasadena, Calif.: Fuller Graduate School of Psychology. Unpublished manuscript, 1974.

Pavlov, I. P. *Selected Works,* edited by K. S. Kostoyants. Moscow: Foreign Languages Publishing House, 1955.

Premack, D. "Toward Empirical Behavioral Laws: I. Positive Reinforcement." *Psychological Review*, 66 (1959), 219–233.

Salter, A. *Conditioned Reflex Therapy.* New York: Farrar, Straus & Giroux, 1949.

Schaefer, H. H., and Martin, P. L. *Behavioral Therapy.* New York: McGraw-Hill, 1969.

Skinner, B. F. *About Behaviorism.* New York: Alfred A. Knopf, 1974.

————. *The Behavior of Organisms.* New York: Appleton-Century-Crofts, 1938.

————. *Walden II.* New York: Macmillan, 1948.

Smith, M. J. *When I Say No, I Feel Guilty.* New York: Dial Press, 1975.

Stampfl, T. G., and Levis, D. J. "Essentials of Implosive Therapy: A Learning-Theory-Based Psychodynamic Behavioral Therapy." *Journal of Abnormal Psychology*, 72 (1967), 496–503.

Thorndike, E. L. *Animal Intelligence.* New York: Macmillan, 1911.

Tolman, E. C. *Purposive Behavior in Animals and Men.* New York: Appleton-Century-Crofts, 1932.

Williams, R. L., and Long, J. D. *Toward a Self-Managed Life Style.* Boston: Houghton Mifflin, 1975.

Wilson, C. *New Pathways in Psychology.* New York: New American Library, 1972.

Wolpe, J. *Psychotherapy by Reciprocal Inhibition.* Stanford, Calif.: Stanford University Press, 1958.

CHAPTER 4 RATIONAL ANALYSIS: TOWARD A LIFE OF REASON

Aristotle called man the thinking animal.

OVERVIEW

OUTLINE

TWO KEY QUESTIONS

What is rational analysis?

Rational analysis represents a point of view that emphasizes the *thinking process.* Its central concerns are decision-making, logic, and how we form judgments. A rational analysis of a personal problem implies the use of sound reasoning to reach an optimal solution to the problem. In brief, the term *rational analysis* may be defined as the application of clear thinking to life's challenges.

How do the principles of rational analysis relate to adjustment and growth?

Proponents of rational analysis assert that a person who has trained himself to think more clearly and more realistically has at least two advantages over less-well-trained persons. First, he will suffer less from undesirable emotional reactions. He will have better coping mechanisms and will thus be somewhat less susceptible to emotionally induced illnesses. Second, he will plan ahead in a realistic manner, which will enable him to avoid some of life's worst blind alleys. He will do more than stumble through existence.

Aristotle called man the thinking animal, suggesting that humans are the only life form on the planet Earth capable of rational thought. Indeed, the very term *homo sapiens*—our self-proclaimed label—means *wise man*. Before we proceed too far with our flattering view of people as rational creatures, it is best that we hesitate a moment to consider that people are not always rational. In an article called "The Rationalizing Animal," social psychologist Elliot Aronson comments, "Man likes to think of himself as a rational animal. However, it is more true that man is a *rationalizing* animal, that he attempts to appear reasonable to himself and to others."

In the novel *Of Human Bondage* by W. Somerset Maugham, the central character, Philip, is confronted by the decision of his friend, Hayward, to volunteer for overseas combat. To Philip, the decision seems unlike Hayward. It is totally against Hayward's stated philosophy of life:

Philip was silent. He felt rather silly. He understood that Hayward was being driven by an uneasiness in his soul which he could not account for. Some power within him made it seem necessary to go and fight for his country. It was strange, since he [Hayward] considered patriotism no more than a prejudice, and, flattering himself on his cosmopolitanism, he had looked upon England as a place of exile. His countrymen in the mass wounded his susceptibilities. Philip wondered what it was that made people do things which were so contrary to all their theories of life. It would have been reasonable for Hayward to stand aside and watch with a smile while the barbarians slaughtered one another. It looked as though men were puppets in the hands of an unknown force, which drove them to do this and that; and sometimes they used their reason to justify their actions; and when this was impossible they did the actions in despite of reason. (p. 452)

Is man a rational animal? Or is man an irrational animal? The answer can only be that man is a rational-irrational animal. There are times when we use intelligent thought to plan ahead, and there are times when we use reason to justify our actions. The proponents of rational analysis discussed in this chapter clearly recognize the tendency of human beings to misuse the thinking process. Indeed, this is, in a sense, their whole point. They feel that although the great mass of people think in murky ways, it is possible to learn new and more effective ways of thinking. They assert that most persons have the potential for rational analysis, but it must be brought forth by specific kinds of educational procedures.

The study of thinking is itself a large subject that covers such diverse areas as concept formation, language acquisition, and problem-solving. It is not the aim of this chapter to offer a general survey of the many facets of the human thinking process. Rather, the goal is the limited one of exploring those approaches specifically designed to enhance adjustment and growth.

Are we rational or irrational beings?

Before we proceed to the topics of this chapter, however, some mention should be made of the work of Jean Piaget, the Swiss researcher who has made great contributions to our understanding of the development of human thought from childhood to adulthood. It would be possible to write a substantial section on Piaget, but I will limit myself to a few observations of particular relevance to rational analysis. Piaget's research provides ample evidence that the consciousness of children is dominated by *stimulus-bound, anthropomorphic*, and *egocentric* thinking. Piaget speaks of a stage of mental development termed the *period of preoperational thought* and notes that it lasts, roughly, from the age of two to the age of seven.

A child's thinking is stimulus-bound when he makes his evaluations on the basis of one and only one outstanding aspect of a stimulus situation. For example, a child may think that a narrow glass with a high water level contains more liquid than a squat glass with a low water level. The squat glass may in fact contain more liquid, but the child responds to the height of the water level alone as the basis of his decision. A child's thinking is anthropomorphic when he perceives processes of nature in human terms. For example, a child may think that the wind is a person and that the leaves are blowing wildly today because Mr. Wind is angry about something. A child's thinking is egocentric when he can see no point of view but his own. For example, say that a very young child is looking at a picture book. You ask the child, "Can I see the picture?"

The child may very well show you the back of the book, holding the picture in such a way that his own view is improved. He thinks that if he can see it more clearly, so can you.

As the child matures, he passes from the period of preoperational thought through an intermediary stage called the *period of concrete operations*. This stage lasts from roughly the age of seven to the age of twelve. During the period of concrete operations, the child elaborates his capacity for symbolical thought and becomes more flexible in his thinking. Finally, the child arrives at the last stage of mental development, the *period of formal operations*. This period begins roughly at age twelve and lasts throughout adulthood. The term *formal operations* is chosen to imply that the mature adult has a number of high-level cognitive capacities. He can reflect, can analyze, can form concepts at a high level of abstraction, can philosophize, and can *think about thinking.*

But the point of my exposition is to suggest that human beings make it to the stage of formal operations in varying degrees. Many of us carry forward into adult life a substantial number of the ways of thought common to the preoperational child. It is not at all unusual to find adults who try to cope with their problems with the outmoded mental tools of children, using stimulus-bound, anthropomorphic, or egocentric thinking. One way of conceptualizing the ideas presented in this chapter is to think of them as psychological catalysts capable of helping a person move increasingly in the direction of Piaget's designation of formal operations. Briefly, the ideas in this chapter are designed to enhance an individual's capacity for clear thinking.

THE TERRITORY
GENERAL SEMANTICS: THE MAP IS NOT

The field of investigation called *general semantics* was the brainchild of a Polish count named Alfred Korzybski (1879–1950). General semantics is an approach to adjustment and growth which asserts that human beings can become more psychologically and emotionally competent if they make an effort to improve their language environment. The phrase "the map is not the territory" was frequently repeated by Korzybski to indicate that *the human nervous system is not external reality.*

Korzybski argued that a person would be "crazy" if he thought a map was identical with an actual physical territory. The map is a guide to the territory, but it leaves much out and may contain errors. Similarly, the human nervous system is a "map" to the external world, but it clearly is not the external world itself. This is an obvious distinction, once made. But Korzybski argued that it is a distinction few people make. He suggested that most people take the ideas in their heads to be identical with the real world. This, he insisted, is a great error and leads to all sorts of defective behavior.

THE WORD IS NOT THE THING

And how are the "maps" in our heads "drawn"? Korzybski's answer was that they are drawn by language. To change the metaphor, think of the brain as a computer. The computer is programmed by a special language, such as Fortran. If the language is accurate and congruent with reality, the "thinking" of the computer will be realistic. If the language is inaccurate, sloppy, or otherwise defective, the thinking of the computer will be similarly inaccurate. Korzybski's thesis was that our brains are programmed by ordinary, everyday language and that ordinary, everyday language contains a host of built-in defects because conventional language is nonmathematical and arose from the thought processes of prescientific people. Archaic and outmoded ways of thinking are retained as residuals in the language patterns of daily usage.

Korzybski felt that a giant step forward could be made in the domain of clear thinking if we would only recognize that the language we use to represent reality to ourselves is not reality itself. A basic slogan of general semantics is "the word is not the thing." Korzybski states:

If we start, for instance, with a statement that "a word is not *the object spoken about," and someone tries to deny that, he would have to produce an actual physical object which would* be *the word,—impossible of performance, even in asylums for the "mentally" ill. (p. 10)*

Let us attempt to provide a lucid example of what Korzybski had in mind. When a child is very young, a parent does a great deal of naming of objects: "This is a spoon." "This is a dog." "This is a saltshaker." These sentences seem harmless enough. Korzybski noted, however, that they contain what he called *the "is" of identity*. The use of the word *is* suggests an identity between the word and the thing and sets up an early confusion in the child's nervous system. "Absurd!" you say. "It is all so innocent!"

"Not so absurd!" says Korzybski. Let's see where the "is" of identity leads. As long as the "is" of identity is used to refer to things that can be pointed at, there is no great problem. Words that refer to things that can be pointed at are called *extensional words*. Such words refer to direct perceptual givens, such as spoon, dog, and saltshaker. But the human language is replete with another category of words: the *intensional words*, and they refer to things that cannot be pointed at. They have no external referent, but exist as processes in the human nervous system. Nonetheless, conventional language has objectified these processes, and they appear in dictionaries as nouns—just as if they too were things. A few examples are *anger, love, beauty, hunger, curiosity, frustration, hope, ecstasy*, and *decency*.

Two friends are standing before a painting in an art gallery. "It's beautiful!" exclaims person A. "No, it's not," protests person B. "It's ugly!" They then begin arguing over whether the painting "is" beautiful or ugly. The way out of the argument is for the individuals involved to recognize that neither beauty nor ugliness are properties of the painting, but perceptual judgments made by human beings. Beauty and ugliness are in the human nervous system, not in the painting. Thus person A can say, "I sure think that looks beautiful!" or "I would call that a beautiful painting," and person B can issue his own opinion—"I would call it ugly"; but there is no foolish argument over whether the painting "is" beautiful. General semantics asserts that it would be a good idea to say, to even very young children, "We call this a dog" or "This is called a saltshaker" to avoid the error of the "is" of identity.

A couple has come to a marriage counselor in great distress. "What seems to be the problem?" asks the counselor. "He doesn't love me any more," says the wife. "That's not true!" says the husband. "I do love you!"

"No you don't" she protests.

"Yes I do," he insists.

"Then why don't you phone me when you're going to be late for dinner?"

"What's that got to do with love? Don't I always bring home the paycheck?"

"What's that got to do with love?" she asks.

A general semanticist would point out that this couple is using the word *love* as if it were a thing. Implicit in their argument is the "is" of identity. Love "is" something—but they aren't sure what! Korzybski would point out that the word *love* refers to a concept, an abstraction without a direct referent in the external world. Thus the couple's argument can only be circular. They need to recognize that there can be more than one concept of love, and that both concepts can be equally valid.

SEMANTIC REACTIONS

Semantics is often defined as the study of the meaning of words. Korzybski invented the term *general semantics* to suggest the idea that the effects of word meanings are not limited to conscious awareness, that they have generalizing, or "spreading," effects on human emotions. The term *semantic reaction* is used to refer to an emotional response to a word. Words can make us happy, sad, angry, frustrated, anxious, or depressed. One of the aims of general semantics is to free people from the direct emotional control of words.

An illustration of the concept of semantic reactions is provided by S. I. Hayakawa, an advocate of general semantics, in an article titled "How Words Change Our Lives."

People suffering from . . . prejudices seem to have in their brains an uninsulated spot which, when touched by such words as "capitalist," "boss," "striker," "scab," "Democrat," "Republican," "socialized medicine," and other such loaded terms, results in an immediate short circuit, often with a blowing of fuses.

Korzybski called such short-circuited responses "identification reactions." He used the word "identification" in a special sense; he meant that persons given to such fixed patterns of response identify (that is, treat as identical all occur- rences of a given word or symbol; they identify all the different cases that fall under the same name). Thus, if one has hostile identification reactions to "women drivers," then all women who drive cars are "identical" in their in- competence. (pp. 9–10)

The terms *identification reactions* and *semantic reactions* are more or less interchangeable. It was, as noted already, Korzybski's contention that emo- tional responses to words take place because of the tendency to treat all members of a class—things with the same name—as identical.

The author Stuart Chase has done much to popularize general semantics. His book *The Tyranny of Words* contains an excellent illustration of how semantic reactions are formed:

Take the word "bad." It probably arose to express a vague feeling of dislike. Rather than go to the trouble of describing the characteristics one did not like in an animal or plot of soil, one said, "It is bad." All right, a useful short cut. Then the word was made into a substantive, "badness." At this abstraction level, it became something ominous and menacing in its own right. One had better not be associated with badness. Badness was incorporated into rigid standards of judgment, especially moral judgment: "This girl is bad." The state- ment implies that she is wholly bad, a veritable chunk of badness. But she may also be a charming girl, kind to children, kind to her parents, and perhaps over- kind to her young man. To cast her out of society as "bad" is the result of a false, one-valued or two-valued appraisal. Adequately to judge this girl, we must make a many-valued appraisal; we must know her other characteristics, the circumstances of the environment in which she was brought up, the status of the moral code at the place and time of the alleged badness, and something about the economic and social prejudices of the judge who calls her "bad." (pp. 77–78)

It does not seem to be the thesis of general semantics that we should dispense with emotions. The person trained to think in the general semantics way does not become a cold-blooded robot. The idea is to free him from false and inappropriate emotional reactions, reactions that plunge him into excessive anger or out-of-proportion depression.

BASIC ERRORS

Korzybski contended that the thinking of the average person is riddled with basic errors. He said that most of us are unsane—not sane and not insane. The term "unsane" was chosen to call attention to the fact that our thinking is not completely delusional, but that it has a rather poor fit with reality as revealed by modern science. For this reason, Korzybski titled his major work *Science and Sanity*. The remainder of this section discusses some of the basic errors noted by Korzybski.

Our logic tends to be two-valued.   The ancient Greeks placed great emphasis on classification as the basis of science, and Aristotle carried the importance of the concept of classes to a fine art in his system of logic. Aristole said that a thing either does or does not belong to a class. An animal is either a fish or a not-fish; a person is either a man or a woman; an individual is either tall or short. A close look at our language reveals many built-in polarities: good-bad, right-wrong, yes-no, up-down, alive-dead, big-small, decent-indecent, success-failure, and so forth. For the sake of simplicity, thinking in two-valued terms can be referred to as *either-or thinking* or *black-white thinking.* The point is that either-or thinking does not do justice to the realities of existence. For example, a man may go brankrupt and think, "I'm a failure." But is this not artificial, two-valued thinking? He may have been a success as a parent, as a husband, as a friend. Is he justified in oversimplifying his existence with two-valued logic?

Korzybski called the two-valued logic of ordinary language *aristotelian* to distinguish it from the multivalued logic—a logic with shades of gray—taught by general semantics. The system of logic advocated by general semantics is called *non-aristotelian*; it calls attention to the fact that many events and processes in nature take place on a gradient having many points. To the general semanticist, a person's height is not adequately described by saying, "He is tall." It is far better to say he is five feet, nine inches, or five feet, eleven inches, or six feet, two inches.

We make the error of treating space–time events as things.   An apple is a fairly solid example of a "thing." Or is it? Once the apple was small and green; now it is red and ripe; in a few days it will be shriveled and decaying. What seems to be a solid object "is" in reality a process of growth and decay taking place as an event in space and time. A somewhat more lucid example is provided by the word *wave*. We look at the ocean and say, "There is a wave coming to shore." "Wave" has the status of a noun and is treated as a thing. But it is evident to us that the wave is temporary and is changing all the time. Clearly, the wave represents a process and is not a thing or an object. Similarly, notes Korzybski, all so-called things are better thought of as space-time events. Note that Korzybski does not say an apple "is" a space-time event, which would be to fall into the trap of the "is" of identity and to make general semantics equivalent to reality; this would be to make the map the territory. The conception of an apple or other "thing" as a space-time event is merely the most adequate conception available, but it is not identical to reality itself.

And what is the value of all this in practical terms? Just this: We too are space-time events. We speak of ourselves as if we were permanent and unchanging objects. "She is a pretty girl," says a young man. She "is" a pretty girl? Does the young man stop to think that the girl may change with time, that she may gain weight, that she may not be pretty when she is forty or fifty years of age? "Tom is so well built!" exclaims

General semantics reminds us that the person is a changing space-time event, not a permanent unchanging thing. (Actor Ray Milland in the 1940's and in the 1970's.)

a young lady. He "is" well built? Will he be well built forever? Perhaps he will have a potbelly in ten years. All this may seem rather obvious and too negative. But the point is that important decisions are often made without conscious recognition that people do change, that what seems permanent today is often gone tomorrow.

I know of a woman who often referred to her husband as "good old Harry—he's my Rock of Gibraltar." When Harry died suddenly of a heart attack, she went into a state of emotional shock. She protested to her relatives, "He's not dead!" and "This can't happen to me!" and "I don't believe it!" Korzybski would say that the woman had failed to recognize that Harry was, like all perceptual objects, not a "thing" but a process. Harry, like the apple and the wave, may be also thought of as a space-time event. He was an infant once, then a child, then an adolescent, then a young adult, then a mature man, and then an organism that died of a heart attack. Such possibilities are in the cards from the very beginning, and it is "unsane" to refer to a human being as "a Rock of Gibraltar" or anything else that suggests absolute permanence.

Korzybski suggested that we remind ourselves of the transient and changing quality of persons and things by dates. For example, we could speak of Harry 1964, Harry 1972, Harry 1975, and so forth.

We incorrectly treat members of a category as identities.   We would find it hard to function without perceptual and conceptual categories. In *A Study of Thinking* by Bruner, Goodnow, and Austin, it is pointed out that the foundation of concept formation revolves around the process of classification. They say, "By categorizing as equivalent discriminably different events, the organism *reduces the complexity of its environment.* It is reasonably clear 'how' this is accomplished. It involves the abstraction and use of defining properties in terms of which groupings can be made. . ." (p. 12)

Unfortunately, the advantage gained by the reduction of complexity is undermined to some extent by the "unsane" idea that there are no differences of importance among members of a group. A person may say, "Teenagers don't respect adults nowadays." But what about *this* teenager? She has a high B average, helps her mother around the house, baby-sits for extra money, and seems to be liked by adults. Someone may comment, "Black people are lazy." But what about *this* black man? He has a profession, supports a wife and two children, mows his lawn every Saturday, and so forth. "Jews are stingy," someone comments. But what about *this* Jewish person? He donates to charity, pays the prices asked by merchants, and has never owned his own business. If we make the mistake of treating members of a group as identities, we will be in for some rude semantic shocks when we encounter discrepancies from our expectancies. Even such a simple statement as "Apples are sweet" can cause trouble. What about *this* apple? You bite into it expecting the familiar sweet taste, and it is sour! This is a bit of a shock. Korzybski warned that we should be careful to avoid building up false expectancies based on the error of identity.

Korzybski suggested that we remind ourselves of the nonidentity of members of a class by the use of index numbers. For example, we could speak of apple$_1$, apple$_2$, apple$_3$, and so forth; we could speak of teenager$_1$, teenager$_2$, teenager$_3$, and so forth. This kind of self-alerting would be likely to reduce the impact of untoward semantic reactions—we would experience fewer rude awakenings.

Conventional language usage overdefines terms by intension and under-defines terms by extension.   You will recall that intensional words refer to things that cannot be pointed at; thus the term *intension* by itself refers to events taking place within the individual. You will also recall that extensional words refer to things that can be pointed at; thus the term *extension* by itself refers to events taking place in the external world. With this introduction, consider the following quotation from Korzybski's *Science and Sanity*:

The dictionaries define "house" as a "building for human habitation or occupation," etc. Let us imagine that we buy a house; this buying is an extensional activity, usually with some consequences. If we orient ourselves by intension we are really buying a definition, although we may even inspect the house, which may appear desirable, etc. Then suppose we move into the house with our furniture and the whole house collapses because termites have destroyed all the wood, leaving only a shell, perhaps satisfying to the eye. Does the verbal definition of the house correspond to the extensional facts? Of course not. It becomes obvious then that by intension the term "house" was over-defined, or over-limited, while by extension, or actual facts, it was hopelessly under-defined as many important characteristics were left out. In no dictionary definition of a "house" is the possibility of termites mentioned. (p. iii)

Stated informally, we overdefine a term by intension when we use a word to "see" things that *are not* there (e.g., perceiving a house to be sturdy that is not in fact sturdy). We underdefine a term by extension when our belief in a word makes us fail to see things that *are* there (e.g., missing the presence of termites).

Korzybski asserted, "Different maladjusted, neurotics, psychotics, etc., orient themselves by intension most of the time." The disturbed person is likely to evaluate by overdefinition. He believes in words and not extensional facts. As a corrective procedure designed to remind ourselves that most words are underdefined in extensional terms, Korzybski suggested we make liberal use of "etc." (*et cetera*), which may mean "and others'' or ''and the rest'' or ''and so forth.'' Etc. reminds us that much has been left unsaid. (You will note that the quotations from Korzybski use etc. It is also interesting to observe that the journal of general semantics is called *ETC.*)

We create verbal divisions where no divisions exist in fact. Language has produced conceptual categories that have no extensional referents. Familiar examples are *mind and body*, and *space and time*. It is hardly possible to point at a mind without a body or a body without a mind. Mind and body are concepts of some convenience, and we may want to make a distinction for certain purposes. But we should remember that they are not separated in nature; they are separated only in our thought processes. Space and time provide another illustration. In *People in Quandaries*, Wendell Johnson, an advocate of general semantics, observes, ''To speak of space *and* time is to imply that it is possible to demonstrate something nowhere at some time, or somewhere at no time!'' (p. 214). Physics underwent a great crisis around the turn of the century, and this crisis was caused partly by physicists speaking of space and time as completely different entities. The Einsteinian revolution brought a new picture of the universe, and in the special theory of relativity it is necessary to speak of space-time, not space and time.

The unfortunate tendency to make arbitrary divisions such as mind and body can have real and undesirable consequences. Say that a man is suffering from ulcers. His physician says he has a medical problem. He is producing too much gastric juice, and the excess secretions are eating a hole in his stomach. His psychologist says he has a mental problem. He worries too much, is hyperanxious, and has to learn to relax. His physician treats him with drugs, and his psychologist treats him with psychotherapy. Perhaps the two professionals communicate little with each other; they may even be a bit hostile to each other's approach. Is the man's problem mental or physical? Is it a ''mind'' or a ''body'' problem? Obviously, the man's problem should not be divided arbitrarily into either a mental or a physical domain. He has a mind–body problem. He is a whole organism and deserves to be treated as such. Ideally, the professionals involved should have open communication with each other and work out a coordinated treatment program.

Love and hate are examples of intensional words that are divided arbitrarily. A client speaking to a counselor may say, ''Sometimes I think I love my husband madly. Then there are times I feel that I hate him. I just can't figure myself out. Do I love him or hate him?'' The problem, according to general semantics, is the attempt to make verbal categories out of a total emotional process. Love and hate do not ''exist'' outside our skins, like a table and a chair. They are at best two aspects of one internal process. Thus the client might be advised to speak of a love–hate relationship toward her husband to help her recognize the ambivalent quality of her feelings.

As you have already noted, the general semantics device for healing arbitrary verbal divisions is the hyphen. Korzybski advised that whenever possible we speak of mind-body instead of mind and body, space-time instead of space and time, love-hate instead of love and hate, and so forth.

EXTENSIONAL DEVICES

The whole thrust of general semantics is to orient the individual toward the external world as revealed by modern science. Korzybski felt that the concepts presented by twentieth-century astronomy, physics, and chemistry were the best "maps" available for the incompletely explored terrain we call reality. And what does modern science reveal? The answer is implicit in the material already presented: Modern science reveals to us a world that cannot be chopped up into static categories; it discloses a world of growth, change, and decay; it tells us that nothing is identical to anything else; and it makes us painfully aware that our knowledge is far from complete. To remind ourselves of these items, Korzybski recommended that we consciously use *extensional devices*, practical techniques designed to orient us toward the external world of our senses as opposed to the internal world of abstract ideas.

These devices have already been used and referred to in the preceding material on general semantics. They are summarized as follows:

1 *Indexes.* Apple$_1$ is not apple$_2$ is not apple$_3$, etc. Teenager$_1$ is not teenager$_2$ is not teenager$_3$, etc.

2 *Dates.* The United States$_{1930}$ is not the United States$_{1945}$ is not the United States$_{1975}$, etc. Adam$_{1960}$ is not Adam$_{1965}$ is not Adam$_{1975}$, etc.

3 *Etc. (et cetera).* Etc. is used to represent non-allness. It was used in No. 1 and No. 2 to suggest that the examples given are incomplete. It could also be used in the following manner: "Mary is a great cook, etc." This is done to suggest that Mary is not completely captured and understood by saying she is a great cook. She may also be a poor seamstress, an effective parent, a good driver, a bad golfer, a loving wife, etc.

4 *Quotation marks.* Quotation marks are used to indicate that a certain word should be qualified and does not mean precisely what it seems to mean. As an example, consider the "is" of identity. The quotation marks are placed around the word "is" to suggest nonidentity between two terms in the same sentence. "This is a delicious cheesecake," we say. Korzybski says that what we really mean is, "This cheesecake tastes delicious *to me*." It may not taste delicious to someone else. If we insist on using the "is" of identity, Korzybski suggests we at least put quotation marks around it.

5   *Hyphens.* Korzybski suggests we speak of space-time instead of space and time, mind-body, not mind and body, etc. In the opening pages of this chapter, the two questions were asked: Is man a rational animal? Or is man an irrational animal? The verbal split created by the questions was healed by the use of the hyphen: The questions were answered by saying that man is a rational-irrational animal.

It is clear that the extensive use of the extensional devices in writing or speech would be cumbersome. On the practical level, it is mainly a matter of awareness. Johnson writes:

It is simply to be understood that words are used and are to be evaluated as though they were indexed and dated, and, where necessary, quoted and hyphenated, with etcetera's *indicating non-allness wherever appropriate. Thus, with no considerable outward or obvious change in language, a tremendous change in language* structure *and in neurosemantic reactions is accomplished.* (*p. 215*)

What does Johnson mean by *neuro-semantic reactions?* He is simply speaking about our psychological-emotional responses to words and their meanings. And this goes to the heart of the general semantics viewpoint. Korzybski and his followers assert that when people use language in a reality-oriented manner, they are less likely to be at the mercy of capricious emotions. Individuals who observe general semantics guidelines thus improve their adjustment and foster their growth as persons.

RATIONAL-EMOTIVE THERAPY: EMOTIONAL SELF-CONTROL

Like general semantics, rational-emotive therapy is designed to prevent the suffering produced by unnecessary emotional reactions. The elimination of excessive guilt, anger, and anxiety is the goal of rational-emotive therapy. Although the term *therapy* is used as a convention, the father of rational-emotive therapy, New York psychologist Albert Ellis, notes that he would prefer a less loaded term, such as *emotional education,* for his system. It is clear from his writings that Ellis conceives of rational-emotive therapy as having broad general applicability to the problems of life. Rational-emotive therapy is a more recent discipline than general semantics. In *Humanistic Psychotherapy: The Rational-Emotive Approach,* Ellis acknowledges the relationship of rational-emotive therapy to general semantics:

RET [rational-emotive therapy], like the science of psychology itself and like the discipline of general semantics, as set forth by Alfred Korzybski, particularly teaches the client how to discriminate more clearly between sense and nonsense, fiction and reality, superstition and science. (p. 63)

IRRATIONAL IDEAS

Ellis contends that excessive guilt, anger, and anxiety are the result of various irrational beliefs. These irrational beliefs are *consciously held* by a person, and he makes himself sick by repeating the ideas over and over again to himself. Thus one factor in emotional illness is the pattern of *self-indoctrination* with false notions. Rational-emotive therapists are *not* passive when they work with clients. They are active, and they aggressively attack unrealistic notions when they hear them.

Ellis believes that human beings suffer largely because they confuse *desires* with *needs.* People say, "I have to have a new dress," "I need to go on a vacation," "I've just got to have a date with Jill," "I just can't live another minute without a drink," and so on. They make their wishes into demands, and they feel miserable if they cannot make their wishes come true. Ellis contends that it is an irrational idea to think that wishes *must* come true or life will not be worth living.

The Ellis theory of human suffering revolves around man's cognitive capacities. People think, they have conscious ideas, and it is these con-

Ellis asserts that human beings often suffer because they confuse desires with needs.

scious ideas that lead to emotional reactions. That is why rational-emotive therapy is sometimes designated as a *cognitive-emotional system,* a system in which thoughts lead to feelings. Say that a young woman thinks to herself, "I just won't be able to endure it if Bill ever leaves me." Suppose that her relationship with Bill is somehow terminated. If she really believes that she must have Bill to endure existence, she will be plunged into depression. Ellis contends that her extreme unhappiness in the present is produced by her earlier unrealistic assumption that life without Bill would not be worth living. The termination of a relationship could, of course, be the occasion for some sadness; but it is seldom "the end of the world" that some people make it into. There is a distinction between being merely unhappy and being desperately unhappy. Mere unhappiness is rational; desperate unhappiness is more often than not irrational.

According to Ellis, people who suffer from chronic negative emotional states do a lot of *catastrophic thinking.* They are like Chicken Little. An acorn hit him on the head and he declared, "The sky is falling!" Similarly, the anxiety-prone person sees an odd discoloration on his skin and thinks, "I've got cancer!" Or he hears a squeak from the wheel while he is driving and thinks, "The car is falling apart!" Or he fails an examination and thinks, "I'll never graduate from college!" The basis of catastrophic thinking is the logical error of *overgeneralizing*, making a single instance of a phenomenon serve as the predictor for a whole set of phenomena. The anxiety-prone person needs to be reminded of the proverb, "One swallow doesn't make a summer." To overgeneralize is to make a blunder in one's thinking, and Ellis asserts that we should make a conscious effort to avoid such blunders.

Another emphasis of rational-emotive therapy is on *long-range hedonism.* Ellis has no argument with a basically hedonistic attitude toward life, the view that pleasure is good and that it is an important end in itself. He contends, however, that much suffering is the result of short-range hedonism—living mainly for immediate gratification. Say that someone drinks too much tonight. When a companion tries to stop him, he declares, "Live today, for tomorrow we may die!" The next day he has a terrible hangover and regrets the indiscretion of the previous night. As the psychologist O. Hobart Mowrer aptly commented, "The trouble with the live today for tomorrow we may die philosophy is that we usually don't die tomorrow!" The rational-emotive philosophy teaches that one should attempt to maximize one's *total* happiness, not just the pleasure of the moment.

In *Humanistic Psychotherapy*, Ellis summarizes the cardinal irrational ideas that lie behind extreme emotional reactions as follows:

1   The idea that it is a dire necessity for an adult human to be loved or approved by virtually every significant other person in his life.

2   The idea that one should be thoroughly competent, adequate, and achieving in all possible respects to consider oneself worthwhile.

3   The idea that certain people are bad, wicked, or villainous and that they should be severely blamed and punished for their villainy.

4   The idea that it is awful and catastrophic when things are not the way one would like them to be.

5   The idea that human unhappiness is externally caused and that people have little or no ability to control their errors and disturbances.

6   The idea that it is easier to avoid than to face life's difficulties and self-responsibilities.

7   The idea that one's past history is an all-important determiner of one's present behavior and that because something once strongly affected one's life, it should indefinitely affect it. (p. 37)

It is evident that the rational-emotive approach has much in common with the doctrine of stoicism as taught by the Greek philosopher Zeno. The Stoics believed that a wise person should be guided by reason and should train himself to be detached from pleasure and pain. Ellis concedes his debt to the Stoics and views the current rational-emotive conceptions as systematic elaborations of Zeno's basic insights. Ellis, however, does not seem to be as extreme as the Stoics. They taught indifference to all emotions; Ellis, instead, teaches indifference to destructive emotions that arise from irrational ideas.

ABCs OF EMOTIONAL SELF-CONTROL

Ellis believes that emotional self-control is possible, that a person need not be the slave of capricious inner storms. Perhaps the term *emotional freedom* would in some ways be preferable to the more familiar term *emotional self-control*; Ellis's idea is to help people find freedom from the constraints of excessive and unnecessary emotions. Toward this end, Ellis proposes a systematic approach called the ABCs of rational-emotive therapy. The ABCs are a convenient device for remembering the basic outlines of the system.

Point A.   Ellis says that at point A there is some *event* that starts an emotion-producing change. This event actually takes place; it is in the real world. For convenience, this event can be called "activity," "action," or "agent." Numerous examples can be given: A person has a fight with his spouse, fails a test, loses a job, is kept waiting by a friend, is disappointed by a child's choice of career, is disappointed by a child's choice of spouse, and so forth. Any one of the examples can be the real-world agent that presses the starter button for one's emotion-generating motor.

Point B. At point B, the person has a *belief* about the activity, action, or agent. If the person has a *rational* belief, there is no problem. For example, a person may think, "It is irritating that Mary and I had to fight this morning," or, "It is annoying that Jim wants to become an accountant instead of a dentist." These are rational thoughts; they reflect an appropriate orientation to reality. Life's disappointments and frustrations should be accepted as irritating, annoying, and so forth.

But the person who is controlled by emotions tends to escalate his belief system beyond the realistic level. Thus at Point B he has an *irrational* belief. He thinks, "It is awful that Mary and I had to fight this morning," or, "It is a catastrophe that Jim wants to become an accountant instead of the wonderful dentist I always dreamed he would become." Ellis argues that an irrational belief cannot be sustained by the facts of life. Such beliefs refer to events that are seldom awful or catastrophic, but merely inconvenient.

Point C. Point C represents the *consequence* of a belief. If the belief is rational, the consequence will be an emotion that is appropriate to the situation. If the belief is irrational, however, the emotion will be something such as excessive guilt, anxiety, depression, or anger. A person who makes a habit out of thinking in terms of irrational beliefs tends to be prone to feelings of self-pity and psychosomatic reactions, such as ulcers and high blood pressure. He is highly defensive and has a great deal of difficulty in seeing his own mistakes. Ellis says:

And he generally experiences what we call "disturbed," "neurotic," or "over-reactive" symptoms. His actions and feelings at Point C are inappropriate *to the situation that is occurring or may occur at Point B, because they are based on magical demands regarding the way he and the universe presumably ought to be. (p. 58)*

Point D. To points A, B, and C, Ellis adds a point D. This is a point that is not usually added by the typical person. Most of us accept our emotional states uncritically. The feeling at point C is one that we deem to be legitimate simply because it is ours. Ellis vigorously attacks the view that all emotions are legitimate. Point D stands for *dispute*, and Ellis contends that the key to emotional education resides in the capacity to energetically challenge the irrational beliefs of point B. Thus a person can ask himself, "Why is it awful that Mary and I had to fight this morning?" There is some likelihood that he will answer himself, "Well, it's not really awful. It's irritating, and it will upset my day for a few hours, but I'm sure to get over it soon enough." Or a parent may ask himself,

"Why is it a catastrophe that Jim wants to become an accountant instead of a dentist?" A realistic attempt to answer the question may produce these sorts of thoughts: "It's not a catastrophe." "I won't starve. He won't starve." "He's still affectionate toward me." "I've been placing all my emotional chips in one bowl and that's nonsense." "I still think it's annoying that he won't take my advice. But it is hardly a catastrophe."

The vigorous dispute of irrational beliefs at point D is not designed to replace negative emotional states with bliss. The goal is more limited: The idea is to bring the emotions into balance, to make them appropriate to one's life circumstances. Ellis understands that human beings will have emotional reactions. He only argues that the level of emotional response should be graded to fit the facts of existence. The emotional slave is hyperemotional. The Ellis ABC system is designed to introduce a corrective element into the domain of human feeling.

Ellis has written a number of books for the layman. In one of these, *A Guide to Rational Living*, Ellis and his coauthor Robert A. Harper give the following advice:

Combat the idea that it is terrible, horrible, and catastrophic when things are not going the way you would like them to go. When conditions are not the way you would prefer them to be, calmly and determinedly try to change them for the better; and when, for the moment, they cannot be changed, the only sane thing to do is quietly to accept them (and wait and plan for the time when they finally can be changed). The greater your loss or frustration is, the more philosophic you must be in regard to it; the more you must accept the fact that it is bad and undesirable—but not *catastrophic or unbearable. (p. 186)*

This quotation contains the essence of the ABC system for emotional self-control.

SELF-ESTEEM AND PERFECTIONISM

One of the important themes in the rational-emotive approach is the teaching that many people suffer needlessly because they expect too much of themselves. You will recall that one of the cardinal irrational ideas residing behind extreme emotional reactions is this one: The idea that one should be thoroughly competent, adequate, and achieving in all possible respects to consider oneself worthwhile. Ellis contends that a person who holds this idea or some version of it is bound to experience low self-esteem *no matter what his objective accomplishments in life.* From the point of view of his family or friends, he may be quite successful. From his own point of view, he has not lived up to his possibilities. His internal standards are simply too high—so high that they are unrealistic; and when he fails to reach his own high standards, he must pay the price in the way of low self-esteem. Ellis thus attacks perfectionism about the self; living one's life by a doctrine of perfectionism is just one more irrational idea to Ellis. It is an idea that does not fit with reality. Any objective analysis of human existence reveals that people are not perfect.

Growth Through Reason, a book edited by Ellis, contains verbatim cases in rational-emotive therapy. One of the case presentations consists of a dialogue between Martha, a twenty-three-year-old girl, and Ellis. Martha has a number of personal problems. One of them is that she is extremely self-punishing. Ellis quickly traces this to her perfectionistic view about how well she *should* do. The following exchange reveals how the rational-emotive therapist assertively disputes an irrational idea held by a client.

Martha. Well, this is the way it was in school, if I didn't do well in one particular thing, or even on a particular test—and little crises that came up—if I didn't do as well as I had wanted to do.

Ellis. Right. You beat yourself over the head.

Martha. Yes.

Ellis. But why? What's the point? Are you supposed to be perfect? Why the hell shouldn't human beings make mistakes, be imperfect?

Martha. Maybe you always expect yourself to be perfect.

Ellis. Yes. But is that *sane*?

Martha. No.

Ellis. Why do it? Why not give up that unrealistic expectation?

Martha. But then I can't accept myself.

Ellis. But you're saying, "It's shameful to make mistakes." *Why* is it shameful? Why can't you go to somebody else when you make a mistake and say, "Yes, I made a mistake"? Why is that so awful? (pp. 247–248)

Ellis takes the position that human beings have intrinsic value to themselves just because they exist and for no other reason. From the inner point of view, aliveness equals worthiness. There is no answer to the question, "What am I worth?" Ellis notes that the tendency of most persons to rate themselves in terms of deeds or acts works only if a person is performing well. But in time one may become less praiseworthy. For example, most of us grow older and eventually less competent. What then? Do we become progressively less worthwhile? The answer is yes if we rate our internal existence in terms of external capacities. The answer is no if we rate ourselves as worthwhile independent of external capacities. Ellis would say that if you must rate anything, rate behavior—not the internal self. It is rational to think, "I failed the test. I'm going to study harder for the next one." It is irrational to think, "I failed the test. I'm a jerk." The first way of thinking is problem oriented and will lead to practical solutions. The second way of thinking is blame oriented and will lead to feelings of worthlessness.

Briefly, Ellis contends that there is rational thinking and there is irrational thinking. He also contends that thinking and feeling are closely linked. Thus irrational thinking leads to such unwarranted emotional states as excessive anger, anxiety, or depression. It is important to note that Ellis contends that we hold our irrational beliefs at a *conscious* level. Unlike the depth psychologists, Ellis does not look for the source of personal distress in unconscious repressed ideas. Ellis finds a sufficient number of personal problems being manufactured out of consciously held irrational beliefs. Thus he encourages people to fight fire with fire, to attack the irrational conscious beliefs with the primary tool at their disposal: Conscious *rational* beliefs. It is asserted that rational thinking frees one from the bonds of negative emotions and helps one become more self-accepting.

REALITY THERAPY: BECOMING A RESPONSIBLE PERSON

The father of reality therapy is William Glasser, a California-based psychiatrist. Early in his career he became disenchanted with the treatment of clients by classical Freudian methods and began developing a treatment approach based on other tenets. His innovations have become reality therapy. Reality therapy has been used in a variety of settings, including institutions for the treatment of disturbed adolescents, mental hospitals, and private practice. It is clear from Glasser's writings that he sees reality therapy as not only a system of treatment, but as a practical set of guidelines for living. In an article coauthored by fellow psychiatrist and reality therapist Leonard M. Zunin, the following observations are made:

> . . . *Reality Therapy is applied not only to the problems of people who are extremely irresponsible and incompetent, but also . . . it can be applied to daily living. It is not a therapy exclusively for the "mentally ill," incompetent, disturbed, or emotionally upset; it is a system of ideas which can help anyone learn to gain successful identity and to help others to do so. Reality Therapy is readily understandable and it may be applied to anyone who understands these principles without prolonged, specific training other than the application of effort, sensitivity, and common sense. (p. 292)*

Reality therapy is included in this chapter on rational analysis because, like general semantics and rational-emotive therapy, it emphasizes clear thinking and the long-run aspects of behavior. The foreword to Glasser's book *Reality Therapy* was written by O. Hobart Mowrer. In that foreword, he suggests that an action can be called "unrealistic" if it gives temporary satisfaction, but a substantial amount of ultimate pain and suffering. On the other hand, an action can be called "realistic" if it yields ultimate satisfaction, even if there is some immediate work or inconvenience required. Mowrer observes, "In the final analysis, it is the capacity to choose wisely between these two types of behavior that we call *reason*" (p. xviii). Thus we see at the outset that reality therapy places a heavy burden on the faculty of reason, the potential capacity of human beings to lead a life of intelligent action.

BASIC ASSUMPTIONS

The central assumption of reality therapy is that *one can have a rewarding life only by living a responsible life*. The essence of responsibility, and of facing reality, is finding effective ways to meet our psychological needs. Glasser specifies two basic psychological needs:

The central assumption of reality therapy is that one can have a rewarding life only by living a responsible life.

1   The need to love and be loved.

2   The need to feel that we are worthwhile to ourselves and others. (p. 9)

It is important to comprehend that Glasser's concept of responsibility includes responsibility to oneself. Glasser feels that irresponsibility, either to oneself or someone else, is the common thread running through all behavioral problems.

In addition to the central assumption concerning responsibility, reality therapy makes a set of corollary assumptions.

1   Reality therapy rejects the value of traditional psychiatric categories such as neurosis, psychosis, and character disorders. These tend to categorize and stereotype people and lead away from understanding the person and his problems. The problem is "explained" by the label; human difficulties are "understood" in terms of word magic instead of processes. To Glasser, the conventional clinical pigeonholes are only descriptions of various forms of irresponsibility—nothing more.

2   The term *mental health* is itself of dubious value because it tends to suggest that there is something organically "wrong" with troubled persons. Glasser, as a physician, notes that a tiny fraction of so-called mental disturbances may be caused by known biochemical disorders or brain damage. He feels, however, that in the majority of cases it would be better to substitute *responsible* for "mental health" and *irresponsible* for "mental illness."

3   The present and the future are more important than the past. Reality therapy rejects the emphasis of classical psychoanalysis on examining a person's past history. Instead,.the philosophy of reality therapy asserts that the important thing in therapy or in daily living is to focus one's attention on the here and the now and where the immediate circumstances of one's existence are leading. If anything is to be analyzed, it is the relationship of the person to his life situation, not to the meaning of events in the past. Thus we may characterize reality therapy as *present/future-oriented* in contrast to *past-oriented.*

4   Insight into unconscious motives is not essential for change. There is greater stress in reality therapy on conscious problems than on unconscious conflicts. One of the pet peeves of the reality therapist is the tendency of people to refer to unconscious motives as excuses for irresponsible behavior. For example, a young man may say, "I guess I just have a lot of repressed hostility toward my father. Maybe that's why I can't turn in assignments on time. Unconsciously, when I reject Professor Smith I also reject my father." Glasser says that this kind of "insight" may be interesting, but it unfortunately makes allowances for irresponsible behavior. The reality therapist insists that behavioral change can *precede* insight. A person can decide consciously to act responsibly because it is in his best interest. Later, as a more effective person, he may reflect and understand why he once acted in an irresponsible manner. Within this framework, insight into unconscious motives is perceived as a kind of psychological excess baggage not having a great deal of importance.

5 Values and moral principles are important in daily living. Reality therapy holds that it is appropriate to think in terms of right and wrong. When people cannot fulfill their needs, their behavior is "wrong." One's task is to confront one's total behavior and *judge for oneself* the quality of one's life. Glasser notes that his approach to morality might not stand the test of scholarly debate with the great moral philosophers of the world; but he feels his approach is practical. He observes:

We believe that almost all behavior which leads to fulfilling our needs within the bounds of reality is right, or good, or moral behavior, according to the following definition: When a man acts in such a way that he gives and receives love, and feels worthwhile to himself and others, his behavior is right or moral. *(p. 57)*

This is why people must do the "right" thing, why they must conform with their own internal standards. It is the way in which a person feels worthwhile.

6 We grow as persons by setting up definite plans and following through with the plans. Of course, a plan is not supposed to be a straitjacket, and some flexibility should be built into the plan. But people need goals, they need something to work for. People without plans just drift, flounder about, and become demoralized. Mowrer, commenting on this aspect of reality therapy, makes an interesting point in his foreword to *Reality Therapy*. He distinguishes between *tragedy* and *folly*. Irresponsible persons are fond of saying such things as, "I knew a guy who went to school for years, never had any fun, was waiting to get married, and then he got killed in an auto accident. What was the point? He should have lived when he had the chance!" Mowrer says that such comments point to the potential of tragedy in human existence. But what is the alternative? If one lives only for the present, and if one continues to live, the individual will experience a substantial amount of long-term suffering.

FACING REALITY

Glasser contends that it is essential for us to face reality. It is the only way we can meet our basic psychological needs, our needs for love and a sense of worth. Every chronically unhappy person suffers from the same basic lack: the inability to satisfy his fundamental needs. Glasser notes that all troubled and troublesome persons deny the reality of the world around them:

Some break the law, denying the rules of society; some claim their neighbors are plotting against them, denying the improbability of such behavior. Some are afraid of crowded places, close quarters, airplanes, or elevators, yet they freely admit the irrationality of their fears. Millions drink to blot out the inadequacy they feel but that need not exist if they could learn to be different; and far too many people choose suicide rather than face the reality that they could solve their problems by more responsible behavior. (p. 6)

You can see from the preceding quotation that Glasser places the responsibility squarely on the individual's shoulders. This may seem harsh. A person may say, "But my mother screamed at me when I was a child, always put me down. That's why I have such a bad self-image. I keep thinking I'm a dumb kid who can't do anything right." Glasser has little patience with such statements. He feels that looking backward can supply a sufferer with endless fuel to keep the engine of irresponsibility turning. Recall that reality therapy is present/future-oriented. The reality therapist says, "You have a brain. You can learn. Put the past behind you and *decide now* to lead a responsible life."

To illustrate how the principles of reality therapy can operate in the case of a particular person, let me briefly relate the story of Dee, one of Glasser's clients. Dee was twenty-five years of age, the mother of two illegitimate children. The children had been given up for adoption, and Dee had also had more than one abortion. She was promiscuous, a sexual pushover who couldn't say no to men. When she came to Glasser, she was living with a man for whom she had little real affection. Dee had a number of positive qualities. She was intelligent, interested in education, and had a warm feeling for people. However, Glasser notes, all of this was obscured by chronic irresponsible behavior.

Glasser saw Dee for about one year. The two of them battled steadily. Dee tried to prove to Glasser that any change in her way of life was impossible. Glasser confronted her with the idea that she had a choice, a *real* choice. It was up to her to decide if she wanted to go on with her old ways or take a new path. Essentially, Glasser helped Dee to see that there was no real payoff in giving into the impulse and/or pleasure of the moment. The payoffs worth talking about all resided in forgoing some of the fun of the present and making some plans for the future. One of the things Glasser helped Dee to see was that she could not meet her need for love through promiscuous sex; such behavior was destroying Dee's hope of ever feeling worthwhile.

Dee eventually went on to finish high school and junior college. She entered the University of California on a scholarship and was preparing to teach in a junior college at the time Glasser wrote about her in *Reality Therapy*. By becoming responsible to herself, Dee was able to turn her life around and discover deeper satisfactions.

IDENTITY

In recent years, Glasser has been stressing the importance of the concept of *identity*, which has different meanings to different theorists. Generally, it has to do with the self, with having a sense of continuity as a person, and with one's social roles. Within the context of reality therapy, the stress seems to be on one's sense of independent selfhood and on social roles. In the article by Glasser and Zunin, identity is defined as a need. They say it is "the need to feel that we are somehow separate and distinct from every other living being on the face of the earth; that no matter where we go we will not find another person who thinks, looks, acts, and talks exactly as we do." They then note that it is not enough to be a distinct identity, but that people seek to have meaning associated with their identity. In other words, they yearn to take their rightful place in society; they seek a relationship with other people.

Glasser feels that the United States has undergone significant social changes in the past twenty or thirty years. We used to be a *survival society*, a society that was fighting to "make it." Such a society produced individuals who were *goal oriented*. They strived to have successful businesses, successful careers. Life was perceived in terms of competitive struggle. With affluence, we have become an *identity society*, a society in which people seek to "find themselves." Such a society produces individuals who are *role oriented*. They need a sensible answer to the question "Who am I?" before they can make a commitment to the pursuit of goals. In his book *The Identity Society*, Glasser observes:

The institutions of our society still operate as if goal took precedence over role. Common examples are our schools, our prisons, and our families. Much parent-child conflict stems from parents' attempts to rear their children the goal-before-role way they were reared. (p. 10)

As a person tries to work through his struggle for an identity within the context of modern society, he tends to form a polarized concept of self. He forms either a *success identity* or a *failure identity*. A person having a success identity feels that he will achieve his goals; thus he is capable of making plans and looking forward to the future. A person having a

With affluence, Glasser says, we have become an identity society, a society in which people seek to "find themselves."

failure identity feels that he cannot achieve his goals, that he is going nowhere. Thus he is incapable of making plans and feels apathetic about the future.

At this point, we can tie in Glasser's concept of responsibility with the concept of identity. To Glasser, individuals are *responsible for themselves*. They can choose their identity. They can decide to become the person they want to be. In spite of society, in spite of changing times, in spite of unfeeling parents, the choice is still within the person. Glasser recognizes that there are many external forces operating to shape a person's self-image. But the person can take a stance against adverse conditions. He does not have to succumb to psychological oppression. This does not mean that a person with a failure identity can say, "Now I have a success identity." He won't have a success identity just because he says he has one. On the contrary, the person can decide that he wants to give up his failure identity and *work toward* a success identity. As noted earlier, he does this by starting to live up to his own standards of conduct by a series of small psychological successes, by changing the *pattern* of his behavior. The success identity will grow out of the *real successes*, small and large, that a person experiences in daily living.

Lest all of this sound much too abstract, let us give at least one practical application. Assume that John had trouble with math in grammar school and junior high school. In high school, he avoided college prep math courses, settling for "bonehead" and review-type courses. When he thinks of doing math, he has a "can't do it" mentality. In this one dimension of his identity, he has a failure identity. He now arrives at college, wants to major in sociology, and finds out to his dismay that his college requires a course in statistics for sociology majors. He now has a choice. He can decide to change his major to a less desirable one to avoid the statistics course, but such a decision will only reinforce his failure identity; in Glasser's terms, John is not being responsible to himself because he really wants to major in sociology. Or John can decide to take the statistics course, thinking, "I'll make it somehow. I'll study twice as hard as other students. I'll get someone to tutor me. I'll even take it twice if I have to." The odds are high that he will pass the course. He may discover, somewhat to his surprise, that he is no longer the child who can't do it. A successful experience with the statistics course will contribute to the formation of John's success identity. In brief, to form a success identity, people have to decide to meet certain challenges directly.

In summary, reality therapy says that to meet the need for love and the need for a sense of worth, we must (1) face reality and (2) be responsible. These are the keys to forming a success identity.

CRITIQUE

On the whole, the approach to living called rational analysis appeals to common sense. It is difficult to take issue with the basic point that clear thinking is of value in making decisions and in formulating plans. The guidelines presented by the thinkers discussed in this chapter are certainly of substantial practical value. Nonetheless, it is possible to take issue with certain general assumptions and specific conclusions made by Korzybski, Ellis, and Glasser.

1 Two of the major forces in modern psychology, psychoanalysis and behaviorism, tend to downplay the significance of rational analysis. As you already know, psychoanalysis stresses the importance of unconscious motives. It sees the power of consciousness as weak when up against the forces of unconsciousness. Behaviorism, of course, gives no credence at all on a formal level to the importance of conscious thought and the use of enlightened reason. The behaviorist sees reason as a poor weapon against entrenched conditioned reflexes and habits. To the extent that a psychoanalyst or a "soft" behaviorist might allow for the importance of reason, it would be only as an *indirect agent* of change, not as a direct agent. In other words, reason can be used as a "thin entering wedge" that sets about to upset the apple cart of unconscious motives or old habits. But it can seldom be used successfully in head-to-head confrontation with the profound processes of motivation or learning. The advocate of rational analysis, on the other hand, seems to suggest that reason can sometimes be used like a hot knife, cutting as if through butter the resistance offered by irrational wishes and undesirable habits.

2 In some ways general semantics seems to perpetuate the very either-or thinking it deplores. Korzybski sets up two-valued categories such as *sane* and *unsane, aristotelian* and *non-aristotelian.* This is peculiar in that general semantics is supposed to be a multivalued system of thought.

3 Perhaps Korzybski is too hard on ordinary language. He would almost seem to suggest that our conventional vocabulary has no extensional devices built into it. But it can be contended that a number of reality-orienting arrows are built into orthodox grammar. For example, adjectives are often used to indicate gradients as opposed to dichotomies. We do not use only the two-fold classes *tall* and *short.* We speak of people as being very tall, medium tall, extremely short, and so forth. The very word *gradient* is itself a part of ordinary English, thus suggesting the common recognition that not all events and things present themselves as dualities. Perhaps the *use* of ordinary language should be criticized, not ordinary language itself.

4 General semantics contends that modern science presents the best map to reality. This is an assumption and one that would not be acceptable to some thinkers. The assumption is based on the philosophy of empiricism, the doctrine that we can only know about reality through our sense organs. It is contended by some that there is a power of intuition or an inner vision that reveals reality directly to a human being and that this view of reality is much more correct than the one grasped indirectly through the sense organs. This point of view has a long tradition, going back in the West to the writings of Plato. It continues as a potent force in transpersonal psychology, Eastern wisdom, and mysticism.

5 The link between thinking as a cause and emotions as an effect is not as well established as general semantics and rational-emotive therapy would suggest. There is a relationship, of course. The history of laboratory experiments on emotion supports a number of theories of emotion, and the role of thought in reference to emotion is not completely clear. We could just as well say that emotion is a cause of thought as say that thought is the cause of emotion. We could also say, as the James-Lange theory proposes, that actions cause feelings. The most accurate statement would seem to be that thoughts, actions, and feelings all interact in a complex relationship in which no one element can consistently be identified as cause and another as effect. This does not discredit the contentions of general semantics and rational-emotive therapy, but it does dampen a bit any tendency to unreservedly accept reason as the absolute king of the psychological jungle.

6   Rational-emotive therapy and reality therapy have an important point of disagreement. Rational-emotive therapy teaches that self-evaluation is unnecessary, that we do not have to judge our inner being on the basis of accomplishments measured against social standards. We are worth something to ourselves merely because we exist. The tendency toward self-evaluation is learned, and it can be unlearned. Reality therapy, on the other hand, argues that the royal road to self-esteem is discovered by setting standards and living up to them. It is inevitable that we will judge ourselves. Thus it is essential that we be at least responsible to our own values. It is not easy to reconcile these two points of view. They seem to be based on entirely different assumptions. Rational-emotive therapy looks on self-evaluation as a learned tendency, a part of the socialization process. Reality therapy seems to suggest that self-evaluation is an innate tendency, an inborn process that is part of all of us. I will not attempt a glib reconciliation of the two points of view. It is an issue you may prefer to think through for yourself.

7   Reality therapy makes a single concept, the concept of responsibility, do too much work. If a person is responsible, he will enjoy mental health and a sense of self-worth. Glasser goes so far as to equate mental illness with irresponsibility. This may be going a bit too far. So much is explained by pinning all of the person's behavior on the responsibility-irresponsibility dimension that nothing is explained. What is the source of the person's capacity for responsibility? Orthodox psychology would point to a person's learning history, his family experiences, his social opportunities, and so forth. Glasser seems to brush all this aside, making the person the prime cause of his own behavior. Even if we accept the doctrine that it is a cop-out to blame parents, unconscious motives, or whatever else for one's problems, it is probably going too far to totally dispense with environmental factors as having relevance for explaining behavior. Skinner, for example, would probably say that irresponsibility is just one more mentalism. For Skinner, the ultimate sources from which behavior springs are to be found in the environment—not within the skin of the individual. If we wish to adopt ideas from both behavioristic psychology and reality therapy, we may adopt the rather complex model that persons have *partial responsibility* for their actions. If you feel that there is some truth in both orientations, you are stuck with having to live with a paradoxical model of human nature.

8   Reality therapy seems to be defective in spelling out specific strategies by which a person can become more responsible. The reality therapist says (1) face reality and (2) act in a responsible way. Presented at this level, however, these are not much better than moral sermons. The *how* needs development in reality therapy.

9   General semantics, rational-emotive therapy, and reality therapy are deficient in making systematic evaluations of their claims. You will find little well-designed research using experimental and control groups. Instead, the main method of evaluation is more often than not the informal —and biased—observations of advocates of the particular methods. This particular criticism can, of course, be leveled at other approaches (e.g., psychoanalysis and humanistic psychology). The criticism is particularly telling in the case of rational analysis, however, precisely because so much stress is placed on the importance of reason. You would think that men who stress rational analysis would want to apply the same methods of evaluation to the worth of their own work that they recommend you apply to daily living. But this is not so.

In spite of some of the difficulties noted, rational analysis holds together fairly well. As one reads the writings of Korzybski, Ellis, Glasser, or their followers, one receives the strong impression that these are thoughtful men of goodwill. As already noted, most of their ideas make a strong appeal to common sense.

IMPLICATIONS FOR ADJUSTMENT AND GROWTH
What can we draw of practical value from rational analysis? What are its implications for our personal lives? The following are several possibilities.

1   One of the values of rational analysis is that it calls attention to the *thinking process.* It reminds us that we are conscious beings and that consciousness is more than a passive element in existence. It is a tool with which we may mold our lives. (The same point is made in different ways by existential-humanistic psychology, discussed in Chapter seven.) On the gateway to Scripps College in Claremont, California, is the following inscription by Ellen Browning Scripps:

The paramount obligation of a college is to develop in its students the ability to think clearly and independently, and the ability to live confidently, courageously, and hopefully.

This statement beautifully summarizes the faith of those who see the individual as capable of adjusting and growing through the exercise of reason.

2   One of the services of general semantics is that it makes us less cocky, it reduces human arrogance. By telling us that the map is not the territory, by saying that the ideas in our heads are not identical with external reality, it makes us a bit more humble. The arrogant person, the bigot, and the person with a closed mind think that they are absolutely right. The person familiar with general semantics can hardly be so naive. (Korzybski's distinction between the map and the territory, between ideas and external reality, is of course not completely unique. Few "modern" ideas are entirely orignial. Korzybski is indebted to classical philosophers such as Plato and Kant as a source of inspiration for the distinction between ideas about things and things-in-themselves.)

3 Of particular practical value are the recommendations and strategies suggested by general semantics and rational-emotive therapy for modifying emotional reactions. Millions of sufferers from emotionally induced illnesses might be able to get at least some partial relief from their afflictions if they could learn and apply principles espoused by Korzybski and Ellis.

4 The focus of both rational-emotive therapy and reality therapy on long-run hedonism would seem to be a matter of substantial importance. The distinction between tragedy and folly is worth remembering. Prudent persons may be unfortunate enough to not collect their just reward for planning ahead and deferring gratification. But imprudent persons are almost certain to suffer the consequences of their impulsivity and inability to wait for their pleasures. The mark of the child and the immature person is the cry, "I want it *now*!"

5 Self-esteem is important. We want to feel that we are worth something as human beings. Both rational-emotive therapy and reality therapy provide ideas that are intended to be useful in maintaining and enhancing our sense of value. As already noted, we do not want to gloss over the differences in the ways rational-emotive therapy and reality therapy approach the subject of self-esteem. But it would seem reasonable, given wide individual differences in people, that some of us might be able to take advantage of one approach and others of us might be able to take advantage of the alternate approach. Both avenues provide "food for thought," thus stimulating our own thinking processes.

There are those who mistrust reason. The famous *Rubáiyát* of Omar Khayyám, twelfth-century Persian poet and astronomer, proclaimed the importance of extracting as much joy as possible from the present moment. In the following quotation from Edward Fitzgerald's translation of the *Rubáiyát* into English, a direct attack is made on reason:

You know, my friends, with
what a brave carouse

I made a second marriage in
my house;
Divorced old barren reason
from my bed.
And took the daughter of the
vine to spouse.

The "daughter of the vine" is wine and is meant to symbolize joyful living—eating, drinking, merrymaking, and lovemaking. Khayyám prefers this to "old barren reason."

By way of contrast, let us consider the view of Kahlil Gibran, a Lebanese poet. Writing in the twentieth century, Gibran had this to say about reason:

When Reason speaks to you, hearken to what she says, and you shall be saved.
Make good use of her utterances, and you shall be as one armed. For the Lord
has given you no better guide than Reason, no stronger arm than Reason. When
Reason speaks to your inmost self, you are proof against Desire. For Reason
is a prudent minister, a loyal guide, and a wise counsellor. Reason is light in
darkness, as anger is darkness amidst light. Be wise—let Reason, not Impulse,
be your guide. (p. 53)

We do not have to make a stark choice between living by desire and living by reason. It is possible to make compromises, to extract some joy from the present while at the same time planning ahead. This seems to be the course recommended by the advocates of reason.

SUMMARY AND SELF-TEST

1 The social psychologist Elliot Aronson said that man is a rational animal, but not a rationalizing animal.
T   F

2 A child's thinking is stimulus-bound when he makes his evaluations on the basis of one and only one outstanding aspect of a stimulus situation.
T   F

3 During the stage of formal operations, a person is incapable of forming concepts at a high level of abstraction.
T   F

4 The phrase "the map is not the territory" was used frequently by Korzybski to indicate that the human nervous system is not external reality.
T   F

5 Korzybski said that there is no such problem as the "is" of identity.
T   F

6 General semantics suggests that the effects of word meanings are limited to conscious awareness; they do not have generalizing effects on human emotions.
T   F

7 Korzybski contended that most of us are "unsane," suggesting that our thinking tends to have a poor fit with reality as revealed by modern science.
T   F

8 One of the basic errors in thinking noted by Korzybski was two-valued logic.
T   F

9 General semantics says that it is appropriate to treat members of a category as identities.
T   F

10   Extensional devices are practical techniques designed to orient us toward the external world of our senses as opposed to the internal world of abstract ideas.

T   **F**

11   Unlike general semantics, rational-emotive therapy is designed to prevent the suffering produced by organic lesions.

T   **F**

12   According to Ellis, one factor in emotional illness is a pattern of self-indoctrination with false notions.

T   **F**

13   Ellis asserts that thoughts often lead to feelings.

T   **F**

14   Ellis notes that people who suffer from chronic negative emotional states do a lot of catastrophic thinking.

T   **F**

15   An important emphasis of rational-emotive therapy is the value it places on long-range hedonism.

T   **F**

16   Ellis asserts that it is easier and more constructive to avoid than to face life's difficulties and self-responsibilities.

T   **F**

17   The Ellis ABC system of emotional self-control requires that the person never dispute his own ideas.

T   **F**

18   The rational-emotive approach contends that many people suffer needlessly because they expect too much of themselves.

T   **F**

19   Glasser believes strongly in the value of treating clients by classical Freudian methods.

T   **F**

20   The central assumption of reality therapy is that one can have a rewarding life only by living a responsible life.

T   **F**

21   Glasser says that the need to love and be loved is not a basic psychological need.

T   **F**

22 An important assumption of reality therapy is that the past is more important than the present in determining behavior.

T   F

23 Glasser feels that the term *mental health* is of great value because it suggests that there is something organically wrong with troubled persons.

T   F

24 Glasser asserts that values and moral principles are important in daily living.

T   F

25 According to Glasser, a survival society is role-oriented.

T   F

ANSWER KEY

1 *False.* The social psychologist Elliot Aronson said that although man likes to think of himself as a rational animal, it is more true that man is a rationalizing animal.

2 *True.* A child's thinking is stimulus-bound when he makes his evaluations on the basis of one and only one outstanding aspect of a stimulus situation.

3 *False.* During the stage of formal operations, a person becomes capable of forming concepts at a high level of abstraction.

4 *True.* The phrase "the map is not the territory" was used frequently by Korzybski to indicate that the human nervous system is not external reality.

5 *False.* Korzybski said that the "is" of identity sets up confusions in the human nervous system.

6 *False.* General semantics suggests that the effects of word meanings are not limited to conscious awareness; they have generalizing, or "spreading," effects on human emotions.

7 *True.* Korzybski contended that most of us are "unsane," suggesting that our thinking tends to have a poor fit with reality as revealed by modern science.

8 *True.* One of the basic errors in thinking noted by Korzybski was two-valued logic.

9 *False.* General semantics says that it is not appropriate to treat members of a category as identities.

10 *True.* Extensional devices are practical techniques designed to orient us toward the external world of our senses as opposed to the internal world of abstract ideas.

11 *False.* Like general semantics, rational-emotive therapy is designed to prevent the suffering produced by unnecessary emotional reactions.

12   *True*. According to Ellis, one factor in emotional illness is a pattern of self-indoctrination with false notions.

13   *True*. Ellis asserts that thoughts often lead to feelings.

14   *True*. Ellis notes that people who suffer from chronic negative emotional states do a lot of catastrophic thinking.

15   *True*. An important emphasis of rational-emotive therapy is the value it places on long-range hedonism.

16   *False*. Ellis says that it is a false idea that it is easier to avoid than to face life's difficulties and self-responsibilities.

17   *False*. The Ellis ABC system of emotional self-control requires that the person dispute his own irrational ideas.

18   *True*. The rational-emotive approach contends that many people suffer needlessly because they expect too much of themselves.

19   *False*. Early in his career, Glasser became disenchanted with the treatment of clients by classical Freudian methods.

20   *True*. The central assumption of reality therapy is that one can have a rewarding life only by living a responsible life.

21   *False*. Glasser says that the need to love and be loved is a basic psychological need.

22   *False*. An important assumption of reality therapy is that the present and the future are more important than the past.

23   *False*. Glasser feels that the term *mental health* is of dubious value because it tends to suggest that there is something organically wrong with troubled persons.

24   *True*. Glasser asserts that values and moral principles are important in daily living.

25   *False*. According to Glasser, a survival society is goal-oriented.

DISCUSSION QUESTIONS

GENERAL SEMANTICS: THE MAP IS NOT THE TERRITORY

1 Can you give some examples from your own experience that demonstrate how you have sometimes confused your mental "map" of reality with the "territory" (external reality)?

2 What are some words that tend to make you happy, sad, angry, frustrated, anxious, or depressed?

3 Do you agree with Korzybski that most of us are unsane, that is, not sane and not insane?

4 Korzybski says we often make the error of treating space-time events as things. Are you aware of one or several instances in which you have made this error?

5 Which of the general semantics extensional devices do you consider to be the most practical ones?

RATIONAL-EMOTIVE THERAPY: EMOTIONAL SELF-CONTROL

1 Are you able to identify any irrational ideas you have?

2 Do you feel that Ellis's ABC system of emotional self-control is anything you might actually be able to apply in your own life? Does it seem practical to you?

3 Does it seem to you that some of your friends suffer needlessly because they expect too much of themselves? Can you offer an example?

REALITY THERAPY: BECOMING A RESPONSIBLE PERSON

1 Are you in accord with the central assumption of reality therapy that one can have a rewarding life only by living a responsible life? Why do you answer as you do?

2 Do you feel that on the whole you face reality?

3 Should traditional psychiatric categories, such as neurosis, psychosis, and character disorders, be rejected in favor of Glasser's responsibility-irresponsibility dimension?

4 Do you feel that you are principally goal-oriented or role-oriented?

REFERENCES

Aronson, E. "The Rationalizing Animal." *Psychology Today* (May 1973), vol. 6, pp. 46–52.

Bruner, J. S., Goodnow, J., and Austin, G. *A Study of Thinking.* New York: John Wiley & Sons, 1956.

Chase, S. *The Tyranny of Words.* New York: Harcourt, Brace & World, 1966.

Ellis, A. *Humanistic Psychotherapy: The Rational-Emotive Approach.* New York: Julian Press, 1973.

————, ed. *Growth Through Reason.* Hollywood, Calif.: Wilshire Book Co., 1971.

————, and Harper, R. A. *A Guide to Rational Living.* Englewood Cliffs, N.J.: Prentice-Hall, 1961.

Fitzgerald, E., trans. *Rubaiyat of Omar Khayyám.* New York: Grosset and Dunlap, 1946.

Gibran, K. *The Voice of the Master.* New York: Citadel Press, 1958.

Glasser, W. *Reality Therapy.* New York: Harper & Row, 1965.

————. *The Identity Society.* New York: Harper & Row, 1972.

————, and Zunin, L. M. "Reality Therapy," in R. Corsini, ed., *Current Psychotherapies.* Itasca, Ill.: F. E. Peacock Publishers, 1973.

Hayakawa, S. I. "How Words Change Our Lives," in *Symbol, Status, and Personality.* New York: Harcourt, Brace & World, 1963.

Johnson, W. *People in Quandaries.* New York: Harper & Brothers, 1946.

Korzybski, A. *Science and Sanity.* Lakeville, Conn.: International Non-Aristotelian Library Publishing Co., 4th ed., 1958.

Maugham, W. S. *Of Human Bondage.* New York: Doubleday & Co., 1915.

Piaget, J. *The Language and Thought of the Child.* New York: Harcourt, Brace & World, 1926.

CHAPTER 5
TRANSACTIONAL
ANALYSIS:
OF STROKES
AND GAMES

Transactional analysis is designed to enhance our understanding of how people communicate.

OVERVIEW

OUTLINE

TWO KEY QUESTIONS

What is transactional analysis?

Transactional analysis is a coherent system of concepts designed to enhance our understanding of how people communicate. The emphasis in transactional analysis is on *interpersonal behavior*, behavior involving two or more people. Transactional analysis also studies how we communicate with ourselves within ourselves, however. This aspect is referred to as *structural analysis*, and it forms the foundation for transactional analysis proper. Thus the scope of transactional analysis ranges from studying communication *within* the individual to exploring communication *between* two or more individuals.

How do the principles of transactional analysis relate to adjustment and growth?

Transactional analysis asserts that human beings have a strong tendency to fall into self-defeating patterns of living. *Rackets, games*, and *losing scripts* are some of the terms used to suggest these patterns. It is important to stress that the patterns usually involve other people in some way. The aim of transactional analysis is to provide us with ways of breaking out of self-defeating patterns so that we can attain greater personal autonomy and intimacy with others.

Consider the following dialogue:

Tom. I don't know how I'm going to keep up my grades and keep my job too. It looks like I'm going to get a D or an F in statistics the way it's going. Got any ideas?

Sue. Why don't you go to bed an hour earlier every night? Then you can get up bright and early and study.

Tom. No, that wouldn't work. I can't relax if I go to bed too early. I've got to unwind with a little TV.

Sue. Well, maybe you could drop one of your courses. Then you could put more effort into statistics.

Tom. I hate to do that. I counted on completing twelve units this semester.

Sue. I know! Let's just cut out the weekend visiting for the rest of the semester. That'll give you plenty of time to study.

Tom. Are you kidding? Do you want to lose all our friends?

Sue. Well, maybe your boss would be willing to cut your hours from twenty to fifteen—that would give you five extra hours to study.

Tom. No, I don't think he would. Besides, we need all the bread we can get.

Sue. Well, why don't you get a tutor for statistics?

Tom. No I don't think so.

The preceding dialogue illustrates a game identified by transactional analysis as *Why Don't You, Yes But*. (The concept of a *game* receives a formal definition later in the chapter. For now, think of a game as a manipulative give-and-take between at least two people.) Tom's statement of his problem would appear to be an adult request for problem-solving suggestions. In actuality it is a psychological trap designed to put down Sue. Tom's ulterior goal is to feel superior to Sue. In the language of transactional analysis, he seeks to be *one up*, to be in a position of psychological power. If he succeeds, Sue is *one down*, in a position of psychological weakness. The seemingly innocent conversation between them in actuality reveals a power struggle initiated by Tom to prove to himself and to Sue that he is the dominant one in their relationship. It is said that *Why Don't You, Yes But* was the first game identified by Eric Berne, the father of transactional analysis. (It is not, however, the basic game. That is identified as *Mine Is Better Than Yours*. More will be said about this game later.)

As noted in Chapter Two, the psychiatrist Harry Stack Sullivan is generally recognized as an important precursor to transactional analysis. Sullivan's ideas were well developed in the 1930s, about thirty years before the publication of Eric Berne's bestselling *Games People Play*.

The psychiatrist Thomas A. Harris, one of the founders of the Institute of Transactional Analysis, notes in the preface of *I'm OK—You're OK* that he first heard the term "interpersonal transactions" under the tutelage of Sullivan. The thrust of Sullivan's theorizing was to emphasize the idea that a personal problem has its source in confused and confusing human relations. The problem is not "in" the person. If the problem "is" anywhere, it is "in" the pattern of communication between two or more persons. It is this basic insight that provided the seed from which transactional analysis grew.

WHO WAS ERIC BERNE?

In an article by writer Hugh Gardner, Eric Berne is referred to as oracle, scientist, healer, humorist, and poet of Everyman's destiny. Never, says Gardner, did he have so much fun with his neuroses as when he read what Berne wrote about them. Gardner says:

There were times in my reading when I actually jumped on my feet, so flush with Berne's insights that had the man been within my reach, I probably would have kissed him right then and there on that magnificent cerebral cortex of his. (p. 25)

Eric Berne was born in 1910 and died in 1970. He received his M.D. degree in Canada in 1935 and subsequently trained as a psychiatrist at

Eric Berne was the father of transactional analysis.

the Yale University School of Medicine. He was married twice and was the father of four children. Fatherhood was an important element in Berne's life; he believed that many parents turn children into *frogs*, children who suffer from low self-esteem. Berne believed that children are born *princes* or *princesses*, that is, children who have a high self-esteem. When Berne separated from his first wife, he moved to Carmel, California. He began to work in both Carmel and nearby San Francisco. As Berne's ideas on transactional analysis formed, he gathered a group of followers. For a number of years he met with a small group of psychiatrists, psychologists, counselors, and social workers interested in expanding on his basic formulations. These informal seminars led to the eventual formation of the International Transactional Analysis Association and the *Transactional Analysis Journal*.

Berne placed a great deal of emphasis on the concept of "cure" as opposed to "making progress" or "getting better." He was suspicious of psychiatrists who kept patients in long-term therapy, who spoke in terms of slow progress. Such psychiatrists, Berne believed, cater to the patient's unconscious wish to remain locked into old patterns. Berne was also impatient with preoccupation with the *why* of behavior. Constantly asking, "Why do I do this?" or "Why am I this way?" places the sufferer on a mental merry-go-round to nowhere. Berne instead said to his patients, "Why don't you get better first, and then find out why afterward?"

It is important to note that Berne spent a substantial period of his life training to be an orthodox Freudian psychoanalyst. Although he eventually broke with the psychoanalytic establishment, he had a high regard for Freudian theory. Many of the concepts in transactional analysis have their roots in ideas espoused by Freud and other psychoanalysts. For example, Berne's formulation of Child, Adult, and Parent ego states is similar to Freud's concept of the id, the ego, and the superego. This is not to say that Berne was not a brilliant and original thinker. But it is best to realize that his work has its place within a certain tradition of psychological thinking.

Berne rose to national prominence in 1964 with the phenomenal best-seller *Games People Play*. For two years the book was at the top of the nation's best-seller lists. It still sells briskly in its paperback version. It has inspired other best-selling books on transactional analysis, such as *I'm OK—You're OK* by Thomas Harris and *Born to Win* by Muriel James and Dorothy Jongeward. Berne himself was surprised by the popular success of *Games People Play* because it was aimed at a basically professional audience. But, Berne's writing and ideas appealed to Everyman. His writing is sprinkled with such colloquialisms as *frog*, *prince*, *game*, *stroke*, *one up*, and so forth in place of ponderous and self-important psychological terminology. Although the heavy use of colloquialisms gave Berne's writing a "flashy" appearance, it was not Berne's intention to write a superficial "pop psychology." He was adamant about the value of colloquial terminology. The following comment is from *Games People Play:*

As I have tried to show elsewhere in discussing colloquial epithets, a whole page of learned polysyllables may not convey as much as the statement that a certain woman is a bitch, or that a certain man is a jerk. (p. 71)

As already noted, Berne died in 1970, of a heart attack. Claude Steiner, a close associate of Berne's, says in his own book, *Scripts People Live,* that he is convinced that Berne himself was living out an unconscious life plan that called for his death of a heart attack in his sixties. Steiner notes that in Berne's books the only cause of death ever mentioned is coronary heart disease. Berne's father died of a heart attack when Berne was eleven years old; Berne's mother, like Berne, died of a heart attack when she was sixty years old. Steiner says, "I believe that he had a limited life-expectancy script which he lived out just as planned" (p. 19). Such a statement is, of course, highly speculative. Nonetheless, it is provocative.

Berne's intellectual child, transactional analysis, is a robust adolescent now. Although Berne himself is dead, the interest in transactional analysis has not died with him.

THE THREE EGO STATES

The English poet William Wordsworth made the famous comment "The child is father of the man." The children we once were contributed to the adults we are today, and the children are retained in our adult personalities in some form. Eric Berne's formulations expand greatly on the foregoing observations. According to him, as adults we have three potential ego states: the Child, the Parent, and the Adult (see Figure 5.1). You will notice that the terms are capitalized. This is done to distinguish them from a living child, parent, or adult. The term *ego states* is used to indicate that from time to time we actually experience ourselves as acting like children, parents, or adults. We "enter into" an ego state as we might enter a room.

THE CHILD

Berne identifies the Child ego state as a set of emotional "recordings" carried forward from childhood. The feelings we felt as children we are

FIGURE 5.1   The basic structure of the human personality according to Eric Berne.

capable of reexperiencing in the present. Transactional analysis makes heavy use of a variety of metaphors to present its case and clarify its meaning. Thus it is said that something pushes your Child "button" and an old "tape" starts playing. For example, say that a married man was a bully when he was a child. When anyone frustrated him, he began pushing and shoving. Now he is having an argument with his wife, and he feels frustrated. He begins to push and shove her about the kitchen, copying the behavior of the little bully he was in grammar school. His wife's behavior pushed his Child button, and he entered his Child ego state. His Child is now determining his behavior, not his thinking Adult.

Of course, husbands are not the only ones who may enter the Child ego state when quarreling with their spouses. Let us say that a particular wife tended to pout and cry as a child when her parents didn't let her have her way. Now, as an adult, her huband may be objecting to plans she made for the weekend without consulting him. She may enter her Child ego state, pouting and crying as she did when she was an actual child.

Many examples can be given of ways we enter the Child. An adult riding the roller coaster at an amusement park may take on the behavior characteristics of a child. His body posture and the expression on his face mimic the way he acted when he was younger. He may use speech patterns that were popular when he was a child: "Wheee! This is keen!" For all practical purposes, this adult has temporarily become a child. He has "lost himself," we say. Transactional analysts would simply say that he is in his Child ego state.

According to Berne, the Child may be divided into three levels: (1) the Adapted Child, (2) the Rebellious Child, and (3) the Natural Child (see Figure 5.2). The Adapted Child represents the part of the Child that conforms, adapts to society's rules, and tries to please "mommy" and "daddy." The question immediately arises, "Why does the child try to adapt at all? Why is it so desperately important to please mommy and daddy?" The answer given by Berne is, essentially, that human beings have a powerful inborn craving for affection. Berne cites the research of Harry Harlow with infant monkeys, which demonstrated that personality development is grossly distorted when the infant monkey is reared in social isolation without mother love. Berne also cites the research of René Spitz with infants reared in orphanages; Spitz demonstrated that ignored infants—infants in a state of psychological-emotional deprivation—developed poorly and had high death rates. As the child grows older, the need for affection translates itself into a *recognition hunger*, a need to have others confirm one's presence and existence. Thus it is common for children to say, "Look at me!" when they do something. As adults, we also want to be recognized.

The preceding observations are captured by the transactional analysis term *stroke*, which is any act that recognizes the presence of another person. An infant is being stroked when his diapers are being changed, when he is being fed, when a parent is tickling him. It is presumed that in terms of the conditioning process, symbolic expressions of attention become associated with actual physical stroking and are eventually capable of replacing it to some degree. Thus an adult is being stroked when someone says, "Hello," when someone listens to a story, when someone says, "Do you think it will rain today?" *Any* form of human recognition has stroke value.

The Adapted Child, then, is the aspect of the Child that earns strokes. If

FIGURE 5.2 The three levels of the Child ego state.

As a child grows older, transactional analysis asserts, the need for affection translates itself into a recognition hunger.

a child's parents are the kind of people who demand that the child be "nice" in order to earn strokes, if strokes are almost always conditional, if affection must be "purchased" by actions, that child will become an adult with an overdeveloped Adapted Child. This would be the kind of person who is supersweet, too goody-goody, and excessively polite. In conventional psychological language, such a person would exhibit neurotic trends.

Let us turn to the second level of the Child identified by Berne, the Rebellious Child. The Rebellious Child also develops out of the human need for strokes. Assume that a child's parents are the kind of people who notice him only when he is acting up. The child is psychologically invisible until he breaks something, says a four-letter word, wets his bed, brings home a poor report card, irritates the neighbors, or engages in any other kind of behavior that automatically commands attention. The parents are *forced* to notice the child by his acts of rebellion. By noticing the child, they stroke him. Although they may hit, shout, scream, or become irrational, these are still strokes. They represent some form of attention, some form of recognition; and anything that makes the parents acknowledge the child's existence is better than nothing. When parents become punitive in words or actions, such strokes are called *negative strokes*. Transactional analysis asserts that negative strokes reinforce the formation of the Rebellious Child.

In an illustrated book titled *T.A. for Tots* by psychologist Alvin Freed, positive strokes are called *warm fuzzies* and negative strokes are called *cold pricklies*. The thesis is that we prefer warm fuzzies, but we will take cold pricklies if we have to. Cold pricklies are better than nothing, and many children and adults are forced to survive on an emotional diet of cold pricklies. If a child has the kind of parents who withhold warm fuzzies, and if they give cold pricklies when the child is being a nuisance, that child will become an adult with an overdeveloped Rebellious Child. This would be the kind of person who always places himself first, has little real affection for others, tends to be highly impulsive, has a hard time waiting for gratification, often breaks rules, and in general tends to "have a chip on his shoulder." In conventional psychological language, such a person would exhibit the traits associated with character disorders.

Let us now turn to the third level of the Child identified by Berne, the Natural Child. The growth of the Natural Child is also fostered by strokes —positive strokes. In addition, these strokes do not have to be earned by "being nice" or by acting in such-and-such a way. Assume that a child is fortunate enough to have parents who give the child quite a lot of spontaneous affection and attention. They like to play with the child, talk to the child, and go places with the child. The child does not have to either earn positive strokes by acting in a particular way nor demand negative strokes by becoming a nuisance. Parents who foster the development of the Natural Child give the child a great deal of *unconditional stroking*, stroking that is not tied to some sort of explicit behavior on the child's part. Unconditional stroking acts on the Natural Child like sunshine acts on a plant. The Natural Child thrives on the warmth of love freely given.

If a child has the kind of parents who give him a great many unconditional positive strokes as he is growing up, that child will become an adult with a well-developed Natural Child. This would be the kind of person who has high self-esteem, likes other people, is autonomous without being a lawbreaker, and is capable of participating in intimate (game-free) human relationships. In conventional psychological language, such a person would exhibit the attributes associated with the healthy personality.

To Berne, adults with an overdeveloped Adapted Child or Rebellious Child were victims of poor parenting. They had been converted from princes or princesses into frogs. Adults with a well-developed Natural Child retain their birthright. They remain princes and princesses.

All this may seem a bit hard on parents, but Berne believed that the experiences of childhood are the prime determiners of the human personality. During the child's formative years, before he can think for himself, the parents shape the child's development. Of course Berne recognized that many children are raised by single parents, stepparents, foster parents, counselors in institutions, and so forth. Such parent surrogates may be loosely labeled "parents" if they have the kind of impact on the child's development usually associated with natural parents.

THE PARENT

Berne describes the Parent ego state as having certain similarities to the Child ego state. Like the Child, the Parent also consists of a set of "recordings" carried forward from childhood. The Parent recordings often have to do with "oughts" and "shoulds." The Parent represents our incorporation of our parents' values, and our personal moral code is based on Parent recordings. We "hear" our parents or parental figures saying, "A penny saved is a penny earned," or "You should always go to church on Sunday," or "Work hard and be thrifty," or "You're never going to amount to anything," or "You're going to be famous someday." The part of the Parent that moralizes and issues advice is called the Controlling Parent. The Parent has another aspect, the Nurturing Parent. Thus the Parent has two levels (see Figure 5.3).

The Controlling Parent is an inner judge. It watchdogs our behavior and says such things as, "You really shouldn't be taking a second helping of dessert; you ought to lose weight," or "You're really a jerk! How could

FIGURE 5.3   The two levels of the Parent ego state.

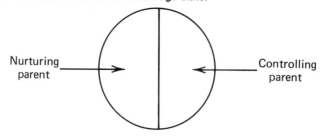

you have gotten a D on that test?'' or ''You're a failure! You had a good chance and you blew it!'' When we blame ourselves, when we criticize ourselves, when we deplore our own behavior, it is the Parent speaking down to the Child that produces inner bad feelings.

The Controlling Parent is also an outer judge. When our Parent button is pushed, we enter the Parent ego state and look down our noses at other people. To illustrate, say that a middle-aged businessman and his wife are driving down the highway in their air-conditioned Cadillac. They pass a young couple hitchhiking. The girl is braless, and the boy has long hair. The businessman mutters, ''Darn hippies! Why don't they clean up and get to work—do something useful with their lives?'' His wife replies, ''They're disgusting. And did you see the girl? What a brazen hussy—revolting!'' Both the businessman and his wife are speaking out of the Controlling Parent. The sight of the young couple pushed their respective Parent buttons, and they ran off some old tapes. When we are in the Controlling Parent, the words that come out of our mouths represent, not thought, *but what we were taught*. It is as if we were robots, reciting old moral lessons. The person who is critical of others is an individual who is often prone to enter his Controlling Parent.

The Controlling Parent is the agent of society. Its aim is to ''keep us in line'' and force us to conform to the norms of the behavior expected of us. Its concern is primarily with the survival of groups to which we may belong, not individual survival. The Controlling Parent seeks to make us resemble good members of an ant colony. We are to do our duty, place others first, and ignore our own feelings. A certain amount of Controlling Parent is probably necessary for a person to become socialized. A person with an overdeveloped Controlling Parent, however, will tend to also have an overdeveloped Adapted Child. Such a person will be too socialized for his own good. He will tend to be uptight, prone to emotionally induced illness, and unable to just relax and have some fun. He will take things too seriously and will lack a spontaneous sense of humor.

The other level of the Parent is the Nurturing Parent. The function of the Nurturing Parent is to provide strokes. Like the Controlling Parent, the Nurturing Parent has its inner and outer aspects. The Nurturing Parent is aimed inward when a person strokes himself. Self-praise would be an example of the inward function of the Nurturing Parent. A person might make a success of a task and give himself a mental pat on the back, saying to himself, ''A job well done.'' The Nurturing Parent is aimed outward when a person strokes someone else. Giving children recognition for their real accomplishments would have its source in the Nurturing Parent. Also, a person with a well-developed Nurturing Parent is capable of genuine concern for the welfare of others, whether they be children or adults. The person with a large Nurturing Parent can give other people strokes freely without necessarily demanding strokes in return. His philosophy is not "If you scratch my back, I'll scratch yours," but "I'll scratch your back because I like to see you feeling good." A well-developed Nurturing Parent is an important component of the healthy personality.

THE ADULT

The Adult ego state is the computer of the personality. Its function is to be rational, plan ahead, and take reality into account. It has no feeling of its own, and an actual adult whose personality is all Adult would be a human iceberg. The science-fiction character Mr. Spock of the Star Trek series portrays the caricature of a person who can think but who has no feeling. The Adult begins to form in early childhood, differentiating itself from the Child and the Parent. You must not confuse the term Adult with an actual adult. Thus a child of five can be said to have an Adult, although this child is not yet an actual adult. This is merely another way of saying that the child has some capacity to think for himself.

In some adults, the Adult is not sufficiently discriminated from the Child

The Adult ego state is the computer of the personality.

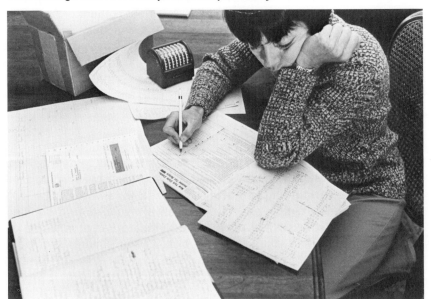

and the Parent. Transactional analysis speaks of such a situation as *contamination*. A person can have an Adult that is contaminated by the Child, an Adult that is contaminated by the Parent, or an Adult that is contaminated by both the Child and the Parent. Say that Bill's Adult is contaminated by his Child (see Figure 5.4). He tends to be impulsive, inappropriate in social situations, and selfish. His Adult and his Child are mixed up with each other, and he has a hard time acting with appropriate maturity. Say that Susan's Adult is contaminated by the Child. In her case, imagine that the Child has almost completely swamped the Adult. Susan tends to exhibit the traits we associate with some psychotic reactions—silliness, flights of fantasy, disorientation, and so forth.

Now assume that Tom's Adult is contaminated by his Parent (see Figure 5.5). He tends to be hard on himself and others; he owns his own business, works ten to twelve hours a day, six days a week; and he seldom takes a vacation. In many ways he is mimicking his father, who used to be fond of saying, "Early to bed, early to rise, makes a man healthy, wealthy, and wise." Tom also tends to be prejudicial in his thinking. "The Republican party is the only true American party," he has said many times. But he has never really thought about this statement; he was raised a Republican, and he is parroting what he heard as a child.

FIGURE 5.4   An example of contamination. In this case the Adult is contaminated by the Child.

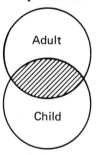

FIGURE 5.5   Another example of contamination. In this case the Adult is contaminated by the Parent.

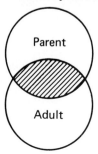

Say that Karen's Adult is contaminated by both the Child and the Parent. Such a state may be defined as *double contamination* (see Figure 5.6). Karen has a hard time thinking for herself. She is a slave to the ideas implanted into her head by her parents and other authority figures. At the same time, she tends to make decisions on an emotional basis. Recently she was a guest at a dinner party and was offered a rich dessert by the hostess. Karen is overweight, and she is always talking about losing weight. In response to the rich dessert, her Parent proclaimed, "It isn't polite to say no." Her Child shouted, "I want it!" Her Adult, heavily contaminated by the Parent and the Child, made no clear expression of its opinion. Karen took the cake and ate it rapidly. Her behavior was unthinking and programmed—determined by messages from the Parent and the Child.

In contrast with contamination of the Adult by a particular ego state, transactional analysis identifies a condition known as *blockage*. Blockage takes place when there is a barrier between one ego state and the Adult. To illustrate, Linda's Adult is contaminated by her Parent, but there is a block between her Adult and her Child (see Figure 5.7). Linda is the martyr-homemaker, constantly cleaning house, running errands for her husband and children, cooking elaborate dinners, and responsible to a fault. She leads a joyless existence, however. There simply isn't any fun in her life; she seldom relaxes or laughs spontaneously. Her potentially happy Child has been locked away in a psychological freezer. In Linda's case, there is a block between her Adult and her Child.

A second kind of blockage takes place when there is a barrier between the Adult and the Parent. From the point of view of civilized living, this second kind of blockage is of more concern than the first. To illustrate,

FIGURE 5.6 An example of double contamination.

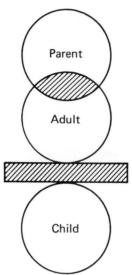

Pete's Adult is contaminated by his Child, and there is a block between his Adult and his Parent (see Figure 5.8). Pete's parents were much too harsh and punitive. Pete's father used to whip the boy with a leather belt for minor infractions of parental law. Pete's mother was a slapper, and she had little emotional self-control. Pete's parents were once investigated for child abuse, but they were not prosecuted. Pete preserved his

FIGURE 5.8 An example in which the Adult is contaminated by the Child and there is a block between the Parent and the Adult.

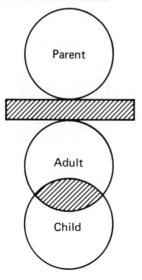

psychological existence by insulating himself emotionally from his parents. He stopped caring about what they thought or felt or wanted of
him. Thus Pete was unable to internalize the little his parents had to give
him in the way of human values. Speaking of people like Pete, Harris
comments in *I'm OK—You're OK:*

*He excludes the painful Parent, but he also excludes what little "good" there is
in the Parent. Such a person does not have available to his current transactions
any tapes which supply data having to do with social control, appropriate
"shoulds" and "should nots," cultural norms, or what, in one sense, may be
referred to as conscience. His behavior is dominated by his Child, which through
the contaminated Adult manipulates other people to his own ends. (p. 103)*

A third kind of blockage occurs when there are *two* psychological barriers, one between the Parent and the Adult and the other between the
Child and the Adult (see Figure 5.9). In such a case, the Adult is not
functioning at all. The person is either in a Parent ego state or in a Child
ego state. Transactional analysis associates this condition with psychosis.
The person with a blocked-out Adult cannot think for himself, is not capable
of rational action, and is not oriented toward reality. We speak of such
people as "crazy," "nuts," "weird," "screwballs," and so forth. Not all
such people are in mental hospitals, but many are. Countless examples

**FIGURE 5.9 In the case of double blockage, the Adult
is out of commission.**

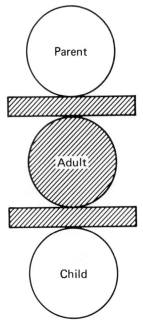

of the person with a nonfunctioning Adult could be drawn from hospital case reports. As a brief illustration, let us again refer to Harris. He offers the case of a female patient in a mental hospital "whose singing of tent-meeting hymns (Parent) was interspersed with obscenities relating to body functions (Child)." Harris states:

The content was bizzare, but seemed to replay an old Parent-Child conflict between good and bad, should and should not, salvation and damnation. The content of these verbal productions quickly revealed a great deal about her Parent and Child. The fact that her Adult was gone indicated the severity of the conflict. (p. 105)

What we have been discussing in the past few pages is formally termed *structural analysis.* Structural analysis is the study of how the three ego states—Parent, Adult, and Child—relate to each other in a single individual. Structural analysis forms the theoretical foundation for transactional analysis proper, the study of how two or more persons communicate with each other.

TRANSACTIONS

A *transaction* is defined by Berne as the unit of social intercourse. As such, a transaction always contains a transactional stimulus and a transactional response. You say "Hello" to a friend you pass in the hallway; the friend responds by saying "Hello" to you. This is an illustration of a simple transaction. Your "Hello" was the transactional stimulus. His "Hello" was the transactional response. Transactions need not be at a verbal level. Say that Tom sees a pretty girl in the school cafeteria and he would like to get acquainted. Tom smiles at her. She sticks out her tongue at him. Their behaviors also represent a transaction with a stimulus and a respose.

Why do we engage in transactions? Berne's answer is that they provide us with strokes. Strokes satisfy the human need for some sort of affection. By being recognized and paid attention to, our affectional drive is gratified. As already noted, strokes may be positive or negative. Although we tend to prefer positive strokes, we will accept negative strokes in preference to no strokes at all. To the transactional analyst, this observation offers an explanation of why people often maintain destructive relationships for long periods of time.

COMPLEMENTARY TRANSACTIONS

If all transactions between human beings were complementary, this would be a rather bland world. The *complementary transaction* is defined

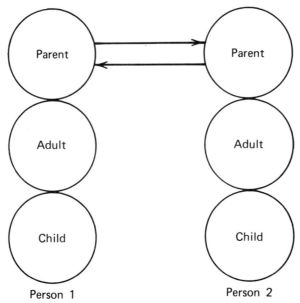

FIGURE 5.10   An example of a complementary transaction. The diagram illustrates a Parent-Parent transaction.

as a no-conflict transaction. On the transactional analysis diagrams, the lines representing the transactional stimulus and the transactional response are parallel (see Figure 5.10). So long as this condition is met, the transaction is complementary. The following are some examples of complementary transactions.

Parent-Parent

Husband. The governor of this state is a jerk! Why can't he get the bums off of welfare?

Wife. I hate to see our tax money go to support a bunch of shameless unwed mothers.

Mother 1. The Smith children are so poorly mannered. I hate to have them play with my children.

Mother 2. I know! The other day I saw Billy Smith picking his nose while he was eating an ice cream cone.

The Parent-Parent transaction often represents an exchange of prejudices. As such, it does not indicate an expression of thought on the part of the speakers; instead, it serves as a pleasant pastime.

Child-Child

Husband. Hey, this is great fun! I haven't been on a roller coaster in years.

Wife. Oh, it's so scary way up here!

Mother. I know I'm on a diet, but I'm going to cheat just this once and have a hot fudge sundae. What do you say, Susan? Would you like to stop at a coffee shop for a treat?

Child. Oh boy! Sounds great!

Child 1 (watching a cartoon). Ha-ha-ha! Bugs Bunny is so funny!

Child 2. Ha-ha-ha! I think so too!

Friend 1. I'm really depressed today.

Friend 2. I know what you mean. Things are really getting me down too.

The Child-Child transaction tends to be an exchange at an emotional level. The feeling expressed can be positive or negative, as indicated in the preceding examples.

Adult-Adult

Boyfriend. Should I pick you up at seven?

Girlfriend. No, it would be better for me if you came over about eight.

Student. What is the length of one meter?

Teacher. A meter is 39.37 inches.

Husband. Honey, where's my favorite blue shirt?

Wife. I put it in the front closet—between two white shirts.

Child 1. Can you come out and play?

Child 2. No, Mom says I have to wash up for dinner.

Prospect. I'm not interested in the savings aspect of life insurance, just the protection aspect.

Salesman. Then you would be interested in a straight-term policy, not an endowment policy.

Mother. I expect you to make your own bed every day.

Child. Do I have to do it before I go to school, or can I wait until I come home?

The Adult-Adult transaction tends to be nonemotional and reality oriented. Its purpose is to make a decision, solve a problem, or to exchange information. As you can see from the preceding examples, Adult-Adult exchanges can take place between children and between a parent and a child. The transaction is Adult-Adult if it is out of the Adult ego states. The person's status as an actual parent, child, or adult has nothing to do with categorizing a transaction.

Parent-child

Husband. You never clean this house! It's beginning to look like a pigpen!

Wife (tearful). I'm sorry, honey. I'm going to try to do better.

Wife. I'm ashamed of you, Fred Jones! Do you realize that you drank like a pig tonight?

Husband. You're right, sweetheart. I'm such a fool. You know I'm weak when it comes to alcohol. Please forgive me.

Mother. You've become a very irresponsible boy, Jimmy. You never pick up your clothes on your own—I always have to tell you.

Son. Please don't be mad at me, Momma. I'll pick them up right away.

Teacher. This essay is sloppy and completely without organization.

Student (hanging head). Yes, ma'am. I'm sorry.

Boss. Is this the way you wipe off a table? Are you a busboy or a zombie? My two-year-old son could get a table cleaner than this.

Employee. Yes, sir. I'm sorry.

Mother (listening to her daughter play the piano). That was fantastic, Julie! You have great talent.

Daughter. Gee! Thanks, Mom.

Boyfriend. You look just great in that dress—terrific!

Girlfriend. Wow! I'm so happy you like it, Bill.

Parent-Child transactions tend to represent either criticism or praise. If the transactional stimulus is out of the person's Controlling Parent, the aim of the speaker is to put down the listener and to be one up himself. If the transactional stimulus comes out of the person's Nurturing Parent, the aim of the speaker is to stroke the listener's Child. Parent-Child transactions are identified as complementary because the person in the Child position *agrees* with the statements made by the person in the Parent position.

CROSSED TRANSACTIONS

A *crossed transaction* takes place when there is conflict between two or more people. On a transactional analysis diagram, the lines representing

A crossed transaction takes place when there is a conflict between two or more people. (Elizabeth Taylor and Richard Burton in a scene from "Who's Afraid of Virginia Woolf?")

the transactional stimulus and the transactional response cross (see Figure 5.11). The following are some examples of crossed transactions.

Adult-Adult, Child-Parent

Teacher. What is seven times eight, Suzie?

Student. It's too hard! Why do you keep picking on me?

Husband. Honey, I'd like to explain my life insurance policies to you.

Wife. Oh, this is so boring! Why do you have to force me to think about things I don't want to think about?

Adult-Adult, Parent-Child

Son. What time is it, Mom?

Mother. You're a pest.

Employee. Can I have off next Tuesday?

Boss. You've been asking for too many privileges, Harry. It's about time you realized that we keep our noses to the old grindstone around here.

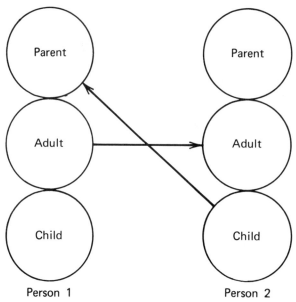

FIGURE 5.11   An example of a crossed transaction. The diagram illustrates an Adult-Adult, Child-Parent transaction.

Husband. Why is the gas tank almost empty? Didn't you have time to stop for gas?

Wife. You're irresponsible too. You didn't put your socks in the clothes hamper today. I always have to pick up after you, just like a little kid.

Parent-Child, Parent-Child

Husband. You never clean this house! It's beginning to look like a pigpen!

Wife. And you never clean the yard! You should get out there right now and start working on it.

Mother. You've become a very irresponsible boy, Jimmy. You never pick up your clothes on your own—I always have to tell you.

Son. You don't do what you're supposed to either. I keep asking for pancakes for breakfast, and all you ever give me is cold cereal. You're lazier than I am!

Parent-Child, Adult-Adult

Husband. You never clean this house! It's beginning to look like a pigpen!

Wife. Billy was sick with the flu today.

Wife. I'm ashamed of you, Fred Jones! Do you realize that you drank like a pig tonight?

Husband. I'm going to call Alcoholics Anonymous and get some help.

Teacher. This essay is sloppy and completely without organization.

Student. I'm going to get some books on composition and study them. And I'm going to get a tutor.

As already noted, the crossed transaction represents conflict. It also represents a break in communication. As such, however, it is not "all bad." There are times when a crossed transaction is preferable to a complementary transaction. Transactional analysis notes that when someone addresses you Parent-Child, one strong tendency is to accept the Child position and engage in a complementary transaction. If you do this, you will feel put down. The other strong tendency is to "flip" from the Child to the Parent. If you then address the other person's Child from your Parent, you will have a harsh crossed transaction (Parent-Child, Parent-Child). The optimal response when addressed Parent-Child would seem to be to come back Adult-Adult. Although this too represents a crossed transaction, it is a fairly moderate one. There may be some confrontation, but it is realistic confrontation.

ULTERIOR TRANSACTIONS

Berne identifies *ulterior transactions* as those involving the activity of more than two ego states simultaneously. Ulterior transactions contain a hidden message, and they underlie most games. Ulterior transactions have a hidden aim or purpose and as such are the real troublemakers of human communication. There are two levels to ulterior transactions: (1) the *social level* and (2) the *psychological level.* The social level contains the manifest message, a message that is being communicated in an obvious sense. The psychological level contains the latent message, a message that hides behind the surface message. The latent message is often the "real" message contained within the transaction.

Two kinds of ulterior transactions are identified by transactional analysis: (1) *angular transactions* and (2) *duplex transactions.* An angular transaction involves three ego states in two persons (see Figure 5.12). Say that an automobile salesman is talking to a customer. The salesman says, "The Hornet-X is the top of our line, but the payments are probably more than you can afford." To simplify what may be an involved set of transactions, say that at some point the customer says, "I'll buy it." What has happened? The salesman has spoken from his own Adult to *two* ego states in the customer, the customer's Adult and the customer's Child. The salesman's messages at the social level are Adult-Adult. They state facts. The Hornet-X *is* the top of the line. And it *is* true that the customer's financial resources will be strained if he buys the Hornet-X. The salesman is also, however, sending a message from his Adult to

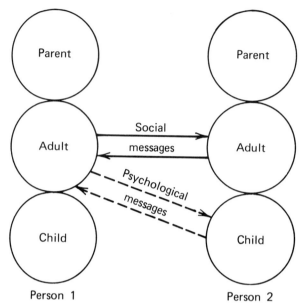

FIGURE 5.12 An example of an angular transaction.

the customer's Child. This unspoken message taunts the customer. It says, "The other kids can have toys you can't have." The unspoken message "hooks the Child" of the customer, makes the Child feel an emotion such as envy, and as such plays a potent part in the customer's decision.

A duplex ulterior transaction involves four ego states in two persons (see Figure 5.13). Berne offers a simple flirtation as an example of a duplex transaction:

Cowboy. Come and see the barn.

Visitor. I've loved barns ever since I was a little girl. (p. 33)

At the social level, the cowboy's Adult is addressing the visitor's Adult, politely inviting her to see a building. But the hidden message from his Child to her Child is, "Let's have some fun." Her Child is apparently saying, "I'd like to have some fun too."

Duplex transactions can take on a variety of patterns. Oftentimes there are Parent-Child messages involved. Harris offers the following example:

Husband says to wife, "Where did you hide the can opener?" The main stimulus is Adult in that it seeks objective information. But there is a secondary communication in the word hide. *(Your housekeeping is a mystery to me. We'd go*

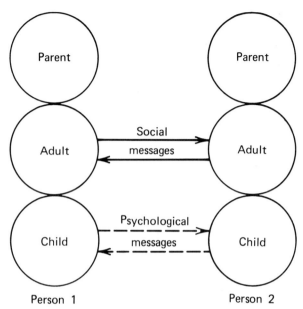

FIGURE 5.13   An example of a duplex transaction.

broke it I were as disorganized as you. If I could once, just once, find some-thing where it belongs!) This is Parent. It is a thinly veiled criticism. (p. 89)

The analysis of transactions is designed to throw a spotlight on the processes of social intercourse. Berne assumes that there are many hidden snares in human communication and that we are somewhat better off when we know something about where and what these snares are.

THE FOUR EXISTENTIAL POSITIONS: ARE YOU OK?

Berne's view that we are all born princes or princesses and that early childhood experiences with parents and authority figures often turn us into frogs has given rise to the analysis of basic outlooks on life. These outlooks are called *existential positions,* stances we take toward our-selves and our relationships with others. Four basic positions are iden-tified: (1) I'm not OK—You're OK, (2) I'm OK—You're not OK, (3) I'm not OK—You're not OK, and (4) I'm OK—You're OK.

I'M NOT OK—YOU'RE OK

''I'm not OK—you're OK'' is a kind of shorthand for saying that some people suffer from low self-esteem and see others as having traits they themselves lack. Such people tend to see themselves as incompetent, unintelligent, not pretty, not handsome, lacking in creativity, unpopular, uncoordinated, or otherwise inferior. If a person is convinced that he is unintelligent, he sees the planet as populated with hordes of people brighter than he is. If a girl has become convinced that she is not pretty, she lives in a psychological world where everyone seems to be prettier than she is.

Inferiority feelings often have little or no relationship to actual inferiorities. A bright person may be convinced that he is not bright. An attractive girl may be sure that she is unattractive. These are matters of self-image—matters that have to do with subjective perceptions, not external reality. This is the point at which Berne's notion of royalty turning into frogs comes into play. The infant is born feeling OK. The growing child will feel OK too if the parents can give unconditional strokes and refrain from being hypercritical. Unfortunately, many parents have a big Controlling Parent, and this Controlling Parent does untold damage to the child's developing self-image. The destructive parent makes many *attributions*, statements to the child that he has such and such personality characteristics. "You're lazy," or "You're rude," or "You're stubborn just like your father," or "Stop being such a clod," or "You're dumb," or "I never thought a child of mine would have such straight hair" are a few examples of ways in which children are made to feel bad about themselves.

Sometimes attributions are unspoken. The criticism is hidden in an ulterior message. To illustrate, Joan read a book called *Between Parent and Child* by Haim Ginott. In that book, Ginott recommends that children be given a choice in matters that affect them. Joan decided this was sound advice and told herself that from now on she was going to allow her five-year-old daughter Carol to do more thinking for herself. A short time later they were in a children's dress shop. Joan found only two dresses she would consider buying for Carol, one pink and one yellow. She had a strong private preference for the yellow dress, but she was determined to allow Carol to do some thinking for herself. She told Carol, "You can have the dress you like better." This was a message from Joan's Adult to her child's Adult. Delightedly, Carol rapidly picked the pink dress. Immediately Joan's face took on an icy look; her posture became rigid. Her facial expression and body posture said, "You have very poor judgment." This message was from Joan's Controlling Parent to Carol's Child.

Joan was following the letter of Ginott's advice, but she was unable to enter into the spirit of the advice. Under these conditions, she was sending her daughter a confusing message. Transactional analysis asserts that if there is a pattern of similar experiences, a child such as Carol will develop, as part of her self-image, the idea "I have poor taste in clothes"—even if her mother never says so at a verbal level.

A traditionalist would identify the person in the I'm not OK—you're OK position as having neurotic patterns of behavior. But transactional analysis prefers not to use conventional psychological labels. The important thing, according to transactional analysis, is not to assign the word "neurotic" to someone, but to understand the underlying process. By recognizing the interpersonal pattern that is typical of "neurosis," there is some possibility of breaking free from the pattern.

It should be noted that transactional analysis sees the majority of people in the I'm not OK—you're OK position. The argument is that the vast majority of parents tend to be overcontrolling. They use put-downs, attributions, and ulterior messages as their way of socializing the child. Also, their strokes are conditional; affection must be earned. Thus Berne saw the vast majority of individuals in the one down position, struggling to overcome feelings of inferiority traceable to early childhood experiences.

I'M OK—YOU'RE NOT OK

The person in the I'm OK—you're not OK position feels that he is superior to other people and that, consequently, he has a right to use others for his own ends. He looks down on others as "worms," "cruds," "jerks," "saps," "dummies," "pigeons," or "suckers." The conscious position is one of smug self-confidence. But it is clear that in some cases this is a mask or a pose designed to cover up inferiority feelings. The person in this position tends to behave in an undersocialized manner. He may be a common criminal, breaking the law to reach his goals. More commonly, however, he would be a criminal from a moral, but not a legal, point of view. He knows what he can get away with. Thus he becomes what is variously described as a "con artist," "wheeler-dealer," "manipulator," "fast-talker," "supersalesman," or "make-out artist." That so many slang terms exist for people who behave out of the second position suggests the common recognition of such persons.

The roots of the second position were described earlier in this chapter. You will recall the transactional analysis formulation of the person with a big Rebellious Child. It is theorized that such persons had to force their parents to pay attention to them by acts of rebellion. Thus persons in the second position probably got their strokes in the form of punishment. If the punishment was excessive or unfair, it tended to reinforce the I'm OK—you're not OK position. The child thought, "It's not fair.

They had no right to do that to me. My parents are a couple of cruds.'' According to transactional analysis, a pattern of harsh punishment tends to backfire. Instead of socializing the child, it sends him into the basically antisocial second position. The traditionalist would associate character disorders with the second position.

I'M NOT OK—YOU'RE NOT OK

People in the I'm not OK—you're not OK position feel that they are inferior in some way. At the same time they also feel that other people are defective in some way. Others are incompetent, have bad intentions, or are conspirators. This third position is a position of no self-trust and no trust of others. Thus it is the ''sickest'' of the life positions. A person in the third position is likely to exhibit highly inappropriate behavior from a conventional point of view. Slang terms used to describe people in the third position are ''crazy,'' ''screwy,'' ''nuts,'' ''cracked,'' ''goofy,'' ''dizzy,'' and so forth. The existence of so many slang terms is significant because it suggests the reality of the third life position. Slang terms arise in response to a need for an everyday descriptive language. In traditional terms, persons in the third position would be associated with various kinds of psychotic reactions.

How do people get into the third position? We must realize that traditional psychologists and psychiatrists see psychotic reactions in terms of a complex interplay of genetic, biochemical, and psychological factors. Transactional analysis concentrates only on the psychological factors. From a transactional analysis point of view, we can infer that persons who in adulthood have arrived at the unfortunate I'm not OK— you're not OK position were subjected to an extra heavy dose of destructive parent-child transactions during early childhood. The parents seldom came on ''straight.'' Ulterior messages were the rule of the day. Stated colloquially, the transactional analyst would say, ''Crazy people were talked to and dealt with in crazy ways when they were kids. They are victims—scapegoats of mom and dad's hang-ups.'' Using Berne's metaphor of the royal person turning into a frog, we could say that people in the third position were not only turned into frogs; they were turned into superfrogs by the superbad magic of mixed-up parents.

I'M OK—YOU'RE OK

A person in the I'm OK—you're OK position is in the healthiest life position. He feels that he is reasonably competent and that life is worth living. He also feels that other people are, on the whole, friendly and likeable. He trusts himself and others. His stance toward others is reminiscent of Will Rogers's remark, "I never knew a man I didn't like." He looks for the best in others, not the worst. The individual in the fourth position does not think of others before meeting them as superior to him, inferior to him, or untrustworthy; such prejudices arise from the traces of early experiences recorded in the Parent and the Child ego states. The person in the fourth position operates out of his Adult, being open to information arising from the present and evaluating people as he goes along. He thus forms his conclusions about others from his transactions with them, not from old transactions with his parents and parental figures.

How does a person get into the fortunate fourth position? There is some controversy among transactional analysts about the correct answer. Harris feels that the fourth position is arrived at only by a conscious decision. The early childhood experience always places us in one of the first three "down" positions. The only way out is to realize that there is an "up" position, to recognize its merit, and to *choose* to be in it. Steiner feels that the fourth position is the natural position, the individual's birthright. It is the destructive transactions with insensitive and unloving parents that shove us into one of the first three positions. The difference between Steiner's and Harris's viewpoint is that Harris feels early childhood experiences inevitably place the child in the down position and make him feel not OK. No matter how loving or understanding are the parents, the child must develop not OK feelings because he in fact knows less than adults, is incompetent compared to adults, is smaller than adults, and so forth. Steiner's position is that early childhood experiences do not inevitably place the child in the down position; a child can be saved from going into one of the unhealthy positions by a rich diet of unconditional strokes and constructive transactions. In other words, the prince or princess does not have to become a frog. Steiner's position would seem to be closer to transactional analysis as originally formulated by Berne.

Perhaps there is more congruence between the Harris and Steiner viewpoints than might be apparent on the surface. Both men would certainly agree that tremendous numbers of people wind up as adults in one of the three down positions. Although Harris would say this is inevitable, and Steiner would say it is not inevitable, the practical question becomes: How does a person move from an unhealthy life position to a healthy life position? There is no categorical answer to this question. The various pathways to adjustment and growth discussed in this book represent different answers to the question. The specific answer given by Harris was already noted: The person must comprehend the value of the healthy life position and make a conscious choice to accept it. In addition, we can say that implicit in transactional analysis is the suggestion that a knowledge of ego states, transactional patterns, games, and life scripts will give a person the self-awareness required to reach the I'm OK—you're OK life position.

PLAYING GAMES

Berne's bestselling book *Games People Play* had so much general impact that it even inspired a popular song by the same title:

Oh, the games people play now,
Ev'ry night and ev'ry day now.
Never meanin' what they say, now
Never sayin' what they mean . . .*

The lyric captures to some degree what Berne had in mind when he used the word *game.* He saw a game in terms of disguised meanings and manipulative ploys. In *Games People Play*, Berne writes:

A game is an ongoing series of complementary ulterior transactions progressing to a well-defined, predictable outcome. Descriptively it is a recurring set of transactions, often repetitious, superficially plausible, with a concealed motivation; or, more colloquially, a series of moves with a snare, or "gimmick." (p. 48)

It is important to realize that Berne was using the word "game" in a serious way. A game may not be fun or even enjoyable. It is often self-destructive and destructive toward others. A game is called a game because it is played by a set of rules. In games played for fun, these rules are usually well defined and made explicit. In serious life games, the rules are often poorly defined and are seldom explicit. Nonetheless, the rules are there; and they are known by the players at a psychological level. Thus the word "game" was chosen by Berne to refer to complex sets of transactions having predictable outcomes.

TIME

Why do people play games? The answer has to do with time. People are alive and they must spend their time on Earth in some way. There thus arises, according to Berne, a need to structure time. Some form must be given to existence. Berne says that the need to structure time arises from three underlying hungers: (1) stimulus hunger, (2) recognition hun-

---

* Joe South, "Games People Play." Copyright 1968 by Lowery Music Co., Inc., Atlanta, Ga. Used by permission. International Copyright secured. All rights reserved.

ger, and (3) structure hunger. *Stimulus hunger* represents itself as the craving for some kind of sensory input. We want to see things, hear voices and music, taste foods, smell odors, touch objects and other people. Prisoners hate solitary confinement because of the sensory isolation. *Recognition hunger* represents itself as the craving for some kind of human attention. The infant needs the cuddling and embraces of nurturing parents. The adult needs other people to say "Hello" and to give him some sort of audience for his behavior. *Structure hunger* represents itself as the craving for something to do or somewhere to go. We feel restless if the day, the week, or life itself seems formless. Games help us satisfy all three hungers. No matter how destructive a game is, it provides us with a certain amount of stimulation, recognition, and structure.

Games are not the only way people structure time. In *Games People Play* and *What Do You Say after You Say Hello*, Berne gives a slightly different list of ways in which people structure time. Let us use the second book as our guide. It was published about eight years after the first book, not long before Berne's death. Thus it reveals his developed thought on the subject of time structuring. In *What Do You Say after You Say Hello*, Berne identifies five basic ways the majority of people structure time for the short run. (Structuring time for the long run is associated with *scripts*; scripts are the subject of the next major section of this chapter.) The five basic ways are (1) withdrawal, (2) rituals, (3) activities, (4) pastimes, and (5) games.

The concept of *withdrawal* states that the first basic choice we make in relating to others is "to play or not to play." We can engage in social interaction, or we can refuse to interact. Withdrawal is common. Berne gives as examples the behavior of people on a subway train and group therapy with withdrawn schizophrenics. Another illustration is provided by the *autistic child*, a child who manifests little interest in relating to other human beings. Still another illustration is provided by the shy adolescent girl who refuses all dates with boys; she is withdrawing from a particular area of her life.

A *ritual* consists of a series of predictable complementary transactions. A ritual may be formal or informal. A Roman Catholic Mass would be an example of a formal ritual. On the other hand, a dinner guest leaving a friend's home would be expected to participate in an informal ritual in which he thanks his host, says how much he enjoyed the dinner, and makes some reference to inviting his host over soon. The proper host would be expected to say how much he enjoyed the guest's company, that he would be glad to accept an invitation to the guest's home, and so forth. This at-the-door leave-taking ritual might take several minutes and is an important part of the evening's behavior. The purpose of rituals

A ritual consists of a series of predictable complementary transactions.

is not to exchange information, but to exchange strokes. Each smile, nod, and word of approval is a stroke.

An *activity* is a form of social interaction in which the transactions are programmed by the nature of the material with which people are working. In other words, a situation or a task tells two or more people how to act together. The word "work" is often used in association with activities. Two men working on a car, a husband and wife working on their income tax return, and two students working on arithmetic problems together provide illustrations of human beings engaged in activities. Like rituals, activities provide a fairly safe way of obtaining strokes.

Slightly riskier than rituals and activities are *pastimes*. Pastimes are a step on the way to games; they represent an intermediary concept between rituals and activities on the one hand and games on the other hand. A pastime may be defined as a series of complementary transactions having to do with a particular subject. As such, a pastime exhibits semiritualistic characteristics. Pastimes are most likely to be manifest at social gatherings; people tend to feel awkward just staring at each other or at their feet. So they search for subjects of general interest and make comments to fill in the void that would otherwise exist. Like games, pastimes may be named. A few names given by Berne are "PTA," "Psychiatry," "Ever Been," "What Became," "General Motors," "Kitchen," and "Wardrobe." Here is an illustration of two people playing "Ever Been":

Person 1. Have you ever been to Italy?

Person 2. No, but I've always wanted to go.

Person 1. We went last summer. It was fabulous.

Person 2. Oh, do I envy you. Did you visit Rome?

Person 1. Yes, and was it fantastic!

Person 2. That's terrific. Tell me, have you ever been to Hawaii?

Person 1. No, but I've always wanted to go.

Person 2. Well, we managed to go last year, and . . .

TRADING STAMPS AND RACKETS

After pastimes, there are games. Games are thus the fifth way the majority of people structure time for the short run. The concept of a game was defined a few pages earlier. The essential characteristic of a game is that at least two people manipulate each other for personal and ulterior ends. Before discussing specific kinds of games, it might be useful to introduce two concepts not previously discussed: *Psychological trading stamps* and *rackets*. They play an important part in games.

The notion of a psychological trading stamp in transactional analysis is similar to the actual trading stamps given by merchants. Stamps can be redeemed for various kinds of "goodies." Similarly, psychological trading stamps can be "cashed" for various kinds of feelings. Also, like actual stamps, psychological stamps come in various colors. Two basic colors are brown and gold: Brown stamps are associated with bad feelings, gold stamps with good feelings. It should be understood that not all people are stamp collectors, although transactional analysis clearly implies that most are. People in the healthy I'm OK—you're OK position would have little need to collect psychological stamps. People in one of the three down positions would be likely to collect stamps. Say that Martha is a habitual brown stamp collector, which means that when she is offended by someone else she collects a favorite bad feeling, such as anger. At a certain point in time she may feel that she wants to cash in her brown anger stamps for a prize. The prize may be a "free" temper tantrum. The word "free" is used because Martha feels justified in throwing her temper tantrum. Another person might save up several books of brown stamps and feel entitled to a guilt-free divorce.

Gold stamps are collected when a person is praised, given a medal, receives a five-year pin, or is otherwise recognized. Like brown stamps, gold stamps are traded in for the right to engage in guilt-free behavior. An employee who has recently received a five-year pin might phone in sick one day, rationalizing that he has earned the time off. A child that has just been given a gold star by his piano teacher for playing a piece particularly well might "goof off" for a few days. We say, "He is resting on his laurels." Some people who have collected many books of gold stamps may just stop working for life. Such might be the case of a great champion. He may have collected so many gold stamps in his twenties and thirties that in his forties and fifties he feels entitled to get fat and be half drunk most of the time. Thus transactional analysis asserts that the collection of and trading in of gold stamps can be just as "sick" as dealing in brown stamps. Again, it is argued that the person in the life-enhancing I'm OK—you're OK position has little need to deal in stamps, either brown or gold.

Transactional analysts say that the individual tends to have a favorite kind of stamp he collects. Cashing in pages or books of stamps is really a form of self-indulgence. The pattern that is peculiar to the particular individual is called his *racket*. Rackets tend to be associated with such negative feelings as inferiority, anxiety, hostility, and guilt. In *What Do You Say after You Say Hello*, Berne defines a racket as follows:

A racket, then, is a feeling, out of all possible feelings, that is habitually turned on by a given person as his payoff in the games he plays. (p. 139)

We see now one of the major reasons people play manipulative and destructive life games. According to Berne, a major aim is to engage in self-indulgent rackets. The other major aim of game-playing is to consolidate one's position. For example, if a person feels I'm not OK—you're OK, he seeks to prove to himself that this is true.

KINDS OF GAMES

Transactional analysis identifies many kinds of games. In addition to the basic category of life games, there are marital games, party games, sexual games, underworld games, consulting room games, and good games. Furthermore, within each category a number of games can be specified. In *Games People Play*, Berne labels and describes more than thirty-five games. And new games have been identified since the publication of *Games People Play*. It is not within the scope of this book to make an exhaustive list of games. Instead, a few games will be named and described to illustrate the way games operate in daily living, according to transactional analysis.

Mine Is Better Than Yours. It was noted earlier in this chapter that "Mine Is Better Than Yours" is the basic game of all the games. The reason is that it best represents the raw power struggle between two or more persons. The aim of the game is to be one up, to place the other person in the one down position, and to consequently obtain a bit of relief from the I'm not OK—you're OK position. The game is evident in preschoolers: "My toy is better than your toy." The game is also evident in school-age children. "I got an A on the test and you only got a C," says Vernon to Edward. "Yeah? So what? I can run faster than you," says Edward to Vernon. "Mine Is Better Than Yours" becomes a full-fledged game when played between intimates. For example, let us say that Al and Jane are a married couple. Both are students working toward higher degrees. They tend to discount each other's achievements, constantly trying to outshine each other. Consequently, they receive little positive stroking in their relationship. Under such conditions, "Mine Is Better Than Yours" is a "sick" game leading nowhere in the long run.

If It Weren't for You. Berne identifies "If It Weren't for You" as a game early in *Games People Play.* He says it is the most common game played by married persons. The game frequently appears in the form of a submissive wife complaining about a domineering husband. She expresses, sometimes to her husband and sometimes to others, that if it weren't for him she might have had a wonderful career or might have realized her art talent or whatever. She blames him for inhibiting her, holding her down, keeping her from realizing her potentialities.

Berne argues that in such a game the husband is peforming a real service for the wife however. Berne notes that the husband forbids her to do something she is deeply afraid of and prevents her from becoming aware of her fears. The wife is really the central figure in the game, and the game is played between the couple primarily because of her unconscious aim to find a justification for her inability to live up to her potentialities as a person. The husband in this game is essentially a fall guy or patsy.

There is, of course, no reason why "If It Weren't for You" can't be turned around in a particular marriage. The husband may be the one who blames his wife for his lack of success, for example. "She stopped me from going into business" or "I would have gone back to school if she had been for it" are typical male laments. The game can also be played between two business partners: "I wanted to expand when interest rates were low. This one store could have been a whole chain. But Joe was against it." Thus we see that the game "If It Weren't for You" can be played by many people under a variety of conditions.

Alcoholic. Transactional analysts tend to regard alcoholism as neither incurable nor a disease. Indeed, the very term "alcoholic" has a different meaning within the context of transactional analysis. In *Games People Play*, Berne says:

In game analysis there is no such thing as alcoholism or "an alcoholic," but there is a role called the Alcoholic in a certain type of game. If a biochemical or physiological abnormality is the prime mover in excessive drinking—and that is still open to some question—then its study belongs in the field of internal medicine. Game analysis is interested in something quite different—the kinds of social transactions that are related to such excesses. Hence the game "Alcoholic." (p. 72)

The two principal players in the game "Alcoholic" are the Alcoholic and the Persecutor. The surface motives for excessive drinking vary with the individual. "I drink to escape from my worries." "I drink just because I like it." "A few stiff drinks are the only thing that relax me when I'm uptight. Then I just seem to lose control." "I drink because I'm depressed." These and other reasons are examples of verbalizations offered by excessive drinkers as explanations of their behavior. Transactional analysts doubt the validity of these stated purposes, however. They see a deeper theme running through the excessive use of alcohol: self-castigation. In game analysis, the Alcoholic is seen as a person who carries around a heavy load of guilt. He is greatly disappointed in himself as a person. The real payoff in the game "Alcoholic" comes when he is having a hangover and his spouse or other significant person takes on the role of Persecutor, heaping abuse on his head. When this happens, the Alcoholic experiences substantial psychological torment. He thus pays some of the price for his past transgressions or failures and in turn feels less guilty about them. Thus we see that the Persecutor is really the Alcoholic's patsy, playing into his hands and reinforcing the pattern of excessive drinking in the long run.

Frigid Woman. "Frigid Woman" is categorized as a marital game. Like "Alcoholism," transactional analysis sees "frigidity" in terms of a role, that role of Frigid Woman. The Frigid Woman is provocative; she teases the male in various ways until he is aroused enough to make an advance. Then she rejects him with accusations that he is little more than an animal and that he is not interested in her as a person—only as a sex object. She is motivated by an unconscious fear of sexual intimacy. The ulterior aim of the game on her part is vindication. She proves to herself that she is a Proper Wife and he is an Inconsiderate Husband. The husband participates in the game because unconsciously he is just as afraid of sexual intimacy as his wife is. The game can, of course, be turned around. Some couples play a game of "Frigid Man"; but Berne argues that this is less common than "Frigid Woman."

Ain't It Awful.   "Ain't It Awful" is classified as a party game. As people become well acquainted, particularly in a given social circle, games begin to make their appearance at get-togethers. "Ain't It Awful" can be broken down into several versions. One of the versions is "Nowadays." It usually consists of a set of Parent-Parent transactions in which the players exchange put-downs of other people.

"Nowadays all teenagers take drugs," says the first player.

"I know. It's just shocking! And the moral decadence!" exclaims the second player.

"Yes! The son of the people next door has one of these vans. And he has girls in it until all hours in the morning."

"My sister's daughter goes out with boys who own vans. I know for a fact what she is doing. In my day we had a name for girls like that."

Persons play "Nowadays" from a form of self-righteous stance. Their remarks tend to be punitive and vicious. The more punitive and vicious the remarks, the more likely it is that the players unconsciously envy those they criticize. The social message emanating from the Parent is, "Ain't it awful." But the psychological message emanating from the Child is, "I wish I could do it."

Uproar. The game "Uproar" is classified as a sexual game. In its most common version, it is played between an authoritarian father and his adolescent daughter. The father plays the role of Judge, finding much fault with his daughter. This leads to anger, and perhaps the girl goes to her bedroom and slams the door. Or they may go to their respective bedrooms and slam the doors. In any event, the slamming of bedroom doors is symbolical. In *Games People Play*, Berne comments:

"Uproar" offers a distressing but effective solution to the sexual problems that arise between fathers and teenage daughters in certain households. Often they can only live in the same house together if they are angry at each other, and the slamming doors emphasize for each of them the fact that they have separate bedrooms. (p. 130)

In brief, transactional analysis sees "Uproar" as a way two relatives who experience a forbidden sexual attraction keep themselves from reaching the point of sexual intimacy.

Cops and Robbers.   "Cops and Robbers" is classified as an underworld game. Some habitual criminals lead a life of crime for profit. They are lawbreakers because they have found a way to make substantial sums of money, and they find numerous ways to avoid prison. Such people are not playing the game of "Cops and Robbers." The protagonist in "Cops and Robbers" is described by Berne as a "compulsive loser."

His Child really wants to get caught. He rarely earns large sums of money from his criminal activities. He plays the role of Robber to seek reassurance. Reassurance may be interpreted as a form of stroking in which parental figures say, "We care enough about you to stop you." The Robber's Child is saying from the psychological level, "You must catch me." Those who play roles such as Cop or Judge are happy to oblige.

I'm Only Trying To Help You.   "I'm Only Trying To Help You" is categorized as a consulting room game. It is played between such professionals as social workers, psychotherapists, and attorneys and their respective clients. The person playing the role of Helper is the hard player in the game, and the person playing the role of Client is his patsy. The Helper's ulterior motive is to prove to himself that people are ungrateful and disappointing. The Helper strenuously works at making suggestions, none of which seem to work. One day the Client may get angry and pour forth bitter criticisms of the Helper. The Helper is bewildered. His words or expression convey the message to the Client, "But I was only trying to help you!" The bewilderment and psychological pain of the Helper are his payoffs for playing the game. Berne feels that a Helper is a person with masochistic tendencies, seeking punishment to relieve chronic feelings of guilt. It is important to note that not all professionals and their clients play "I'm Only Trying To Help You." The legitimate helper who charges a fair fee for services rendered, does not raise false expectations in his clients, and relates on an Adult-Adult basis must be distinguished from the game-playing Helper.

Cavalier.   Most games are "bad" because they involve ulterior motives, manipulation, and exploitation of at least one of the players (the patsy) by the other player. It is not easy to find "good" games. A good game also involves ulterior motives and a certain degree of manipulation, or it is not a game in transactional analysis terms. A good game is one in which the players are not hurt or used and in which one or both players derive some benefit. "Cavalier" is an example of a good game.

The game "Cavalier" is played between a man who adopts the role of Poet and a woman who adopts the role of Appreciative Subject. The Poet must be a man who is not under sexual pressure. He may be an older man, a man with a satisfactory marriage, or a celibate content with his state. In brief, the Poet and the Appreciative Subject do not have sexual designs on each other. Within the bounds of good taste, the Poet seeks out numerous opportunities to admire, praise, and flatter the female in question. He is eloquent. She in turn reinforces his behavior with responsive appreciation. Their joint aim is mutual admiration, and that is why they play the game.

ENDING THE GAMES

Are we doomed like chess pieces to play games for life? The answer given by Berne and other transactional analysts is no. People need not go on playing games indefinitely. The purpose of game analysis is to shine a harsh spotlight on games, reveal their hidden nature, and thus make it possible for people to give up destructive transactional patterns. The principal player in a game, once he recognizes the nature of his role, can ask himself, "Do I want to keep playing this part? Is this the real me, or is it just a cardboard character going through stale moves to achieve ulterior aims?" The patsy in a game, upon discovering that he has been allowing the principal player to manipulate him, can ask himself, "Do I want to keep on being a patsy? How can I stop the other person from conning me?" Games end when one or both of the players "blows the whistle" on the game by refusing to play any more. This can be done in various ways. Sometimes a player just stops responding in predictable ways. Other times a player may confront the other player with the facts of the game.

Although much of Berne's writing about games seems to be exceedingly pessimistic, Berne was a long-range optimist. He believed in the power of human awareness. By comprehending the nature of games, by seeing the way rackets work, by recognizing the roles that they play, persons can proceed to a better existence beyond games. The nature of this better existence will be detailed shortly, when autonomy and intimacy are discussed.

LIFE SCRIPTS: YOUR FATE IS NOT IN YOUR STARS

Long before the appearance of Eric Berne and transactional analysis, Shakespeare penned these well-known lines:

All the world's a stage,
And all the men and women merely players:
They have their exits and their entrances;
And one man in his time plays many parts . . . (As You Like It, *Act II*)

Shakespeare clearly reveals in these lines a view of human nature that finds its parallel in the current formulations of transactional analysis. Specifically, transactional analysis asserts that we not only tend to live by games, but we also tend to live by *scripts*. A script is defined as an unconscious life plan.

In another play by Shakespeare, *Romeo and Juliet*, the two central characters are referred to as "star-crossed lovers." This implies that their personal destinies can be understood in astrological terms, a view popular in both Shakespeare's time and ours. Transactional analysis, however, does not see one's life script in terms of an impersonal fate determined by planetary bodies. On the contrary, the life script is the person's own choice. It represents a *decision* made in early childhood out of the Child ego state. As such, it is difficult to change. Nonetheless, because it does represent a decision, it is something for which the person must take responsibility if he wishes to modify it.

KINDS OF SCRIPTS

You will recall that games are one of the ways that people structure time for the short run. Scripts represent a way that people structure time for the long run. As already noted, a script represents an unconscious life plan adopted by the Child ego state. According to Berne, the script is adopted in early childhood. If it is a losing script, and many are, at least one of the child's parents was functioning much like a witch or an ogre in a fairy tale, "hexing" the child and making him feel that he was destined to be a loser. The child was made to feel that he was not lovable or competent, and this turned him into a frog. The frog-child then made a statement to himself such as, "I'll never amount to anything no matter how hard I try," "I'll hurt them someday the way they're hurting me," or "If they think I'm crazy, then I'll just be crazy." One of these thoughts, depending on the particular child, represents a decision to live life in a certain way. This decision is the *script protocol*, a crude image of the way the future will be. In adulthood, the script protocol is replaced with the *shooting script*, complete in dramatic detail and filled out with a cast of characters.

In *What Do You Say after You Say Hello*, Berne sets up a basic script typology. He says that there are (1) winning scripts, (2) nonwinning scripts, and (3) losing scripts. Persons who have adopted winning scripts are called princes and princesses. They will accomplish their goals in life. To illustrate, if a winner's script calls for retiring by age forty, earning an M.D. degree, or marrying the prettiest girl in town, he will do it. Persons who have adopted nonwinning scripts stand somewhere between royalty and frogs. They are the also-rans, the at-leasters. To illustrate, say that Tom sets out to have $100,000 saved by the age of forty. When he is forty, he has saved $10,000 and he can say, "Well, at least I saved $10,000." Persons who have adopted losing scripts are called frogs. They do not reach their goals in life. Berne observes, "The typical, classical loser is the man who makes himself suffer sickness or damage for no good cause" (p. 205).

In *Scripts People Live*, Steiner expands on Berne's concept of the losing script and notes that in his own study of unhappy life-styles, three kinds

Berne says that winners accomplish their goals in life.

of losing scripts seem to stand out: (1) the depression, or no love, script, (2) the madness, or no mind, script, and (3) the drug addiction, or no joy, script. Persons living out a *depression script* experience a chronic lack of adequate stroking. The theme of their life is lovelessness, and they often feel unworthy of love. In extreme cases, the depression script may end in suicide. Persons living out a *madness script* suffer from a chronic fear that they will go crazy. Some persons in the grips of a madness script are eventually hospitalized; others are relatively incompetent and have a difficult time coping with the problems of daily living. Persons living out a *drug addiction script* may be dependent on such obvious drugs as alcohol or heroin, or they may rely heavily on the drugs found in coffee, aspirin, and sedatives. The aim of chronic drug-taking is to block feelings, to dim one's awareness that life is a joyless affair.

Steiner notes that the three losing scripts are not necessarily mutually exclusive. A person can suffer from a mixture of two or even three scripts in which one of the scripts forms a major theme and the other one or two form minor themes. Steiner also notes that in everyday life many of the persons acting from a losing script live it out in what is described as a *banal manifestation*, meaning a version of the script that is nondramatic— a rather dull and featureless version of what might have been an exciting and tragic script. Illustrations given by Steiner of banal manifestations are the spinster or bachelor, the cigarette-and-coffee-addicted unhappy person, or the individual who is almost always in a crisis because of an inability to manage ordinary problems.

SCRIPT VARIATIONS

Scripts can vary in ways other than along the winning–losing dimension. Two principal script variations from the basic script are (1) the counterscript and (2) the antiscript. The *counterscript* represents the social message sent by a parent, parents, or parental figures. It is what a child was *told* to do in words, as opposed to what he was *programmed* to do by ulterior psychological messages. The counterscript represents the "oughts" and the "shoulds" of the Right Path and, consequently, may be taken only half-seriously by the Child ego state of a person who has adopted a losing script. For example, assume that Albert is a chronic alcoholic. His script calls for him to drink himself to death. His counterscript calls for him to abstain from alcohol forever. From time to time he makes a presumably iron resolution to never touch a drop of liquor again. He may observe the resolution for days, weeks, or longer. But he feels like a puppet acting out a farce, and at a deeper level he knows he will eventually return to the bottle. While he is "being good" he is living out the counterscript. The counterscript provides a bit of temporary relief from the script, and it makes the individual's life less featureless; but it is not to be taken seriously. It is just a lull in the action.

The *antiscript* is the mirror image of the script. Say that a person has become aware that he has a particular kind of script. He says, "I don't want to play the role the script calls for." He then decides to oppose every instruction in the script. If the script says "Stop," he goes. If the script says "Speak," he is quiet. If the script says "Be polite," he is nasty. If the script says "Work hard and make a lot of money," he quits his job and joins a commune. He may delude himself that he has freed himself from the script, but this is an illusion. The script is still determining everything he does.

AUTONOMY AND INTIMACY

The principal goals of transactional analysis are autonomy and intimacy for the individual. Within the context of transactional analysis, *autonomy* may be defined as game-free and script-free living. The autonomous person tends to be nonmanipulative in his personal relations. He is not a put-down artist. He does not live his life like a character in a play, rigidly acting out unconscious directives as if he is a hypnotized subject. At this point it should be noted that living out a winning script is *not* the same as script-free living. A script is by definition an unconscious life plan. Thus even a winning script may be a kind of straitjacket that confines a person to a narrow set of acceptable behaviors. A person with a winning script is *programmed* to be top dog, to achieve his goals, and so forth. Thus, in a sense, having a winning script is not quite the same thing as being a "real" winner. A real winner is a person who has broken free from the script. He is not living out of unconscious script directives, but out of conscious decisions. This is not to say that a person without a script has no plans and no goals. On the contrary, he has flexible plans and realistic goals made out of his thinking Adult, not his irrational Child.

The other principal goal of transactional analysis, *intimacy*, is defined by Berne in *What Do You Say after You Say Hello* as follows: "A game-free exchange of emotional expression without exploitation" (p. 443). The concept of intimacy is particularly important when it is applied to the way we relate to *significant others*—parents, husbands, wives, children, and close friends. When there is intimacy in a relationship, there is mutual respect for each individual's status as a real person. Berne saw intimacy as a function of the Natural Child. Thus autonomy and intimacy are closely

Transactional analysis defines intimacy as a game-free exchange of emotional expression without exploitation.

related. The autonomous person, living in a game-free and script-free way, liberates his Natural Child. The liberated Natural Child finds intimacy a rewarding way of life.

CRITIQUE

Transactional analysis has become the most widespread system used for understanding the communication process between two or more people. It has tremendous popularity. Books on transactional analysis have sold millions of copies to persons in all walks of life. Transactional analysis should not be accepted and used without any critical reservation whatsoever, however. The following are some thoughts to consider:

1 A large number of psychologists remain relatively unimpressed by transactional analysis. A common comment is, "Transactional analysis is just warmed-over psychoanalysis." It is certainly correct that much of transactional analysis grew directly out of psychoanalysis. Berne's concept of ulterior aims is approximately the same as Freud's idea of unconscious motivation. Berne's formulation of the Parent, Adult, and Child is detected by many critics as a copy of Freud's superego, ego, and id. Berne argued that there are important differences. The Parent, Adult, and Child are *ego states*; thus they are *directly experienced* by the person. The superego, ego, and id are abstract concepts; they are hypothetical contructions *about* the person. In spite of Berne's protests, the similarities between the Parent, Adult, and Child and the superego, ego, and id seem to outweigh the differences. The charge that transactional analysis is just warmed-over pychoanalysis seems somewhat appropriate when applied to structural analysis, the analysis of ego states. It seems unfair, though, when directed at transactional analysis proper. The idea that one person's ego states communicate with the ego states of other persons is not evident in the writings of Freud or his followers. Their primary concern was with processes within the individual, not the dialogue between two or more persons. It is in the area of interpersonal communications that transactional analysis makes its original contributions.

2 Transactional analysis itself can become a game. Berne himself warned against this danger. A person may learn and use most of the jargon of transactional analysis as an elaborate way of avoiding legitimate insight. He talks at length *about* autonomy and intimacy, but never becomes autonomous or intimate. He intellectualizes transactional analysis to such a degree that it is of no service to him in his quest for greater adjustment and growth.

3 Transactional analysis lends itself readily to those who wish to exploit others. Persons of ill will who seek to manipulate other people may use the concepts of transactional analysis to further their own selfish aims. Steiner calls attention to this hazard in *Scripts People Live.* The hazard is hardly the fault of transactional analysis itself. A knife can be wielded by a thug or by a surgeon. Like the knife, transactional analysis can cut two ways, depending on the intentions of the user. But it is important to realize that in certain people's hands, transactional analysis may have adverse effects.

4   The heavy use of slang by transactional analysts has led some thinkers to see transactional analysis as a slick, superficial psychology. The slang terms do indeed seem to encourage an oversimplified either–or kind of thinking. People are either frogs or princes. They are either getting positive strokes or negative strokes. They are either game-bound or game-free. They are either script-bound or script-free. They are either one up or are one down. Parents are either nurturing parents or they are witches and ogres. The reflective reader of transactional analysis will realize that slang terms and two-valued logic are used because they have impact. They make the system more accessible to persons having a limited background in psychology. Berne felt that more was gained than was lost by presenting ideas in sharp black-and-white images as opposed to shades of gray. This is a debatable point. From a practical point of view, however, we should be cognizant that gradients usually underlie two-valued terminology. For example, persons cannot be classified simply as frogs or princes. The frog image is invoked to suggest low self-esteem. The prince or princess image is invoked to suggest high self-esteem. Self-esteem can be conceptualized as a gradient with low self-esteem at one end and high self-esteem at the other, with an infinite number of points in between. An individual may have low self-esteem, slightly below average self-esteem, moderate self-esteem, somewhat higher than average self-esteem, and so forth. The actual person defies a label such as frog or prince.

5   Perhaps transactional analysis overemphasizes the importance of early childhood. Reading Berne and his followers, one would think that human destiny is determined by the time a child is five or six years of age. In contrast to Berne's formulations, several lines of research suggest that the school-age years (from about six to twelve years of age) are of particular importance in shaping one's sense of competence versus one's sense of inferiority. Also, experiences with peers appear to be of enormous importance during the adolescent period. These experiences have a great deal to do with the development of one's identity and one's capacity for intimacy. Berne overlooks the role of later childhood and adolescence in personality development. Even if experiences during the first five or six years of life may have more impact than the subsequent years of development, it seems an oversimplification to give the early years as much weight as Berne gives them.

6 Is Berne too hard on Parents? Thomas C. Oden, author of *Game Free: The Meaning of Intimacy*, writes:

Although Berne denies that he is being unkind to parents, the logic of his language and the force of his rhetoric lands almost without exception on the side of children against parents. Always the parenting voice is the witch, devil, ogre, or pig.

At a time when actual parents and children are having tough times communicating on the same wavelength, TA comes on with what to many seems to be a steady put-down of the necessary constraining parent inputs into the formulation of consciousness. (p. 87)

Oden goes on to note that Berne does in fact distinguish between the Controlling Parent and the Nurturing Parent. Berne is not, of course, critical of all parents, just those parents who set up irrational injunctions for their children. Oden observes, however, that in the heat of rhetoric the crucial distinction between the Controlling Parent and the Nurturing Parent tends to get lost.

7 Transactional analysts are against clinical name-calling. They say that they consider it insulting to label people with such terms as "neurotic" or "psychotic" or to say that certain people have character disorders. Yet transactional analysts do not hesitate to coin a new form of name-calling in which people are referred to as bitches, jerks, witches, ogres, winners, losers, frogs, princes, and princesses. Although it may be complimentary to refer to someone as a winner, a prince, or a princess, is it not insulting to refer to someone else as a bitch, jerk, witch, ogre, loser, or frog?

8 Like most approaches to more effective living derived from clinical experiences, transactional analysis does not derive its conclusions from rigorous experimental designs. There is a general consensus among psychologists that the clinical method is a weak method. Thus observations derived from the clinical method should be looked on more as hypotheses than as facts. Unfortunately, Berne and his followers tend to use a fact-oriented language, which gives readers the feeling that they are reading about the one and only system for understanding human behavior. A more sophisticated view would be to say that transactional analysis presents us with a set of penetrating insights and plausible hypotheses. As such, they may be helpful in furthering our understanding of human behavior.

9 Such concepts as autonomy and intimacy are on a high level of abstraction. They are such global terms that it is sometimes difficult to anchor them in reality. Although they are pregnant with intuitive and emotional meaning, it is often difficult in daily living to ascertain with any accuracy to what degree one is living an autonomous life or to what degree one has achieved intimacy. There are no objective criteria. Because there are no objective criteria, the person who quizzes himself too diligently about his own attainment of autonomy or capacity for intimacy may conclude he is falling short of some theoretical ideal and may experience a sense of failure as a person. Again, the language of transactional analysis tends to perpetuate either–or thinking. A person is either game-bound and script-bound or autonomous. A person is either emotionally distant from or intimate with another person. It would seem more accurate to suggest that individuals are more or less autonomous and more or less capable of intimacy, that there are stages of development in these areas. We should not set up such words as autonomy and intimacy as unrealistic standards by which we harshly judge ourselves.

IMPLICATIONS FOR ADJUSTMENT AND GROWTH

The foregoing critique does not discredit transactional analysis. In spite of some of the problems noted, transactional analysis remains a useful psychological tool. The following are some of the ways in which transactional analysis can contribute to our adjustment and growth.

1 The greatest single element of value in transactional analysis is its focus on the communication process. It explicitly suggests ways of improving the quality of messages exchanged by human beings. The primary emphasis is on the importance of Adult-Adult messages when there is a problem in a human relationship. Name-calling in the form of Parent-Child put-downs, bickering in the form of crossed transactions, and ulterior messages with hidden meanings do little to move a human relationship toward a more positive position. Transactional analysis shows us some ways of breaking out of old and valueless communication patterns.

2 Transactional analysis helps us to see the destructive and self-destructive traps of larger patterns identified as games and scripts. By throwing a harsh spotlight on these patterns, their outlines are brought into our consciousness. Such awareness is a first step on the road to greater personal freedom.

3 The insights offered by transactional analysis suggest practical ways of coping with destructive and manipulative people. We see more clearly how they are trying to be one up or to exploit us. Transactional analysis gives us strategies for defense. You may say to yourself, "He's putting me in the role of patsy. But I won't play his game." You might give an Adult response when someone sends a message to your Child, not allowing yourself to be placed in the one down position. Sometimes we might be willing to run some of the risks inherent in a confrontation if we feel it is necessary to "blow the whistle" on a game. The assertiveness skills defined and explained in Chapter Three are congruent with the transactional analysis idea of speaking out of your Adult. They can be combined with the transactional analysis formulations to help us avoid being used by other persons.

4   Transactional analysis gives us an explicit model for analyzing communication processes within ourselves. If a person is momentarily depressed, he might use the insights of structural analysis to reflect as follows: "Why am I depressed? Because I was expecting a promotion. I've been looking forward to it for a year, and the boss passed me over for Harry. Why does that depress me? Well, obviously I'm blaming myself, telling myself that something's wrong with me. And that's coming out of my Controlling Parent. My Controlling Parent is putting down my Child. It's scolding me. What does my thinking Adult have to say about all this? My thinking Adult says that I'm OK, that I did all I could to earn the promotion. At a rational level, I shouldn't blame myself. I'm still disappointed. No use kidding myself about that. But maybe I can use my Adult to keep my Parent from pounding on my Child. That's only making me feel worse, and there's just no point to it." Such a thought chain when we are feeling depressed, worried, anxious, or angry can clarify the source and content of the messages we are sending to ourselves within ourselves.

5   The transactional analysis goals of autonomy and intimacy create powerful images of what the Good Life can be. As such, they have both positive and negative aspects. As already noted in the critique section, the goals of autonomy and intimacy can create problems if we think of them in either–or terms. If we place autonomy and intimacy on gradients, however, we can think of ourselves as growing as persons as we gradually increase our sense of personal freedom and our capacity for emotional closeness.

6   One of the main themes of transactional analysis is: *You were meant to be a winner.* Again, this can create problems if conceptualized in strictly either–or terms. On the positive side, though, the theme of winning can be useful if we think of it in terms of personal growth. A "real winner" is a person who learns from experience, broadens his horizons, has a capacity for rational action, and enjoys life. Winning, in the transactional analysis sense, has nothing whatsoever to do with getting the best of others or with being the leading rat in the proverbial rat race. This is a point that is often misunderstood.

7   Transactional analysis gives us many ideas for becoming more effective parents. Examples of transactional analysis guidelines for parents are as follows: (1) Whenever possible, correct a child by addressing the

Adult in the child. (2) Give a substantial number of unconditional positive strokes to children; this is another way of saying that children should feel that the love of their parents is not something they have to purchase by "right" action. (3) Avoid sending ulterior messages that confuse children and place them in double binds. (4) Be aware that criticisms of a child's character are attributions that all too often "stick" and adversely affect a child's self-image. Muriel James, author of *Transactional Analysis for Moms and Dads*, ends her book for parents with a free-verse poem simply titled "A Further Thought":

It's pretty well known that:
What you give is what you get.

If you're a parent who gives wishy-washy strokes to
Children, you're likely to get wishy-washy strokes in
return.

If you're a parent who gives critical strokes to children,
you're likely to get critical strokes in return.

If you're a parent who gives warm, loving, golden strokes to
children, you're likely to get warm, loving, golden
strokes in return:
—and hugs
—and kisses
—and more love.*

In brief, transactional analysis is a coherent system for clarifying communication processes within and between ourselves. It throws a spotlight on ulterior games and unconscious scripts, suggesting ways of breaking free from these often destructive patterns. It tells us that we are basically OK as persons, that we are meant to be real winners. And it indicates that movement in the direction of greater autonomy and greater intimacy is desirable.

SUMMARY AND SELF-TEST

1 In the language of transactional analysis, the person who is one up is in a position of psychological power.
T   F

2 The psychiatrist Harry Stack Sullivan is generally recognized as an important precursor to transactional analysis.
T   F

3 Eric Berne was the father of transactional analysis.
T   F

4 Berne placed a great deal of emphasis on the value of "making progress" or "getting better" as opposed to the concept of "cure."
T   F

5 The three ego states identified by transactional analysis are the Child, the Parent, and the Adult.
T   F

6 The Natural Child represents the part of the Child that conforms to society's rules.
T   F

7 Psychologist Alvin Freed refers to positive strokes as "warm fuzzies."
T   F

8 The Controlling Parent tends to act as a judge.
T   F

9 A person can have an Adult that is contaminated by the Child, but the Adult cannot be contaminated by the Parent.
T   F

10 The term *blockage* is used as a synonym for contamination of the Adult.
T   F

11 Structural analysis is the study of how two or more persons communicate with each other.
T   F

12 According to Berne, a transaction is the unit of social intercourse.
T   F

13 An Adult-Adult transaction tends to be nonemotional and reality-oriented.
T   F

14 Parent-Child transactions tend to represent either criticism or praise.
T   F

15 A crossed transaction is never preferable to a complementary transaction.
T   F

16 Ulterior transactions involve the activity of one and only one ego state at a time.
T   F

17 The phrase "I'm not OK—you're OK" is a kind of shorthand for saying that some people suffer from low self-esteem and see others as having traits they themselves lack.
T   F

18 An *attribution* in transactional analysis is a statement to another person that he has such and such personality characteristics.
T   F

19 In traditional terms, persons in the I'm not OK—you're not OK existential position would be associated with various kinds of neurotic reactions.
T   F

20 Berne defined games in terms of explicit meanings and authentic human relationships.
T   F

21 Psychological trading stamps and rackets play little or no part in games.
T   F

22 The aim of the game called "Mine Is Better Than Yours" is to be one up and to place another person in the one down position.
T   F

23 Transactional analysts tend to regard alcoholism as a disease.
T   F

24 Transactional analysis sees "frigidity" in terms of a role, the role of Frigid Woman.
T   F

25 Transactional analysis sees the game "Uproar" as a way two relatives who experience a forbidden sexual attraction keep themselves from reaching the point of sexual intimacy.

T   F

26 Although much of Berne's writing about games seems to be exceedingly pessimistic, Berne was a long-range optimist.

T   F

27 In transactional analysis, a script is defined as an unconscious life plan.

T   F

28 Berne says that there are only two kinds of scripts: (1) winning scripts and (2) losing scripts.

T   F

29 The counterscript represents the social message sent by a parent, parents, or parental figures; it is what a child was *told* to do in words, as opposed to what he was *programmed* to do by ulterior psychological messages.

T   F

30 The principal goals of transactional analysis are autonomy and intimacy for the individual.

T   F

ANSWER KEY

1 *True*. In the language of transactional analysis, the person who is one up is in a position of psychological power.

2 *True*. The psychiatrist Harry Stack Sullivan is generally recognized as an important precursor to transactional analysis.

3 *True*. Eric Berne was the father of transactional analysis.

4 *False*. Berne placed a great deal of emphasis on the concept of "cure" as opposed to "making progress" or "getting better."

5 *True*. The three ego states identified by transactional analysis are the Child, the Parent, and the Adult.

6 *False*. The Adapted Child represents the part of the Child that conforms to society's rules.

7 *True*. Psychologist Alvin Freed refers to positive strokes as "warm fuzzies."

8 *True*. The Controlling Parent tends to act as a judge.

9 *False*. A person can have an Adult that is contaminated by the Child, by the Parent, or by both the Child and the Parent.

10 *False*. *Blockage* takes place when there is a barrier between one ego state and the Adult.

11 *False.* Transactional analysis, not structural analysis, is the study of how two or more persons communicate with each other.

12 *True.* According to Berne, a transaction is the unit of social intercourse.

13 *True* .An Adult-Adult transaction tends to be nonemotional and reality-oriented.

14 *True.* Parent-Child transactions tend to represent either criticism or praise.

15 *False.* There are times when a crossed transaction is preferable to a complementary transaction.

16 *False.* Ulterior transactions involve the activity of more than two ego states simultaneously.

17 *True.* The phrase I'm not OK—you're OK is a kind of shorthand for saying that some people suffer from low self-esteem and see others as having traits they themselves lack.

18 *True.* An *attribution* in transactional analysis is a statement to another person that he has such and such personality characteristics.

19 *False.* In traditional terms, persons in the I'm not OK—you're not OK life position would be associated with various kinds of psychotic reactions.

20 *False.* Berne defined games in terms of disguised meanings and manipulative ploys.

21 *False.* Psychological trading stamps and rackets play an important part in games.

22 *True.* The aim of the game called "Mine Is Better Than Yours" is to be one up and to place another person in the one down position.

23 *False.* Transactional analysts tend to regard alcoholism as neither incurable nor a disease.

24 *True.* Transactional analysis sees "frigidity" in terms of a role, the role of Frigid Woman.

25 *True.* Transactional analysis sees the game "Uproar" as a way two relatives who experience a forbidden sexual attraction keep themselves from reaching the point of sexual intimacy.

26 *True.* Although much of Berne's writing about games seem to be exceedingly pessimistic, Berne was a long-range optimist.

27 *True.* In transactional analysis, a script is defined as an unconscious life plan.

28 *False.* Berne says that there are (1) winning scripts, (2) nonwinning scripts, and (3) losing scripts.

29 *True.* The counterscript represents the social message sent by a parent, parents, or parental figures; it is what a child was *told* to do in words, as opposed to what he was *programmed* to do by ulterior psychological messages.

30 *True.* The principal goals of transactional analysis are autonomy and intimacy for the individual.

DISCUSSION QUESTIONS

THE THREE EGO STATES

1 Do you agree that the actual child you once were is retained in your adult personality in some form?

2 If you agree that you have a Child ego state, what are some of the "buttons" that make you play childhood "tapes"?

3 In what way is the concept of the Parent ego state similar to Freud's concept of the superego?

4 What are some of the functions of the Adult? Think of a close friend. Do you feel that his or her Adult ego state is functioning well?

TRANSACTIONS

1 On the whole, do you tend to prefer complementary no-conflict transactions? What does your answer suggest to you in terms of your own personality structure?

2 A crossed transaction takes place when there is conflict between two or more people. Have you recently been a participant in a crossed transaction? What was the situation? What was the outcome?

3 Why are ulterior transactions major troublemakers in human communication? What damage do they do?

THE FOUR EXISTENTIAL POSITIONS: ARE YOU OK?

1 Do you identify with one of the life positions?

2 In your family circle, does one of the life positions seem to be exhibited by a majority of the family members?

3 Do you feel that you have ever been conned by a person in the I'm OK —you're not OK position? What is the best way to protect ourselves against the manipulative tendencies of such persons?

4 Transactional analysis asserts that the I'm OK—You're OK life position is the healthiest life position. Is this consistent with your view of life?

PLAYING GAMES

1 What are some of the rackets you recognize in other people? Do you have any rackets of your own?

2 Is there a particular game or set of games you tend to play? Or do you feel that your own behavior is game-free?

3 Ending a game may call for a crossed transaction. Are there times when such a transaction is desirable?

LIFE SCRIPTS: YOUR FATE IS NOT IN YOUR STARS
1 Think of at least one person you know well. Do you feel that person is living his or her life by a script? What kind of a script is it?

2 According to transactional analysis, a script represents an unconscious life plan adopted by the Child ego state. Does this have the ring of truth to you?

3 Do you know anyone who has been been hospitalized for mental illness? If so, does it seem to you that this person is living out a madness script?

AUTONOMY AND INTIMACY
1 The principal goals of transactional analysis are autonomy and intimacy for the individual. Why do these seem to be particularly valuable goals?

2 How would you contrast the concept of a winning script with script-free living (autonomy)?

3 Do you feel that you have attained psychological-emotional intimacy with at least one other person?

REFERENCES
Berne, E. *Games People Play.* New York: Grove Press, 1964.

————. *Principles of Group Treatment.* New York: Grove Press, 1966

————. *Sex in Human Loving.* New York: Simon & Schuster, 1970.

————. *Transactional Analysis in Psychotherapy.* New York: Ballantine Books, 1961.

————. *What Do You Say after You Say Hello?* New York: Grove Press, 1972.

Chapman, A. H. *The Games Children Play.* New York: G. P. Putnam's Sons, 1971.

Freed, A. *T. A. for Tots.* Sacramento, Calif.: Jalmar Press, 1973.

Gardner, H. "Hello Up There, Dr. Q." *Human Behavior* (January 1975) vol. 4, pp. 24–29.

Ginott, H. G. *Between Parent and Child.* New York: Avon Books, 1969.

Harris, T. *I'm OK—You're OK.* New York: Harper & Row, 1967.

James, M. *Transactional Analysis for Moms and Dads.* Reading, Mass.: Addison-Wesley Publishing Co., 1974.

James, M. and Jongeward, D. *Born To Win.* Reading, Mass.: Addison-Wesley Publishing Co., 1971.

Meininger, J. *Success Through Transactional Analysis.* New York: Grosset & Dunlap, 1973.

Oden, T. C. *Game Free: The Meaning of Intimacy.* New York: Dell Publishing Co., 1974.

Steiner, C. *Games Alcoholics Play.* New York: Ballantine Books, 1971.

———. *Scripts People Live.* New York: Grove Press, 1974.

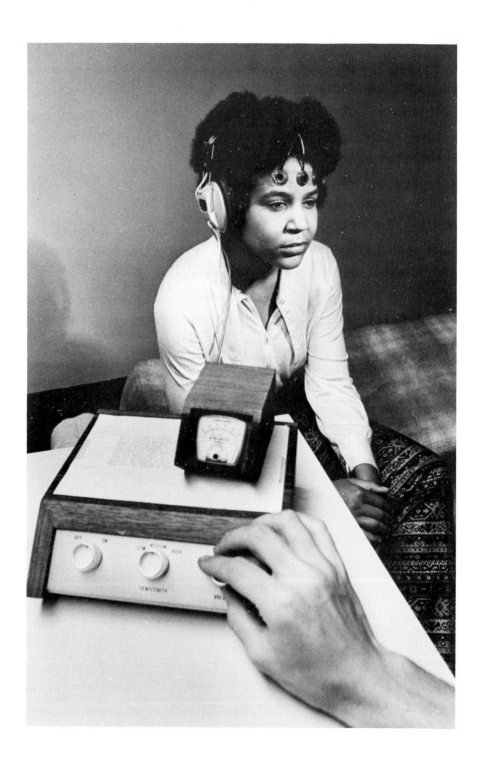

CHAPTER 6
PSYCHO-
TECHNOLOGY:
FROM
PSYCHOSURGERY
TO BIOFEEDBACK

OVERVIEW

OUTLINE

TWO KEY QUESTIONS

What is Psychotechnology?

The word *technology* taken by itself means applied science. Thus the best translation of psychotechnology into a meaningful phrase would be "applied behavioral science." In general terms, psychotechnology suggests a wide domain of exploration in which the orthodox distinctions among psychology, the physical sciences, and the biological sciences become blurred. Specifically, in this book the study of psychotechnology is defined as including the following subjects: psychosurgery, nutrition and behavior, drugs, and biofeedback.

How does psychotechnology relate to adjustment and growth?

Advocates of psychotechnology point to its useful features. Persons prone to violence, worry, depression, or hyperactivity may find relief from their conditions through psychosurgery, drugs, or changes in diet. Individuals with chronic migraine headaches, hypertension, and other psychosomatic problems can sometimes learn to reduce the impact of these problems via the route ot biofeedback training. Also, some researchers believe that psychotechnology can be used to greatly augment human abilities. Critics of psychotechnology, however, point to its many possibilities for abuse and arbitrary behavior control.

Psychotechnology is as new as today's headlines and as old as the dawn of civilization. *The Egyptian*, a highly popular novel in the late 1940s written by Mika Waltari, tells the tale of Sinuhe, physician to the Pharaoh. The action takes place about three thousand years ago, and yet brain surgery is described. Sinuhe is called on to relieve the distress of a man who constantly hears the roar of the sea in his ears, who is "given to swooning," and who suffers from excruciating pains in his head. The novel is written in the first person, and Sinuhe describes the brain surgery as follows:

I tapped him with the hammer at different points, and he made no sign until suddenly he cried out and fell to the ground senseless. I concluded from this that I had found the spot where it would be best to open his skull.

. . . I began my work. Slitting up the scalp, I stanched the copious bleeding with red-hot irons, though I was uneasy at the agony this caused him. . . . I had given him plentiful draughts of wine in which narcotics were dissolved so that his eyes protruded like those of a dead fish and he was cheerfully disposed. Next I opened the bone as carefully as I could with the instruments I had at my disposal, and he never even fainted but drew a deep breath and told me it already eased him when I removed the piece of bone. Now my heart rejoiced, for just where I had opened his head either the devil or the spirit of disease had laid its egg. . . . It was red and hideous and the size of a swallow's egg. With the utmost care I removed it, burning away all that held it to the brain. . . . I closed the skull with a silver plate and stitched the scalp over it, and the patient never lost consciousness at any time. When I had finished, he rose and walked about and thanked me with all his heart, for he no longer heard the terrible roar in his ears, and the pains also had ceased. (pp. 140–141)

The passage from *The Egyptian*, presumably a well-researched novel, is instructive in several ways. It suggests that perceptual delusions such as a roaring in the ears, can be caused by a diseased brain. It proposes that the ancient Egyptians did more than drill holes in the skull to "let out evil spirits." Possibly they understood something about the removal of brain tumors. It notes that *trepanning*, making a perforation in the skull, is an ancient art. And, lastly, the patient was conscious during the surgery! This may seem farfetched, but it is not. Patients are sometimes conscious during modern brain surgery. For example, the famous neurosurgeon Wilder Penfield performed numerous operations on sufferers from epilepsy in the 1930s and 1940s. During the course of the operations, he stimulated the brains of his *conscious* subjects with electrodes. Such stimulation often produced experiences of sights or sounds within the subject; sometimes the patient experienced a vivid recall of memories. Other points of stimulation produced motor movements, such as the involuntary clenching of a fist. Penfield was not merely using his patients as guinea pigs. Their reports were valuable feedback to him; they guided his hand. Fortunately, Penfield systematically collected his observations,

Motor and sensory areas of the human cortex have been mapped during brain surgery. (Open-brain surgery by Wilder Penfield. A record is made of the patient's behavior and subjective experience as each of the numbered areas is stimulated by an electrode.)

and his findings have played a large part in the contemporary mapping of the motor and sensory areas of the cortex in human beings.

In contemporary times, psychotechnology has had several precursors. One set of precursors was the *shock therapies*, therapies in which the treatment involves sending the organism into a state of shock by electrical or chemical means. The shock therapies played an important role in the development of psychotechnology because their wholesale use for several decades in mental hospitals paved the road for the use of other psychotechnological applications.

There are three principal forms of shock therapy: (1) Metrazol therapy, (2) insulin coma therapy, and (3) electroconvulsive therapy. *Metrazol therapy* utilizes Metrazol, a drug prepared from camphor, to induce convulsions. The method was pioneered by L. J. Meduna in the mid-1930s. Metrazol therapy never won a large following. It is of historical interest in that it stimulated the search for other ways of inducing seizures. *Insulin coma therapy* is another method of inducing a state of shock by chemical means. The patient is injected with insulin. This burns up his blood sugar at a rapid rate, and the patient goes into a state of shock. He is left in a coma and watched closely for about one hour. Then he is brought out of the coma by an injection of glucose. The method was developed by Manfred Sakel, also in the 1930s.

Why did Meduna, Sakel, and other psychiatrists seek to induce seizures in mental patients? The answer is based on their day-to-day observations, not on an elaborate psychological theory. It was noted that epileptic patients, patients subject to involuntary seizures, were seldom psychotic. There seemed to be a relationship between mood and nervous system "storms." It was also noted that following accidental insulin comas, diabetic schizophrenic patients sometimes improved psychologically. It was thus reasoned that the artificial induction of shock might be an effective treatment for psychosis.

By far the most widespread form of shock therapy was and is *electroconvulsive therapy,* a form of treatment in which an electric current is briefly passed through the frontal lobes of the brain. This induces a *grand mal seizure,* a large convulsion similar to the kind manifested by epileptic persons. Electroconvulsive therapy was introduced in 1937 by two Italian psychiatrists, Ugo Cerletti and Lucia Bini. It is reported in an article by psychiatrist Robert L. Taylor (p. 7) that their first electroconvulsive patient said after coming out of his seizure, *"Non una seconda! Mort fera."* ("Don't give me a second treatment. It's going to kill me.") His statement expresses the fear shared by most patients of having their brains "zapped" by electricity.

The principal value of electroconvulsive therapy appears to be its use in cases of psychotic depression, particularly when the patient is suicidal. Advocates of electroconvulsive therapy also recommend it for breaking up bizarre patterns of action, thought, or perception. Some psychiatrists give electroconvulsive treatments to patients with neurotic reactions, but the consensus seems to be that electroconvulsive therapy is not appropriate with neurotic sufferers.

Unfortunately, electroconvulsive therapy lends itself to a substantial amount of questionable use. In *The Making of a Psychiatrist*, an autobiographical account by psychiatrist David S. Viscott, is a chapter titled "Quacks, or Nobody's Perfect But . . ." In it, Viscott takes his colleagues to task for the excessive application of electroconvulsive therapy. He argues that various organic conditions can produce symptoms that mimic psychotic reactions. Such patients cannot benefit from shock treatments. He says:

One afternoon I became extremely upset thinking about all of this. I went down to my car and not knowing what else to do I drove to the zoo. At least this zoo wasn't disguised as a hospital. I bought two bags of peanuts, one for the elephant and one for me. . . .

It's not that I don't believe in electroshock. I do, but I think its use is limited. I simply had no idea EST was being abused this much. (p. 360)

Viscott's dismay is shared by many others who note the potential for abuse in electroconvulsive therapy and similar treatments. We will return to this point in the critique section of this chapter. For now, let us take a close-up look at key aspects of psychotechnology.

PSYCHOSURGERY: WILL SOCIETY BECOME PSYCHOCIVILIZED?

Visualize the following train of action: A man is standing in a bullring in Spain, facing a charging bull. The man is unarmed. He holds a small radio transmitter in his hands. Before the bull can reach him, the man presses a button on the radio transmitter. The radio message activates an electrode planted deep in the bull's brain, and the bull stops in his tracks! Is this science-fiction, a glimpse of the psychotechnology of the future? No, the demonstration actually took place a few years ago. The man was the Yale Medical School neurophysiologist, José Delgado.

Delgado has done a substantial amount of research on electrical stimulation of the brain and is the author of *Physical Control of the Mind: Toward a Psychocivilized Society*. We will return to Delgado and his work in a few pages. The material in the following section is applicable only to serious and/or chronic behavioral disturbances, not to the common problems of adjustment faced by most people in daily living.

EARLY PSYCHOSURGERY

As already noted, it is possible to stretch the history of psychosurgery back to the ancient Egyptians. But the story of modern psychosurgery begins in 1935 with the work of the Portuguese physician Egas Moniz. Moniz was impressed by research reports that severance of the frontal lobes of the brain calmed a chimpanzee prone to violent temper tantrums. Moniz decided to try the same kind of brain surgery on hostile and aggressive mental patients. Thus was born the *lobotomy*, a surgical procedure in which the connections between the frontal lobes of the cortex are severed from the subcortex. This, of course, makes the frontal lobes nonfunctional. It has been hypothesized that the frontal lobes of the cortex have a great deal to do with the higher thought processes in man. Thus the mental patient who is "thinking too hard for his own good" may be pacified by a lobotomy. The crude theory of lobotomy seems to be that hyperthought, or mental overactivity, tends to make certain mental patients hostile, assaultive, aggressive, uncontrollable, compulsive, depressed, and so forth.

The medical colleagues Walter Freeman and James Watts jointly introduced the lobotomy to the United States in 1936. By the 1940s lobotomies were a firmly established form of psychiatric treatment; thousands of lobotomies were performed during the 1940s. They were performed primarily on patients who were aggressive and assaultive, but their use was not limited to such patients. All sorts of patients received lobotomies, including patients having such symptoms as compulsion or depression.

By the early 1950s the proverbial honeymoon was over. Lobotomy patients were not "cured" of mental illness and restored to normalcy. Often, they were more impulsive, unable to plan for the future, and had fragmented self-images. As one patient's wife complained, "You have removed the devil in him, but you have also destroyed his soul." The lobotomy patient often loses his coherent sense of self, the feeling that one is basically the same person one was yesterday. The appearance of tranquilizers on the psychiatric scene also contributed to the growing disenchantment with the lobotomy procedure. Behavior control of mental patients with drugs was obviously a less drastic procedure than cutting into their brains. Lobotomies have fallen into disrepute and are seldom performed today. As we shall see presently, however, more sophisticated forms of psychosurgery are emerging.

ELECTRICAL STIMULATION OF THE BRAIN

To appreciate the nature of modern psychosurgery, it is important to know something about research that utilizes a procedure known as *electrical stimulation of the brain* (ESB). ESB requires that tiny holes be drilled in the skull of the subject. *Electrodes* (insulated wires with small uninsulated tips) are inserted through the holes, pushed through brain tissue, and implanted in selected areas of the brain. Electrodes can be cemented to the skull with an exposed plug. Thus the subject can be connected or disconnected to a source of current at the researcher's convenience.

The electrodes are usually implanted in various regions of the subcortex and brain stem, which are often hypothesized to be the site of primal drives and basic emotions. Sending small amounts of current through the electrodes to specified regions of the brain stimulates neurons of that region to "fire," and various nervous system pathways are consequently activated. The subject, particularly an animal subject, can be made into a "puppet" controlled by the electricity.

To illustrate, let me cite the research, initiated in the 1920s, of the Swiss physiologist Walter R. Hess. Hess, the first researcher to use ESB, implanted electrodes in a cat's hypothalamus, a region of the subcortex just above the brain stem. When Hess sent a mild current through a selected electrode, the cat acted as if an enemy were present. It went through a patterned fright reaction—spitting, growling, and arching its back. Repeated stimulation of the same brain region elicited the same pattern over and over. Hess experimented with more than one cat, of course. Indeed, his work with chemical and electrical stimulation of the brain eventually earned him a Nobel Prize. Hess found that by stimulating different regions of the subcortex, each region only a slight distance removed from another region, it was possible to induce a variety of responses in his experimental cats.

A dramatic example of the power of ESB is provided by the research of James Olds and Peter Milner. They reported in 1954 on ESB of the septal area and nearby regions of the rat brain. The Olds and Milner setup was unique. For the first time, the experimental rat was allowed to stimulate its own brain. The rat was placed in a Skinner box. Whenever it pressed the box's bar, a small amount of current was delivered to the rat's septal area. Thus was introduced a new concept in ESB research, self-stimulation of the brain. It was discovered that a specific region of the septal area was highly reinforcing, and this region has been nicknamed "the pleasure center." A rat allowed to self-stimulate its own pleasure center may press the bar as many as seven thousand times in a single hour! Many rats will engage in this behavior for hours on end, often dropping of exhaustion eventually.

In one experiment, Olds trained rats to cross a shock grid to obtain food. When the grid was electrified, the rats would starve to death before crossing the grid to eat. When given the opportunity to cross an electrified grid to reach a self-stimulation bar, however, the rats scampered across it. The motive to engage in self-stimulation was stronger than the hunger motive!

Other researchers have explored what might be called "pain centers." In 1954 José Delgado, Neal Miller, and W. W. Roberts reported an experiment that suggested that the amygdalae are triggers for the experience of pain. The *amygdalae* are small brain structures located near the hypothalamus. There is a right amygdala and a left amygdala, one located in each hemisphere of the brain. When a chimpanzee has one of its amygdalae stimulated, the chimpanzee grimaces and acts as if it has been whipped.

The research on ESB of the amygdalae has reached an advanced stage. A device called the *stimoceiver* has been perfected; it is an electrode-radio-unit implant that receives activating messages and transmits information about brain states. A chimpanzee with a stimoceiver becomes a receiving-transmitting organism without wires.

Paddy, one of Delgado's experimental subjects, is such a chimpanzee. When he began to act in an aggressive manner, a nearby computer noted that the electroencephalogram patterns from Paddy's amygdalae were displaying brief bursts of intense activity. The computer automatically sent a signal that activated the stimoceiver, and Paddy was quickly pacified. His aggressive impulse was inhibited before he had a chance to act on it. The potential for behavior control of the stimoceiver-computer combination is enormous. Aside from its potential for behavior control, there are other possibilities in ESB. The research of Lawrence Pinneo of the Stanford Research Institute suggests that with the aid of electrode implants and a computer, it is possible to give an organism a partially artificial brain. Pinneo took out a portion of the cortex of an experimental monkey, which resulted in a paralysis of its right arm. Then Pinneo placed a set of electrodes in selected positions in the monkey's brain stem. By stimulating the electrodes in a certain sequence, the monkey could be made to raise its usually paralyzed arm. The monkey was then trained to press a bar that activated a computer programmed with the correct stimulation sequence. When the monkey pressed the bar with his good left arm, he was able to move his right arm.

The long-run implications of Pinneo's research are great. It may be possible someday, with the aid of computers and stimoceivers, to restore lost brain functions in stroke victims or individuals with other kinds of brain damage. The term "artificial brain" is not quite as farfetched as it sounds.

ESB WITH HUMAN BEINGS

The *Terminal Man* by physican-author Michael Crichton tells the story of Harry Benson, an epileptic patient prone to violence, and how a surgical team outfits him with a computerized stimoceiver. Whenever Harry starts to go into a violence-epilepsy pattern, the computer directs the stimoceiver to deliver a short pulse of current to Harry's pleasure center. The resulting pleasant experience aborts the unwanted brain-behavior pattern. Unfortunately, Harry—like Olds's rats—seeks to produce the pleasurable stimulation. The epileptic pattern is the instrumental response that brings the current to the pleasure center. So Harry begins to produce more and more seizures, and the stimoceiver–brain system goes wild. The *Terminal Man* is usually dismissed as "just science fiction." But how close does it come to reality? The answer is: *The Terminal Man* does not go far beyond actual psychosurgery that has taken place with human beings.

The problem with doing ESB research with human beings is that it evokes passionate emotional responses and raises a considerable number of moral-ethical questions. Hostile critics of ESB often think of the brain as an inviolable organ, and they see no value in ESB research. Indeed, they feel that the whole area of ESB research is fraught with potential dangers for humanity. Let us not evade the moral-ethical problems raised by ESB and other forms of psychotechnology, but let us wait until the critique section of this chapter to make an evaluation. For now, let us simply establish the existence of ESB with human beings by presenting a few illustrations of actual work that has been done.

"I guess, Doctor, that your electricity is stronger than my will." This statement was made to Delgado by a human subject who had electrode implants. When Delgado applied current to a certain subcortical region, the man's hand closed. Delgado asked the subject to try to keep his hand open when the current was applied, and he couldn't do it. Thus he made the statement that his will was weaker than ESB. Delgado notes that ESB *always* overwhelms the will of human subjects if a sufficiently intense current is applied! He has demonstrated with more than one human subject the power of ESB over conscious intention. In a great many cases of ESB-induced behavior, the subjects rationalize their behavior *after the fact.* They justify their actions, offering to Delgado superficial "cover" explanations for their behavior.

Robert Heath, a psychiatrist at the Tulane University School of Medicine in New Orleans, has used ESB with a number of patients. Two of his patients are identified as Patient No. B-7 and Patient No. B-10 in an article by Heath called "Electrical Self-stimulation of the Brain in Man." Note that the term *self-stimulation* appears in the title of the article. Heath has given to the patients themselves the power to push the buttons that operate implanted electrodes. They, not a remote computer, stimulate their own brains.

Patient No. B-7 was twenty-eight years old. One of his main problems was *narcolepsy*, an involuntary tendency to fall asleep at inappropriate times. He had not responded to standard treatments. Fourteen electrodes were implanted in various brain regions. Three buttons operated the electrodes, and the patient wore the operating unit on a belt. It should be understood that the patient had a severe case of narcolepsy. Heath states that within seconds the patient would go from an alert state to a deep sleep.

Patient No. B-7 wore the stimulator for seventeen weeks. Whenever he felt unwanted sleep approaching, he would press one of the three buttons. It soon developed that he pressed only one of the buttons, the one that stimulated the septal region of his brain. This is the same region self-stimulated by Olds's rats. Patient No. B-7 found that stimulation of the septal region kept him from falling asleep. The feeling he got from ESB was like the feeling of an approaching orgasm, although a climax was not reached. Perhaps this explains why self-stimulation of the septal region tends to occur at a high rate. The anticipation of great pleasure is evoked, but the peak is not achieved.

Patient No. B-10 was twenty-five years old and suffered from *psychomotor epilepsy*, a form of epilepsy in which the "seizure" takes a peculiar form: The patient is conscious, but lacks voluntary control over his actions. He may see things, hear things, steal items of value impulsively, walk for hours, or become violent. (Crichton's *Terminal Man* suffered from a form of psychomotor epilepsy.) Patient B-10 tended to engage in brief episodes of uncontrolled impulsive behavior. Heath reports that fifty-one leads were implanted into seventeen brain sites. Like patient No. B-7, patient No. B-10 was outfitted with a portable belt-stimulator that permitted him to send a brief current to various self-selected sites. And also like Patient No. B-7, Patient No. B-10 reported pleasurable sexlike feelings from stimulation of the septal area. This, however, for Patient No. B-10 was not the most frequently stimulated brain region. Another region, one that seemed to bring back an elusive memory, was preferred. Both Patient No. B-7 and Patient No. B-10 achieved partial control over their problems with the use of self-controlled ESB.

The range of potential applications of ESB is quite great. In *Physical Control of the Mind,* Delgado explores a wide range of applications and future possibilities. Here is a brief listing:

1 *Localization of tumors.* ESB can be used to pinpoint the location of tumors without opening the skull.

2 *Treatment of Parkinson's disease.* "Freezing" certain areas of the thalamus is a form of brain surgery used to treat Parkinson's disease. With the use of ESB techniques, it is possible to avoid the destruction of important motor pathways during surgery.

3 *Treatment of pain.* Intractable pain, such as the pain of certain cancer victims, can be partially controlled with ESB to selected brain sites.

4 *Control of severe mental disturbances.* Anxiety, fear, compulsive obsessions, and aggressive behavior are among the symptoms Delgado associates with severe mental disturbances. He notes that the use of ESB to treat the listed symptoms is controversial. Delgado comments, "Some investigators report a remarkable therapeutic success in obsessive patients; others are more skeptical about the usefulness of depth electrodes and electrocoagulations in treating mental illness" (p. 199).

5 *Control of tremors.* ESB can be used to help control the severe tremors associated with multiple sclerosis. Patients can operate a self-stimulation ESB unit to attain partial control over their involuntary movements.

6 *Treatment of anorexia nervosa.* The treatment of *anorexia nervosa*, a condition in which the patient loses his appetite and may starve to death, is presented by Delgado as a possible application. With ESB, the patient may self-stimulate an excitatory region of the hypothalamus associated with hunger.

7 *Restoration of destroyed senses.* Blind persons and deaf persons have been given visual and auditory experiences with the use of ESB and auxiliary devices. An example is provided by the work of the Mexican researcher, Armando del Campo. Using a device called an *amaroscope*, an instrument made up of photo-electric cells, del Campo has been able to transmit visual patterns through the lower brain to the visual cortex. Crude pattern vision is possible even in patients who do not have eyes! The amaroscope is the first "artificial eye," and it is an exciting development. Lest we become too enthusiastic, however, a great deal more research is needed before such devices will be of any real value to persons with sensory difficulties.

The English poet John Milton wrote, in *Paradise Lost*:

The mind is its own place,
and in itself
Can make a heaven of hell, a
hell of heaven.

Delgado makes a similar comparison. One of the chapters of *Physical Control of the Mind* is titled "Hell and Heaven within the Brain." In another chapter, Delgado uses the phrase "magic window" in referring to electrode implants. ESB gives us a deeper glimpse into that poetic heaven-hell described by Milton.

NUTRITION: FOOD FOR THOUGHT

What does nutrition have to do with psychology? Just this: Remember that the psychotechnologist first and foremost sees a human being as an organism. An organism is made up of living cells. The brain is the principal organ of what we call mental or psychological phenomena—thinking, remembering, reflecting, and so forth. These processes can be no more "healthy" than the health of the organism in which they take place. In other words, we *are* what we eat in the most complete sense. Our bodies and our thought processes are so closely associated that distinctions between the two domains are primarily linguistic conveniences, not physical realities. Food is literally "food for thought."

Perhaps humankind recognizes a profound connection between personality and food. Maybe what follows is not much more than idle speculation.

But have you ever noticed the number of food words that are used in common slang to describe the human personality? The *Pocket Dictionary of American Slang* lists many such words. Here are just a few: A *top banana* is a comedian in a burlesque show; an *egghead* is an intellectual; a *peach* is a pretty girl; *honey* refers to one's beloved; a *nut* is an insane or crazy person; a *cold fish* is a person who is too reserved or withdrawn; and a *big cheese* is an important person. Also, folklore provides many associations between traits of character and food. For example, some people believe that oysters increase a person's sex drive. Others say that fish is "brain food." And a Zen koan teases us with this question: When does the food you eat become you?

PROTEIN AND THE BRAIN

When does the food you eat become you? There is no categorical answer. There is general agreement, however, that the food you eat *does* eventually become you. (At least it becomes that aspect of you that is you-the-organism.) Thus it is important to attain some understanding of the way food relates to the development and health of the organism. It would be beyond the scope of this book to explore all the ways nutrition relates to health. But it is appropriate to give some attention to those aspects of nutrition that are most closely related to dimensions of human behavior. Let us first take a look at the relationship between protein and the brain.

One of the principal ways of categorizing foods is to identify all foods as proteins, carbohydrates, and fats. *Proteins* are the principal "building blocks" of the muscles and body organs. *Carbohydrates* and *fats* are fuel; they "burn" and supply us with energy. The brain is made up mainly of protein. Thus children who do not receive sufficient protein during their developing years cannot have as large or as physically healthy a brain as they might have had. In turn, they will exhibit less general intelligence as a consequence of their stunted brains. Adults also need a steady supply of protein to maintain and rebuild their bodies and their brains. Incidentally, the relationship of protein supply to the health of the brain gives oblique support to the folklore notion that fish is brain food. Fish is an important source of protein. Many other foods also supply protein, however. There is no particular magic power in eating fish.

Are the people of the world getting enough protein? It depends on the country you are talking about. The United States and the industrialized nations in general have adequate protein supplies. But about one-half of the countries of the world are spoken of as "underdeveloped countries." In *The Population Bomb* by biologist Paul Ehrlich, it is stated that half the people of the world are undernourished or malnourished. Such people and their children have little hope of reaching relatively normal levels of intellectual functioning.

Nutritional problems exist even in the United States. In the preceding paragraph, a distinction is made between *undernourished* and *malnourished*. According to Ehrlich, an undernourished person does not get enough food; in contrast, a malnourished person does not have a properly balanced diet. In an affluent country such as the United States, it is possible for a family to have enough money to eat well. Yet, because of an ignorance of the basic facts of nutrition, its members may be malnourished.

To illustrate, in many families sugar cereals are purchased for and eaten by children. The protein content of such cereals is about 4 percent. If, by some stretch of the imagination, a child had to live on sugar cereals alone, the child would be severely malnourished—even if he got enough calories. It is generally said that we need a minimum of about 14 percent protein to avoid malnourishment. Fortunately, adding milk to a bowl of sugar cereal brings the total protein content of the breakfast to about 14 percent. Whole grain cereals have about 14 percent protein, and adding milk to them brings the protein content to about 25 percent. Millions of people in the world's underdeveloped countries subsist on about 8 percent protein, not enough for proper physical and mental health.

The richest sources of protein are meat, fish, and meat by-products such as milk, eggs, and cheese. In the developed countries, these have been the favorite mainstays of a protein-rich diet. With rising food costs and less availability of the high-protein foods, however, we are faced with a problem: How can we obtain an adequate protein supply from less expensive and more available foods? To answer this question, it is important to know about the principle of *protein complementarity*, the fact that one protein can supplement another one. Protein is a complex food made up of *amino acids*, complex organic molecules that are the building blocks of protein itself. Meat, fish, and meat by-products tend to contain most of the important amino acids. (Eggs are almost a "perfect" protein food, containing almost all the amino acids.)

If a person is forced to live on grains and various kinds of legumes, such as beans, getting all the essential amino acids can be a problem. This is where the principle of protein complementarity comes in. In *Diet for a Small Planet*, Frances Moore Lappé points out that beans eaten with wheat equal a nearly complete protein in terms of amino acids. The important point is that beans and wheat have *different* amino acids. Eaten together *at the same meal*, they enhance each other. Understanding and utilizing such principles as protein complementarity can help us avoid protein malnourishment.

All the body organs depend on a steady supply of high-quality protein. Our principal concern here is with the brain, however. The brain, like the other organs, needs protein in the proper quantity and of the proper quality for continued efficiency. The capacity for clear thinking is related to getting enough protein. It is important in childhood; and it continues to be important in adulthood.

LOW BLOOD SUGAR OR NEUROSIS?

Bernard R. is a thirty-three-year-old stockbroker. Lately he has been complaining of depression and insomnia. He is irritable and has difficulty concentrating on his work. Sharon C. is a twenty-eight-year-old home-maker. Recently she has found herself prone to unaccountable anxiety and crying spells. She has never before had any serious problem with muscle pains, but now she has developed a chronic backache. What is wrong with Bernard and Sharon? Are they suffering from neurotic reactions? It would certainly seem so from the presenting symptoms. But some researchers who study the relationship of nutrition to behavior claim that a condition of chronic low blood sugar can produce symptoms that mimic the classical symptoms of neurotic reactions. Although we should not dispense with the orthodox psychological approach to understanding the neuroses, it is certainly a tenable hypothesis that an undetermined num-

It has been hypothesized that chronic low blood sugar can produce symptoms that mimic the classical symptoms of neurotic reactions.

ber of persons having neurotic symptoms are actually victims of chronic low blood sugar.

The technical label for chronic low blood sugar is *hypoglycemia*; it may have several causes. For example, a tumor in the pancreas gland may induce the gland to secrete too much insulin. The oversecretion of insulin too quickly oxidizes the blood sugar, and blood sugar concentrations may fall far below normal. The victim of this condition may, in extreme cases, go into a state of coma; too much insulin can induce a coma. Most victims of hypoglycemia, however, do not suffer from a tumor in the pancreas gland. Thus there is a kind of hypoglycemia that has come to be called *functional hypoglycemia*, hypoglycemia *not* caused by a detectable organic condition. Seale Harris, the pioneer researcher on hypoglycemia, indicated in the 1930s that he believed hypoglycemia to be more common than diabetes, its opposite pathological condition. Indeed, it has been suggested that years of low-grade hypoglycemia may precede a diabetic condition.

Some nutritionists (Fredericks and Goodman, 1969; Abrahamson and Pezet, 1971) suggest that functional hypoglycemia is a common condition and that it underlies many symptoms mistakenly taken to be neurotic reactions. Although this is not the majority view among most nutritionists, the thesis has aroused sufficient interest that it should not be dismissed lightly. At any rate, if hypoglycemia is as common as some nutritionists think it is, what is the reason? And what can be done to correct the condition?

It is proposed that the intake of *refined carbohydrates*, primarily highly processed flour and sugar, overstimulates the pancreas gland. Refined carbohydrates are digested quickly and assimilated into the blood stream as sugar. The brain is constantly scanning blood sugar levels. When the blood sugar level is too high, the brain sends a message to the pancreas to secrete insulin to burn up the excess sugar. If the blood sugar "spikes" (i.e., rises too high too fast), the brain's alarm message is too strong and the pancreas overreacts, thus oxidizing too much sugar and sending the individual into a low blood sugar state. Paradoxically, eating too much sugar produces a low blood sugar condition!

It is argued that citizens of the United States and England are massive users of refined carbohydrates, and this may be the source of much functional hypoglycemia. John Yudkin, a professor of nutrition and dietetics at Queen Elizabeth College of London University and author of *Sweet and Dangerous*, states that the average American and Briton eat two pounds of sugar or more a week! He comments:

One of the reasons why some people find it difficult to accept that on average

Americans and Britons eat two pounds of sugar or more a week is that they think only of the sugar that is brought into the home as visible sugar. But an increasing proportion of sugars is now bought already made up into foods by the manufacturer.

Industrial sugar goes to the factory and comes to us in the form of candy, ice cream, soft drinks, cakes, cookies, and nowadays also in a very wide range of other items, especially the fancily packaged "convenience foods." (p. 47)

If a person suspects that he is suffering from hypoglycemia, he should consult with a physician. If in turn his physician suspects the presence of hypoglycemia, he will order a *glucose-tolerance test*, a six-hour test in which the blood is sampled for sugar content at regular intervals. When an individual is found to suffer from functional hypoglycemia, a diet that restricts refined carbohydrates is often recommended. The patient is also asked to reduce his intake of caffeine and alcohol; these are said to stimulate the pancreas. And he is encouraged to take in an adequate amount of protein.

For our purposes, it is important to observe that the claim of a relationship between neurotic symptoms and chronic low blood sugar makes us appreciate that the division between "psychological problems" and "medical problems" is to some degree arbitrary. This observation brings us naturally to the next topic, orthomolecular psychiatry.

ORTHOMOLECULAR PSYCHIATRY

The Greek word *orthos* means "right." Thus *orthomolecular psychiatry* may be thought of as an approach to mental health in which it is deemed important that mental patients receive the "right molecules." In practice, this refers to *megavitamin therapy*, a regimen that prescribes massive doses of selected vitamins for a patient.

The current high level of interest in orthomolecular psychiatry was initially sparked by Linus Pauling, a famous biochemist and Nobel laureate. In 1968 Pauling published an article on megavitamins in *Science* magazine. In 1972 he and David Hawkins, a physician, coauthored a book titled *Orthomolecular Psychiatry*.

The theory behind megavitamin therapy is that mental disorientation is caused by a deficiency in certain enzymes. These enzymes are needed to carry out crucial chemical reactions that take place at the level of the brain cells. Megavitamins help the suffering individual overcome his enzyme deficiency by acting as catalysts. They facilitate enzyme production. The emphasis in megavitamin therapy is on the B-complex vitamins, which are believed to be crucial ones.

The relationship of sugar intake to orthomolecular psychiatry is note-worthy. Richard Passwater, a research biochemist, writes in his book *Supernutrition*, "Sugar-restricted diets are used in megavitamin therapy for schizophrenia because sucrose unnecessarily consumes valuable nicotinamide during its metabolism" (p. 48). Nicotinamide is a coenzyme (part of an enzyme), and it is formed by vitamin B_3 (niacinamide of nico-tinic acid). Briefly, sugar "uses up" the products of vitamin B_3. Thus refined sugar is tagged as a culprit again. It was hypothesized earlier that a high sugar intake might contribute to hypoglycemia and symptoms that mimic neurosis. Now it is suggested that sugar depletes the body of the products of vitamin B_3, products essential for efficient functioning of the central nervous system. It should be mentioned that the nutritionists who are down on sugar are not critical of *fructose*, the natural sugar found in fruits. They are concerned about *sucrose*, refined sugar.

What about people who are not hospitalized, people who are "normal?" The implication is clear in the writings on orthomolecular psychiatry that "what is sauce for the goose is sauce for the gander." The line between normal and abnormal is often hard to find, and many persons who are not hospitalized as out-and-out mental patients may suffer some symp-toms of mental disorientation because of poor nutrition. It is thus con-cluded that proper nutrition is important for all of us, not just for people branded with such labels as "schizophrenic." In *Nutrition against Dis-ease*, biochemist Roger Williams, the first man to identify pantothenic acid (B_5), writes:

If you who read these words have never been afflicted with mental disease, it is not because you have undergone shock treatments or have consumed the right tranquilizers; it is because you have received in your food enough of all the minerals, amino acids, and vitamins that brain cells need to maintain them in reasonably good working order. . . .

If any one of a number of nutritional items had been received by your brain in, what would be for you, inadequate amounts, you would have been afflicted with mental disease. (p. 155)

One of the unfortunate side effects of the enthusiasm for orthomolecular psychiatry has been the tendency of some people to self-prescribe massive doses of vitamins. It is one thing to eat correctly and to take some vitamins judiciously. It is quite another thing to embark on an unsuper-vised megavitamin regimen. It is often said, "Oh well, it does no harm. It all goes out in the urine. So the worst that can happen is you'll have expensive urine." This is not completely true. In the first place, not all vitamins are water soluble and their excessive intake may be toxic. In the second place, even the water-soluble vitamins may have untoward effects if consumed in great quantities. The simple truth is that the long-run effects of years of taking megavitamins is unknown. Megavitamin therapy is a *treatment*, not a way of life.

Advocates of orthomolecular psychiatry make grand claims for their approach. They speak of emptying mental wards, restoring shattered lives, bringing families together again, and saving taxpayers millions of dollars in mental hospital bills. There are less enthusiastic voices, as we shall see later.

ARTIFICIAL FOOD FLAVORS AND COLORS

Ralph Nader and "Nader's Raiders," consumer advocates, have called the American way of eating "the chemical feast." They are referring, of course, to the many substances added to our foods. In particular, it has been suggested that artificial food flavors and colors play an important role in the behavior of *hyperkinetic children*, children who strongly manifest such characteristics as impulsivity, distractability, excitability, and perceptual and motor coordination problems. Such children are also said to be resistant to discipline and to be domineering in their social behavior.

Several theories have been expounded to account for hyperkinesis in children. The first theory advanced was that hyperkinetic children suffer from *minimal brain damage*, a condition in which the nervous system damage is so slight that the child incorrectly seems to be organically normal. Another theory is that most hyperkinetic children are basically of sound body, but their unique behavior is caused by inborn temperamental differences. This theory is presented by Paul H. Wender, a professor of psychiatry on the staff of the College of Medicine at the University of Utah, in his book *The Hyperactive Child*. He asserts that the majority of hyperkinetic children are not brain-damaged. A third theory is that the term "hyperkinetic child" is a wastebasket term which includes a host of possible states. In an article titled "We're Too Cavalier about Hyperactivity" in a 1974 issue of *Psychology Today*, Sydney Walker, III, a neuropsychiatrist who has private medical practice, asserts that a variety of conditions ranging from hypoglycemia to heart problems may underlie hyperactive behavior.

The leading advocate of the principal theory that concerns us in this section is Benjamin Feingold, a pediatrician and allergist. In *Why Your Child Is Hyperactive*, Feingold presents the thesis that artificial food flavors and colors play an important role in hyperactivity. Feingold does not indict food preservatives as culprits, with the possible exception of butylated hydroxytoluene (BHT), an antioxidant used in many foods; he says that an occasional child may show a reaction to BHT. Essentially, though, Feingold's theory is an allergic-reaction theory. Hyperkinesis results as a side effect of allergic reactions to artificial flavors and colors. Feingold's work has created a substantial amount of interest, and he was invited to testify before Sen. Edward Kennedy's Subcommittee on Health.

Feingold asserts that the problem of hyperactive children has reached epidemic proportions. Several sources place the estimated percentage of hyperactive children between 10 percent and 15 percent of the children in the United States. Converted to numbers, these percentages suggest about five million children. These figures are probably too high, however. The Department of Health, Education, and Welfare estimates that about 10 percent of the nation's children are emotionally handicapped. This percentage includes problems other than hyperkinesis (e.g., autism, schizophrenia, mental retardation, etc.). Nonetheless, the number of children that get tagged with the label "hyperkinetic" *is* large. A December 1975 edition of *People Weekly* contains an interview with Feingold. Asked about the upsurge in the problem of hyperkinesis, he comments:

I correlate this increase with the increased consumption of food chemicals and in particular the artificial colors and flavors, of which there are 1,500 to 1,800 on the market. If you project a graph for the estimated incidence of hyperkinesis and then compare it with the Standard and Poor's table for the dollar value of soft drinks over the past decade, you'll find it is identical. Circumstantial evidence, but interesting. (p. 65)

There is also the clear implication in Feingold's work that adults are not immune to the effects of artificial colors and flavors. Irritability, restlessness, and various symptoms associated with neurotic reactions may be related to the ingestion of artificial colors and flavors. Feingold's approach may be classified as a variety of orthomolecular psychiatry: The usual approach to orthomolecular psychiatry is, "Let's get the right substances *into* the organism"; Feingold's theme is, "Let's get the wrong substances *out* of the organism."

The saying "You are what you eat" is a familiar one. The nutritionist would add, "You think and behave as you eat." This section on nutrition has revealed the possible links between protein intake and brain functioning, sugar usage and hypoglycemia, megavitamin therapy and mental illness, and artificial colors and flavors and hyperkinesis. Many of the statements about nutrition and behavior should be accepted only at the level of provocative hypotheses, not established facts. Nonetheless, it is clear that the disciplines of nutrition and psychology have something to say to each other.

DRUGS: THE TRANQUILIZED MIND

The following excerpt is from an article titled "Coping with Depression" by Matt Clark in a 1973 issue of *Newsweek.*

Carl Schwartz, a 61-year-old New York lawyer, spent nearly 40 years swinging between the highs and lows of endogenous manic-depressive illness. "I literally enjoyed the manic phases," he recalls. "I was a big shot, on top of the world. I spent not only my own money, but everybody else's I could get my hands on— I bought six suits at a time, a lot of stupid unnecessary things. I usually left home and set up my own apartment." But in between the highs, there were frightening plunges into depression. "I feared getting out of bed, and was anxious to get into bed at night because I could block out the horror of my daily life." For the last three years, Schwartz has been free of his illness, thanks to daily doses of lithium carbonate. (p. 53)

The excerpt reveals one of the ways a drug can be used to treat mental illness. Like the nutritional approach, the drug approach assumes that psychological problems often have a biochemical basis. In this section we will review chemotherapy as a form of psychotechnology.

WHAT IS CHEMOTHERAPY?

In the broadest possible sense, *chemotherapy* may be defined as the use of drugs to treat either organic or mental illnesses. In this section, our concern is with mental illnesses. Chemotherapy used against psychological-emotional problems is itself a subclass of a larger subject, *psychopharmacology*—the study of how drugs affect psychological and emotional processes. When the knowledge from psychopharmacology becomes applied, then we speak of chemotherapy. Our concern in this chapter is with technology, which implies applications of general knowledge.

The use of chemotherapy to treat people's ills is not new. This chapter opened with a quotation from *The Egyptian* designed to reveal the antiquity of psychotechnology. Similarly, records of chemotherapy can be traced to the time of the pharaohs. One of the most famous medical documents in history is the *Papyrus Ebers.* It was compiled in Egypt around 1500 B.C., and it summarizes the knowledge of physicians and priests about treating various illnesses. A list of "chemicals" from the *Papyrus Ebers* is frightening indeed to the modern mind! The list includes: The excretion of animals, teeth crushed in honey, rotten meat, the blood of lizards, and other readily available organic substances. From the time of the ancient Egyptians to the present, humankind has used drugs in many ways. A complete presentation would itself make a long book. Let us content ourselves with a few illustrations.

Galen is one of the most famous physicians in history. A Greek scientist, he lived and worked about a century after the days of Christ. His teachings had a tremendous impact on medicine, lasting for many centuries. Our interest in Galen here is in his use of chemotherapy. In a sense, he was the father of the modern prescription drug that contains more than one ingredient. Galen combined various drugs to form mixtures called *galenicals.* The authority of today's physician to prescribe drugs descends from the prestigious practices of the great Galen.

The ancient Eastern world also has a history of drug use for the treatment of illnesses. For centuries, Hindu healers have used the roots of the plant *Rauwolfia serpentina* to treat both organic and psychological problems. *Reserpine*, a drug sometimes used today against psychotic reactions, is extracted from the serpentina plant.

In the Americas, Indians fought malaria by ingesting the juice from the bark of the cinchona tree. They chewed cocoa leaves for greater strength when confronted with difficult tasks; cocoa leaves contain cocaine. Our chronical has been brief. But you can see that drug use is nothing new. The great nineteenth-century physician Sir Wiliam Osler once commented, "A desire to take medicine is, perhaps, the great feature which distinguishes man from other animals."

KINDS OF DRUGS USED IN CHEMOTHERAPY

The three principal kinds of drugs used in chemotherapy for psychological problems are (1) antipsychotic agents, (2) sedative-hypnotic agents, and (3) stimulants.

Antipsychotic agents.   Antipsychotic agents are drugs used to combat the effects of psychotic reactions. This class of drugs is used extensively. In *Pharmacology*, Michael Gerald, a member of the faculty of the College of Pharmacy at Ohio State University, notes that the incredibly large number of *fifty million patients* were given *chlorpromazine* (Thorazine) from 1955 to 1965! He also states that it has been the subject of more than ten thousand publications. These figures reveal the tremendous impact of chemotherapy on the treatment of mental illness. (Don't be confused by the fact that two names are often given for the drug. The first name, uncapitalized, is the generic, or proper, chemical name. The second name, capitalized and in parenthesis, is the trade name. Trade names are given because they are popularized and are often the only name you will associate with the drug.)

Chlorpromazine is used so extensively because of its great calming effect on mental patients. Physical restraints and heavy sedation with barbiturates was the order of the day in mental hospitals of yesteryear.

Chlorpromazine's greatest value is thus with patients who are prone to violence. But make no mistake. None of the drugs herein discussed, including chlorpromazine, are cures for psychotic reactions. They make the patient more manageable and, in some cases, more amenable to psychotherapy.

There are several other antipsychotic agents in addition to chlorpromazine. The most well known of these is reserpine (Serpasil), the drug made from the roots of the serpentina plant. Reserpine is of historical interest because it was one of the first antipsychotic agents to win recognition and wide use. This took place in the early 1950s. But reserpine is seldom used today because of undesirable physical side effects and because chlorpromazine has proven itself to be a more effective antipsychotic agent.

There are various theories of how the antipsychotic agents work. The principal theory concerns *norepinephrine* (NE), one of the main transmitter substances found in the brain. When a neuron "fires," it releases the chemical substance NE. NE makes its way across the *synapse*, the gap between two neurons, and stimulates an adjacent neuron to fire. If the brain has too much or too little NE, there can be effects on thought processes and moods. It is hypothesized that depression is associated with insufficient NE and that manic states of great excitement are associated with too much NE. It is believed that the antipsychotic agents act in such a way as to interfere with the arrival of NE to adjacent neurons. Thus antipsychotic agents are of greatest value when the NE levels are too high and the patient is manifesting manic symptoms.

Sedative-hypnotic agents. The principal physiological effect of sedative-hypnotic agents is to depress the action of brain-arousal mechanisms. Small doses of sedative-hypnotic agents make a person drowsy and sometimes somewhat less reserved in social situations. Let us discuss two general kinds of sedative-hypnotic agents, *barbiturates* and *antianxiety agents*.

Some well-known trade names for barbiturates are Nembutal, Seconal, and Pentothal. Primarily, barbiturates are used as sedatives. They are prescribed for neurotic reactions ranging from anxiety to insomnia. They are also sometimes prescribed for high blood pressure when it is suspected that the high blood pressure is associated with chronic anxiety. One of the principal uses of barbiturates, the treatment of insomnia, is currently subject to review. Some researchers believe that the "hangover symptoms" of barbiturates the morning after are too high a price to pay for the night's sleep. It is argued that the side effects of frequent barbiturate usage include listlessness and prolonged depression. A well-known researcher on sleep is William C. Dement, widely recognized for his investigations of rapid-eye-movement (REM) sleep. He and his coauthors comment in the December 1975 issue of *Psychology Today*:

Almost every sedative, if used regularly, will aggravate the insomnia that it is intended to cure. Anyone who has become dependent on drugs for sleep may need to go through a carefully managed withdrawal program and endure a string of restless, even miserable, nights. (p. 46)

Turning to the antianxiety agents, some well-known trade names are Miltown, Equanil, Librium, and Valium. The antianxiety agents are referred to as the *minor tranquilizers* in contrast to the *major tranquilizers*, the earlier discussed antipsychotic agents. The antianxiety agents are widely used to treat neurotic patients. There is some controversy over the wisdom of treating so many people with antianxiety agents. Some pharmacologists argue that all sedative-hypnotic agents, including the antianxiety agents, are subject to abuse and addiction. Others argue that many people operate automobiles and other machinery with the false idea that a "tranquilizer" allows one to remain completely clearheaded. Such is not the case. Antianxiety agents tend to affect alertness and vigilance. It is also noted by some critics that a substantial number of persons use the antianxiety agents in irresponsible ways. For example, it is not uncommon for excessive drinkers to combine alcohol with an antianxiety agent. Although a large number of pharmacologists now hold that the antianxiety agents are no more effective for treating anxiety than barbiturates, the use of these agents has become extremely popular. They do have one big advantage over the barbiturates: In general, they are less toxic.

Stimulants. Stimulants are drugs that tend to increase one's alertness. A moderate dose of a stimulant may temporarily make a person feel stronger, more capable, in a better mood, and optimistic about the future. An excessive dose of a stimulant may produce an anxiety reaction or a transient psychotic reaction. The widespread use of drugs is illustrated by the fact that *caffeine* and *nicotine*, both stimulants, are found in coffee and cigarettes respectively. Millions of people who do not consider themselves drug users are addicted to stimulants via the route of the intemperate use of coffee and cigarettes. *Cocaine*, mentioned earlier, is also a stimulant. An interesting historical note is that Freud went through a brief period of enthusiasm for the use of cocaine, proclaiming its marvelous ability to elevate mood and increase strength. His enthusiasm was brief when he discovered that some cocaine users become addicts.

The two principal drug groups of interest to us here are the ones used in chemotherapy. These are the *amphetamines* and the *clinical anti-*

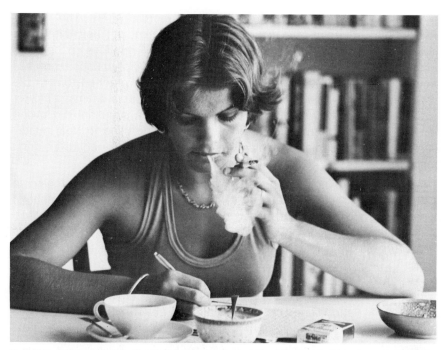

Caffeine and nicotine, both stimulants, are found in coffee and cigarettes respectively.

depressants. The action of both kinds of drugs can be in part explained by reference to the norepinephrine theory of mood. You will recall that the antipsychotic agents interfere with the arrival of NE to adjacent neurons. Thus, with antipsychotic agents, the effects of NE are reduced. The opposite happens with the stimulants under discussion. Amphetamines have a structure that closely resembles the brain's own NE. Thus amphetamines *copy* the NE action. Taking amphetamines has an effect similar to increasing the amount of NE in the brain. Clinical antidepressants, on the other hand, do not have the structure of NE; but they facilitate NE production. Consequently both amphetamines and clinical antidepressants have similar effects, and these effects can be understood in terms of the norepinephrine theory.

Well-known trade names for amphetamines are Benzedrine, Dexedrine, and Methedrine. The principal clinical uses of amphetamines are for the treatment of narcolepsy, hyperkinesis, and obesity. One can clearly see the value of amphetamines in the treatment of narcolepsy. The narcoleptic individual tends to fall asleep at inappropriate times; a stimulant helps him to stay awake.

In the case of hyperkinesis, the logic is a bit more obscure. The hyperkinetic child is already too active. How can a stimulant help him? The stimulant seems to have a paradoxical effect. The relationship between arousal and stimulation appears to be an inverted *U*. Stimulation increases arousal, *but only to a point*. An arousal "crest" is reached, and more stimulation brings the arousal level down. Thus, odd as it seems, a hyperkinetic child may very well be "tranquilized" with a stimulant. Following this logic, it may be noted that caffeine can also be used to treat hyperkinetic children. Some physicians prescribe that such children drink coffee instead of taking amphetamines.

A substantial amount of reservation exists among persons interested in mental health about the wide use of amphetamines for the treatment of hyperkinesis. As noted earlier, hyperkinetic symptoms may be caused by more than one factor. Critics of chemotherapy argue that the effects of a drug may mask important symptoms, thus allowing an underlying illness to get worse. Others, such as Feingold, feel that taking a hyperkinetic child off artificial food flavors and colors is preferable in many cases to prescribing amphetamines. Peter Schrag, an editor of the *Saturday Review*, and Diane Divoky, an editor of *Learning* magazine, argue in their book *The Myth of the Hyperactive Child* along the following lines:

By early 1975 between 500,000 and 1,000,000 American children and adolescents were taking amphetamine-type drugs and other psychostimulants by prescription. . . . A small percentage of those children suffer from some diagnosable medical ailment sufficiently serious to warrant chemotherapy. Most do not; they are being drugged, often at the insistence of schools or individual teachers, to make them more manageable. (p. xiii)

Amphetamines have also found large-scale use in the treatment of obesity. They act as appetite suppressants, thus helping the person to stay on a diet. They also give the taker a feeling of well-being and they combat anxiety. Some overweight people are said to eat out of negative emotional states, such as anxiety and depression. Thus the "lift" obtained from an amphetamine may work against tendencies to eat associated with low moods. There are, however, problems. After several weeks of usage, a tolerance builds up to the drug, and its appetite suppressant qualities are lost. Larger doses are required to obtain the desired effect. Although there is some question about the degree to which amphetamines are addictive, it certainly seems to be the case that some users develop a psychological dependence on them. And this is certainly undesirable. All in all, it can be argued that the beneficial effects of amphetamines for weight control are short-lived. They are probably of little value for the long-range control of obesity.

CHEMOTHERAPY AND PSYCHOSOMATIC ILLNESSES

Psychosomatic illnesses are literally "mind-body" disorders. The word "psychosomatic" comes from two Greek words: *psyche*, meaning mind or soul, and *soma*, meaning body. A practical definition of a psychosomatic illness is that such an illness is either caused by psychological-emotional factors or greatly aggravated by them. In popular language, "Your mind can make you sick."

By now, most people have heard it said that ulcers can be psychosomatic. In addition to ulcers, the list of psychosomatic illnesses is long indeed. In *None of These Diseases* by physician S. I. McMillen, a list of fifty-one illnesses are given a psychosomatic label. Disorders of the digestive system, the circulatory system, the genitourinary system, the nervous system, the glands of internal secretion, the muscles and joints, the eyes, and the skin may all be complicated by psychological-emotional factors. Also, various allergic disorders are often thought of as psychosomatic.

What is the appropriate treatment for the long list of psychosomatic illness? One answer has been chemotherapy. Ulcer patients are often given an antianxiety agent because it is believed that anxiety aggravates ulcers. Another illustration is provided by *primary hypertension*, high blood pressure of unknown origin. About 85 percent of all high blood pressure falls into this category. It is estimated that about twenty million Americans suffer from primary hypertension. Presently, this condition is usually treated with *antihypertensive agents*, drugs that tend to have the effect of reducing blood pressure. Similar statements can be made about other psychosomatic illnesses. Current practice places a heavy reliance on drug treatment.

The question arises, "If we are willing to accept the assertion that your mind can make you sick, would it not be logical to accept the converse assertion that your mind can make you well?" Of course, that is the thesis underlying much of this book. Psychologists work on the assumption that behavioral strategies, those that contribute toward greater adjustment and growth, can act as counterforces against psychosomatic disorders. Advocates of counseling and psychotherapy feel that these approaches may afford better long-run treatment of psychosomatic illness than chemotherapy.

OPIATES AND HALLUCINOGENS

Our concern with opiates and hallucinogens is not so much with their addictive potential or possible abuse, but with their role in chemotherapy. An *opiate* is a narcotic agent, a drug that has a two-way action: (1) sedation and (2) pain relief. Well-known opiates are opium, heroin, morphine, codeine, and methadone. In moderate doses, several of the opiates produce *euphoria*, a sense of well-being. In *Confessions of an English Opium-Eater*, published in 1822, author Thomas DeQuincey writes, "Here was a panacea . . . for all human woes; here was the secret of happiness, about which philosophers had disputed for so many ages" (p. 179). You can see why some people have mistakenly believed that opium was a cure for their mental problems. Opiates sometimes play a proper role in the relief of pain, and are appropriate for other specific medical purposes. But the sad fact is that they are not useful for the responsible treatment of mental illness.

A *hallucinogen* is a drug that tends to alter conventional perception and thought. Sometimes these drugs are called *psychotomimetic agents*, drugs that "mimic" psychotic reactions. Still another name for these drugs is *psychedelic agents*. The psychiatrist Humphry Osmond coined the word "psychedelic" to suggest a mind-manifesting action, an expanding of consciousness and an enlarging of vision. It is apparent that "psychotomimetic" is a negative label and that "psychedelic" is a positive label. The labels themselves reveal the controversy that has surrounded the use of hallucinogens. Familiar hallucinogens are lysergic acid diethylamide (LSD), psilocybin, mescaline, and cannabis (marijuana).

There was, during the late 1950s and early 1960s, quite a bit of interest in hallucinogens as adjuncts to psychotherapy. LSD was used to treat alcoholics, the depression brought about by terminal illnesses, and other kinds of problems. A number of favorable reports were published. During the 1960s, however, LSD was also taking on negative associations and receiving a bad press. Many people disapproved of Timothy Leary and others who spoke in positive terms about hallucinogens. Terms such as *bum trip* and *flashback* came into prominence. In the absence of responsible guidance, panic states and psychotic reactions were sometimes reported. The bad press rubbed off on researchers, and experiments with hallucinogens as potential psychotherapeutic tools all but stopped. By 1969 the *Annual Review of Medicine* had little good to say about LSD as a means of looking within one's self.

A small amount of research with the use of psychedelic agents in connection with psychotherapy still goes on. There are still a number of psychiatrists who feel that drugs may be potent enhancers of experience. For example, psychiatrist Claudio Naranjo, in *The Healing Journey*, tells of his research with psychedelic drugs. He describes two classes of drugs: feeling enhancers and fantasy enhancers. *Feeling enhancers* augment emotional responses. *Fantasy enhancers* increase imaginative capacities. Thus Naranjo speaks of these drugs as psychedelic or mind-manifesting, but *not* hallucinogenic; they do not produce sensory delusions. Naranjo writes:

If both the agony and the ecstasy of drug experiences have a potential for psychological healing, it is important for us to know the place and promise of each in the treatment of an individual and the best way to deal with each when it occurs. . . . (p. 13)

Naranjo notes that there is a widespread tendency to see drug experiences and psychotherapy as unrelated. He and a relatively small number of researchers make a case for the use of psychedelic drugs in psychotherapy. There is little professional enthusiasm for that point of view, however. At present, chemotherapy for psychological disorders seldom includes the use of psychedelic agents.

In brief, there are five kinds of *psychopharmacological agents*, drugs that affect perception, thought, and emotion: (1) antipsychotic agents, (2) sedative-hypnotic agents, (3) stimulants, (4) opiates, and (5) hallucinogens and psychedelics. It should be noted that although hallucinogens and psychedelics are grouped in the same formal class, some researchers (e.g., Naranjo) assert that not all psychedelics are hallucinogenic. Of the drugs in the five classes just cited, those in the first three classes are the principal ones used in the treatment of mental illnesses and other psychological disorders.

BIOFEEDBACK: UNIFYING MIND AND BODY

Imagine an accomplished yogi sitting in a psychophysiological laboratory. Electrodes are attached to his body. An electrocardiogram unfolds a moment-to-moment record of his heart beats. He states that he can consciously control the pumping action of his heart. The yogi focuses his attention, and the EKG shows that his heart is fibrillating rapidly, making it unable to pump blood. He has made good his claim.

Is the preceding description merely a speculative scenario? No; the event actually took place in a laboratory supervised by Elmer Green, a physiological psychologist at the Menninger Foundation. The yogi was Swami Rama from India, and for years he had been practicing meditation and self-control of the body. But what the yogi was able to do seems to be within the capacities of most people. Self-control of various visceral responses of the body is possible with a procedure known as biofeedback.

WHAT IS BIOFEEDBACK?

Biofeedback is a procedure by which a subject can learn to bring physiological processes under voluntary control; this is facilitated by providing

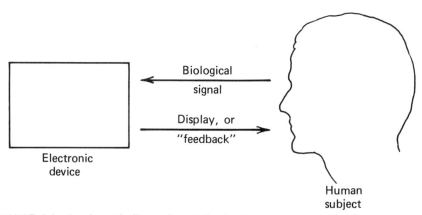

FIGURE 6.1 A schematic illustration of the basic structure of biofeedback training.

the subject with high-quality, moment-to-moment information about the state of such processes. In practice, the information—or feedback—is provided by electronic devices that augment biological signals (see Figure 6.1). The principal response measures that have been used in biofeedback research are (1) the electroencephalogram (EEG), which is associated with "brain waves"; (2) the electrocardiogram (EKG) and other measures associated with the heart's behavior; (3) the electromyograph (EMG), which is associated with muscle tension; (4) the galvanic skin response (GSR), which is associated with emotional responses; and (5) skin temperature, which is associated with the dilation and constriction of small blood vessels.

On a more informal level, biofeedback represents an exciting break-through in man-machine systems. For the first time human beings can learn to "play" organs of the body much like a musician can play a piano. Biofeedback has been described with such phrases as *electronic yoga*, *visceral learning*, and *mind over body*. Biofeedback in its present form did not make its appearance on the psychological horizon until the late 1960s. When it did appear, it generated a substantial amount of interest among scientists and laymen alike.

The basic principle on which biofeedback is based has been known to psychologists for years. The early learning theorist, Edward L. Thorndike, called the principle *knowledge of results*, which states that learning is greatly facilitated if learners are provided with information about the outcomes of their actions. Imagine yourself sitting blindfolded before a typewriter. Assume that you don't know how to type. You practice, but your practice means nothing because you can't associate keys with letters. Say that a teacher is willing to call out each letter as you strike it. Could you learn the keyboard now? Of course, because you are obtaining knowledge of results. The knowledge of results allows you to shape your behavior, dropping out those responses that do not contribute to your learning goal and keeping in those responses that do contribute. In a sense, we have all been "blind" when it comes to having knowledge of results about the actions of organs of our body. We have not been able to control them voluntarily because we couldn't "see" (or "hear," or otherwise sense) what they were doing.

A traditional distinction in physiology and psychology has been the distinction between the somatic and the autonomic nervous system. The *somatic nervous system* is said to control the muscles attached to the skeleton. Thus such actions as walking, moving a hand, turning the head, and so forth are thought of as voluntary. We can will these actions, and most of us are able to acquire rather precise control over them. On the other hand, the *autonomic nervous system* is said to control the smooth muscles associated with the body's internal organs and endocrine glands. Such internal events as heart rate, blood vessel changes, gastric juice secretion, and thyroxine production are thought of as involuntary. It is usually said that we cannot will these events, and most of us live our whole lives with no conscious control over them.

At present the whole distinction between what is voluntary and what is involuntary is breaking down. It was one of B. F. Skinner's accomplishments to demonstrate that much behavior that is classified as voluntary could just as well be classified as involuntary. Instrumental conditioning deals with the conditioning of overt movements, visible actions, the kinds of behavior usually thought of as voluntary. Thus many people felt that Skinner's work downgraded the importance of conscious control, or what we refer to as the human will. Now biofeedback makes its appearance and says, "Yes, the distinction between voluntary and involuntary *is* arbitrary. People can gain control over so-called involuntary processes." Thus biofeedback upgrades the importance of conscious control, or the human will.

Let us conduct a thought experiment to illustrate how voluntary control over a visceral reaction can be acquired. Imagine yourself sitting in a chair in a biofeedback laboratory. Before you is a television screen. Electrodes have been pasted to your body; the electrodes convey information about heart activity to an EKG apparatus; the data are quickly analyzed by a computer; and then heart-rate information is projected on the television screen. The televised picture provides you with high-quality information about heart-rate activity. A moving dot and a line across the middle of the screen are the essential elements in the picture. When the dot is moving above the line, your heart rate is above a previously established standard. When the dot is moving below the line, your heart rate is below the standard. Your task is to be able to move the dot from above the line to below the line, or vice versa, at will.

You stare at the display in dismay. You do not have the slightest idea how to control your heart rate, and you express your feeling to the experimenter in charge. He gives you gentle assurance that most people can develop some internal strategy for getting the dot to move at will. It is a matter of trial and error, and that is why the feedback is so important. So you look at the dot, concentrate, and various thoughts and images come and go. They seem to have only a minimal connection with the display on the screen. Little by little, however, you begin to feel that something is happening. By the end of the session, it seems that you have acquired some modicum of control over the movement of the dot.

Say that you return to the laboratory twice a week for a period of time. After five or ten sessions, it is quite clear that something is happening. Perhaps within ten or twenty sessions you begin to feel quite adept. You can often "drive" the dot at will. You have acquired a degree of voluntary control over your heart rate.

The preceding example was hypothetical. But similar research has been conducted by Peter Lang of the University of Wisconsin. He has taught a number of subjects to control heart rate. Such research has great promise. Persons suffering from heart problems may be able to relieve some of their symptoms with the help of biofeedback training. There have already been some clinical applications, but so far these have been relatively limited in number.

BIOFEEDBACK RESEARCH

One of the first reports of a successful biofeedback study dealt with the instrumental conditioning of heart rate in rats. The experiment was conducted by experimental psychologists Neal Miller and Leo DiCara, and it was reported in 1967. In the experiment, heart rate was the instrumental response and electrical stimulation to a rat's pleasure center was the reinforcer. Some of the rats learned to speed up their heart rates for the electrical stimulation; others learned to slow down their heart rates for the electrical stimulation.

This pioneer demonstration of the reality of visceral learning was not produced easily. To rule out the possibility that the rats were controlling heart rate indirectly through changes in breathing or muscular activity, they were injected with curare, a drug that paralyzes skeletal muscles. The results were clear. The rats were able to attain direct voluntary control over heart rate. Indeed, so powerful was the direct control that seven out of forty rats trained to slow down their heart rates died a sudden death. Upon hearing these results, a student in one of my psychology classes exclaimed, "What next? Now there are even yogi rats!"

DiCara and other researchers working with Miller have gone on to show that rats can acquire voluntary control of a spectrum of visceral responses, including urine flow and systolic blood pressure. They have also demonstrated that salivation in dogs, usually thought of as an involuntary response, can be instrumentally trained and brought under voluntary control.

It would certainly seem that if rats and dogs can take advantage of biofeedback, so can human beings. And such is, of course, the case. One of the first reports of biofeedback research with human beings were the alpha rhythm studies conducted by Joseph Kamiya. Kamiya, at the time a psychologist at the Langley Porter Neuropsychiatric Institute in San Francisco, first trained human subjects to recognize their own alpha rhythms. The *alpha rhythm* is one of several brain-wave patterns. The term "brain wave" is informal usage for the electroencephalographic records (EEG) produced by changing electrical potentials of the brain. There are several prominent frequency bands. These are designated by letters of the Greek alphabet, including *alpha, beta, delta*, and *theta*. The terminology can be slightly confusing because *alpha* is the first letter of the Greek alphabet. But of the four waves just noted, it is ranked second in terms of cycles per second.

One response measure used in biofeedback is the electroencephalogram, associated with "brain waves."

This is the order in terms of cycles per second: (1) The *beta rhythm* occurs at the rate of about fourteen cycles per second or more and is associated with alertness and high arousal. (2) The *alpha rhythm* occurs at the rate of about eight to fourteen cycles per second and is associated with mental relaxation and what has been described as "passive alertness." (3) The *theta rhythm* occurs at the rate of about four to eight cycles per second and is associated with a reverie-fantasy state in which mental imagery is high. (4) The *delta rhythm* occurs at the rate of about four cycles per second or less and is associated with deep sleep (see Figure 6.2).

After Kamiya discovered that people could reliably recognize alpha states, he wondered if they could learn to increase their production of the alpha rhythm. The task given the experimental subjects was to maintain the sound of a tone. When subjects were in an alpha state, the tone was on; when subjects slipped out of the alpha state, the tone went off. The majority of subjects were able to learn the voluntary control of the alpha rhythm. Kamiya had verified with objective data what meditators have claimed for generations: It is possible to develop self-control of mental states. One of the exciting things about EEG-biofeedback is that the typical subject can make rapid progress in the direction of voluntary mental control, accomplishing in months what might take years without the aid of the biofeedback equipment. This finding has led popularizers to speak of "instant Zen" and the like. (Zen is discussed in Chapter Eight.)

But make no mistake. Reasonable researchers, such as Kamiya, make no rash claims for EEG training. For now, it can be said that the alpha

FIGURE 6.2 Schematic illustration of the differences in cycles per second among beta, alpha, theta, and delta rhythms.

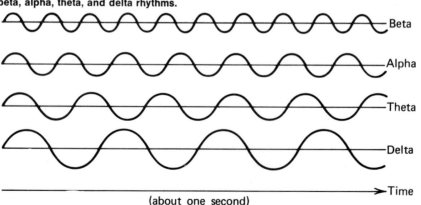

(about one second)

state does seem to be associated with a kind of quiet awareness without many visual images. As such, learning how to produce the alpha rhythm at will can be useful in helping a person learn how to relax.

One of the questionable things about alpha training is that it has spawned the production of home units for self-supervised learning. The value of such units, advertised for sale for a few hundred dollars, is dubious. For example, the problem of "noise" or incorrect information in the system is considerable. The movements of the eyes, the wrinkling of the brows, and so forth also produce changing electrical potentials of the muscles; these may give false signals that are misinterpreted. Many persons who are convinced that they are masters of alpha control are simply deceiving themselves.

Relaxation is associated with biological signals other than the alpha rhythm. Indeed, the alpha rhythm may not be the best measure of relaxation. A more direct measure is the *electromyograph* (EMG), a record of muscle tension. Starting in the early 1960s, Thomas Budzynski, an electronics engineer and psychologist, and Johann Stoyva, a psychophysiologist with a special interest in relaxation techniques, have worked together at the University of Colorado Medical School. They have combined autogenic training with EMG feedback; *autogenic training* is a method of inducing relaxation developed in Germany in the 1920s. The method calls for the subject to give himself suggestions that he is feeling less fatigued and less tense. It is an autosuggestive method. Budzynski and Stoyva have found that the combined results of autogenic training and biofeedback can be impressive.

It appears from the research of Budzynski and Stoyva that anxiety and deep muscle relaxation are antagonistic responses. If a person is deeply relaxed, it is hard for that person to simultaneously feel anxious. The two researchers have found that an important muscle associated with deep relaxation is the *frontalis,* the forehead muscle. It is a relatively difficult muscle to learn to control voluntarily. If a subject does learn to control it, however, he generally gets a spread of relaxation involving the rest of the head and the upper part of the body. Working with a substantial number of subjects over a period of years, Budzynski and Stoyva have been able to help subjects find relief from anxiety, tension headaches, and other woes that have no organic basis.

Tension headaches are not the same as migraine headaches. A tension headache appears to be caused by excessive muscle contraction. A migraine headache is probably caused by temporarily enlarged blood vessels, and this condition produces a pulsing pain. At the Menninger Foundation, Elmer Green (mentioned earlier in connection with the Swami Rama) Alyce Green, and E. Dale Walters have been conducting research on the relief of migraine. Their method involves skin temperature as the feedback measure. In a typical experiment, a subject sits with a highly sensitive thermometer taped to one hand. The thermometer provides information to a biofeedback device, and the device provides the subject with a visual display that gives skin temperature readings to one-tenth of a degree. Using autosuggestion and the information from the machine, the subject learns voluntary control over his skin temperature. After a substantial amount of training, it is not at all unusual for a subject to be able to voluntarily alter the skin temperature of a particular hand by several degrees.

What does this have to do with migraine headaches? If the skin temperature goes up, it means that the subject is enlarging the blood vessels in his hand. When the blood vessels in the hand enlarge, the blood vessels in the muscles surrounding the head constrict. The migraine was caused by temporarily enlarged blood vessels in the head muscles; thus raising the skin temperature of the hand brings about relief from the migraine. The Greens have reported promising results using the skin temperature method for treating the pain of chronic migraine. There is evidence that once the subject learns voluntary control of skin temperature, the learning persists for quite some time without the support of the machine. Thus the sufferer is not constantly dependent on the laboratory equipment for relief. This last statement applies not only to skin temperature control, but to biofeedback learning in general.

Biofeedback research has blossomed and expanded on many fronts in the 1970s. It is beyond the scope of this book to present summaries of the many biofeedback studies that have been conducted. But the picture is already clear in many ways. Biofeedback has tremendous practical implications, particularly in the area of treating psychosomatic disorders.

CLINICAL APPLICATIONS AND BEYOND

New Mind, New Body by Barbara Brown, a leading biofeedback researcher, details the promise of biofeedback in the area of clinical applications. The following are a few of the possibilities gleaned from her book and the biofeedback literature in general.

1 It has already been noted that subjects can learn to control their heart rates. This capacity can be of value in treating persons with *cardia arrhythmias*, odd patterns in the usual pumping action of the heart.

2 We have also already noted that biofeedback can be useful in treating headaches, both the tension and the migraine varieties.

3 Primary hypertension, high blood pressure of unknown origin, was discussed in the section on chemotherapy. High blood pressure is usually treated with drugs. It is hoped that biofeedback techniques will eventually lead to a reduction in the use of antihypertensive agents, replacing drugs with voluntary blood pressure control.

4 Ulcers are believed to be associated with anxiety. If chronic anxiety can be reduced with EEG training or muscle relaxation techniques, the ulcer sufferer may sustain substantial benefits.

5 The EEG has been useful for years in diagnosing epilepsy. There is now the hope that EEG training may be useful in reducing the severity of some epileptic conditions. It appears that by gaining self-control over their brain waves, some epileptics can learn to abort seizures.

6 It is widely held that asthma is complicated by episodes of anxiety and other emotional factors. Biofeedback training, by giving the sufferer greater self-control over emotional states, may alleviate some of the more severe symptoms associated with asthma.

7 Spastic colitis, a painful and sometimes dangerous condition in which the colon undergoes involuntary contractions, offers possibilities for biofeedback training. Again, biofeedback techniques allow the subject to gain voluntary control over autonomic functions traditionally thought of as beyond the reach of the conscious will.

It is clear that biofeedback training offers a large range of possible clinical applications. Many conditions that have been treated by psychosurgery and drugs may eventually fall within the domain of biofeedback technology. This trend, although weak now, is expected to grow as we learn more about biofeedback and as improvements in the electronic devices continue. The use of biofeedback techniques, when possible, seems to be advisable over psychosurgery or drugs. Biofeedback training has more than one advantage over other treatment modalities. It is certainly not as drastic as psychosurgery. It does not bring with it the problems of addiction and unwanted side effects associated with chemotherapy. Finally, biofeedback training allows sufferers to play the part of *active agents* in their own therapy; this is of great value for self-esteem. They are not the passive victims of their illnesses. Instead, with the aid of the biofeedback technology, they can assert themselves against their ailments.

The alleviation of suffering resides primarily within the domain of adjustment. If we broaden our scope to the wider horizons of personal growth, biofeedback offers some intriguing possibilities for maximizing human potentialities. To illustrate, some research suggests that the theta rhythm is associated with creativity, that persons with a high spontaneous production of theta waves are somewhat more likely to produce original thoughts. If this lead is sustained, it may be possible to increase an

Some researchers suggest that biofeedback may be used to expand the range and power of consciousness.

individual's creativity level by training him to produce the theta state voluntarily. Similarly, Brown speaks of expanding mind abilities by becoming aware and *becoming aware of becoming aware* with biofeedback. There are many "brave new world" proposals suggesting that biofeedback may be used to augment various psychological processes, such as memory, perception, and learning. The general idea is to use biofeedback to expand the range and power of consciousness. Brown compellingly concludes *New Mind, New Body* with the following words:

The excitement that bio-feedback has generated is deserved. It is a powerful and effective tool for the future of the mind. Its potential may be unlimited, or it may be merely a step toward a new reality. Beyond this we cannot predict. What new resources man will find within the depths of his mind cannot be foretold. One can but guess that new forces of mental energy will be unleashed, for we are all familiar with the repressive constraints exerted upon our minds during the entire age of materialism and technology. Now technology has come full circle and is allowing us to begin the exploration of the recesses of our inner space. (p. 408)

CRITIQUE

Somewhat more than one hundred years ago, the English poet and essayist Charles Colton said, "Tyrants have not yet discovered any chains that can fetter the mind." With the advent of psychotechnology, Colton's statement becomes outdated. A tyrant *can* control the "mind" via its physical organ, the brain. Let us examine some of the problems associated with psychotechnology:

1   The principal problem is the one expressed in the opening paragraph of this section: the problem of *uninvited behavior control.* This is the biggest single specter raised by psychotechnology. Drugs and electrical stimulation to the brain represent the two most powerful forms of psychotechnology, and it is feared that ESB and drugs can be used against people as well as for people. As techniques of behavior control become increasingly potent, the question arises: Who will control the controllers? There is no easy answer to this question. ESB in particular has been the target of attacks by worried journalists, who see it as the potential right arm of an Orwellian Big Brother. The following frightening commentary appears in *The Second Genesis* by Albert Rosenfeld, science editor of *Saturday Review:*

It has been suggested that a dictator might even implant electrodes in the brains of infants a few months after birth—and they would never know that their thoughts, moods, feelings, and all-around behavior were not the results of their own volition. Where then is free will, and individual responsibility? (p. 229)

Delgado, ESB's most outstanding spokesman, disagrees. He indicates that the complexities of electrode implants and the problem of individual differences in reactivity make it unlikely that ESB on a grand scale as an agent of social or political control will ever be practiced. He feels that ESB will be restricted mainly to clinical uses. Nonetheless, fears persist.

2   Physiological and chemical treatments of psychological disorders tend to take less of a professional person's time than does psychotherapy. It is faster and seemingly more efficient to shock, drug, or cut a person than to help him tease apart the complexities of inner conflicts, maladaptive habit patterns, or faulty styles of social interaction. Critics of psychotechnology argue that its methods grossly oversimplify the human condition and that psychotechnology "things" the person by viewing him only in biological terms. The living individual is reduced to a kind of high-grade puppet that can be pushed and pulled by electricity and drugs. This in turn can lead to monetary abuses by individuals in private practice. They can charge high fees for remedies that take up little of their professional time, running large numbers of patients through their psychotechnological turnstiles with little regard for each patient's individual personhood.

3   In spite of years of experience with electroconvulsive therapy (ECT), there is still serious debate among psychiatrists as to its value. It is true that a majority of psychiatrists consider ECT a valuable therapeutic tool. But a large and vocal minority of psychiatrists, supported by many psychologists and ex-patients, insist that ECT is barbaric. The mixed feelings about ECT are illustrated by these two letters, both of which appeared in *Psychology Today* (December 1975):

Letter 1. *I came home after ECT completely disoriented and frightened. I lived in a three-room apartment and couldn't remember where my vacuum cleaner was. I needed to be shown how to use make-up and how to cook. I played a violin all through my school years, won a medal in fact, but I can't even read music now. This memory loss would be only temporary I was told, but it has lasted 16 years.*

Letter 2. *I was so depressed that I couldn't even pull together a successful suicide plan and after all the horror stories I had heard about ECT from psychologists, I agreed to have it and thought for sure I would die on the table. It seemed as good a way to go as any. After the treatments were over, though, I found I no longer wanted to die. Thus I call the treatments very effective and successful for me.*

What is the answer? There is no such thing as *the* answer. ECT may be helpful or harmful, depending on a host of variables, not the least of which is individual differences in psychiatric patients. Presumably, in the hands of a responsible and qualified psychiatrist, ECT has a proper place among various modes of therapy.

4   Megavitamin therapy, potentially a promising avenue of investigation, has failed to establish its thesis with a large percentage of mental health professionals. The main problem seems to be that most of the research conducted on megavitamin therapy has been conducted by "true believers," people who are anxious to find what they set out to find. The experiments have usually been poorly designed, often lacking adequate controls. The results of megavitamin therapy are often mixed with the results of psychotherapy, ECT, drugs, and vocational rehabilitation. When dramatic "mind cures" are announced, it is impossible for the unbiased observer to decide whether megavitamin therapy was the essential factor in the patient's improvement.

5   If used judiciously, there is little question that drugs can play a proper role in therapy. Chemotherapy has been of particular value in treating the more severe forms of mental problems, the psychotic reactions. Antipsychotic agents have played a big role in reducing the population sizes of overcrowded mental hospitals. Since the advent of chemotherapy, there has been less reliance on ECT and physical restraints to control difficult patients. Thus chemotherapy is in its own way contributing to the more humane treatment of mental patients. In the case of neurotic reactions, character disorders, and hyperkinetic children, however, the picture is less clear. The drugs used to treat these conditions are often addictive and may have harmful physical side effects. Opponents of chemotherapy believe that when drugs are used to control the conditions cited, the underlying problems often get worse. They argue that the real difficulty is masked and often goes untreated. The antidrug voices say that answers to problems in living seldom come in convenient bottles. It may be of some value to note that emotions are reactions to life situations. In bad situations, they are alarm signals. The person knows through his "gut reaction" that *something is wrong.* His emotions confirm the knowledge of his intellect that his business is failing, that his marriage is unhappy, or that he cannot communicate with his adolescent children. The commonsense approach is to alleviate the intensity of the emotional reaction by doing something about the life situation. In a sense, the use of a drug has us short-circuiting this process. It numbs us to the situation, providing us with a way of not giving the normal biological response. This may be desirable in persons who are overreactive. But the optimal response to a chronic destructive emotion is to take some realistic action to change a negative life situation into a more positive one.

6   There are even a few dark clouds in the blue sky of biofeedback. As already noted, a gullible public often wastes its money on next-to-worthless equipment of questionable reliability. One practical difficulty with biofeedback training is that it is time consuming, requires a motivated subject, and also requires an interested biofeedback-oriented therapist. In the actual world of day-to-day clinical work, these are not conditions that are particularly easy to meet. Many people with psychosomatic complaints want something done to them; they don't want to do something to themselves. They see their problems as afflictions that are visited upon them, not as stress reactions to difficulties in coping with the challenges of existence. Unless a substantial amount of time is invested in reeducating such individuals prior to biofeedback training, the biofeedback training in and of itself is likely to be of slight value. Another problem with biofeedback training is the tendency to regress to prior behavior patterns. Although the capacity for voluntary control of autonomic responses is a fact, and although there is obviously some persistence of learning in the absence of the machine's support, there will usually be a slow loss of benefits gained. Several sets of retraining sessions over a period of years may be required before the learning can be regarded as more or less permanent.

IMPLICATIONS FOR ADJUSTMENT AND GROWTH

Zealous opponents of psychotechnology speak of it in the harshest terms. They present many tales of its abuses and thus view it as an unmitigated evil, a tool of the Devil himself. Loving advocates of psychotechnology speak of it in glowing language. They see a bright world of the future in which psychosurgery, proper nutrition, drugs, and biofeedback training bring into existence a behavioral Utopia for mankind. It is doubtful that exaggerated statements in either direction are valid. Although a number of problems are inherent in psychotechnology, it has a proper place among the adjustment-growth pathways. Let us note several positive aspects of psychotechnology.

1 Psychotechnology properly reminds us that the mind-body distinction is arbitrary. Its techniques compellingly reveal that the mind and the body are two aspects of the same unity. This point of view is known as *holism,* the assertion that an organism is an organized whole which cannot be meaningfully divided into parts. Although many behavioral scientists pay lip service to holism, in practice they often forget about it. Psychotechnology takes holism seriously.

2 Many people in this country suffer behavioral afflictions caused by stroke damage or other organic impairments. For them, computer-assisted ESB offers tremendous possibilities. Also, there are a number of additional ways ESB can be beneficially used in clinical settings. These include applications in epilepsy, narcolepsy, the treatment of chronic pain, the localization of tumors, and so forth.

3 In spite of the perhaps too grand claims of orthomolecular psychiatry, it is certainly clear that good nutrition is important for physical-mental health. If the mind-body distinction is arbitrary, then it is certainly obvious that the health of the brain is important. A physically ill brain can hardly produce clear thoughts. The person who seeks after adjustment and growth will not rely solely on psychological strategies. He will get enough protein, avoid excessive amounts of refined carbohydrates, be alert to the possible side effects of artificial food additives, and be realistically concerned about his vitamin intake. He need not become a food faddist, of course; but correct eating is certainly a reasonable thing to practice.

4 Although, as already noted, there are drawbacks to using drugs for treating psychological problems, there are times when chemotherapy is advantageous. It would certainly seem to have a proper role in the treatment of psychotic reactions. But what of the person who is not hospitalized, who suffers from excessive anxiety or depression? In such a case, the individual should realize that drugs may be helpful as a *temporary crutch.* In other words, the proper use of tranquilizers and other medications is to get the person through a *transient* situational disturbance. But if the taking of drugs becomes a key element in one's life-style, then something is seriously amiss.

5   Of the psychotechnological approaches discussed in this chapter, biofeedback training appears to offer the greatest long-run hope for both adjustment and growth. In the domain of adjustment, biofeedback training may help alleviate conditions often treated by drugs (e.g., anxiety and muscle tension). Also, biofeedback training has numerous clinical applications in the war against psychosomatic illnesses. In the domain of growth, biofeedback training points to ways the individual can move past an adjusted norm. By building a partial bridge between modern technology and Eastern ways of thought, biofeedback training provides access to strategies for personal growth that have often been disdained by tough-minded Western psychologists. More will be said about Eastern philosophy and its relation to personal growth in Chapter Eight.

In an address given at the California Institute of Technology, Albert Einstein said, "Why does this magnificent applied science, which saves work and makes life easier, bring us so little happiness? The simple answers runs: Because we have not yet learned to make sensible use of it." Einstein's observation is also pertinent to the area of applied science called psychotechnology in this book. It is obvious to thinking persons that psychotechnology is neither good nor bad in and of itself. It can possibly improve the quality of human life if, as Einstein notes, we can learn to make sensible use of it.

SUMMARY AND SELF-TEST

1 The ancient art of trepanning involves making a perforation in the skull.

T   F

2 The systematic observations of the neurosurgeon Wilder Penfield have played an important part in the contemporary mapping of the motor and sensory areas of the cortex in human beings.

T   F

3 Metrazol therapy, utilizing a drug prepared from camphor, is not a kind of shock therapy.

T   F

4 Electroconvulsive therapy was introduced in 1897 by the French physician Pierre Janet.

T   F

5 The term *psychocivilization*, as used by Delgado, tends to suggest a Utopia of the future in which each person "does his own thing."

T   F

6 The lobotomy is a surgical procedure in which the connections between the frontal lobes of the cortex are severed from the subcortex.

T   F

7 In electrical stimulation of the brain (ESB), electrodes are usually implanted in various regions of the subcortex and brain stem.

T   F

8 The amygdalae are small brain structures located near the hypothalamus.

T   F

9 A stimoceiver is an electrode-radio unit that receives activating messages, but cannot transmit information about brain states.

T   F

10 It is much too farfetched to suggest that it may be possible someday,

with the aid of computers and stimoceivers, to restore lost brain functions in stroke victims or individuals having other kinds of brain damage.
T   F

11   Narcolepsy is an involuntary tendency to fall asleep at inappropriate times.
T   F

12   Electrical self-stimulation of the brain in human beings is up to this time a science-fiction fantasy.
T   F

13   Children who do not receive sufficient protein during their developing years cannot have as large or as physically healthy a brain as they might have had.
T   F

14   The principle of protein complementarity states that one protein cannot be used to supplement another one.
T   F

15   All nutritionists reject the hypothesis that functional hypoglycemia may underlie symptoms associated with neurotic reactions.
T   F

16   Orthomolecular psychiatrists tend to be hostile to megavitamin therapy.
T   F

17   The pediatrician and allergist Benjamin Feingold theorizes that artificial food flavors and colors play an important role in hyperactivity.
T   F

18   Antipsychotic agents are in fact seldom used.
T   F

19   Antianxiety agents are widely used to treat neurotic patients.
T   F

20   Caffeine is a stimulant, but nicotine is not.
T   F

21   Odd as it seems, a hyperkinetic child is sometimes "tranquilized" with a stimulant.
T   F

22   Advocates of counseling and psychotherapy feel that these approaches may afford better long-run treatment of psychosomatic illness than chemotherapy.

T   F

23 A hallucinogen is a drug that tends to alter conventional perception and thought.

T   F

24 Drugs classified as "fantasy enhancers" augment emotional responses, but do not increase imaginative capacities.

T   F

25 The psychiatrist Claudio Naranjo asserts that not all psychedelics are hallucinogenic.

T   F

26 Self-control of various visceral responses of the body is possible with a procedure known as "biofeedback training."

T   F

27 The basic principle upon which biofeedback is based is called the "law of exercise."

T   F

28 The somatic nervous system is said to control the smooth muscles associated with the body's internal organs and endocrine glands.

T   F

29 Rats are unable to acquire voluntary control of visceral responses.

T   F

30 Voluntary control of heart rate can be of value in treating persons with *cardia arrhythmias*, odd patterns in the usual pumping action of the heart.

T   F

ANSWER KEY

1 *True*. The ancient art of trepanning involves making a perforation in the skull.

2 *True*. The systematic observations of the neurosurgeon Wilder Penfield have played an important part in the contemporary mapping of the motor and sensory areas of the cortex in human beings.

3 *False*. Metrazol therapy, utilizing a drug prepared from camphor, is a kind of shock therapy.

4 *False*. Electroconvulsive therapy was introduced in 1937 by two Italian psychiatrists, Ugo Cerletti and Lucia Bini.

5 *False*. The term *psychocivilization*, as used by Delgado, tends to suggest a society in which it is possible to have remote control over impulsive, aggressive, or otherwise unorthodox persons.

6 *True.* The lobotomy is a surgical procedure in which the connections beween the frontal lobes of the cortex are severed from the subcortex.

7 *True.* In electrical stimulation of the brain (ESB), electrodes are usually implanted in various regions of the subcortex and brain stem.

8 *True.* The amygdalae are small brain structures located near the hypothalamus.

9 *False.* A stimoceiver is an electrode-radio unit that receives activating messages and also transmits information about brain states.

10 *False.* It may be possible someday, with the aid of computers and stimoceivers, to restore lost brain functions in stroke victims or individuals having other kinds of brain damage.

11 *True.* Narcolepsy is an involuntary tendency to fall asleep at inappropriate times.

12 *False.* Electrical self-stimulation of the brain in human beings is a reality.

13 *True.* Children who do not receive sufficient protein during their developing years cannot have as large or as physically healthy a brain as they might have had.

14 *False.* The principle of protein complementarity states that one protein can be used to supplement another one.

15 *False.* Some nutritionists accept the hypothesis that functional hypoglycemia may underlie symptoms associated with neurotic reactions.

16 *False.* Orthomolecular psychiatrists endorse megavitamin therapy.

17 *True.* The pediatrician and allergist Benjamin Feingold theorizes that artificial food flavors and colors play an important part in hyperactivity.

18 *False.* Antipsychotic agents are used extensively.

19 *True.* Antianxiety agents are widely used to treat neurotic patients.

20 *False.* Both caffeine and nicotine are stimulants.

21 *True.* A hyperkinetic child is sometimes "tranquilized" with a stimulant.

22 *True.* Advocates of counseling and psychotherapy feel that these approaches may afford better long-run treatment of psychosomatic illness than chemotherapy.

23 *True.* A hallucinogen is a drug that tends to alter conventional perception and thought.

24 *False.* Drugs classified as "fantasy enhancers" increase imaginative capacities.

25 *True.* The psychiatrist Claudio Naranjo asserts that not all psychedelics are hallucinogenic.

26 *True.* Self-control of various visceral responses of the body is possible with a procedure known as "biofeedback training."

27 *False.* The basic principle upon which biofeedback is based has been known to psychologists for years; the early learning theorist, Edward L. Thorndike, called the principle "knowledge of results."

28 *False.* The somatic nervous system is said to control the muscles attached to the skeleton.

29 *False.* Rats are able to acquire voluntary control of visceral responses.

30 *True.* Voluntary control of heart rate can be of value in treating persons with *cardia arrhythmias*, odd patterns in the usual pumping action of the heart.

DISCUSSION QUESTIONS

PSYCHOSURGERY: WILL SOCIETY BECOME PSYCHOCIVILIZED?

1 What kind of an emotional response does a word such as *psychocivilized* evoke from you?

2 Do you have a basic objection to psychosurgery of any kind on moral-ethical grounds? Or do you feel that psychosurgery is sometimes justified?

3 Do you feel that electrical stimulation of the brain (ESB) is a threat to a free society?

4 What are some of the potential applications of ESB to medical-psychiatric problems?

NUTRITION: FOOD FOR THOUGHT

1 Do you get enough protein to maintain and rebuild your body and brain? About what percentage of your diet is protein? Do you feel that you are getting a proper balance of protein, carbohydrate, and fat?

2 Do you know anyone who is a "sugar freak"? Does that person display what appear to be neurotic symptoms? Do you accept the hypothesis that chronic low blood sugar can produce symptoms that mimic neurotic reactions?

3 Does the approach of orthomolecular psychiatry bring forth a positive reaction from you? Or do you think it is a false trail?

4 Do you personally know of a hyperactive child? Does the contention that artificial food flavors and colors are associated with hyperactivity seem to be a plausible explanation of that child's behavior?

DRUGS: THE TRANQUILIZED MIND

1 Do you agree with the drug approach that psychological problems often have a biochemical basis?

2 Do you personally know anyone who has taken or is taking drugs for a psychological-emotional problem? What advantages and/or disadvantages do you assign to the drug treatment?

3 Are you addicted to popular stimulants, such as caffeine or nicotine? If so, does your addiction seem benign to you? Or do you think it has adverse effects on your feelings and behavior?

4   Do you think that drugs are relied on too heavily to treat psychosomatic illnesses? Or do you think that at present there is no other large-scale practical way of managing these illnesses?

5   Do you consider it unfortunate that at present little research investigates the possibility of using hallucinogens as adjuncts to psychotherapy?

BIOFEEDBACK: UNIFYING MIND AND BODY

1   Do you consider biofeedback training an exciting breakthrough in the psychology of self-control? Or do you think that much of the excitement it has generated is unjustified?

2   Do you know anyone who has experienced biofeedback training? If so, what kind of training was it? Was the training for demonstration purposes, an experiment, or for a specific problem?

3   Can you think of any potential clinical applications of biofeedback training not mentioned in the book?

REFERENCES

Abrahamson, E. M., and Pezet, A. W. *Body, Mind, and Sugar*. New York: Pyramid Books, 1971.

Brown, B. *New Mind, New Body*. New York: Harper & Row, 1974.

Budzynski, T., and Stoyva, J. "An Instrument for Producing Deep Muscle Relaxation by Means of Analog Information Feedback." *Journal of Applied Behavior Analysis*, 2 (1969) 231–237.

Clark, M. "Coping with Depression." *Newsweek*, January 8, 1975.

Colton, C. C. As quoted in *The Great Quotations*. New York: Pocket Books, 1967.

Crichton, M. *The Terminal Man*. New York: Alfred A. Knopf, 1972.

del Campo, A. "Blind Can 'See' the Shape of Things." *Med. World News* (Oct. 7, 1966) 142–143.

Delgado, J. M. R. *Physical Control of the Mind: Toward a Psychocivilized Society*. New York: Harper & Row, 1969.

Delgado, J. M. R., Roberts, W. W., and Miller, N. E. "Learning motivated by Electrical Stimulation of the Brain." *American Journal of Physiology*, 179 (1954), 587–593.

Dement, W. C. et al. "Sleeplessness, Sleep Attacks and Things That Go Wrong in the Night." *Psychology Today* (December 1975).

DeQuincey, T. *Confessions of an English Opium-Eater*. New York: E. P. Dutton & Co., 1907.

Ehrlich, P. R. *The Population Bomb*. New York: Ballantine Books, 1968.

Einstein, A. As quoted in *The Great Quotations*. New York: Pocket Books, 1967.

Feingold, B. F. "An Interview." *People Weekly*, December 8, 1975.

————. *Why Your Child Is Hyperactive*. New York: Random House, 1974.

Fieve, R. R. *Moodswing: The Third Revolution in Psychiatry*. New York: William Morrow & Co., 1975.

Fredericks, C., and Goodman, H. *Low Blood Sugar and You*. New York: Constellation International, 1969.

Freeman, W., and Watts, J. W. *Psychosurgery in the Treatment of Mental Disorders and Intractable Pain*. Springfield, Ill.: Charles C. Thomas, 1950.

Gerald, M. C. *Pharmacology*. Englewood Cliffs, N.J.: Prentice-Hall, 1974.

Green, E. E., Green, A. M., and Walters, E. D. "Voluntary Control of Internal States: Psychological and Physiological." *Journal of Transpersonal Psychology*, 2 (1970), 1–26.

Heath, R. G. "Electrical Self-stimulation of the Brain in Man." *American Journal of Psychiatry*, 120 (1963), 571–577.

Jonas, G. *Visceral Learning*. New York: Viking Press, 1972.

Kamiya, J. "Conscious Control of Brain Waves." *Readings in Experimental Psychology Today*. Del Mar, Calif.: CRM Books, 1970.

Karlins, M., and Andrew, L. M. *Biofeedback*. New York: Warner Books, 1972.

Kline, N. S. *From Sad to Glad*. New York: Ballantine Books, 1974.

Lang, P. "Autonomic Control." *Psychology Today* (October 1970), vol. 3, pp. 37–41.

Lappé, F. M. *Diet for a Small Planet*. New York: Ballantine Books, 1971.

McMillen, S. I. *None of These Diseases*. Old Tappan, N.J.: Fleming H. Revell Co., 1973.

Miller, N. E., and DiCara, L. V. "Instrumental Learning of Heart-Rate Changes in Curarized Rats: Shaping and Specificity to Discriminative Stimulus." *Journal of Comparative and Physiological Psychology*, 63 (1967), 12–19.

Naranjo, C. *The Healing Journey*. New York: Ballantine Books, 1973.

Olds, J., and Milner, P. "Positive Reinforcement Produced by Electrical Stimulation of Septal Area and Other Regions of the Rat Brain." *Journal of Comparative and Physiological Psychology*, 47 (1954), 419–427.

Passwater, R. *Supernutrition*. New York: Dial Press, 1975.

Pauling, L. C. "Orthomolecular Psychiatry." *Science*, 160 (1968), 265–271.

Pauling, L. C., and Hawkins, D. *Orthomolecular Psychiatry*. San Francisco: W. H. Freeman, 1973.

Pines, M. *The Brain Changers*. New York: Harcourt Brace Javanovich, 1963.

Rosenfeld, A. *The Second Genesis*. New York: Vintage Books, 1969.

Schrag, P., and Divoky, D. *The Myth of the Hyperactive Child.* New York: Pantheon Books, 1975.

Taylor, R. L. "Electroconvulsive Treatment (ECT): The Control of Therapeutic Power." *The Thin Edge: A Mental Health Newsletter for San Bernardino County* (November 1975), 1, 4–7.

Viscott, D. S. *The Making of a Psychiatrist.* Greenwich, Conn.: Fawcett Publications, 1972.

Walker, S., III. "We're Too Cavalier about Hyperactivity." *Psychology Today* (December 1974), vol. 8, pp. 43–48.

Waltari, M. *The Egyptian.* New York: G. P. Putnam's Sons, 1949.

Wender, P. H. *The Hyperactive Child.* New York: Crown Publishers, 1973.

Williams, R. J. *Nutrition against Disease.* New York: Pitman Publishing Corp. 1971.

Yudkin, J. *Sweet and Dangerous.* New York: Peter H. Wyden, Inc., 1972.

CHAPTER 7
EXISTENTIAL-HUMANISTIC PSYCHOLOGY: THE SEARCH FOR AUTHENTICITY

The principal underlying assumption of existential-humanistic psychology is that self-awareness can make a crucial difference in the way we behave.

OVERVIEW

OUTLINE

TWO KEY QUESTIONS

What is existential-humanistic psychology?

Existential-humanistic psychology asserts the importance of human consciousness. The principal underlying assumption is that self-awareness can make a crucial difference in the way we behave. Existential-humanistic psychology says that we are capable of voluntary action, that we are more than reflex machines. It agrees that we are organisms, but argues that we cannot be understood in strictly biological terms. Instead, we must be understood in terms of those human characteristics that set us apart from other organisms.

How do the principles of existential-humanistic psychology relate to adjustment and growth?

According to existential-humanistic psychology, individuals shape themselves.

We are thus responsible for our own adjustment and growth. We are challenged by existential-humanistic psychology to adjust, not to arbitrary norms set by our culture, but to our own internal standards. We are also challenged to grow, to become the persons we are capable of becoming in terms of our unique talents and potentialities.

Imagine that you are watching an animated cartoon. Coyote is chasing Road Runner, is deceived, and runs off a cliff. Coyote continues running, oblivious to the fact that he has lost his support. Suddenly he stops, looks down, appears puzzled, and runs a few more steps. Then he looks down again, and his expression changes as he becomes aware that he is running on thin air. At this point he begins falling. This sort of thing is standard fare for animated cartoons. The cartoon seems to be saying that reality is defined by consciousness, that something is not real until we are aware of it. One almost believes that Coyote can run on the air as long as he thinks he is running on a road. This illustrates the tremendous implicit importance generally attached to consciousness. Although we seldom verbalize it, we take it for granted that awareness has enormous significance. This is the principal assertion of existential-humanistic psychology: Consciousness counts.

Existential-humanistic psychology has been called a Third Force in psychology. The reason for this label is that the two dominant forces in psychology in this century have been psychoanalysis and behaviorism. Both, each in its own way, downgrade the importance of consciousness. Recall Freud's famous statement that the mind is an iceberg, that the unconscious domain is much larger and more significant than the conscious domain. The individual only thinks that consciousness is important. In actuality, invisible forces rule his life, not his conscious mind. The radical behaviorist denies the existence of consciousness. The soft behaviorist says that consciousness may be real, but that it has no explanatory power. It is there, but only as an interesting side effect of the fact that we are reacting organisms. Consciousness has no causative value. It can't make anything happen. Existential-humanistic psychology categorically denies the validity of the way that psychoanalysis and behaviorism look at consciousness.

Existential-humanistic psychologists say that psychoanalysis and behaviorism have gone too far down a wrong road. They ask these questions: How do you experience your life? Do you experience it as ruled by unconscious forces? Do you experience it as a set of conditioned responses? To these questions, most of us would answer, "Of course not." How then do you experience your life? If you experience your life as a self-aware human being capable of taking action and making decisions, then trust this experience. Believe in this firsthand information before you believe in the theories of psychoanalysis and behaviorists. Existential-humanistic psychologists agree that we are organisms, that we react, and that many of the insights of psychoanalysis and behaviorism make sense. However, they assert that we are conscious human beings and that *we act as well as react.*

EXISTENTIALISM: CREATING YOURSELF

To appreciate the present status of existential-humanistic psychology, it is important to know something about the philosophical movement that spawned it, existentialism. Existentialism is not a philosophy; it is a movement within philosophy. Its broad current includes several kinds of existentialism. Let us use the word *existentialism* to refer to a general point of view in philosophy that places greater value on subjective experience than on objective data. The existentialist says that what you actually experience within yourself is far more important than what any expert can tell you about yourself.

ROOTS OF EXISTENTIALISM

Who was the first existential philosopher? The question defies a categorical answer. Some say it was Saint Thomas Aquinas because he said man has a free will. Others say it was René Descartes because he said, "I think, therefore I am!" Thus both men in their own way emphasized the importance of human consciousness. There can be no doubt that there was some thread of existentialism in these early philosophers. The modern existential movement, however, is generally regarded to have begun with the writings of Sören Kierkegaard somewhat more than one hundred years ago. Kierkegaard, a resident of Denmark, has been nicknamed "the lonely Dane" because his musings had a gloomy quality. He is a significant figure in the history of philosophy because he turned philosophy on its proverbial head. European philosophy in Kierkegaard's day was under the influence of such men as Immanuel Kant and Georg Hegel. These men were highly organized thinkers and constructed grand systems of philosophy. They were attempting to describe objectively the essence of human nature and man's place in the universe. Kierkegaard in effect asked the impertinent question, "What does all of this have to do with me?" He disputed the value of orthodox philosophy, arguing that on a personal level it did little to relieve anxiety and that it left the most important questions about the human condition unanswered.

Two ideas stand out like bright lights in Kierkegaard's works: (1) the importance of the individual and (2) the significance of personal emotions. Kierkegaard asserted that the single person is important, that he has importance in and of himself, that his unique characteristics should be valued. Kierkegaard was disconcerted that society was progressing in the direction of stamping out individuality, of placing too much value on the "agreeable person" who is a good member of the team. Kierkegaard fought the idea of conformity with a passion, indicating that an increasingly organized and complex society was making people behave like

Kierkegaard fought the idea of conformity with a passion.

well-regulated ants in an ant colony. His fear was that this trend was destroying the inner life, the very soul, of the individual.

The second idea, the significance of personal emotions, runs like a black thread through Kierkegaard's works. The thread is black because he was concerned with the "dark" emotions, anxiety and depression. Kierkegaard felt that anxiety and depression were more than neurotic symptoms; they were an inevitable part of the human condition. As we face the future, who cannot feel anxiety? As our illusions are shattered, who cannot feel depressed? One of Kierkegaard's principal works is titled *Fear and Trembling and Sickness unto Death*, which illustrates the tremendous importance he attached to the emotion of anxiety. Although Kierkegaard did not believe that complete relief from the dark emotions was possible, he did believe that they could be alleviated to some extent by *authentic living*: by pursuing a life in which one is true to oneself as an individual, not pledging false allegiance to the values and standards arbitrarily imposed by other people or one's culture. Kierkegaard said that for his tombstone he would prefer only these words: *The Individual.*

Kierkegaard was the fountainhead from which modern existentialism sprang. Let me briefly outline a few of the developments in existential thought following Kierkegaard. The concepts represented by these developments reside behind today's existential-humanistic psychology. My sketch will focus on the ideas of three men: Friedrich Nietzsche, Martin Heidegger, and Jean-Paul Sartre. It is not my purpose to present a coherent exposition of the thought of these men, but merely to pluck out of their works those ideas that have been adopted as core ones by contemporary existential-humanistic psychology.

The German philosopher Friedrich Nietzsche, writing shortly after Kierkegaard, also placed great importance on the individual. Indeed, he glorified and celebrated the potentialities of the individual with his idea of the superman, a person with the strength and the will to rise above the gray existence of the masses. Nietzsche felt that life is not worth living unless one has heroic values; the superman is a person with a sense of mission in life, a feeling that there are great things to be accomplished.

Associated with the idea of the superman is Nietzsche's concept of the *will to power*, an inborn tendency in all of us to gain ascendency over others. The will to power springs from biological evolution, the struggle of each animal to survive in competition with other animals. Charles Darwin expressed this idea with the phrase *survival of the fittest*. Nietzsche adopted Darwin's formulations and made them part of his philosophy of life. Only the fit deserve to survive, said Nietzsche. Thus in many people the will to power is blocked and destroyed by other people and/or the larger culture. Nietzsche scorned such persons, admiring the "lone wolf" who could preserve his individuality agains great odds. We shall see that Nietzsche's concept of the will to power plays an important part in the psychology of Alfred Adler, an important precursor of existential-humanistic psychology.

With the appearance of Martin Heidegger, also a German philosopher, existential philosophy took a turn in the direction of greater complexity. It is generally agreed that Heidegger's thought is extremely sophisticated. Much of it is opaque to the person having a limited background in philosophy. Heidegger's most significant book is *Being and Time*, published in 1927. Let us comment on only two ideas in Heidegger's thought, the idea of Being and Being-in-the-world. You will note that the word *Being* is capitalized. This is done to indicate that Being is a concrete reality, not an abstraction. To Heidegger, the most important thing about a person is the simple fact that he exists. He exists *before* he is anything else. Heidegger argues also that this is the way we experience our lives. We are always conscious of Being, or existence itself, prior to all other experiences. To illustrate, let us say that you are tasting an ice-cream cone. Residing behind the fact that you are *tasting* the ice-cream cone is the fundamental fact that you *are* tasting the ice-cream cone. The word *are* is a form of the verb *to be*. Thus Being is fundamental to experience and is primary.

Working forward from the crude concept of Being, Heidegger introduces the more complex concept of Being-in-the-world. This concept is captured in German with the single word *Dasein*. In English, *Dasein* must be rendered by the clumsy four-letter hyphenated form. Heidegger says that we not only have Being; we have *Dasein*. We are "thrown" here on this planet in a particular place and time; this is our human condition of Being-in-the-world. And we are challenged to make the best of it. It is as if each person is a Robinson Crusoe, cast away on an island. He must survive and make do with what he finds. Robinson Crusoe could have been thrown by the sea onto a better island. But he was not. Thus he has to work within the constraints of his actual condition. There is no point in asking a blind Fate, "Why didn't I land on a better island?"

Similarly, the individual must work within the constraints of his own particular Being-in-the-world. It is his responsibility to make the most of himself within the conditions of his life. For Heidegger, the human condition offers possibilities, but not unlimited possibilities. Possibilities are limited by one's particular *Dasein*, one's particular set of circumstances. The crucial point is this: If the person does not make the most of his possibilities within the framework of realistic constraints, he will eventually fall into existential despair, a state of great disappointment with himself. Essentially, Heidegger has returned us once again to the idea of authentic living.

The writings of Jean-Paul Sartre, a French existential philosopher, became influential after World War II. The destruction and waste of the great struggle among nations suggested to men such as Sartre that the other side of Being is *Nothingness*. Nothingness is capitalized, like Being, to suggest that it also represents a concrete reality. Without Nothingness to provide it with definition, there could be no Being. The individual is confronted, says Sartre, with a constant choice between Nothingness and Being. He can choose the road of nonexistence, plunging himself ever deeper into a meaningless dead-end existence. Or he can *consciously* choose to give value to his actions, to *decide* that his individual life has meaning—and thus nurture his Being. This was a stark choice for Sartre and other existential thinkers. They saw many of their friends commit suicide or select the slow suicide of alcoholism and/or purposeless living. Sartre and other existentialists could see no rational purpose to life. They believed in no Higher Purpose or value-giving God. Thus they faced a blank wall and thought that perhaps their suicidal friends were not particularly irrational.

The choice they faced is essentially the choice between life and death. Sartre decided to choose life, to affirm his existence. Why? The choice is based on Being against Nothingness. Sartre says that man has *Being-for-itself*, implying that the individual has a right to exist simply *because he* exists, not because he serves the purposes of others or of God. In other words, life has *intrinsic value*; it is an end in itself. Others have argued that life is not worth living unless it has *extrinsic value*, suggesting that one's existence must contribute to some larger dimension of meaning. Sartre opposes this view, asserting that a life is worth living even if it is only for itself.

Sartre says that individuals have freedom, that they are conscious, and that they can make real choices. We are very unlike things and animals. They have *Being-in-itself*, meaning that they cannot change their given characteristics. They are what they are, and they cannot create or mold themselves into new images. Man, on the other hand, having Being-for-itself, can create himself by his own hand. Man, unlike things and animals, has no given qualities. ". . . existence comes before essence," writes Sartre. This means that for a given person he *is* before he is *anything*. Because he is conscious and has the capacity for choice, the person can mold himself, even change his character. If we take Sartre seriously, he is saying, "Life isn't something that happens to you. The quality of your life and the very nature of your personality are your responsibility."

INFLUENCE ON PSYCHOLOGY

At this point it might be well to make a distinction between existential psychology and humanistic psychology. Until now we have been using the hyphenated form existential-humanistic psychology, and we will return to this form as the preferred one as we progress. But to understand why the form is hyphenated, why the two words *existential* and *humanistic* have been joined, it might be well to suggest the different connotations of the two words.

Existential psychology is a direct outgrowth of existential philosophy, inspired primarily by the writings of such men as Kierkegaard, Nietzsche, Heidegger, and Sartre. The aim of existential psychology is to help the individual move from a negative state of existence into at least a more or less neutral one.

Humanistic psychology, a current development in psychology, is a combined outgrowth of existential psychology and the traditional achievement orientation of the United States. Humanistic psychology stresses the positive side of life, personal growth, maximizing one's talents and potentialities. Existential psychology tends to stop at the neutral line; humanistic psychology boldly crosses it and stresses the significance of positive factors in human existence. Both psychologies, however, stress the importance of consciousness, the capacity for choice, the reality of responsibility. Both deal with the subjects of existence and the quality of human life.

Before American humanistic psychology bloomed, the seed of European existential psychology was transplanted to these shores. The existential orientation of psychology was introduced to the United States about twenty years ago with the publication, in 1958, of *Existence: A New Dimension in Psychiatry and Psychology*. Prior to that time, existential themes were virtually unknown in American psychology. The principal editor of *Existence* was Rollo May, and he has become a prominent existential psychologist in his own right. *Existence*, and books like it, made American psychologists aware of the thinking of two men in particular: Ludwig Binswanger and Medard Boss, both of whom can be properly thought of as pioneers of existential psychology.

Binswanger was a personal friend of Freud; but he gradually moved away from psychoanalysis and developed an approach of his own that is called *Daseinsanalysis*, or the analysis of Being-in-the-world. When working with a disturbed person, Binswanger does not give major emphasis to the past, to childhood experiences, and the like. He is more interested in helping the person understand his way of experiencing reality *now*. Thus the analysis is the analysis of *one's present existence*, not the analysis of the *psyche* or personality. An anecdote may help to clarify the similarities and differences between *Daseinsanalysis* and psychoanalysis. Binswanger gave a talk in 1936, commemorating Freud's eightieth birthday. In the talk, Binswanger noted that Freudian psychology overemphasized the view of man as an animal, that it tends to forget that there is an "upper story" to the human mind, a level concerned with religion and the arts. Freud wrote to Binswanger a warm and somewhat tongue-in-cheek reply in which he indicated that man has always known he possesses a spiritual side and that Freud's task was to reveal to man the importance of biological forces.

Like Binswanger, Boss is also concerned with man's Being-in-the-world. It is clear that both men were greatly influenced by Heidegger's philosophy. One of Boss's principal concerns is *guilt*. To the orthodox psychoanalyst, guilt is the result of violating an injunction of the superego. The superego is acquired via the socialization process, and it punishes us for acting upon or being tempted to act upon our animal urges. Boss feels this is a superficial view of guilt. He certainly agrees that such guilt exists, but he suggests that a more basic kind of guilt can be identified: existential guilt.

Existential guilt refers to the kind of guilt one experiences when one does not fulfill his possibilities in life. It is the feeling that one's life is being wasted. The guilt is very deep under such conditions. The standard that one should not waste one's life is not acquired from authority figures; it is not a part of a learned superego. Boss maintains that it is inborn, an indivisible portion of the fabric of human existence. Thus existential guilt is not neurotic, and it cannot be analyzed away. A person suffering from existential guilt can reduce it only by beginning to act upon his possibilities, by making the most of what he has to work with.

The American psychologist Rollo May has augmented and clarified existential themes for students of behavior and experience in this country. In *Existential Psychology*, May contrasts the existential approach with other approaches in the following manner:

The existentialist emphasis in psychology does not . . . deny the validity of conditioning, the formulation of drives, the study of discrete mechanisms, and so on. It only holds that we can never explain or understand any living human being on that basis. And the harm arises when the image of man is exclusively based on such methods. There seems to be the following "law" at work: the more accurately and comprehensively we can describe a given mechanism, the more we lose the existing person. The more absolutely and completely we formulate the forces or drives, the more we are talking about abstractions and not the living human being. For the living person . . . transcends the given mechanism and always experiences the "drive" or "force" in his unique way. The distinction is whether the "person has meaning in terms of the mechanism" or the "mechanism has meaning in terms of the person." The existential emphasis is firmly on the latter. (p. 14)

At the risk of oversimplifying, existential psychology says that a person has unconscious motives, drives, and habits, but they do not necessarily have him! Augmenting this point in one of his principal works, *Love and Will*, May makes a distinction of some value between the concepts *driven* and *driving*. The orthodox psychoanalyst sees man as a driven creature, controlled by unconscious forces. The existential psychologist sees man as potentially a driving creature, the agent of his own destiny. The lament of Rollo May is that so many people in today's world have lost their driving capacity and have fallen prey to the impersonal forces that make them into rather pathetic driven creatures.

This section has elaborated on the meaning of existential psychology. American humanistic psychology will be more completely described when we review the work of Abraham Maslow and Carl Rogers later in this chapter. However, as already noted, there is no essential distinction to be made between existential psychology and humanistic psychology. Existential psychology represents the dark side, and humanistic psychology represents the bright side, of the same general domain: human

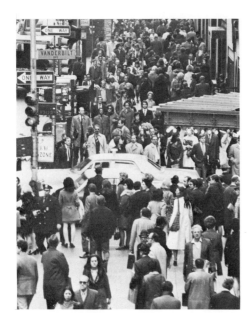

The lament of Rollo May is that many people have fallen prey to impersonal forces that make them into rather pathetic driven creatures.

existence. Indeed, no less an authority than May, in the preface to the second edition of *Existential Psychology*, notes that existential psychology is not a separate school in itself. He says, ". . . it is allied to the new 'Third Force' psychology, so that most initiates in the field speak of 'existential-humanistic' psychology, the two words hyphenated" (p. vi).

INDIVIDUAL PSYCHOLOGY: THE WILL TO POWER

It is becoming increasingly conventional to think of Abraham Maslow as the father of American humanistic psychology. His writings gained increasing popularity In the late 1950s and the 1960s, and he was clearly a leading voice of the Third Force. However, more than thirty years before the advent of Third Force psychology, Alfred Adler was expressing ideas that today we could classify in the existential-humanistic domain. Thus Adler was an important precursor of contemporary themes in psychology, and his contributions should not be overlooked.

WHO WAS ALFRED ADLER?

It is traditional to classify Alfred Adler as one of the founders of depth psychology. Usually he is associated with Freud and Jung. It is true that in his early professional years Adler worked together with Freud and Jung and was a member of Freud's weekly discussion groups. But within a few years, Adler broke with Freud and the psychoanalysts over questions of theory and established his own approach. That approach, called *individual psychology*, emphasizes the uniqueness of the individual and the individual's capacity to direct his own life. It does *not* emphasize the significance of unconscious mental processes; it refuses to see the person as a helpless victim of invisible forces. Thus Adler is not properly classified as a depth psychologist, and for this reason was not discussed in Chapter Two. He is included in this chapter on existential-humanistic psychology because the principal theme in Adler's writings is a stress on the importance of consciousness in human existence.

Adler was born in 1870, the second son of a successful merchant. He spent his childhood and most of his professional life in Vienna, Austria. In the 1930s he emigrated to the United States; he died in 1937 in Scotland while on a lecture tour. His initial medical specialty was ophthalmology. His observations while working with persons with eye defects contributed to the formulation of two of his important principles, those of inferiority and compensation. He noted that patients with a visual problem (e.g., difficulty in focusing without the aid of corrective lenses), or an organ inferiority, often put their eyes to better use than persons with no defects. For example, a patient might become an excellent reader and a scholar. This is the principle of compensation at work. He needs to prove to himself that he is competent as a person in spite of his physical defect. The range of Adler's observations in time went far beyond these beginnings. For example, he eventually came to observe that inferiority feelings could be based on *imagined* defects as well as real ones.

Adlerian psychology has been quite influential. There is an American Society of Adlerian Psychology, and it has branches in a number of major cities. There is also a journal, the *American Journal of Individual Psychology*, which disseminates the thought and research of Adlerians. In a book published five years before his death, *What Life Should Mean to You,* Adler offers the following description of individual psychology:

In Individual Psychology . . . we are considering the psyche itself, the unified mind; we are examining the meaning which individuals give to the world and to themselves, their goals, the direction of their strivings, and the approaches they make to the problems of life. (p. 48)

The quotation has a modern ring to it and quite clearly establishes that Adler's vision of the scope of psychology was similar to that proclaimed by contemporary existential-humanistic psychology.

THE WILL TO POWER

Initially, Adler was impressed by the writings of Nietzsche and his concept of the will to power. Adler argued that the will to power was the basic theme in human existence. He thus set himself against the Freudians, who were at the time proclaiming the importance of sexuality. Adler said that all of us have an inborn will to power. If the will to power is not frustrated, it is the driving force behind the development of autonomy and skills. The child "would rather do it himself." He grabs the spoon out of his mother's hand and tries to feed himself. This is the raw will to power at work. Unimpeded, it is a natural drive in the direction of competence. If the will to power is not distorted by arbitrary demands, it will play a positive role in normal development. The will to power resides behind what Adler called *superiority striving*, a striving to make the most of oneself. In normal persons, superiority striving leads to self-improvement. In neurotic persons, superiority striving leads to the wish to dominate others.

It is the frustration of the will to power that leads to the *inferiority complex,* which is a set of beliefs about oneself, all revolving about a central core. It is for this reason that Adler used the word *complex*. He wanted to indicate that there was more than one aspect to a negative self-image. If a person thinks of himself as stupid, he may also see himself as unable to learn mathematics, as uncreative, as unattractive to the opposite sex, and so forth. He will avoid situations in which he is required to display any intelligence at all. For example, he might keep putting off taking a driver's examination, convinced that he will fail. The core of the complex is the basic belief in his own stupidity. Revolving around the core like a set of moons are other negative beliefs, and these make up the elements of the complex.

How does the frustration of the will to power lead to the inferiority complex? Say that a preschool child expresses a wish to dress himself, comb his own hair, wash his own hands, and so forth. Most preschoolers will demonstrate a desire to learn how to perform these tasks, and this is a natural expression of the will to power. The child wants to take the initiative, become more responsible for himself. Adler believed that this is an inborn tendency in children. But say that a particular child has a mother who is a "perfectionist." After the child dresses himself, she comments, "You look sloppy. Here, let me tuck your shirt in. And let me pull up your pants." After the child washes his hands, she says, "You'll never learn how to wash your hands. They're still filthy. Here, hold them out while I go over them again with the washcloth." Instead of making the child responsible for his own appearance and requesting that he repeat unsatisfactorily performed behaviors, she arbitrarily takes over and reduces the child to a passive role. Under such conditions, if continued, the child will gradually form the idea "I'm incompetent," "I'm not coordinated," or some similar idea.

The core idea of a complex is just that, an *idea.* It does not necessarily reflect reality, but an abstraction *about* reality. The child may not in fact be incompetent or uncoordinated, but he imagines that he is. Thus the negative idea becomes part of the self-image. An imagined defect can be as devastating as a real defect. Note the similarity between the words *imagine* and *image*; they are derived from the same root. One's self-image is thus what one *imagines* to be true about oneself, not necessarily what *is* true. This, Adler felt, is one of the great tragedies of human existence. Great numbers of people without actual inferiorities have inferiority complexes. These complexes are in large part derived from the way one was perceived and treated by one's parents. Relationships with peers, particularly during the highly formative grammar school years, also have much to do with self-image formation, however.

The existence of an actual inferiority or of an inferiority complex does not necessarily imply the defeat of the individual. On the contrary, if the flame of the will to power has not been completely extinguished in a person, the principle of *compensation* will begin to operate. A person will strive to offset his real or imagined defects. It has already been mentioned how a person with an eye defect might go on to become an excellent reader and scholar. Many other examples of compensation can be given. Raymond is shorter than average; he takes up body-building. Sally is a somewhat plain girl, or thinks she is; she takes a course in beauty and self-improvement. Charles feels that he is bad in mathematics in college; he spends triple time on his math course and earns an A. All these individuals are compensating, struggling to overcome inferiority complexes of various kinds and degrees. Adler applauded their efforts. He said that one of the great things about human beings is their capacity to turn a minus into a plus.

GOALS AND STYLE OF LIFE

Ask a student, "Why are you going to college?" Say that he answers, "Because I want a B.A." Notice that he replies in terms of a goal, an event that resides in the future. This is typical of human beings. They explain their behavior in terms of goals, not the events of the past. Adler said that for human beings, a future event is perceived as causing the present action. From an objective point of view, this is inaccurate. The future cannot reach backward in time and cause things to happen in the present. But from a *subjective* point of view, the frame of reference from which life is actually lived, the future is real and has causative power. Adler felt that this was the way the behavior of the person had to be understood, in terms of his inner experience of the world.

Adler thus proposed a doctrine of *fictional finalism.* The word "finalism" is used to suggest that a future event is used to explain a present event. The word "fictional" is used because from an objective point of view, *the future is not real.* It may never come to be. The future is a soap bubble that may pop at any instant. A person could die at any hour, and one who feels rich with future might be suddenly bankrupt. It is intolerable to constantly think this way, and we thus construct a fictional future. Adler developed this idea from his reading of the German philosopher Hans Vaihinger's book *The Philosophy of As If.*

As we strive toward goals, we develop a style of life. The *style of life* is made up of the unique set of strategies the individual develops to cope with situations and attain his goals. As such, one's style of life develops early and is often fairly well set by the grammar school years. One of Adler's methods for ascertaining a person's style of life was to ask for the person's earliest memory. He says, in *What Life Should Mean to You:*

The first memory will show the individual's fundamental view of life; his first satisfactory crystallization of his attitude. It offers us an opportunity to see at one glance what he has taken as the starting point for his development. I would never investigate a personality without asking for the first memory. Sometimes people do not answer, or profess that they do not know which event came first; but this itself is revealing. (p. 75)

Adler tells of a woman who said that her first memory is that of her father buying two ponies when she was three years old, one for her and one for her older sister. The older sister, who was about six years old, led her pony triumphantly down the street. The woman recalls, "My own pony, hurrying after the other, went too fast for me and trailed me face downward in the dirt. It was an ignominious end to an experience which had been gloriously anticipated." Adler notes that the woman's life-style was characterized by the suspicion that she was always behind others. The theme of her existence was "I am always at the back, I must try to get ahead. I must surpass the others. If any one is ahead of me I am endangered. I must always be the first."

Adler believed that each of us has a style of life. Some people are overly aggressive. Like the woman in the example, they feel they must constantly strive to be first. Some people are passive. They feel they can attain their goals by being parasites, by "freeloading" off others. One person thinks he can best attain his goals in life by being a "good sport," by joining clubs and being sociable. Another person thinks he can best attain his goals in life by being a "lone wolf," by keeping to himself and maintaining cool human relations. There are many life-styles, and all of them can be understood in terms of the person's psychological goals.

SOCIAL INTEREST AND THE CREATIVE SELF

As Adler grew older, his thinking mellowed. His early writings emphasized the will to power and the principle of compensation. In his later years, he placed greater emphasis on two concepts: (1) social interest and (2) the creative self. The concept of *social interest* asserts that humans are basically gregarious, that there is an inborn drive in the direction of companionship. More than this, inborn social interest is the fundamental source of the desire to make a contribution to the welfare of mankind. Granted, there are persons who do not manifest social interest.These people, contended Adler, suffer from some form of psychopathology. Their personality development has been stunted and distorted. Normal persons care about their fellows and want to feel that their lives play some meaningful part in the larger story of humankind.

It is important to stress that Adler's concept of social interest is at variance with psychoanalytic and behavioristic theory. Psychoanalysis sees social interest as part of the superego; as such, it is a thin veneer over animal impulses. Behaviorism sees social interest as a result of conditioning; in various ways we are reinforced for being concerned about other people.

According to Adler, we have an inborn social interest.

Thus both psychoanalysis and behaviorism tend to define social interest as something that is *acquired*. Adler, on the other hand, sees social interest as *natural*, as a built-in part of the human personality.

With his concept of the creative self, Adler clearly entered the domain that we today call humanistic psychology. The concept of the *creative self* suggests that individuals are, to a large extent, the shapers of their own personality and their own destiny. Man not only reacts, he *acts*. The human vocabulary contains such words as *will, volition, spontaneity, self-determination, intention*, and *voluntary*. Adler would have said that these words exist for good reason. They describe realities of human experience and, as such, cannot be discredited by labeling them "unscientific" or "subjective." Of course, Adler was not the first person to say that voluntary action is a reality. We have already seen that Saint Thomas Aquinas, Jean-Paul Sartre, and others expressed similar views. Indeed, almost two thousand years ago the Greek philosopher Epictetus asserted that the mind is self-contained, and he is credited with having said, "No one can rob us of our free will." Thus Adler was in good company. He and a number of other thinkers were the forerunners of today's Third Force psychology.

THE SELF-ACTUALIZATION PROCESS: MAXIMIZING HUMAN POTENTIALITIES

On the opening page of Chapter One of this book appeared the following question: Are you making the most of your talents and potentialities as a human being? The challenge posed by this question was the prime concern of Abraham Maslow. He was intensely interested in the self-actualization process. He defined *self-actualization* as an inborn tendency to make the most of one's possibilities as a person.

Maslow had a substantial impact on psychology. As you already know, he is sometimes thought of as the father of American humanistic psychology. He was born in 1908 and died in 1970. For a number of years Maslow was the guiding light of the Third Force, articulating the importance of understanding human behavior in terms of awareness, choice, and responsibility as opposed to unconscious motivation and conditioned responses. The *Journal of Humanistic Psychology* was established in 1961, and there is also an Association of Humanistic Psychologists.

HUMAN MOTIVATION

In *New Pathways in Psychology*, Colin Wilson reports the story of a young woman who came to see Maslow with a personal problem. The time was

For a number of years, Abraham Maslow was the guiding light of Third Force psychology.

1938, during the depression. She had a job as an assistant personnel manager in a chewing-gum factory, and she was earning fifty dollars a week. During the depression this was considered quite a good income, and she was supporting the members of her unemployed family with it. The girl complained of insomnia, lack of appetite, disturbed menstruation, and sexual frigidity. She was extremely depressed, bored with life, and said that she was unable to enjoy anything.

In Maslow's discussions with the girl, it became evident that she felt her life was being wasted. She had been an outstanding psychology student in college. Maslow suggested to her that she was frustrated and angry because she was not being her own very intelligent self. He told her that her talents and capacities were motivations in their own right, that they represented needs. The proposal Maslow made was that she pursue graduate studies in the evening, working toward her higher purposes in life. The girl was able to follow Maslow's suggestions, and he reports that she became more alive, happier, and that most of her physical symptoms disappeared. This anecdote illustrates the concept of self-actualization in action. The girl was in the doldrums because she was not making the most of herself.

According to Maslow, there is a hierarchy of motives (see Figure 7.1).

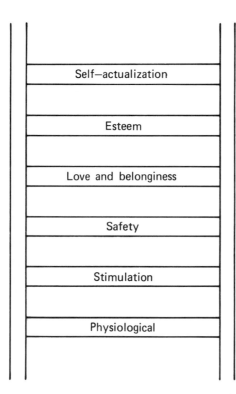

FIGURE 7.1 Maslow's hierarchy of motives is like a ladder.

Imagine a ladder with basic physiological needs on the bottom rung and the motive for self-actualization at the top of the ladder. Self-actualization does not become a pressing need until the "lower" needs are satisfied. The six rungs on our imaginary ladder are as follows:

1 *Basic physiological needs.* These include such needs as food, air, water, temperature, elimination, rest, and pain avoidance.

2 *Stimulation needs.* Stimulation needs include the need for activity in general, exploration and manipulation of the environment, and novelty-seeking behavior.

3 *Safety needs.* Human beings seek security from the hazards of their environments, as do all organisms. For example, it is natural to wear something warm or to look for a shelter when it is cold.

4 *Love and belongingness needs.* We want the affection of relatives and friends. Also, we usually wish to identify with one or several social groups, such as a family, a faculty, a fraternity, a sorority, a club, or a church.

5 *Esteem needs.* We tend to seek status and careers that have prestige. In addition, we are motivated in the direction of self-esteem, wanting a good opinion of ourselves.

6 *Self-actualization.* Maslow felt that this was the highest need on the scale.

Self-actualization has already been defined as an inborn tendency to make the most of one's possibilities as a person. Sometimes the metaphor of a seed is used to get across the idea of self-actualization as Maslow meant it. Say that the seed for a particular flower is planted in hard soil, receives insufficient water, and doesn't get enough sunshine. The plant that grows from the seed will be stunted, and inferior flowers will bloom. On the other hand, assume that the seed is planted in excellent soil, receives an adequate amount of water and sunshine. The plant will be lush and green, and beautiful flowers will bloom. An *optimal* environment has allowed the plant to *maximize* its potentialities. Similarly, if the lower needs of the person are not met, his personality development will be stunted. Like the plant seed, the seed of the personality needs adequate nurturance to free one to become the best self one can become.

The concept of self-actualization implies that each person has an essential inner nature. Maslow believed that the impulses arising from this inner nature are *instinctoid*, meaning similar to an instinct. He said that they were intrinsic, given, and natural. But he also believed that even though the inner core of the self is biologically based, or instinctoid, it is weak. He notes that it can all too easily be overcome or repressed. Learning, fear, cultural expectations, and disapproval may dampen or distort the self-actualizing tendency. Maslow comments, in *Toward a Psychology of Being:*

Authentic selfhood can be defined in part as being able to hear these impulse-voices within oneself, i.e., to know what one really wants or doesn't want, what one is fit for and what one is not fit for, etc. It appears that there are wide individual differences in the strength of these impulse-voices. (p. 179)

Maslow made a distinction between deficiency motivation and growth motivation. He sometimes spoke of deficiency-needs in contrast to being-needs. *Deficiency-needs* are represented by the basic needs for food, water, safety, belongingness, love, respect, and self-esteem. They are activated by deficits. Maslow compared them to empty holes in one's existence that must be filled for the sake of health. *Being-needs* emerge when the deficiency-needs are met; the being-needs are aspects of the basic need for self-actualization. To illustrate, a person may feel that he has an important mission in life. He chooses a certain career, works long hours, lives in a certain part of the world—all because of his feeling that he has a call to do a particular sort of thing with his life. This individual's sense of mission is a being-need, and it is part of his larger need for self-actualization.

It is also important to realize that self-actualization is a *process,* not an end state. Self-actualization represents growth and becoming. Thus it is proper to speak of self-actualizing persons, but not self-actualized persons. There is always room for more growth. As long as the person is living, as long as he has being, there is space for more becoming. The human personality is never a complete project. Only a fool would smugly announce, "Well, I'm self-actualized now. At last I'm perfect."

CHARACTERISTICS OF SELF-ACTUALIZING PERSONS

Maslow felt that psychologists over the years had paid a great deal of attention to defining and understanding psychological sickness, but that not enough attention had been paid to the concept of psychological health. Thus he studied healthy personalities in an effort to ascertain their core attributes. It should be stressed that Maslow believed that self-actualization was a positive force, a growth force, in human nature. Thus self-actualizing people are healthy. The concept of the healthy personality and the self-actualizing person are essentially synonymous in Maslow's writing.

Maslow published several lists of the characteristics of self-actualizing persons; the number of items on the list varied from ten to fifteen. As he himself willingly admitted, he was groping with the concept of self-actualization himself, seeking the best ways of articulating it. In *Toward a Psychology of Being*, he published a list of thirteen characteristics of psychologically healthy people:

1 Superior perception of reality.

2 Increased acceptance of self, of others and of nature.

3 Increased spontaneity.

4 Increase in problem-centering.

5 Increased detachment and desire for privacy.

6 Increased autonomy, and resistance to enculturation.

7 Greater freshness of appreciation, and richness of emotional reaction.

8 Higher frequency of peak experiences.

9 Increased identification with the human species.

10 Changed (the clinician would say, improved) interpersonal relations.

11 More democratic character structure.

12 Greatly increased creativeness.

13 Certain changes in the value system. (p. 23)

We could go over the list item by item, attempting to define and illustrate exactly what Maslow meant by each statement. He did not mean anything *exactly* by each statement, however. He was trying to present a global sketch, to suggest in a few bold strokes the outlines of the healthy personality. Although Maslow wrote extensively about the healthy personality, his writing consisted of expansive discourses, not limiting essays. Thus we will miss the whole concept of self-actualization if we try to look at the list through a microscope. We have to stand back from the list, receiving a general impression from it. The general impression we receive is that Maslow was describing a person who is *alive* in the fullest sense of the word.

There is only one technical term on the list that is unique to Maslow's thought: the reference to peak experiences (item 8). A *peak experience* takes place when a person has a wonderful moment in his life, a moment of ecstasy, rapture, or creativity. Such an experience is an emotional high point, and that is why the word *peak* is used. In addition, the moment is imbued with meaning. One is suddenly "hit" by a book or a painting. Or one suddenly realizes that he or she is really in love. A parent watching his child take his first steps may suddenly feel that life is indescribably mysterious. Sometimes people "cry for happiness." They are so carried away by joy, their experience is so moving, that they find themselves sobbing. Maslow believed that the peak experience is a growth experience. Because it is meaningful, it helps the individual to gain a broader perspective on life.

A peak experience takes place when a person has a wonderful moment, a moment of ecstasy, rapture, or creativity.

In brief, Maslow presented an optimistic view of the nature of human beings. He saw us as having an inborn self-actualizing tendency. Although the tendency can be repressed and distorted, there is hope. Many individuals become self-actualizing, and Maslow passionately wished that as society improves, as human understanding increases, more and more persons will become self-actualizing. He spoke enthusiastically of a *synergic society*, a society in which people cooperate for mutual advantage. He felt that our society is at best only average in terms of synergy. It was his hope that the future would bring a society with greater synergy, thus making it possible for more and more individuals to become self-actualizing personalities.

CLIENT-CENTERED COUNSELING: BECOMING A PERSON

One day I asked one of my psychology classes to answer this question: What does the phrase *becoming a person* mean to you? I asked for brief responses in writing, and the following are some of the answers:

Becoming a person, to me, means being aware of what is going on inside me, understanding myself, so I know what to do to improve myself. It means developing as fully as I possibly can.

Finding out about yourself, and being yourself, not what you think other people expect you to be. Showing one's true feelings.

Being able to make my own decisions. Having my own profession that I enjoy doing. I feel this question should be becoming your own individual.

To mature in every sense of the word. To know ourselves in order to understand somebody else.

I think the phrase becoming a person *means to know yourself, what your potentialities and goals are, and to try with all your strength—both physical and mental—to reach your aims. Becoming a person also means to stand on your own feet or to carry your load—sort of independent.*

On Becoming a Person is the title of a book by Carl Rogers, the principal exponent of client-centered counseling. Let us compare the student responses with the meaning Rogers attaches to the phrase "becoming a person." In the book, he tells about his work at the Counseling Center of the University of Chicago. He worked with people who presented a variety of problems. He speaks of the student who is failing in college, the housewife who is disturbed about her marriage, the individual who is on the edge of a psychotic reaction, the professional man who spins sexual fantasies that interfere with working efficiently, the bright student who is afraid he is inadequate, the parent upset by a child's behavior, and so forth. Rogers says he could go on and on citing specific cases of personal problems, but he indicates that there is a theme running through all the problems. He states that he has come to believe that there is perhaps only one problem:

As I follow the experience of many clients in the therapeutic relationship which we endeavor to create for them, it seems to me that each one is raising the same question. Below the level of the problem situation about which the individual is complaining—behind the trouble with studies, or wife, or employer, or with his own uncontrollable or bizarre behavior, or with his frightening feelings, lies one central search. It seems to me that at bottom each person is asking, "Who am I, really? How can I get in touch with this real self, underlying all my surface behavior? How can I become myself?" (p. 108)

Rogers goes on to point out that as the individual grows, he begins to drop the false fronts, or the masks, or the roles, with which he has faced life. Rogers says, "He appears to be trying to discover something more basic, something more truly himself" (p. 109). We thus see that the formal meaning attached by Rogers to the phrase "becoming a person" is similar to the intuitive meanings expressed informally by members of the psychology class. The central theme is expressed by such familiar and informal phrases as *finding yourself, being real*, and *growing up*. The very familiarity and informality of such phrases suggests that the task of becoming a person is one that all of us face.

Rogers was for a number of years a professor of psychology at the University of Chicago where he established the Counseling Center. He was president of the American Psychological Association from 1946 to 1947. Rogers was born in 1902 and is still active as a psychologist. He is currently associated with the Center for Studies of the Person at La Jolla, California.

PERSONALITY THEORY

Person to Person is a book authored by Rogers and writer Barry Stevens (a woman). The book opens with these remarks by Stevens:

In the beginning, I was one person, knowing nothing but my own experience.

Then I was told things, and I became two people: the little girl who said how terrible it was that the boys had a fire going in the lot next door where they were roasting apples (which was what the women said)—and the little girl who, when the boys were called by their mothers to go to the store, ran out and tended the fire and the apples because she loved doing it.

So then there were two of I.

One I always doing something that the other I disapproved of. Or other I said what I disapproved of. All this argument in me so much.

In the beginning was I, and I was good.

Then came in other I. Outside authority. This was confusing. And then other I became very confused because there were so many different outside authorities. (p. 1)

The quotation is useful in that it illustrates important concepts in Rogers's theory of personality. Rogers postulates the existence of two selves in many of us. These two selves are the self-concept and the ideal self. The *self-concept* may be defined as the way the person sees himself. It consists of the attributes he perceives himself as having. For example, a girl may feel that she is quite bright, not very creative, fairly popular, friendly, moderately religious, and so forth. These traits make up her self-concept. The self-concept can range from very negative to very positive. Thus on an informal level we speak of some people who have a "bad" self-concept and of others who have a "good" self-concept.

In contrast to the self-concept, there is the *ideal self*, the self one feels he would like to be or ought to be. It is the "higher" self, the self of one's dreams and aspirations. The ideal self presents goals and standards of behavior. If moderate, these have motivational value to the person. If impossibly high, they will play an important role in personality disturbances.

According to Rogers, the important thing for the person is not so much the external objective world; it is the internal subjective world. The term *phenomenal field* is used by Rogers to refer to the world *as the individual perceives it*. The concept of a phenomenal field is taken from the writings of existential philosophers. Recall that they placed greater importance on subjective evaluations than on objective data. *Phenomenology*, the study of the way the individual perceives and constructs his own version of reality, plays an important part in the tradition residing behind Rogers's formulations. It was Immanual Kant who made the distinction between a noumenon and a phenomenon. He said that a *noumenon* refers to a thing in itself, a part of the external reality. A *phenomenon* refers to the appearance of a thing in the mind, an aspect of human experience.

The self-concept and the ideal self reside in the domain of phenomena, the world of experience. The important thing about these two selves is *not* their questionable objective status; it is that they are *ideas* in the human mind. As such, they have a powerful influence on emotions and behavior. Although the self-concept and the ideal self are subjective, Rogers argues that they can be measured and evaluated. He uses a method devised by William Stephenson (1953) called the Q technique.

Imagine that you are a subject in a study of personality utilizing the Q technique. The researcher hands you a set of cards. On the cards are such self-reference statements as, "I tend to be shy," or "I like to socialize," or "I am very ambitious," and the like. You are instructed to sort the cards into categories, ranging from "Very unlike me" to "Moderately like me" to "Very much like me." An evaluation of your *Q*-sort is made, and this represents your self-concept.

Now you are given the same set of cards again, but this time with different instructions. You are instructed to sort the cards into similar categories on the basis of *how you would like to be.* The evaluation of this *Q*-sort represents your ideal self.

At this point the researcher can make a measurement of the magnitude of agreement between your self-concept and your ideal self. Rogers refers to this measurement with the word *congruence.* Rogers felt that congruence between the self-concept and the ideal self is identified with psychological health. If a person's idea of who he is bears a great similarity to what he wants to be, that person will be relatively self-accepting and at peace with himself. If, on the other hand, there is *incongruence*, a large gap between the self-concept and the ideal self, that person will manifest the kinds of reactions generally associated with psychological sickness.

An important concept in Rogers's formulations is the need for *self-regard,* the need to have a reasonably positive estimate of oneself. When there is substantial incongruence between the self-concept and the ideal self, self-regard will be low. Rogers thus formulates a motivational tendency in the direction of increasing self-regard. If this is so, why are there so many people with low self-regard? The answer is that many barriers may stand in the way of a positive motivational tendency. There may be emotional conflicts, odd ideas, residual inferiority feelings from childhood, the interference of family, the influence of society, and so forth.

In spite of the barriers, Rogers is an optimist about personal growth. Like Maslow, Rogers also speaks of a self-actualizing tendency, a disposition within the individual to "discover himself," to "become real," or, as already noted, "to become a person." In addition, Rogers is a practical optimist, and he is concerned with these questions: How may the barriers to personal growth be removed? What conditions foster self-actualizing tendencies? Let us now examine Rogers's way of answering these questions.

COUNSELING

We can gain an understanding of how Rogers believes personal growth is fostered by familiarizing ourselves with his approach to counseling. Rogers sees the counseling situation as a slice of life itself. The relationship between a client and his therapist is *not* a patient-doctor relationship in which the patient passively submits to something that is done *to* him by the healer. On the contrary, the relationship should be a person-to-person relationship in which the therapist talks *with* the client. It is for this reason that Rogers uses the word *client* instead of *patient.* He wants to indicate that the client is not sick in any organic sense, that psychological "sickness" is of a different nature than physical sickness.

The name that Rogers prefers for his approach to counseling is *client-centered counseling,* which indicates that the person himself is the subject of interest, not his symptoms and problems. An older name (no longer in vogue) for client-centered counseling was *nondirective counseling.* That name is still instructive because it reveals something about the Rogerian approach. Client-centered therapists do not give explicit advice to their clients about how to conduct their lives or how to solve a personal problem. The person is not directed to do this or that. Client-centered therapists refrain from trying to be all-seeing and all-knowing wizards. Instead, they adopt the position that in the final analysis the client and only the client is the expert about his life. After all, only he has all the information about his existence. Only he lives his life from the inside. The role of the therapist is to create a human relationship in which the client feels he can safely explore his inner world.

To create this atmosphere of psychological safety, Rogers recommends that the therapist provide the client with *unconditional positive regard;* that is, the person himself must not be judged by the therapist. If the client feels that his character is being evaluated, he will put on a false front or perhaps leave therapy altogether. A judgmental approach on the part of the therapist shuts off the capacity of the person to reveal his deeper concerns. You will recall that low self-regard is typical of persons who seek counseling. Rogers feels that this low self-regard is itself the result of the way the person was treated in the past. Parents, teachers, and other authority figures often act as if the child has no intrinsic value as a person unless he behaves as they say he ought to behave. Thus they do not give the child unconditional positive regard. On the contrary, their regard is *conditional.* "I will love you *if* you act the way I want you to act" is frequently the message that comes across to the child. A person who has had a long history of being acceptable to others only on their conditions will be the one who tends to manifest a substantial incongruence between his self-concept and his ideal self. The Rogerian therapist gives unconditional positive regard during the counseling sessions as a partial antidote for the person's earlier experiences.

Another important condition for successful counseling is *empathic under-*

standing. Rogers says that empathic understanding takes place when the therapist can sense the client's world as if it were his own. Rogers notes, however, that the *as if* quality must never be lost by the therapist. The therapist must sense the client's emotions without getting bound up in them. Empathic understanding is fostered by two processes, reflection and clarification. *Reflection* takes place when the therapist repeats fragments of what the client has said with little change, conveying to the client a nonjudgmental understanding of his statements. *Clarification* takes place when the therapist abstracts the core or the essence of a set of remarks by the client. Of course, reflection and clarification are not techniques that can be applied mechanically, or they will backfire. The therapist's interest in the client must be genuine, or none of Rogers's methods will work.

The following excerpt from one of Rogers's cases is instructive. The client is a Mrs. Oak, descibed by Rogers as a housewife in her late thirties who is having problems in her marriage and in her family relationships. The dialogue is taken from a portion of a taped interview from her thirteenth session with Rogers (*Becoming a Person*, p. 81). (Note: The client uses the word "thing" to make a general reference to the process of therapy.)

Client. Well, I made a very remarkable discovery. I know it's—(*laughs*) I found out that you actually *care* how this thing goes. (*Both laugh*) It gave me the feeling, it's sort of well—"maybe I'll let you get in the act," sort of thing. It's—again you see, on an examination sheet, I would have had the correct answer, I mean—but it suddenly dawned on me that in the—client-counselor kind of thing, you *actually care* what happens to this thing. And it was a revelation, a—not that. That doesn't describe it. It was a—well, the closest I can come to it is a kind of relaxation, a—not a letting down, but a— (*pause*) more of a straightening out without tension if that means anything. I don't know.

Therapist. Sounds as though it isn't as though this was a new idea, but it was a new *experience* of really *feeling* that I did care and if I get the rest of that, sort of a willingness on your part to let me care.

Client. Yes.

Several observations may be derived from the dialogue. In Rogerian therapy, the client does most of the talking; the therapist acts as a sounding board for the client's thoughts and feelings. The client is allowed to express ideas in a trial-and-error manner, searching for his own best way to arrive at a psychological position. The primary purpose of the therapist's remark was clarification; he briefly summarized the client's position. And he did it in a warm way that conveyed to the client empathic understanding.

PARENTS, CHILDREN, AND COMMUNICATION

Although Rogers does not have a formal theory of child development, his basic principles have inspired psychologists to apply them to the communication process between parent and child. Followers of Rogers indicate that the home should be neither child-centered nor parent-centered; it should be person-centered. The household should be run on a democratic basis, not on an authoritarian or a permissive basis. In the *authoritarian home*, the parent is a dictator, treating the children with little respect. In the *permissive home*, the child is the dictator, often treating the parents with little respect; the child has license to do almost anything he wants to do. In the *democratic home*, there is a feeling of mutual respect between the child and his parents. These ideas are not unique to Rogers and his followers, of course. The methods of client-centered counseling, however, suggest some quite explicit ways that a democratic atmosphere can be fostered.

These explicit ways are the basis of two bestselling books on child rearing, *Between Parent and Child* by Haim G. Ginott and *Parent Effectiveness Training* by Thomas Gordon, both psychologists. Ginott's book speaks of

Adults sometimes act as if a child has no intrinsic value. (Scene from the film "Oliver Twist.")

giving children a "voice and a choice" in matters that affect them. He places a great emphasis on *respect for a child's feelings*, stressing that parents do not have a right to invalidate a child's emotional world. Parents do have a right and a responsibility, however, to place practical limits on a child's behavior. Ginott's book is of greatest value for parents who are having difficulty communicating with school-age children.

Gordon's book is aimed at all age levels, but it seems to be of particular value for the parents of adolescents. An emphasis is placed on the principle of *active listening*. The argument is that many parents do not actually really hear their children. They hear the words; but they do not "hear" the emotional message behind the words. The parent is instructed to *decode,* to translate a child's surface message into its real meaning. Here is an example of active listening from Gordon's book.

Child. Daddy, when you were a boy what did you like in a girl? What made you really like a girl?

Parent. Sounds like you're wondering what you need to get boys to like you, is that right?

Child. Yeah. For some reason they don't seem to like me and I don't know why (p. 53)

If the father in the example had not decoded, he would have responded to the literal question. He might have answered, "What made me really like a girl was when she had a winning personality. And I have to admit I really went for blondes too—tall ones." Or he might have given any number of equally irrelevant answers, answers that did not touch on the concern behind the daughter's question. Gordon comments:

In active listening, then, the receiver tries to understand what it is the sender is feeling or what his message means. Then he puts his understanding into his own words (code) and feeds it back for the sender's verification. The receiver does not send a message of his own—such as an evaluation, opinion, advice, logic, analysis, or question. He feeds back only what he feels the sender's message meant—nothing more, nothing less. (p. 53)

We can see that Gordon's concept of active listening is a way of achieving the empathic understanding spoken of by Rogers.

To summarize the Rogerian approach to becoming a person, the approach asserts that there is an impulse within the individual to "become real" or to "find himself." He seeks to reduce any incongruency that may exist between his self-concept and his ideal self. This impulse is at root a self-actualizing tendency, similar to the one postulated by Maslow. If the self-actualizing tendency is allowed to blossom, the individual will develop self-regard, he will respect himself as a person. The conditions which tend to foster the undistorted growth of the person are unconditional positive regard and empathic understanding. These conditions are important in both the family atmosphere and in counseling settings.

THE SEARCH FOR MEANING: EXISTENCE AND VALUES

The European psychiatrist Viktor Frankl agrees with Maslow and Rogers that self-actualization is important. But he asks the hard questions, "Is there a 'higher' motive than self-actualization? Or does the human being exist for self-actualization? Is it the purpose of existence?" Frankl asserts that it is a mistake to regard self-actualization as the highest motive of man. He says that to do so is to confuse being with meaning. He writes (1967) that ". . . meaning must not coincide with being; meaning must be ahead of being. Meaning sets the pace for being. Existence falters unless it is lived in terms of transcendence toward something beyond itself" (p. 12). Thus Frankl believes there is a motive that is one step above self-actualization: the will to meaning.

Frankl is thought of as an existential psychiatrist, and he has taught and lectured extensively in the United States. A number of his ideas were formulated out of his experiences as a concentration-camp prisoner in Nazi Germany. *Man's Search for Meaning* is based on Frankl's experiences, and a cornerstone of his way of thinking is to resist all efforts to dehumanize persons.

THE WILL TO MEANING

A phrase sometimes used to describe our modern world is "changing times." Traditional values are up for grabs. For example, we hear people questioning orthodox models of marriage. Alternate life-styles, such as open marriage, contract cohabitation, and swinging are being examined seriously. Without cataloging the details, it is rather clear that today's society is not particularly tradition-oriented. There has been an increasing emphasis on thinking for oneself and living autonomously. This emphasis is not necessarily to be decried. For a substantial number of people, however, it has played an important role in an increasingly pervasive *nihilism*—the view that nothing, including existence, is of any value. Frankl's system of thought, logotherapy, sets itself against nihilism.

Logotherapy asserts that human beings, unlike animals, have an inborn will to meaning. The *will to meaning* is an impulse that motivates us to do things that make sense to us in terms of our place in the larger scheme of things. We seek to live not only for ourselves, but to contribute something of worth to other people and to the world we live in. Although it is evident that the individual's existence is to a certain degree an end in itself, it is more than that. It is also a means to an end, an agent of a bigger destiny than its own. For example, it is typical that responsible parents are as concerned with the welfare of their children as with their own welfare. Indeed, it is not at all uncommon for parents to be more concerned about their children than they are about themselves. Such parents see themselves as having a meaning to fulfill in life: making a success of raising their children.

If a person's will to meaning is frustrated, he finds himself in an *existential vacuum*, which may be described as the feeling that one's life is a void. In the song "What Kind of Fool Am I," the singer proclaims that he is an "empty shell." This phrase aptly captures the essence of the existential vacuum. The person who can see no purpose to life, who thinks that all values are absurd, is said to be suffering from *existential neurosis*. Frankl argues that an existential neurosis arises from a faulty worldview, a deadend way of looking at the process of living. The tenets of logotherapy are designed to point a way out of the deadend.

These are the three principal tenets of logotherapy:

1   Man has an inborn will to meaning.
2   Man has a free will.
3   Life has meaning.

You are already familiar with the first tenet, the assertion that man has an inborn will to meaning. Let us turn our attention to the second and third tenets. The view that man has a free will has a long tradition, reaching back to Saint Thomas Aquinas and beyond. But the view lost favor among psychologists during the rise of psychoanalysis and behaviorism. These orientations saw behavior in strictly cause-and-effect terms. Toughminded determinists make no allowance for free will. They say that this is tantamount to proclaiming that the will is an unmoved mover. In contrast, Frankl notes that the freedom of the will is a *firsthand experience*, and as such can hardly be denied. He comments, in *The Will to Meaning*, "Man's freedom is no freedom from conditions but rather freedom to take a stand on whatever conditions might confront him" (p. 16). Thus we must act within constraints. If Frankl is correct, however, we can make real choices and real decisions within the constraints of our particular life situation. It is his contention that the human quality of a human being must not be disregarded and neglected, that the "machine model" and the "rat model" (understanding the behavior of human beings in terms of the behavior of rats) of man are woefully inadequate.

The third tenet of logotherapy, that life has meaning, calls attention to the importance of values. Frankl says that values are real, that they actually exist. They are not merely created or invented to satisfy the will to meaning. He puts it this way in *The Doctor and the Soul:*

If I see a lit lamp, the fact that it is there is already given along with my perception of it, even if I close my eyes or turn my back to it. In the perception of an object as something real is already contained the implication that I recognize its reality independently of its perception by myself or anyone else. The same is true of the objects of value perception. As soon as I have comprehended a value, I have comprehended implicitly that this value exists in itself, independently therefore of whether or not I accept it. (p. 33)

If accepted, this view of values restores great dignity to human existence. Life is *not* "a tale full of sound and fury, told by an idiot, signifying nothing." On the contrary, life can be seen as a great adventure, filled with challenges, and imbued with high purpose. This is the view of life proposed by Frankl.

KINDS OF VALUES

Frankl says that there are three kinds of values:

1   Creative values
2   Experiential values
3   Attitudinal values

Creative values are those that are realized by productive action. The clearest example is provided by the person who feels that he has a calling or a mission in life. He perceives his actions as having objective importance. To illustrate, imagine a scientist who works long hours seeking a cure for a dreaded childhood disease. Assume that he is not the kind of person who questions the value of life. He loves children and hates to see them in pain. Providing them with relief from suffering is a real value to him. Such a person does not work long hours because it gives him any immediate pleasure or personal reward. His eyes are set on higher sights. He dreams of the day when his discoveries can reduce human misery. Such a person is in the process of realizing a creative value.

Of course, one does not have to have a profession or an exalted calling to realize creative values. Anyone doing an ordinary job who takes his work seriously, and who sees it as a worthwhile contribution to his fellows, is realizing a creative value. Some examples are the mother who serves nutritious meals, the auto mechanic who renders honest service, and the farmer who lovingly tends his fields.

Experiential values are those that are realized by being open to impres-

Experiential values are those that are realized by being open to impressions from the world.

sions from the world. Frankl gives as examples surrendering to the beauty of nature or of art. He says, in *The Doctor and the Soul:*

Imagine a music-lover sitting in the concert hall while the most noble measures of his favorite symphony resound in his ears. He feels that shiver of emotion which we experience in the presence of the purest beauty. Suppose now that at such a moment we should ask this person whether his life has meaning. He would have to reply that it had been worth while living if only to experience this ecstatic moment. (p. 35)

Attitudinal values are those that are realized by taking a courageous stance toward limiting conditions. A person may find himself facing an unpleasant destiny, a destiny that must be accepted. Examples are the person whose business is going bankrupt, the patient who knows he has a terminal illness, the prisoner in a concentration camp. Even in extreme situations, when it is not possible to realize either creative or experiential values, the realm of attitudinal values remains open. Frankl says that the measure of the person's human fulfillment is given by the dignity he displays in suffering. If he can retain his humanity under the harshest of conditions, his life will continue to have meaning.

To illustrate the importance of attitudinal values, Frankl tells of an old doctor who consulted him in Vienna. The old doctor had been depressed ever since the death of his wife. Frankl asked him what would have happened if he had died first and his wife would have had to survive without him. The old man replied that this would have been terrible, that his wife would have suffered very much. Frankl then said, "You see, Doctor, such a suffering has been spared her, and it is you who have spared her this suffering; but now you have to pay for it by surviving and mourning her." Frankl reports that the old man perceived his condition in a new way. He saw that his suffering was meaningful.

In brief, Frankl asserts that life has meaning, that the will to meaning is inborn, that we have the free will to realize values in various ways, and that the frustration of the will to meaning plunges the person into an existential vacuum. Thus, for Frankl, one of the built-in challenges of existence is the directive that we should take an affirmative stance toward life, not allowing ourselves to fall victim to those forces that would rob life of its intrinsic meaning.

RADICAL PSYCHOLOGY: OF MENTAL ILLNESS AND ALIENATION

Why are so many people finding it hard to lead meaningful lives in the modern world? Frankl would reply in terms of the breakdown of traditions and the failure of people to use free will and to realize values. *Radical psychology*, a counterculture movement within psychology, goes a step further than Frankl. It asserts that most existential suffering is caused by oppressive aspects of familiar social institutions. Its attacks are leveled against the family, marriage, the school, the church, and the Establishment in general. Many of radical psychology's criticisms are overstated, are too categorical, and have a hysterical quality. Nonetheless, a number of interesting points are made by radical psychology, and it quite definitely has something important to say about adjustment and growth.

IS MENTAL ILLNESS A MYTH?

Contemporary radical psychology owes a debt to the psychiatrist Thomas Szasz. His book *The Myth of Mental Illness* dropped like the proverbial bombshell, somewhat more than fifteen years ago, in the midst of orthodox psychologists and psychiatrists; it challenged many unexamined assumptions about "mental illness." In *The Myth of Mental Illness*, Szasz says that so-called mental illness is a metaphor used to describe people who do not "fit in" with established social patterns and who manifest various problems in living. Such people are labeled "sick," as if they have physical afflictions. It should be noted that Szasz is not talking about psychological disturbances due to organic causes. He is speaking of the *functional* disturbances, those that have no evident physical basis. People having such disturbances, insists Szasz, are not sick at all and should not be so labeled.

Szasz hastens to point out that although he maintains mental illness does not exist, he does not wish to suggest that the various behavior patterns to which the label is attached do not exist. They are real; people *do* have difficulties in coping with life. The question thus arises, Whose agent is the psychiatrist, psychologist, or mental health worker? Is he the agent of the sufferer, helping him to constructively work out his problems in living? Or is he the agent of relatives, the school, the military services, a business organization, or a court of law? Szasz answers that all too often the "therapist" is the agent of these other entities: He does not seek to adjust the person to himself, to those values that are of deepest importance to him. The therapist thus cannot really be a factor in the sufferer's personal growth.

One of Szasz's principal quarrels is with institutional psychiatry, as distinguished from contractual psychiatry. *Contractual psychiatry* is voluntary. The sufferer seeks help, feels distressed, and may find relief. When practiced with intelligence, contractual psychiatry is of value to the individual. *Institutional psychiatry* is involuntary. It is imposed on those who deviate from established norms of behavior. Szasz thus sees it as oppressive, unfair, and the enemy of the person. Institutional psychiatrists are not necessarily on the side of the person; they are more clearly on the side of the group. In a relatively recent book, *The Second Sin*, Szasz notes that ". . . much of what now passes as psychiatry is also force and fraud —the so-called psychiatric physician trying to coerce others by pretending to be a healer combating a pestilential epidemic" (p. 78).

ANTIPSYCHIATRY AND ALIENATION

The counterculture movement against institutional psychiatry has acquired the label *antipsychiatry.* The movement has gathered quite a bit of momentum in the past few years. Several collections of articles in book form have appeared: *Going Crazy, The Radical Therapist, Radical Psychology,* and *R. D. Laing and Anti-Psychiatry.* The unifying theme of these books is the thesis that established institutions and orthodox psychiatry often oppress and deceive the person. Of course, antipsychiatrists are not against psychiatry per se. Indeed, they are often practicing psychiatrists themselves, and therefore the label may be somewhat confusing. Antipsychiatrists are against many current psychiatric practices. They are *for* an existential-humanistic approach to patients' problems, an approach in which an effort is made to understand patients' worldviews.

A principal champion and poetic spokesman for antipsychiatry is the British psychiatrist Ronald D. Laing. His writings have a compelling quality, and he has served as a fountainhead of inspiration for the antipsychiatry movement. Laing is not a grand-scale social revolutionary. He is interested in producing what he terms *microrevolutions*, significant modifications in family patterns and institutional psychiatry. It is Laing's hope that the effect of these changes will spread and have a beneficial effect on society in general.

Laing indicts the family as the prime source behind psychological disturbances. He asserts that people are often driven into madness by a false benevolence and fake kindness exuded by well-meaning parents. In *The Politics of Experience*, he writes:

From the moment of birth, when the Stone Age baby confronts the twentieth-century mother, the baby is subjected to these forces of violence, called love, as its mother and father, and their parents and their parents before them, have been. These forces are mainly concerned with destroying most of its potentialities, and on the whole this enterprise is successful. By the time the new human being is fifteen or so, we are left with a being like ourselves, a half-crazed creature more or less adjusted to a mad world. This is normality in our present age. (p. 58)

In a book of free verse poems called *Knots*, Laing writes in the first person, attempting to capture the mood of the child experiencing a psychological tangle.

My mother loves me.
I feel good.
I feel good because she loves me.

I am good because I feel good.
I feel good because I am good.
My mother loves me because I am good.
My mother does not love me.
I feel bad.
I feel bad because she does not love me
I am bad because I feel bad
I feel bad because I am bad
I am bad because she does not love me
She does not love me because I am bad.* (p. 9)

If this mental maze makes little sense to you, that is precisely the point. It makes as little sense to the child in the family, and yet somehow he must cope with it.

Laing uses the phrase the *mystification of experience* to describe what happens to the child: He is spellbound, believing that his way of seeing the world is wrong and that he must adjust somehow to the world as others tell him it is. To a lesser extent, Laing argues that the school and other traditional institutions do violence to the growing child's experience of himself. The person who succeeds in coping with the double-bind messages of the family and society in general becomes *self-alienated*. This means that his personality is torn apart and that two selves form out of one. In *The Divided Self*, Laing argues that the "adjusted" person in our society must present a false outer self and repress his real inner self.

If the person cannot manage to become "well adjusted," his other option is to become alienated from others. The person begins to behave oddly, and he begins to deviate from established norms of behavior. If the deviations are too severe, he acquires labels such as *psychotic* or *schizophrenic.* Laing feels that these labels are just that, *labels.* They are brands that a society places on its psychological untouchables. Laing much prefers the older word *madness* to the clinical labels, thus suggesting the anger and frustration of the disturbed person in contrast to his presumed pathology.

Like Szasz, Laing does not see the "psychotic" patient as sick. He does not have a disease; instead, disease becomes *dis*-ease. The "crazy" person lacks ease in his way of being-in-the-world; he is not comfortable with his way of existing. He is seeking a way out and must make a "journey through madness" to find the exit.

To help the "psychotic" patient overcome his sense of alienation, the antipsychiatrist believes that the "patient" must be allowed to make his journey through madness. A clarifying analogy is the metamorphosis of a caterpillar into a butterfly. To become a butterfly, the caterpillar must be allowed to spin its cocoon and go through a profound inner change. Similarly, the antipsychiatrist asserts that the "psychotic" person must be allowed to draw into himself, perhaps regress to an infantile level of behavior, and rebuild his personality along different lines. The drugs, shock treatments, and psychosurgery used by institutional psychiatry only abort the self-healing process, making it impossible for the disturbed person to overcome his state of alienation.

Laing's theories are more than idle speculation. In 1965 he helped establish Kingsley Hall, a "therapeutic" community located in an old London settlement house. Laing lived with the "patients." Somewhat more than one hundred people lived in Kingsley Hall between 1965 and 1969. Although a large number of the residents of Kingsley Hall were originally from conventional mental hospitals, only a small percentage returned to a mental hospital when Kingsley Hall closed its doors. *Mary Barnes: Two Accounts of a Journey through Madness* by Mary Barnes and antipsychiatrist Joseph Berke provides a vivid account of how one resident of Kingsley Hall was allowed to be and become herself. There are currently some efforts to establish communities like Kingsley Hall in the United States.

In brief, the radical psychologist does not see the disturbed person as sick in any conventional sense. His "disease" is *dis*-ease, a lack of comfort with his way of being in the world. The source of his *dis*-ease is viewed as the influence of the family and other social institutions. Underlying his discomfort are two kinds of alienation: (1) self-alienation and (2) alienation from others. To overcome alienation and achieve psychological wholeness, the radical psychologist asserts that the sufferer must be allowed to change and grow in his own way.

THE GESTALT APPROACH: GETTING IT ALL TOGETHER

Like radical psychology, the gestalt approach identifies self-alienation as a common existential problem. Frederick S. Perls, the father of Gestalt therapy, often spoke of the fragmentation of the personality. He felt that inner splits were common, that most people living in Western society are "neurotic." Perls used the word *neurotic* in a general, nonclinical sense to indicate his contention that most people today are "dead" inside. So when Perls speaks of "the neurotic" in his writings, it is almost as if he is speaking of Everyperson.

In the foreword to *Man, the Manipulator* by psychologist Everett L. Shostrom, Perls writes:

Modern man is dead, a puppet. This corpse-like behavior is a part of every modern man. He is deliberate and without emotions—a marionette. He is reliable, but without live intentions, wishes, wants, and desires. He controls and manipulates others and is caught in the web of his own manipulations. (p. vii)

Unlike the radical psychologists, Perls was not particularly interested in tilting against social institutions, blaming them for the individual's state of self-alienation. Instead, Perls's principal concern was to devise constructive ways to help the individual return to being alive and being fully human.

Perls was sometimes described as a "bad boy" because he was an iconoclast, willing to impolitely poke holes in the theories of other thinkers and sometimes behaving in a rude fashion. No one can doubt that he was "fully alive." The title of his own autobiography, *In and Out the Garbage Pail*, reveals the ambivalence he had about his own behavior. His wife, Laura, once described him as a cross between a prophet and a bum, and Perls agreed with her description. Toward the latter part of his life, Perls was associated with the Esalen Growth Center in California. Although he worked in groups, his groups were not *encounter groups*, groups in which people communicate with each other. Perls did individual therapy in a group setting; the person in the group encountered himself. Perls acquired the affectionate nickname *Fritz*, and that is the title of an irreverent biography of Perls by psychiatrist Martin Shepard. Perls died in 1970 at the age of seventy-six.

PAPER PEOPLE AND WHOLENESS

In his last book, *The Gestalt Approach and Eye Witness to Therapy*, Perls writes, "The idea of Gestalt therapy is to change paper people to real people" (p. 118). Perls was fond of metaphor, and he used the phrase *paper people* to describe people who lack inner vitality, people for whom life is a lackluster affair with little zest, joy, or meaning. Unfortunately, as already noted, Perls was convinced that most individuals living in the modern world are paper people.

What can be done to help paper people? Perls's answer is: They must be restored to wholeness. Inner fragmentation between various aspects of the personality is what makes people go dead inside. A prime example of inner fragmentation is the split between the *top dog* and the *underdog,* two different aspects of the personality. Perls called these the two clowns of the personality because they play a self-torture game on the stage of human fantasy. The top dog is similar to Freud's concept of the superego and Berne's concept of the Parent. It tends to be righteous, authoritarian, and a bully, and it is fond of issuing phrases such as "You should," "You ought," and "If you don't, then . . ." The underdog bears a closer resemblance to Berne's concept of the Child than it does Freud's concept of the id. The underdog tends to play the crybaby. It tries to "win by losing," using such strategies as apology, defensiveness, cussing, whining, and the like. There is little peace for the person as long as he continues with a personality fragmented into top dog and underdog.

The way to end the war between top dog and underdog is not for one of them to become the victor. This will not happen. It is an illusion that one or the other can win. And for this reason, in the neurotic person the struggle between the two often goes on for a lifetime. The way out of the dilemma is for the two to make a truce, to make concessions to each other, to recognize that the demands of each are legitimate in their own way. Perls had clients role-play each part, speaking sometimes as top dog and sometimes as underdog. The two "clowns" thus entered into a dialogue with each other and tried to work out a truce.

We can now appreciate why Perls called his approach Gestalt therapy. The German word *Gestalt* can be roughly translated as "organized whole." The classical school of Gestalt psychology, associated with the names of Max Wertheimer, Wolfgang Köhler, and Kurt Koffka, studied human sensory processes in terms of organized wholes in perception. It asserted that our rich perceptual world cannot be explained by reducing Gestalten, organized wholes in experience, into parts-processes (e.g., individual color sensations or specific pitch sensations). To illustrate, a melody is the same melody played in different keys. Thus the melody is not explained in terms of its "parts," specific pitch sensations. It must be understood at a higher level of organization. In contrast to common sense, the Gestalt is *first* in perception and gives to the parts their qualities within the Gestalt. It is not the parts that give a particular quality to the Gestalt.

Gestalt therapy bears only slight resemblance to early Gestalt psychology. Basically, Perls borrowed the word *Gestalt* to suggest his idea that a paper person becomes real by integrating fragmented parts of his personality into organized and meaningful wholes. The early Gestaltists also spoke of the principle of *closure*, a tendency for a Gestalt to want to finish itself in perception. For example, a 340-degree arc tends to *not* be defined that way in perception. Instead, it is usually seen as a circle with a gap in it. The tendency to see the finished figure, the Gestalt, is quite strong. Perls worked forward from this principle and spoke of *unfinished business.* The neurotic person is constantly mulling over old problems that have never been satisfactorily resolved. For example, he may harbor resentments toward his parents, still bearing out-of-date grudges. He struggles toward closure, and this aspect of the struggle is a sign of psychological health. But he cannot achieve closure because of what Perls termed the *impasse.*

The impasse is a psychological block, a form of self-induced blindness that keeps the individual from seeing the true nature of his problem. It is one of the many ways a person may keep himself from "being real." He is being a phony with himself, kidding himself. The only way to deal with the problem is through *awareness.* According to Perls, the person needs to see how he is stuck. Once he sees how he is stuck, he can deal with the impasse.

Say that John is stuck in an unhappy marriage. This is the impasse. He pretends to himself, however, that the marriage is not unhappy. The pretense is supported by being in love with a fantasy, an idea of what the marriage and his wife should be like. This is the basis of the blaming game, in which his wife is told in various ways that she should be different,

An impasse in life may be supported by being in love with fantasy, an idea of what life should be like. (From the Walt Disney production of "Cinderella.")

that she should change. John complains and criticizes, but he never faces the bald fact: "I'm unhappy in my marriage." He tries to get around this fact. If John faces the stark reality of his unhappiness, he is in a position to do something about it. He may seek marriage counseling, divorce his wife, or do something else. But he will never take any action if he remains at the fantasy level.

According to Perls, the only way to deal with an impasse is to go through it. Paper people try to go around impasses, never facing them squarely. They are thus on an endless psychological merry-go-round. They are filled with unfinished business, incomplete Gestalten in the form of resentments, chronic complaints, and unresolved ambitions. Perls says that real people, people who are psychologically whole, face their problems and take constructive action.

GESTALT TECHNIQUES
Perls, in conjunction with a number of colleagues such as R. F. Hefferline, Paul Goodman, Abraham Levitsky, and Laura Perls, formulated a number of *Gestalt techniques.* These are techniques used to help individuals

integrate fragmented parts of themselves and to recognize the nature of impasses in their lives. A basic principle running through the Gestalt techniques is what Perls called the *principle of the now.* The client is instructed to stay in the "here and the now," to speak in the present tense as much as possible. For example, if a client is narrating the story of something that happened in the past, he might say, "My father slapped me, and I ran out of the house." Instead, he is asked to say, "My father slaps me, and I run out of the house." Thus he is encouraged to relive his memories, not merely relate them. The aim is to avoid what Perls called *aboutisms*, bland intellectualizations about one's existence.

There is quite a formidable list of Gestalt techniques, and it is beyond the scope of this book to list and discuss all of them. Let us content ourselves with discussing three techniques: (1) dialogue, (2) playing the projection, and (3) concentration.

Dialogue.   Dialogue is used to help an individual deal with splits in the personality. The most obvious split is the one between top dog and underdog. The person is encouraged by the Gestalt therapist to verbalize a dialogue between his top dog and his underdog. This helps him to comprehend clearly the demands of each and may make evident the ways a compromise can be reached.

Assume that a young mother named Marian is verbalizing the conflict between her top dog and her underdog. Marian's top dog says, "Marian, you've got to stop taking college classes and thinking about a career as an illustrator. Your husband and your children come first. Stay home and do your duty! Don't be selfish!" Her underdog replies, "But what about me? I have feelings too! I feel like I'm going to die and just wither up to nothing inside if all I'm going to do with my life is cook, clean, and take care of children!" After a series of such expressions, Marian may spontaneously express the following thought, a thought that reconciles opposites: "I see now that I don't have to make a choice between expressing myself and being a responsible mother. I've been trying to carry a full college load, and I've been feeling guilty about Tom and the kids—the way they've been eating, and the house has been a mess. So top dog is halfway right. But underdog is halfway right too. I'm just *not* going to sit home and be a drudge, the typical little wife. I'm going to carry a half-load and keep plugging away, developing my talent for drawing and painting."

The split between top dog and underdog is not the only possible split in the human personality. Other splits that might exist are those between the feminine self and the masculine self, the introverted self and the extroverted self, the aggressive self and the passive self, and so forth. Any of these divided selves can participate in the Gestalt technique of dialogue.

Playing the projection.   The technique called "playing the projection" is of particular value in helping a person to integrate the meaning of a dream. Perls believed that the elements of a dream which appear as non-self, as things or as other people in the dream, are in actuality projections, alienated parts of the self. As an example, Perls was working with a woman named Linda in one of his dreamwork seminars. Linda reported a rather long dream in which she watched a lake drying up. She said that she felt there should be a treasure at the bottom of the lake, but there was only an old license plate. The following exchange is from *Gestalt Therapy Verbatim:*

Fritz. Will you please play the license plate.

Linda. I am an old license plate, thrown in the bottom of a lake. I have no use because I'm no value—although I'm not rusted—I'm outdated, so I can't be used as a license plate . . . and I'm just thrown on the rubbish heap. That's what I did with a license plate, I threw it on a rubbish heap.

Fritz. Well, how do you feel about this?

Linda (quietly). I don't like it. I don't like being a license plate—useless.

Fritz. Could you talk about this. That was such a long dream until you come to find the license plate, I'm sure this must be of great importance.

Linda (sighs). Useless. Outdated . . . The use of a license plate is to allow— give a car permission to go . . . and I can't give anymore permission to do anything because I'm outdated . . . (p. 86)

Through the technique of playing the projection, Linda was able to discover what Perls referred to as the "existential message" of the dream, that at a profound level of her being she felt useless and outdated. Perls asked Linda to play the lake, and as Linda went deeper into the dream she discovered another existential message, the message that there was still hope in her life. The exchange between Perls and Linda ends as follows:

Fritz. . . . On the surface, you find something, some artifact—the license plate, the artificial you—but then when you go deeper, you find the apparent death of the lake is actually fertility . . .

Linda. And I don't need a license plate, or a permission, a license in order to . . .

Fritz (gently). Nature doesn't need a license plate to grow. You don't have to be useless, if you are organismically creative, which means if you are involved.

Linda. And I don't need permission to be creative . . . Thank you. (p. 87)

Concentration.   The Gestalt technique called "concentration" requires that the person focus on the here and now. One of Perls's clients, a man who stuttered, was asked by Perls what he felt in his throat when he stuttered. He replied that he felt like choking himself. Perls gave the man his arm, asking him to choke it. The man was thus able to concentrate on his anger, bringing it into the center of his awareness. As he got in touch with his anger, he began to speak loudly without a stutter. Perls comments (1969a), "I showed him he had an existential choice, to be an angry man or be a stutterer" (p. 80).

The concentration technique can be used to help overweight people. Many overweight persons eat rapidly, gobbling their food with little conscious awareness of what they are eating. The concentration technique requires that they slow down, taste their food, masticate it thoroughly, and swallow one mouthful before placing more food in the mouth. Some overweight people feel that they are spellbound by food. The concentration technique helps them "break the bubble." Eating with awareness helps them feel less spellbound.

BEING REAL

The phrase Perls used to describe authentic living was *being real*. Although he was responsible for developing a number of Gestalt techniques, he said that they were merely tools of somewhat limited value. The important thing to Perls was not technique; it was "not being a phony." He detested phoniness on any level, as he indicates by this short poem (1969a):

A thousand plastic flowers
Don't make a desert bloom
A thousand empty faces
Don't fill an empty room* (p. 2)

One of the important distinctions Perls made was between self-actualization and self-image actualization. Perls believed in self-actualization, in the importance of making real one's talents and potentialities. He felt that many people were on a "bum trip," however. They were not actualizing themselves; they were actualizing an *image*, something that had been "laid on them" by other people. The person who is trying to live out a life planned for him by parents or by other authority figures is not actualizing himself; he is actualizing his image of what they expect him to become. This is another way in which a person may fail to be real.

---

* *Gestalt Therapy Verbatim.* Copyright 1969 by Real People Press. Reprinted by permission of Real People Press, Lafayette, California.

Perls indicated that being real could be divided into two domains: (1) being real with yourself and (2) being real with others. He was against manipulative relationships in which one person attempts to con or use the other person. This is, of course, a familiar theme in existential-humanistic psychology and is not unique to Perls. Perhaps the best expression of the importance of being real with others is found in the theologian Martin Buber's phrase, the *I-thou relationship.* The I-thou relationship recognizes that the other individual is a real person, that he has feelings and a world view of his own. This is contrasted with the *I-it relationship*, a relationship in which the other individual is reduced to a thing or an object in the first person's environment. According to Perls, the fake person who chooses a manipulative life-style pays a heavy price for his use of other people. He forsakes the aliveness and spontaneity of a real relationship for the control and deadness of a deceptive one.

Perls is the author of the famous *Gestalt Prayer:*

I do my thing, and you do your thing.
I am not in this world to live up to your
expectations
And you are not in this world to live up to
mine.
You are you, and I am I.
And if by chance we find each other, it's
beautiful.
If not, it can't be helped. *

The *Gestalt Prayer* has received its share of criticism. Perls's wife Laura, herself a Gestalt therapist, is quoted in *Fritz* as saying that she finds herself "rather unhappy about it. Particularly the last sentence, for it abdicates all responsibility to work on anything" (p. 4). On the positive side, the *Gestalt Prayer* seems to say, between its lines, "Nobody owns anyone else in this world. No one has a right to manipulate anyone else. And some relationships are too far gone to save. Under such circumstances they should be realistically terminated."

In brief, the basic aim of Gestalt therapy is aptly summarized by the informal phrase "getting it all together." The Gestalt approach seeks first and foremost to integrate fragmented parts of the self into an organized and meaningful whole. Gestalt techniques can be of some value. But more importantly, wholeness requires a philosophy of life in which the person places a prime value on being real, on leading an authentic life.

---

* Copyright 1969 by Real People Press. Reprinted by permission of Real People Press, Lafayette, California.

CRITIQUE

Although existential-humanistic thought represents a rich vein of psychological ore, it is not pure gold. Indeed, psychologists who have a strong psychoanalytic or behavioristic orientation would argue that although existential-humanistic psychology glitters attractively, much of its content is fool's gold. As usual, extreme positions are seldom correct. The existential-humanistic point of view has much to recommend it. A number of reservations can be expressed, however.

1 The two principal approaches running contrary to existential-humanistic thought are the psychoanalytic and behavioristic schools of thought. So let us allow them their say first. The orthodox psychoanalyst would say of existential-humanistic psychology, "Its principal difficulty is that it attempts to completely discredit the significance of unconscious motives. It makes the conscious mind king. This is absurd in view of what we know about people from years of observation. We have all kinds of clues—slips of the tongue, everyday errors, and dreams—that suggest to us that there is an important unconscious level to life that cannot be discounted."

The radical behaviorist would say of existential-humanistic psychology, "It is completely unscientific, denying the importance of laboratory research and experimental work in psychology. In particular, it has little to say about the learning process, the single most important process underlying human behavior. Existential-humanistic psychologists seldom talk about conditioned responses and habits, and when they do they tend to brush them away as if they had no real significance in determining behavior. The convinced existential-humanistic psychologist reminds me of an ostrich. He thinks that because he sticks his head in the sand of his own ideas and refuses to look at the learning process, it will go away. What folly!"

2 Sometimes the existential-humanistic psychologist talks about the human will as if it were absolutely free. Reading Frankl, for example, one feels that he has not progressed much past the thinking of Aquinas in regard to the powers of the will. Even if the freedom of the will is granted, serious thinkers would be unwilling to say that there are not many constraints on its action.

3 There are contradictions within the existential-humanistic tradition. To illustrate, Sartre says that we create our own personalities, that an individual does not have an inborn essence. On the other hand, Maslow, speaking of self-actualization, suggests that each person has an inborn set of talents and potentialities which can be looked on as a "seed." This seed, if nurtured, will blossom into the real self. Thus Sartre says that we do not have an inborn essence, and Maslow says that we do. It is not our task here to attempt to resolve contradictions. But it is important to note that the threads of existential-humanistic thinking are of different colors and make up a variegated fabric.

4   Existential-humanistic psychology stresses the importance of the subjective point of view. We live our lives from the inside, and this internal frame of reference is asserted to be more valid than an external one. Traditional academic psychology disagrees. Humans are not only subjects, but they are the *objects* of their own study. The scholarly orientation in psychology has held for years that, to a large extent, human behavior can be studied as objectively as the motions of planets or the movements of atoms. Of course, neither the subjective point of view nor the objective point of view needs to be adopted as the one true point of view. The two views may be regarded as complementary, together forming a meaningful whole.

5   The existential-humanistic approach returns us to a philosophical-speculative kind of psychology. The rise of scientific psychology has been a long struggle against nebulous concepts. Existential-humanistic psychology is replete with such misty ideas as *Being*, the *will*, the *creative self, consciousness, self-actualization, authentic living*, and so forth. Although these are powerful ideas, they are also somewhat hazy. As such, they do not easily give rise to testable hypotheses. To a large extent, existential-humanistic psychology consists of a set of assertions not really amenable to scientific validation.

6   Radical psychology overstates its case. It presents too harsh an attack on such age-old institutions as marriage, the family, and the school. Certainly, there are problems with institutions. But one would almost think from reading the radical psychologists that minds are being destroyed haphazardly, that almost everyone is mad or self-alienated. These contentions seem doubtful to more cautious thinkers.

7   If leading an authentic life, or "being real," is made into an absolute value, it may lead to various sorts of practical problems in daily living. Such familiar notions as being polite, having good manners, and telling a white lie may be branded as unauthentic. Yet, many persons find it difficult to function without some sort of facade, some set of pretenses. Also, it is possible for some persons to use "being real" as an excuse for leveling insults at others. Such people fail to see that they are scapegoating aggressions and that the concept of authentic living has become a rationalization for their actions.

These comments do not exhaust the possible list of problems we might identify within the existential-humanistic approach. They do, however, point out the general direction that additional criticisms might take.

IMPLICATIONS FOR ADJUSTMENT AND GROWTH

Yes, existential-humanistic psychology has its defects. Nonetheless, it stands as a psychological giant, a growing giant, in spite of the scars of its own inconsistencies and inherent difficulties. It is possible to discover a host of positive implications for adjustment and growth within the domain of existential-humanistic psychology. The following are a few implications.

1 One of the principal values of existential-humanistic psychology is that it reminds us of our humanity. It thus imbues life with a depth and richness of quality that goes far beyond the limited range of early academic psychology.

2 The existential-humanistic approach teaches us to respect our own experience. Our anxiety, anger, or joy is not explained away by psychological jargon. Feelings are taken to be real, and there is an insistence on their validity. We are advised to respect our own feelings and the feelings of others.

3 The stress placed on the importance of the individual by existential-humanistic psychology is important. The person is not reduced to an element in a category. Instead, each person is seen as having a universe within himself, a universe of thought and feeling. The value of one life is seen as immeasurable.

4 If we accept the idea that we have at least a partial free will, this can have a salutary effect on our existence. With such acceptance, life is not perceived as something that merely happens to us. This view says that we are, to a certain extent, in the driver's seat and that we can shape our own destinies. We are seen, not as the passive victims of fate, but as the authors of our own future.

5 The Third Force in psychology gives us a set of positive images about the way life can be. It speaks of the self-actualizing person, the person who is leading a meaningful life, and the integrated person. These images have a pacesetting quality. They set a standard, suggesting that authentic living is important.

6 Although existential-humanistic psychology is grounded in the black mood of early existential philosophy, it has risen above its own origins. It points upward to a life beyond the gray zone of mundane existence. It says that life can be meaningful and joyful. Contemporary existential-humanistic psychology sounds an optimistic note about the possibilities of human existence.

7 Existential-humanistic psychology asserts that it is our responsibility to make the most of our possibilities. It challenges us to become the "best and the brightest'' that we may become. It says that we can consciously choose to live a life that is rich and rewarding.

The formulations of existential-humanistic psychology make up a rather large tent capable of covering a large conceptual territory. The region included is so wide that neither psychoanalytic nor behavioristic formulations are totally rejected. They are merely subsumed and included in a world view having a larger scope. Tough-minded psychologists will resent being smothered by the affectionate inclusion of the tender-minded existential-humanistic psychologists. But included they will be.

In brief, existential-humanistic psychology says that we are conscious beings, that we are capable of voluntary action, that we can shape our own destinies, and that we are capable of growing and becoming authentic persons. It asserts that we did not choose to be in this world, but we can choose to make the best of it. Some years ago the author William Henley ended his poem *Invictus* with these words: "I am the master of my fate; I am the captain of my soul." Henley's stirring lines portray the essential theme in existential-humanistic psychology: Individuals shape the quality of their own existence.

SUMMARY AND SELF-TEST

1 The principal assertion of existential-humanistic psychology is that consciousness counts, that it has enormous significance.
T   **F**

2 The existential-humanistic psychologist says that although we are conscious human beings, we never act voluntarily; we always react.
T   **F**

3 Existentialism places greater value on objective data than it does on subjective experience.
T   **F**

4 Kierkegaard asserted that a single person has importance in and of himself.
T   **F**

5 Kierkegaard believed that some relief from the dark emotions was possible by pursuing an authentic life.
T   **F**

6 Nietzsche's concept of the will to power asserts that there is an inborn tendency in all of us to gain ascendency over others.
T   **F**

7 For Heidegger, the human condition offers unlimited possibilities.
T   **F**

8 Sartre asserts that a life is worth living even if it is only for itself.
T   **F**

9 When working with a disturbed person, Binswanger gives major emphasis to the past and to the analysis of childhood experiences.
T   **F**

10 Existential guilt refers to the kind of guilt one experiences when one does not fulfill his possibilities in life.
T   **F**

11 May makes a distinction of some value between the concepts "driven" and "driving."
T   F

12 Adler completely rejected the writings of Nietzsche and his concept of the will to power.
T   F

13 Adler said than an inferiority complex is a set of negative beliefs about oneself, all revolving about a central core.
T   F

14 One's self-image is what is true about oneself.
T   F

15 The doctrine of fictional finalism suggests that from an objective point of view, the future is not real.
T   F

16 According to Adler, social interest is an acquired trait in human beings.
T   F

17 According to Maslow, self-actualization does not become a pressing need until the "lower" needs are satisfied.
T   F

18 Maslow said that the individual does not have an essential inner nature.
T   F

19 A peak experience takes place when a person has a wonderful moment in his life, a moment of ecstasy, rapture, or creativity.
T   F

20 Rogers points out that as an individual grows, he becomes more adept at using the false fronts and masks with which he faces life.
T   F

21 For Rogers, congruence between the self-concept and the ideal self is identified with psychological health.
T   F

22 Unconditional positive regard in a counseling setting means that the client should be judged by the therapist.
T   F

23 Active listening requires that one person decode another person's message, translating the surface message into its real meaning.

T   F

24 Logotherapy asserts that people, unlike animals, have an inborn will to meaning.

T   F

25 According to Frankl, experiential values are those that are realized by productive action.

T   F

26 Frankl asserts that we have the free will to realize values in various ways.

T   F

27 Szasz is against contractual psychiatry.

T   F

28 Szasz argues that persons who suffer from functional psychological disturbances are sick and should be so labeled.

T   F

29 Laing indicts the family as the prime source behind psychological disturbances.

T   F

30 According to Laing, the person who succeeds in coping with the double-bind messages of the family and society in general becomes self-alienated.

T   F

31 The antipsychiatrist believes that the "patient" must be allowed to make his journey through madness.

T   F

32 Perls said that the idea of Gestalt therapy is to change paper people into real people.

T   F

33 The top dog as formulated by Perls is similar to Freud's concept of the id and Berne's concept of the Child.

T   F

34 According to Perls, the impasse is a psychological block, a form of self-induced blindness that keeps the individual from seeing the true nature of his problem.

T   F

35   In the Gestalt technique known as "playing the projection," a client role-plays alienated parts of the self.

T   F

ANSWER KEY

1   *True.* The principal assertion of existential-humanistic psychology is that consciousness counts, that it has enormous significance.

2   *False.* The existential-humanistic psychologist says that we are conscious human beings and that we act voluntarily as well as react.

3   *False.* Existentialism places greater value on subjective experience than it does on objective data.

4   *True.* Kierkegaard asserted that a single person has importance in and of himself.

5   *True.* Kierkegaard believed that some relief from the dark emotions was possible by pursuing an authentic life.

6   *True.* Nietzsche's concept of the will to power asserts that there is an inborn tendency in all of us to gain ascendency over others.

7   *False.* For Heidegger, the human condition offers possibilities, but not unlimited possibilities.

8   *True.* Sartre asserts that a life is worth living even if it is only for itself.

9   *False.* When working with a disturbed person, Binswanger does not give major emphasis to the past, to childhood experiences, and the like.

10   *True.* Existential guilt refers to the kind of guilt one experiences when one does not fulfill his possibilities in life.

11   *True.* May makes a distinction of some value between the concepts "driven" and "driving."

12   *False.* Adler was impressed by the writings of Nietzsche and his concept of the will to power.

13   *True.* Adler said that an inferiority complex is a set of negative beliefs about oneself, all revolving about a central core.

14   *False.* One's self-image is what one imagines to be true about oneself, not necessarily what is true.

15   *True.* The doctrine of fictional finalism suggests that from an objective point of view, the future is not real.

16   *False.* According to Adler, social interest is an inborn trait in human beings.

17   *True.* According to Maslow, self-actualization does not become a pressing need until the "lower" needs are satisfied.

18   *False.* Maslow said that the individual has an essential inner nature.

19   *True.* A peak experience takes place when a person has a wonderful moment in his life, a moment of ecstasy, rapture, or creativity.

20   *False.* Rogers points out that as the individual grows, he begins to drop the false fronts, or the masks, or the roles with which he has faced life.

21   *True.* For Rogers, congruence between the self-concept and the ideal self is identified with psychological health.

22   *False.* Unconditional positive regard in a counseling setting means that the client must not be judged by the therapist.

23   *True.* Active listening requires that one person decode another person's message, translating the surface message into its real meaning.

24   *True.* Logotherapy asserts that people, unlike animals, have an inborn will to meaning.

25   *False.* According to Frankl, experiential values are those that are realized by being open to impressions from the world.

26   *True.* Frankl asserts that we have the free will to realize values in various ways.

27   *False.* Szasz has little quarrel with contractual psychiatry; he does have harsh criticisms of institutional psychiatry.

28   *False.* Szasz argues that persons suffering from functional disturbances are not sick at all and should not be so labeled.

29   *True.* Laing indicts the family as the prime source behind psychological disturbances.

30   *True.* According to Laing, the person who succeeds in coping with the double-bind messages of the family and society in general becomes self-alienated.

31   *True.* The antipsychiatrist believes that the "patient" must be allowed to make his journey through madness.

32   *True.* Perls said that the idea of Gestalt therapy is to change paper people into real people.

33   *False.* The top dog as formulated by Perls is similar to Freud's concept of the superego and Berne's concept of the Parent.

34   *True.* According to Perls, the impasse is a psychological block, a form of self-induced blindness that keeps the individual from seeing the true nature of his problem.

35   *True.* In the Gestalt technique known as "playing the projection," a client role-plays alienated parts of the self.

DISCUSSION QUESTIONS

EXISTENTIALISM: CREATING YOURSELF

1 Kierkegaard asserted that the single person is important, that he has importance in and of himself, that his unique characteristics should be valued. What kind of response does this assertion call forth from you?

2 The existential approach defines authentic living as pursuing a life in which one is true to oneself as an individual, not pledging false allegiance to the values and standards arbitrarily imposed by other people or one's culture. To what extent do you feel you are capable of authentic living in these terms?

3 Do you agree that if persons do not make the most of their possibilities within the framework of realistic constraints that they will eventually fall into existential despair?

INDIVIDUAL PSYCHOLOGY: THE WILL TO POWER

1 Looking within yourself, do you see the will to power at work? In what ways do you strive to make the most of yourself? Are there ways you attempt to dominate others?

2 Do you know someone who seems to you to suffer from an inferiority complex? If so, what seems to be the core of the complex? What are some of the associated beliefs that revolve around the core?

3 What are your principal goals in life?

4 How would you describe your life-style? Does the description give any insight into your own personality?

THE SELF-ACTUALIZATION PROCESS: MAXIMIZING HUMAN POTENTIALITIES

1 Do you think that there actually is an inborn self-actualizing tendency, a tendency to make the most of one's possibilities as a person?

2 In your own life, what needs on Maslow's hierarchy of needs are being or not being met?

3 Can you relate to the concept of a peak experience? If so, can you give an example of a peak experience in your own life?

CLIENT-CENTERED COUNSELING: BECOMING A PERSON

1   How would you answer this question: What does the phrase "becoming a person" mean to you?

2   Do you feel that your self-concept and your ideal self are close together or far apart?

3   Do you feel that members of your family and/or close friends give you unconditional positive regard? Are you able to give unconditional positive regard to them?

4   Do you feel that you have much skill at active listening? Are you able to decode messages from other people?

THE SEARCH FOR MEANING: EXISTENCE AND VALUES

1   Frankl says that the will to meaning is one step above self-actualization. Do you agree?

2   Do you feel that changing times and the loss of many traditional values have played an important role in an increasingly pervasive nihilism, the view that nothing, including existence, is of any value? If so, can you think of specific persons who seem to manifest this negative philosophy?

3   Do you know anyone who seems to have fallen into what Frankl terms the "existential vacuum"?

4   In your opinion, what is the highest value in life?

5   Do you agree with Frankl that human beings have the free will to realize values?

RADICAL PSYCHOLOGY: OF MENTAL ILLNESS AND ALIENATION

1   Do you share Szasz's hostility toward institutional psychiatry? Have you or your loved ones had any direct experiences with institutional psychiatry? If so, were they positive or negative?

2   What are the pros and cons of antipsychiatry?

3   Do you know someone who seems to be self-alienated in Laing's terms?

4   To help the "psychotic" patient overcome his sense of alienation, the antipsychiatrist believes that the "patient" must be allowed to make his journey through madness. How do you react to this point of view?

THE GESTALT APPROACH: GETTING IT ALL TOGETHER

1   Perls felt that most people living in Western society are "neurotic." He used the word *neurotic* in a general, nonclinical sense to indicate his contention that most people today are "dead" inside. What are your reactions to Perls's point of view?

2 Are you aware of a top-dog personality and an underdog personality within yourself?

3 Perls felt that the only way to deal with an impasse is by going through it. Do you agree? Can you think of any other way to deal with an impasse?

4 How does self-actualization differ from self-image actualization? Why is the distinction important?

REFERENCES

Adler, A. *Practice and Theory of Individual Psychology.* New York: Harcourt, Brace & World, 1927.

―――. *What Life Should Mean to You.* London: George Allen & Unwin, 1932.

Agel, J., ed. *The Radical Therapist.* New York: Ballantine Books, 1971.

Barnes, M., and Berke, J. *Mary Barnes: Two Accounts of a Journey through Madness.* New York: Harcourt Brace Jovanovich, 1971.

Barrett, W. *Irrational Man: A Study in Existential Philosophy.* New York: Doubleday Anchor Books, 1962.

Binswanger, L. *Being-in-the-World.* New York: Harper & Row, 1963.

Boss, M. *Psychoanalysis and Daseinsanalysis.* New York: Basic Books, 1963.

Boyers, R., and Orrill, R., eds. *R. D. Laing and Anti-Psychiatry.* New York: Harper & Row, 1971.

Brown, P., ed. *Radical Psychology.* New York: Harper & Row, 1973.

Fagan, J., and Shepherd, I. L., eds. *Gestalt Therapy Now.* New York: Harper & Row, 1970.

Frankl, V. E. *Man's Search for Meaning.* Boston: Beacon Press, 1962.

―――. *Psychotherapy and Existentialism.* New York: Washington Square Press, 1967.

―――. *The Doctor and the Soul.* New York: Alfred A. Knopf, 1955.

―――. *The Will to Meaning.* New York: The New American Library, 1969.

Ginott, H. G. *Between Parent and Child.* New York: Avon Books, 1965.

Goble, F. *The Third Force.* New York: Pocket Books, 1971.

Gordon, T. *Parent Effectiveness Training.* New York: Peter H. Wyden, 1970.

Heidegger, M. *Being and Time.* New York: Harper & Row, 1962.

Kierkegaard, S. *Fear and Trembling and Sickness unto Death.* New York: Doubleday, 1954.

―――. *Kierkegaard Anthology.* New York: Modern Library, 1959.

Laing, R. D. *Knots.* New York: Random House, 1970.

———. *The Divided Self.* London: Penguin Books, 1965.

———. *The Politics of Experience.* London: Penguin Books, 1967.

Maslow, A. H. *Toward a Psychology of Being.* Princeton, N.J.: D. Van Nostrand, Co., 1962.

———. *Motivation and Personality.* New York: Harper & Row, 1954.

May, R. *Love and Will.* New York: Dell Publishing, 1969.

———, ed., *Existential Psychology.* New York: Random House, 1960.

———, Angel, E., and Ellenberger, H. F., eds. *Existence: A New Dimension in Psychiatry and Psychology.* New York: Basic Books, 1958.

Nietzsche, F. *The Portable Nietzsche.* New York: Viking Press, 1954.

Perls, F. S. *Gestalt Therapy Verbatim.* Lafayette, Calif.: Real People Press, 1969a.

———. *In and Out the Garbage Pail.* Lafayette, Calif.: Real People Press, 1969b.

———. *The Gestalt Approach and Eye Witness to Therapy.* Palo Alto, Calif.: Science & Behavior Books, 1973.

Rogers, C. *On Becoming a Person.* Boston: Houghton Mifflin Co., 1961.

———, and Stevens, B. *Person to Person.* New York: Pocket Books, 1971.

Ruitenbeek, H. M., ed. *Going Crazy.* New York: Bantam Books, 1972.

Sartre, J. P. *Being and Nothingness.* New York: Philosophical Library, 1956.

———. "Existentialism Is a Humanism." In *Existentialism from Dostoevsky to Sartre,* W. Kaufman, ed. New York: The World Publishing Co., 1956.

Shepard, M. *Fritz.* New York: E. P. Dutton, 1975.

Shostrom, E. L. *Man, the Manipulator.* New York: Bantam Books, 1968.

Stephenson, W. *The Study of Behavior.* Chicago: University of Chicago Press, 1953.

Szasz, T. S. *The Myth of Mental Illness.* New York: Harper & Row, 1974.

———. *The Second Sin.* New York: Doubleday, 1974.

Vaihinger, H. *The Philosophy of As If.* Trans. by C. K. Ogden. New York: Harcourt, Brace, 1925.

Wilson, C. *New Pathways in Psychology: Maslow and the Post-Freudian Revolution.* New York: New American Library, 1972.

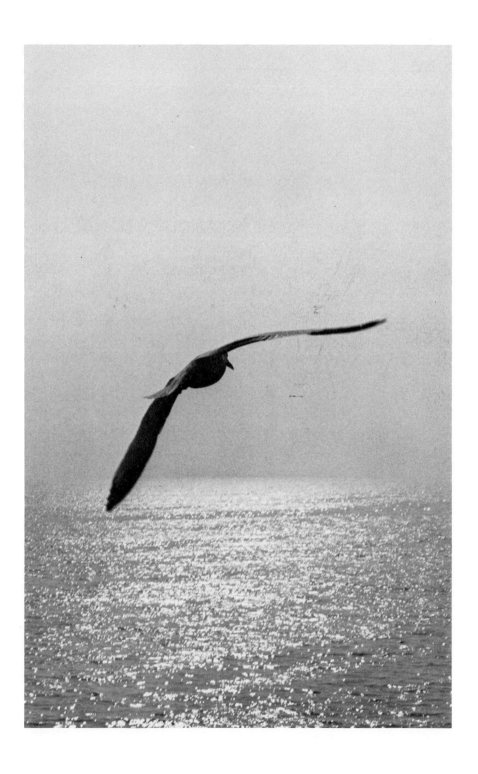

CHAPTER 8
TRANSPERSONAL PSYCHOLOGY: OF BLISS AND COSMIC AWARENESS

The insights and techniques represented within the body of transpersonal psychology are often called "ways of liberation."

OVERVIEW

OUTLINE

TWO KEY QUESTIONS

What is transpersonal psychology?

Transpersonal psychology represents a blend of Eastern philosophy, esoteric knowledge, and Western psychology. It draws heavily from such traditions as Yoga and Zen. We may thus characterize transpersonal psychology as "mental science" in contrast to tough-minded behavioral science. The approach is sometimes described as intuitive in comparison to rational.

How do the principles of transpersonal psychology relate to adjustment growth?

The insights and techniques represented within the body of transpersonal psychology are often called "ways of liberation." The individual is shown that much of his suffering as a human being is needless. Escapes from the chains of anxiety, tension, depression, anger, and petty ambition are revealed. Advocates of transpersonal psychology hold out the promise of finding serenity, bliss, and ecstasy. Opponents of transpersonal psychology reject it with such phrases as "hazy mysticism" and "cloudy occultism."

Transpersonal psychology is being called a Fourth Force in psychology because it is bringing a new look to orthodox psychological thinking. Interest in transpersonal psychology is anything but new, however. For example, *Lost Horizon* by novelist James Hilton was published in 1933, more than forty years ago. The book is still in print and is now in its seventy-ninth printing! And two motion pictures have been made from the novel. *Lost Horizon* tells the story of Hugh Conway and his involuntary journey to the valley of Shangri-La, an enchanted place, hidden deep in the Himalaya mountains of Tibet. The residents of Shangri-La age very slowly and live for centuries. The High Lama of Shangri-La is described as spending most of his time in clairvoyant meditation, seeing into the future of the world. He also has powers of telepathy. The task the High Lama sets for Shangri-La is the preservation of things of beauty and important knowledge against the destruction of a future great war. *Lost Horizon*, although a novel, is rich in Eastern philosophy. Perhaps this accounts for its perennial popularity.

The forty-odd years of popularity enjoyed by *Lost Horizon* are small though when contrasted with the span of the centuries. The history of Yoga, for example, can be traced to the *Upanishads*, sacred Hindu texts,

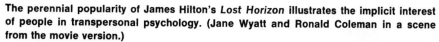

The perennial popularity of James Hilton's *Lost Horizon* illustrates the implicit interest of people in transpersonal psychology. (Jane Wyatt and Ronald Coleman in a scene from the movie version.)

dated about 400 B.C. But what of the Western world? Is not the mystical way of thinking relatively new to its residents? The answer is no. One of the founders of Western philosophy, Plato, was a mystic. Writing also around 400 B.C., Plato said that the mind has an intuitive power. It can grasp reality directly without the aid of the sense organs. But it must be admitted that this aspect of Plato's thought was not augmented by the philosophers who followed him.

The mystical tradition in the Western world was kept alive for centuries not by philosophers, but by devout religious practitioners. There is, for example, a definite tradition of Christian mysticism. A few of the names that are usually cited in connection with this tradition are Dionysius the Areopagite, Meister Eckhart, Jan van Ruysbroeck, Saint Teresa of Avila, and Saint John of the Cross.

A *mystic* is a person who believes that through the use of intuition he can have a direct experience with Ultimate Reality. Sometimes this Ultimate Reality is called God. Others refer to it as the All, the One, the Eternal, the Supernatural, the Transcendental World, and so forth. There is a distinct similarity in the reports of mystics when they come "back to Earth." They consistently report the mystical union with Ultimate Reality to be a blissful and ecstatic experience. It is said that they more than intellectually realize, they actually *know*, that the distinction between one's self and the rest of the universe is an arbitrary construction of time-bound mortals.

Coming closer to the present, the American essayist-poet-philosopher Ralph Waldo Emerson can be cited as a forerunner of transpersonal psychology. Writing in New England about one hundred years ago, Emerson's philosophy came to be known as "transcendentalism." He preached the doctrine of *pantheism*, a belief system which asserts that there is no distinction between the universe and God. Pantheism says that God is not a being, but Being itself. It should be noted that this view is essentially the same one that underlies the Yoga and Zen traditions.

The first major figure in modern psychology to recommend a transpersonal approach in psychology was Carl Jung. As you already know, Jung was one of the giants of twentieth-century psychological thinking and a principal founder of depth psychology. As noted in Chapter Two, Jung was a scientist; but he was also a mystic. Jung had a great respect for Eastern philosophy. In *Autobiography of a Yogi* by Paramahansa Yogananda, Jung is quoted as follows:

Quite apart from the charm of the new and the fascination of the half-understood, there is good cause for Yoga to have many adherents. It offers the possibility of controllable experience and thus satisfies the scientific need for "facts"; and, besides this, by reason of its breadth and depth, its venerable age, its doctrine and method, which include every phase of life, it promises undreamed-of possibilities. (p. 264)

In spite of Jung's enthusiasm for Yoga and other Eastern disciplines, Western psychology remained hostile to Oriental ways of thought. Indeed, Freud spoke with disdain of the "black mud of occultism." In spite of the hostility of tough-minded psychologists, transpersonal psychology has made slow but steady inroads into academic psychology. Quasi-respectability was achieved when Abraham Maslow founded, with Anthony Sutich, the *Journal of Transpersonal Psychology*. This event occurred just one year before Maslow's death and suggests that he was moving into a broader domain of thought than the one represented by existential-humanistic psychology. The *Journal* identifies some of its concerns as *metaneeds, ultimate values, unitive consciousness, ecstasy, mystical experience, bliss, transcendence of the self, oneness, cosmic awareness,* and related concepts.

If existential-humanistic psychology may be identified as a Third Force in psychology, let us again note that transpersonal psychology is a Fourth Force. Transpersonal psychology, hailed as the newest star on the psychological horizon, is in actuality the reappearance of one of the oldest stellar bodies in the philosophical firmament: the star of mental science. Let us begin our exploration into transpersonal psychology by familiarizing ourselves with one of its basic themes, the doctrine that we live in a world of appearances.

PERCEPTION: THE SPELL OF *MAYA*

A *Star Trek* episode called "The Menagerie" tells the story of a crippled starship captain who chooses to return to an unusual alien planet. The inhabitants of the planet are master hypnotists, capable of creating illusions so strong they are taken for reality. He decides to live out the rest of his life on the planet, being restored in his mind to physical health. He prefers the illusion to the reality. On a deeper level, the episode asks the philosophical question: What is reality? If an illusion is so strong that it shuts out all other experience, does it become reality?

THE DOCTRINE OF MAYA

Eastern philosophy maintains that all of us, like the injured starship captain, live in a kind of waking dream, taking our perceptions for reality. This is the doctrine of maya. In the *Zen Dictionary* compiled by scholar Ernest Wood, the following definition of *maya* is given:

An old Hindu and especially Vedantic teaching, referring to the creation of all manifest things, of both the mind and the body, from ignorance, through the two processes of (1) veiling the reality, and then (2) building on the basis of the veiling by projection. The product—the whole world of body and mind—is then called maya. The word *maya* is often translated "illusion," which is not to be confused with "delusion." Strictly, in modern terms, it seems very closely related to the idea of relativity or relative truth, which is never *really* correct. (p. 80)

Edward Albertson, author of *Spiritual Yoga for the Millions*, says that maya is not so much untruth, as it is our limited view of the truth. We experience reality through limited sense organs and mistakenly take our experiences for reality itself. He tells the following anecdote to clarify his point:

Once at a museum exhibition I saw a device which gave a superlative illustration of maya. The whole thing was contained in a six-foot-high cabinet, the front of which was blank except for a narrow vertical slot opening into the interior. A plate which could be moved down along this slot had a small hole in it, giving a limited view of what was going on, or seemed to be going on, behind it. As the machine was activated, the little opening descended, and one could see through it what appeared to be a blue light revolving about a red one, much like a miniature planet revolving around a sun.

Then I was invited to step around to the side of this device, which was entirely covered by a sheet of glass, according a full view of the cabinet's insides. Nothing was in motion, absolutely nothing at all. There were only two neon tubes—a blue one in the form of a spiral, and a straight red one standing in the center of that blue spiral. What had caused me to think there was motion occurring inside that cabinet? My own limited view of the proceedings. Once I had become illumined—that is, once I had seen the whole device in its entirety and without limitation—the truth became clear. (pp. 22–23)

The doctrine of maya thus says that the world we experience is our mental construction, not reality itself (see Figure 8.1). Behind the world of experience stands the real world—unchanging, eternal, infinite. The world of experience might be compared to the countless items that can be made from a vast amount of clay. The clay itself is impersonal, formless, and has no character. But from the featureless clay all kinds of interesting objects can be made. The One, the All, is like the featureless clay. It resides behind everything. We take the momentary patterns of the clay for eternal forms, when in fact they are merely temporary appearances out of the clay.

Another way of understanding maya is to define it as our classification and measurement schemes. Indeed, *maya* is derived from the Sanskirt

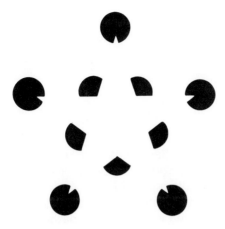

FIGURE 8.1 The doctrine of maya says that the world is our mental construction. Is there a star in this picture? Or is it constructed out of our acts of perception?

root *matr-*, which means "to measure." Human beings speak of things as being big and small, heavy and light, good and bad, right and wrong, and so forth. The doctrine of maya says that measurement and classification may be necessary to function and deal with the world. We should not, however, confuse our classification schemes with reality itself. Classification chops up reality into arbitrary parts, chops the flow of events into bits and pieces, and creates dualities where none exist. For example, are there right and wrong deeds? Common sense would answer of course. But what of the classic case of the poor man who steals milk and bread to feed his starving children? Was he right or wrong? He was wrong to break the law. But he was right to feed his starving children. The dilemma is created by maya, by the way we chop up the world into dualities such as good and bad. Eastern philosophy would not force us to make a logical choice.

The major value of the doctrine of maya resides in what it has to say about human suffering. If we take the doctrine seriously, all suffering occurs because the person attaches himself to maya instead of reality. He takes his personal world of experience for the All. He is spellbound by his own expectations, learnings, and values. He thinks that his finite world of perception is Everything, and this leads to all kinds of negative emotional reactions. There is the feeling that "things *must* go my way. It is essential!" Naturally, things do not always go the way the person wishes, and then there is frustration, anger, and disappointment. We are attached to our property, our jobs, our marriages, our parents, our children, our loves, our hopes, our plans, and so forth. And yet these are all aspects of maya. None of them, including ourselves, are permanent. Everything appears momentarily out of the universal "clay," and everything will once again merge into it. All experiences and appearances are temporary. Thus Eastern philosophy asks, "Why be troubled?" It advises, "Relax and do not attach yourself to maya."

THE WORLD VIEW OF DON JUAN

If, as the doctrine of maya teaches, the everyday reality of the average person is illusion, it is possible that there are other "realities." This is precisely the point of view espoused in a series of widely read books by University of California anthropologist Carlos Castaneda. *The Teachings of don Juan: A Yaqui Way of Knowledge, A Separate Reality,* and other books by Castaneda tell of his adventures with a Yaqui Indian from northwestern Mexico. Castaneda refers to him as "don Juan." Don Juan is a *brujo*, meaning a sorcerer, medicine man, and curer. Castaneda became don Juan's apprentice and for a number of years explored the secrets of Mexican sorcery. Peyote (referred to by don Juan as *Mescalito*), mushroom powder, and psychotropic mixtures, were used by don Juan to open the doors of perception to other realities.

A distinction is made in the Castaneda books between ordinary reality and nonordinary reality. *Ordinary reality* is the consciousness of the average individual; it refers to the consensual world, the one that most of us agree on. It is the reality of everyday society, of one's culture. *Nonordinary reality* appears when the person is in an altered state of consciousness. It is a strange psychological domain described by Castaneda (1971) as "incomprehensible and impossible to interpret by means of our everyday mode of understanding the world" (p. 18). According to don Juan, it takes an unusual person, a "warrior," to be able to enter and leave nonordinary reality successfully. Thus Castaneda's ability to face his experiences in nonordinary reality with will and courage became a test to his mettle as a person.

One of Castaneda's ventures into nonordinary reality involved a meeting with a strange creature called the *guardian*:

I was looking at an unbelievably enormous animal. It was brilliantly black. Its front was covered with long, black, insidious hair, which looked like spikes coming through the cracks of some slick, shiny scales. The hair was actually arranged in tufts. Its body was massive, thick and round. Its wings were wide and short in comparison to the length of its body. It had two white, bulging eyes and a long muzzle. This time it looked more like an alligator. It seemed to have long ears, or perhaps horns, and it was drooling.

. . . It made a wide circle before stopping in front of me; its mouth was wide open, like a huge cavern; it had no teeth. It vibrated its wings for an instant and then it charged at me. It actually charged at my eyes. I screamed with pain and

then I flew up, or rather I felt I had ejected myself up, and went soaring beyond the guardian, beyond the yellowish plateau, into another world, the world of men, and I found myself standing in the middle of don Juan's room. (pp. 158–160)

And what, in ordinary reality, was the guardian? Merely a tiny gnat! When Castaneda discussed this with don Juan, the sorcerer pointed out that in nonordinary reality the gnat actually became the guardian, and it could have killed Castaneda. Even in terms of conventional psychological formulations, don Juan's assertion is plausible. It is easy to imagine that experiences in altered states of consciousness might produce emotional shocks strong enough to induce death. Voodoo deaths, in which tribal members expire from a witch doctor's curse, provide another example of the way an individual's particular construction of reality may induce tragedy. This is why don Juan warned Castaneda that only the brave dare enter the world of nonordinary reality. And it is also why Castaneda needed the steady support, wisdom, and experience of don Juan to guide him safely into and out of the other world.

An important theme in the Castaneda books is the doctrine of *seeing*, and it is closely related to what has already been said about reality. Don Juan tells Castaneda that the average person merely looks, but the "man of knowledge" *sees*. Responding to things in terms of their surface appearance is what don Juan means by merely looking. Responding to events in terms of a larger space-time perspective is what don Juan means by seeing. The art of seeing can be used to exercise what don Juan refers to as *controlled folly* when one faces a personal disappointment, a deliberate shifting of one's attention beyond the immediate event.

For example, say that a businessman loses all his money in a stock-market crash. If he merely looks at the situation, he is despondent; some people have been known to commit suicide during such a period of despair. But if he practices controlled folly, he will *see* that there may be many tomorrows, that his health is still good, that his wife still loves him, and so forth. If he is really skilled at controlled folly, he might even laugh at his misfortune. Thus he is a "fool" in a sense, but a wise fool. Don Juan's idea of seeing as opposed to looking would seem to be similar to the Eastern idea of "piercing the veil of maya." It seems that the esoteric teachings of Indian sorcerers and the doctrines of Eastern philosophy suggest that freedom from much psychological-emotional suffering is possible. Release from suffering requires that the individual be made aware of the fact that he lives in a psychological soap bubble of his own making.

THE STUDY OF PERCEPTION

The age-old doctrine of maya has its counterpart in orthodox psychology. You are already familiar with the term *phenomenal world*, the world as perceived, from the chapter on existential-humanistic psychology. This is a familiar idea in Western philosophy and psychology. It can readily be traced all the way back to Plato's famous allegory of the person imprisoned in a cave. He sees shadows on the wall projected from outside the cave and mistakenly takes these for reality. Plato used the allegory to suggest that we are forced to construct a limited reality, a psychological world, from the small bits of data available to us from Reality itself. As noted in Chapter Seven, a similar formulation can be found in the writings of the philosopher Immanuel Kant.

Students of perception sometimes distinguish between sensation and perception. *Sensation* refers to the raw data of experience. In the case of vision, these might be patches of color and brightness. *Perception* refers to the meaningful whole organized out of the raw data. The bits and pieces of sensation are organized, like the bits and pieces of a jigsaw

Is all perception, even "normal" perception, a kind of illusion or maya? ("The Magician" by Hieronymous Bosch.)

puzzle, into a coherent pattern. Thus when looking at a painting of a landscape, we do not see a random jumble of colors, but the water and the woods.

Perceptions also differ among individuals, however. A basic finding derived from experiments in perception is that motives, expectancies, and attitudes affect perception. Thus David might look at a particular painting in an art gallery and say, "It is beautiful." His companion, Deborah, might look at the same painting and say, "It is ugly." They might even start arguing about whether the painting "is" beautiful or ugly. But they are not debating the "isness" of the painting. They are merely having incongruent perceptions. If they can really appreciate this, their pointless debate might end quickly.

Over and over in the research on perception, we encounter the idea that the person constructs his own reality. This is true even in the domain of tough-minded research. For example, one of the more modern conceptual models for understanding perception is the Tanner-Swets theory of visual detection. W. P. Tanner, Jr., and J. A. Swets found that subjects required to identify visual signals in laboratory experiments report many false positives and false negatives. A *false positive* occurs if the subject says, "A light flashed," when in fact no light flashed at all. A *false negative* occurs if the subject says, "I see no light," when in fact a light flashed. Here is the important point: *Both false positives and false negatives change as a function of the subject's motives and expectancies.* If the subject has a good reason to see or not see a light flash, or if his past experience has led him to believe that a light will or will not flash, his perception is directly altered. In more dramatic terms, he misses things that are clearly evident and "hallucinates" things that are not there. In short, a wide spectrum of formulations, including Eastern philosophy, the teachings of don Juan, Platonic doctrine, and experimental psychology, suggest that the individual constructs his psychological world. As philosopher-author Joseph Pearce says in *The Crack in the Cosmic Egg*, ". . . we represent the world to ourselves, and *respond* to our representations" (p. 2).

YOGA: AN ANCIENT MENTAL SCIENCE

The aim of Yoga is to carry the person beyond maya into a perfect union with the All. Indeed, the word *Yoga* is derived from *yuj*, a Sanskrit root meaning "to yoke." Literally, Yoga means that the individual self is yoked with the Divine Self, thus attaining a sense of oneness with all creation and a state of cosmic awareness. To the cynic, it is amusing that Yoga is a contemporary rage, one of the ''in'' things to be doing, one of the fads of modern times. In actuality, this ''new'' technique is one of the oldest kinds of ''mental science'' known to the human race.

Yoga is easily traced to 300 B.C. and the writings of the great teacher Patanjali. *Raja* Yoga, or Royal Yoga, is associated with Patanjali, and is described in the next section. A *yogi* is one who practices Yoga; the term suggests that he has attained a certain level of expertise. A *swami* is a master; the word connotes one who has attained mystical union with the All. The holy Swami Order has existed in India for more than one thousand years.

KINDS OF YOGA

Yoga is a complex discipline with a variety of techniques. All the techniques have the same general aim, spiritual growth, but they operate in different ways. In *Awakening* by scholar C. William Henderson, the specific methods are described as follows:

They can be likened to the separate cars, buses, trucks, and motorcycles on any highway. The road leads in the direction you want to go, but the vehicles get you there. There are many of these yoga vehicles. Some are similar, some overlap, and a few are the same things going under different names. (p. 121)

A yogi is one who practices yoga; a swami is a master.

The variety of techniques exist to deal with the realities of human temperament. We all have different personalities; thus the different kinds of Yoga appeal to different people. For example, an action-oriented person might find that he is unsuited for sedentary meditation. He might, however, be suited for *Karma Yoga*. Let us identify five basic kinds of Yoga: (1) *Raja Yoga*, (2) *Jnana Yoga*, (3) *Karma Yoga*, (4) *Bhakti Yoga*, and (5) *Hatha Yoga*.

Raja Yoga. Raja Yoga is "Royal" Yoga and is the oldest form of Yoga. It is the one that demands a substantial amount of sedentary meditation. Meditation, as conceived by Raja Yoga, is a skill that requires long hours of intense concentration. The mind of the unskilled meditator is like an unfocused lens. The sun shines through it, but there is no pinpoint of light. The skilled yogi, however, learns to focus the lens of his mind, making consciousness into a small ray of intense energy. This ray "burns" through the veil of maya and carries the yogi into ecstatic union with the All.

Jnana Yoga. Jnana Yoga suggests that harmony with the Infinite can be acquired through self-knowledge. The individual examines himself, his motives, his ambitions, his emotions, and so forth. He gives up practices of self-deception, a kind of inner maya that keeps him from knowing himself completely. Jnana Yoga is similar to the teachings of depth psychology, particularly the teachings of Carl Jung. A disciple of Eastern philosophy might say that such men as Freud and Jung rediscovered in their own way and in their own words the ancient practice of Jnana Yoga.

Karma Yoga. Karma Yoga asserts that self-realization can be attained by leading a responsible life, by being of service to other people. The decent person who is doing his work and raising his children is living according to the principles of Karma Yoga. The idea of *selfless action*, action that has no obvious external reward for the individual, is the core of Karma Yoga. Frankl's logotherapy bears a strong resemblance to Karma Yoga.

Bhakti Yoga. The emphasis of Bhakti Yoga is on devotion. We thus have the image of a person who prays, who chants, who adores his *guru*, his spiritual teacher on Earth. The key concept in Bhakti Yoga is fervent worship, which suggests that practicing great reverence for the All is one way that mystical union can be achieved.

Hatha Yoga. Hatha Yoga is perhaps the most popular form of Yoga in the Western world. Its purpose is to help the individual attain better physical health. This is accomplished through a variety of methods. There are *asanas*, postures that are essentially isometric or "static" exercises; these are designed to strengthen the muscles of the body. There is *pranayama*, or Yogic breathing; this is designed to capture for the body *prana*, or vital energy, believed by yogis to be in the air we breathe. There are also recommendations for correct eating and cleansing of the body. Hatha Yoga is based on the premise that the human being has three aspects—body, mind, and spirit. The thesis is that mental and spiritual growth requires a healthy body. Thus the true yogi does not get "stuck" at the Hatha Yoga level; he does not become preoccupied with physical culture for its own sake. For him it is a mere stepping-stone to higher levels of development. *The Complete Illustrated Book of Yoga* by Swami Vishnudevananda is one of the better introductions to Hatha Yoga.

In addition to the various Yogas just described, there is Integral Yoga. *Integral Yoga* was conceived by the Indian sage Sri Aurobindo, and it seeks to combine the best elements of the five principal Yoga systems.

MENTAL-SPIRITUAL GROWTH

According to Yoga philosophy, mental-spiritual growth takes place via a set of seven stages. These stages are represented by *chakras*, Sanskrit for "disks." The *chakras* are said to be wheellike patterns of energy located at various places in the body. A poetic language is used to describe the process of psychological awakening. A female serpent called the Kundalini is said to be asleep at the base of the spine of the ordinary person. Yogic techniques are designed to awaken the Kundalini, and she slowly ascends from the first *chakra* to the seventh *chakra*. The seven *chakras* are (1) the root, or basic, *chakra*, located at the base of the spine; (2) the spleen *chakra*; (3) the navel *chakra*; (4) the heart *chakra*; (5) the throat *chakra*; (6) the brow *chakra*; and (7) the crown *chakra*, located on the top of the head. It should be understood that it might take a number of years of Yogic study and practice before the Kundalini reaches the crown *chakra*.

When the Kundalini reaches the crown *chakra*, the yogi experiences *samadhi*. In *Yoga Sutras* by Rammurti Mishra, a Sanskrit scholar, the following definition of *samadhi* is given:

> State of superconsciousness; highest state of existence; iden-
> tification of mind with Supreme Consciousness; state of union
> of individual consciousness with Cosmic Consciousness. (p.
> 532)

Thus *samadhi* is the supreme goal of Yogic training. Phrases such as "torrential bliss," "blessed experience," and "ecstatic union" are used to describe *samadhi*. In his later years, the Swami Paramahansa Yogananda wrote a poem called *Samadhi*. Here is a brief excerpt from the poem as it appears in his *Autobiography of a Yogi*:

I, in everything, enter the Great Myself.
Gone forever: fitful, flickering shadows of mortal
memory;
Spotless is my mental sky—below, ahead,
and high above;
Eternity and I, one united ray.
A tiny bubble of laughter, I
Am become the Sea of Mirth Itself. (p. 171)

Although *samadhi* is the goal of Yogic training, the yogi is enjoined to return from *samadhi* and show others the way of mental-spiritual growth. The danger of *samadhi* is presented in Yoga philosophy by telling the story of the salt doll who wanted to discover the depth of the ocean. Obviously, the doll melted into the ocean and never came back. In other words, the yogi should not get "hooked" on *samadhi*. He has a responsibility to his fellow human beings.

It should be understood that the ascension of the Kundalini may be accepted as a case of poetic license. A student of Yoga does not necessarily believe that a real serpent rises from the base of the spine. When Perls spoke of paper people, he did not mean that if snipped such persons would not bleed. The Kundalini and the paper person are metaphors used to get across concepts. In fact, Maslow's formulation of a hierarchy of motives rising in stages from basic drives to self-actualization is remarkably similar to the rise of the Kundalini from the root chakra to the crown chakra.

YOGA AND PARANORMAL PHENOMENA

Yoga takes paranormal phenomena for granted. In the *Autobiography of a Yogi*, Yogananda speaks of materializations, astral projection, and clairvoyance as matter-of-factly as a Western person might speak of making a telephone call or watching television. To the yogi, the common view that we live in a universe limited by the three dimensions of space and the one dimension of time is just another case of maya. The example is given by Swami Vishnudevananda of a ship sailing on the ocean. It can travel in only two dimensions—longitude and latitude. Assume that the captain of the ship is unfamiliar with air travel. An airplane appears

---

* Copyright 1974 by Self-Realization Fellowship. Reprinted by permission of the American publisher, Self-Realization Fellowship, Los Angeles, Calif.

overhead. Then it "disappears." Much to the captain's amazement, he finds the airplane at his destination. The airplane has traveled in the third dimension—a dimension unknown to the captain. Thus its behavior seemed incredible and paranormal. Similarly, the yogi believes that the *astral body,* a "second" body made of a finer matter than the ordinary body, can travel in higher dimensional planes. Extrasensory perception and other paranormal phenomena are understood in such terms.

Of late, the seemingly incredible world view of Yoga has received some support from such unlikely quarters as astronomy and theoretical physics. In *The Amazing Universe,* authored by Herbert Friedman, pioneer in rocket astronomy, and published by the National Geographic Society, you can read about *black holes,* regions of space only a few miles wide that trap all matter and/or light entering their domain. Where does the matter and light go? Some astronomers and physicists speculate that the existence of black holes suggests the complementary existence of white holes, perhaps in another universe. As matter passes out of our universe into the black hole, it travels through a "wormhole" in space and reemerges out of a white hole located in the other universe.

The following quotation was not written by a yogi. It was written by Jack Sarfatti, holder of a Ph.D. in theoretical physics from the University of California. In *Space-Time and Beyond,* he says:

I believe the gravitational distortion of space and time predicted in Einstein's general theory of relativity provides a possible scientific explanation of precognition, clairvoyance, and astral projection, provided we accept the additional postulates that individual consciousness can alter the biogravitational field of a living organism and that the biogravitational field distorts the local subjective space-time of the conscious observer. Thus, a participator in a high state of consciousness can artificially create blackholes and whiteholes in his local biogravitational field. (p. 153)

The existence of paranormal phenomena is an unsettled question within the profession of psychology. There is a body of experimental work on *psi abilities,* capacities of the mind asserted to transcend its normal limits. The pioneer psychologist in the area was J. B. Rhine. His findings are available in the *Journal of Parapsychology* and in his books, including his most famous, *The Reach of the Mind.* In brief, Rhine was convinced of the reality of psi abilities and presented various experiments with statistical analyses to support his contentions. More recently, in an article titled "Telepathy Could Be Real," author Paul Chance reported on a series of telepathy experiments conducted by Charles Tart of the University of California at Davis. Tart's data suggest that many subjects score significantly above chance when given the opportunity to exhibit psi abilities.

The research on parapsychology is extremely difficult to evaluate objectively, however. There are all sorts of problems in experimental design, fine points of statistical analysis, and experimenter bias that enter in to discredit the research in the minds of the psychological community. The case in favor of paranormal phenomena has *not* been made in the halls of academic psychology. At present, it can only be said that a large number of psychologists keep an open mind about parapsychology. They do not give it categorical rejection or categorical acceptance.

In either case, an interesting proposition emerges from the point of view of Yoga. Instead of making much of paranormal phenomena, we find that the serious yogi tends to discount them! He discounts them not because he supposes they are not real, but because he feels they interfere with mental-spiritual growth. In other words, they are a trap. They tend to appear *before* the Kundalini reaches the seventh *chakra*. If the novice becomes distracted by his supernormal mental powers, he may be delayed in reaching *samadhi*. Yoga warns that even if psi abilities are real, they are hardly ends in themselves.

Yoga sees itself as having a responsibility to humanity. In the *Autobiography of a Yogi*, Yogananda writes:

The Western day is nearing when the inner science of self-control will be found as necessary as the outer conquest of Nature. The Atomic Age will see men's minds sobered and broadened by the now scientifically indisputable truth that matter is in reality a concentrate of energy. The human mind can and must liberate within itself energies greater than those within stones and metals, lest the material atomic giant, newly unleashed, turn on the world in mindless destruction. (p. 265)

Briefly, Yoga teaches that it is possible to pierce the veil of maya and attain mystical union with the All. This produces a state of bliss known as *samadhi*. Several kinds of Yoga exist, but they are not thought of as mutually exclusive. As an ancient science, Yoga teaches that it is possible to attain tremendous levels of inner self-control over the body and the mind. It should be understood, however, that the techniques of Yoga are merely instruments in the whole scheme. The real purpose of Yoga is spiritual growth.

ZEN: THE ENLIGHTENED LIFE

Like Yoga, Zen seeks to break the spell of maya. But there are important differences between Yoga and Zen. Yoga is "upward bound." It takes the person into the psychological stratosphere. It is truly *trans*personal in that it takes the person "out" of himself. Zen, on the other hand, is "down to Earth." It returns the individual to himself. This is evident in that a prime goal of Zen is to see into one's own true nature. In Zen poetry, one finds a love of and a closeness to the Earth itself—to the land, the trees, the flowers, the animals, the rivers, and so forth. Zen holds that our true nature is *not* divided from Nature itself. We are part of Nature. More than a part of Nature, we are an indivisible aspect of Nature. Ringing Western phrases such as "the conquest of space" are nonsense to the Zen mind. They artificially pit man against the universe.

Use of the single word *Zen* is technically incorrect. The proper term is *Zen Buddhism*, a meditative approach to Buddhism. But Zen Buddhism is a sufficiently unique school of thought that informal usage allows the single word *Zen* to stand alone. Zen is a Japanese word derived from the Chinese word *Ch'an*, meaning "meditation." *Ch'an* itself is derived from the Sanskrit word for meditation, *Dhyana*. Thus the core meaning of Zen is simply meditation. Zen was brought to Japan, where it flourished, about eight hundred years ago by traveling monks. There are presently about twenty thousand Zen temples in Japan.

THE TAO AND THE FOUR NOBLE TRUTHS

Because Zen is derived from *Taoism*, the ancient religion of China, and also from Chinese Buddhism, it would be well to examine these roots of Zen. In the words of the great Chinese sage Lao-tzu:

There are ways but the Way is uncharted;
There are names but not nature in words:
Nameless indeed is the source of creation . . .

These words are said to have been written in the fourth century B.C. A paraphrase of the quotation is offered by the Eastern scholar R. B. Blakney:

None of the ways observed or described by us, in which things happen or events occur, is the Master Way by which nature works. No word or name can disclose nature's deepest secret. Creation began in an event which is not identified and therefore has no name. (p. 53)

The Tao is thus the Way, the Master Way, of existence. It is inexorable in its course, and it must be accepted. Taoism teaches that there is nothing we can do to change it. Like a great river, it carries everything along in its forceful flow. Deep acceptance of the Tao is said to be the key to tranquillity and a nonartificial life.

Another root of Zen is the set of Four Noble Truths proposed by Chinese Buddhism. It should be understood that Buddhism and its variant, Zen, are psychologies as well as religions. As earlier noted, they are "ways of liberation." They aim to free human beings from unnecessary suffering. The Four Noble Truths are intended to contribute to this goal:

1   The First Noble Truth is the simple admission that suffering exists. Human beings experience pain, despair, frustration, and decay of the body. These are inevitable.

2   The Second Noble Truth is that suffering originates with excessive desire. A person may want too much sexual activity, too much money, too much food. Also, the Second Noble Truth asserts that some people have too strong a desire to save their own souls. Such spiritual craving is also seen as a source of suffering.

3   The Third Noble Truth is that suffering can be eliminated. This can be done by getting rid of excessive desire. By focusing on the reality of the Tao, the inevitability of the great cycle of birth, growth, and decay, one can gain a great perspective. One sees that excessive desire is folly in terms of the great course of existence.

4   The Fourth Noble Truth is that there is an Eightfold Middle Path between excessive desire and excessive self-denial. In *Selling Water by the River*, a manual of Zen training by the Abbess Jiyu Kennet, the following eight aspects of the Middle Path are designated: (1) right understanding, (2) right thought, (3) right speech, (4) right action, (5) right livelihood, (6) right effort, (7) right mindfulness, and (8) right concentration (p. 10). The Middle Path is essentially the path of moderation.

The teachings of Taoism and Buddhism are the underpinnings of Zen, and contemporary Zen still incorporates these basic orientations. They are implicit themes in all the Zen literature.

THE WORLD VIEW OF ZEN

It is easy to be glib about Zen. But serious students of Zen quote the words of Lao-tzu:

Those who know do not speak;
Those who speak do not know.

Assume that you pick up a small book titled *What Is Zen?* by no less an authority than D. T. Suzuki, one of the principal persons responsible for awakening the Western mind to the possibilities in Zen. This is what you find on the opening page:

You ask, "What is Zen?"

I answer, "Zen is that which makes you ask the question, because the answer is where the question arises. The answerer is no other than the questioner himself."

"Do you then mean that I am Zen itself?"

"Exactly. When you ask what Zen is, you are asking who you are, what your self is. It is for this reason that the Zen masters often tell you not to ask where the donkey is when you are right on it, or not to seek for another head when

yours has been on your shoulders ever since you were born. It is the height of stupidity to ask what your self is when it is this self that makes you ask the question."

Now, you know what Zen is, for it is Zen that tells you what your self is, and that that self is Zen. This now saves you from asking such a stupid question. (p. 1)

Do you feel vaguely disgusted, insulted, and confused? You read on and soon feel like throwing the book away. That is the whole point! When Suzuki says you should not "seek for another head," he simply means *think for yourself.* He is asking you, "Why turn to me or to any other authority for ideas about right living? You have a head. Use it!" Zen seeks to teach by example, and Suzuki is perfectly willing to turn you away from him if this will contribute to your self-sufficiency.

Zen has a great mistrust of abstract thinking, the forte of the Western rational mind. In a book called *Zen Buddhism and Psychoanalysis*, co-authored with Erich Fromm and Richard DeMartino, a book much less obscure than the one already cited, Suzuki clarifies the Zen mistrust of analytical thought. He quotes a *haiku*, a seventeen-syllable poem, written about three hundred years ago by Basho, a great Japanese poet:

When I look carefully
I see the nazuna *blooming*
by the hedge! (p. 1)

The *nazuna* is a wild plant, the sort that most people might not even notice as they walk by. The poem does not seem to be much of a poem at all by Western standards, hardly the work of a great poet. But Suzuki points out that the poem is intended to convey a depth of feeling and an appreciation for nature just as it is. Basho has an emotional reaction to the *nazuna*—perhaps admiration or a transient sense of joy—and he records the feelings. Suzuki contrasts Basho's poem with a superficially similar poem by the Western poet, Alfred, Lord Tennyson:

Flower in the crannied wall,
I pluck you out of the crannies;—
Hold you here, root and all, in my hand,
Little flower—but if I could understand
What you are, root and all, and all in all,
I should know what God and man is.

The difference between the minds of Basho and of Tennyson is indeed great. Tennyson cares nothing for the flower itself—his act must kill the flower. He is interested in understanding the world he lives in, grasping it intellectually. Consequently, he both destroys and alienates himself from that world. Basho is interested in appreciating the world he lives in; thus he does not set himself against it. Tennyson's approach is used to symbolize the approach of Western rational thought. Basho's approach is used to symbolize the approach of Zen.

Suzuki summarizes the world view of the Western mind with such words as analytical, discriminative, differential, inductive, individualistic, intellectual, objective, scientific, generalizing, conceptual, schematic, impersonal, power-wielding, and self-assertive. In contrast, the world view of Zen is described with such words as synthetic, totalizing, integrative, nondiscriminative, deductive, nonsystematic, dogmatic, intuitive, subjective, spiritually individualistic, and socially group-minded.

PRINCIPLES OF ZEN

Perhaps we can make the world view of Zen more explicit by formulating some of the teachings of Zen in the form of principles. Three principles will be specified: (1) the principle of no-thingness, (2) the principle of no-twoness, and (3) the principle of no-mind. These principles would probably not be abstracted formally from the flow of Zen, as we have done, by a Zen master interested in instructing a student. The listing of principles is itself a categorizing process toward which Zen is indifferent. Thus let us proceed with at least the awareness that our procedure does some violence to the Zen way of thinking.

The principle of no-thingness. As we look about the world, we see the familiar environment of *things*, objects of perception. We see pencils, cups, tables, houses, cars, and so forth. Zen teaches that these are not things, but abstractions we have made from the great flow of the Tao. It is our perceptual processes that create the world of things. They are psychological constructions, created by our sense organs. There was a time when they were not. There will be a time when they are not. Things merely appear and disappear out of the current of existence. It is thus a form of maya to think that the world is made up of hard, enduring objects. The same can be said of ourselves. We are not things. We too appear and disappear, produced by and swallowed up by the Tao. It is thus folly to attach too much importance to material possessions or to the "ultimate" possession—life itself. For life itself will dissolve into the river of the Way.

The same thinking is applied by Zen to the *ego*, the conscious self. It is not a thing either, but a construction abstracted from space-time events. Not being a permanent thing, the Zen view would make no assertions about the survival of the ego after one's death. A Zen *koan*, a "puzzler" or thought-provoking paradox used to foster enlightenment, asks: "Where does your fist go when you open your hand?" The word *fist* is a noun and seems to refer to a thing. Yet the "thing" disappears merely by opening the hand! And yet we see, from our larger frame of reference, that nothing

The Zen principle of no-thingness teaches that familiar objects are abstractions from the great flow of the Tao.

was lost. Indeed, there never actually existed a "thing" called the fist in and of itself. Similarly, Zen teaches that to ask, "Where does the ego go after death?" is like asking about the fist. The ego is not a thing in and of itself any more than the fist is. It doesn't "go" anywhere. There is only a change of form. The human ego, says Zen, is a temporary organization emerging briefly from the restless changes of existence itself.

Alan Watts, author of *The Way of Zen* and a number of other books about Eastern ways of thought, offers the following example to illustrate how the Zen view of the ego fits into the principle of no-thingness. We say the ocean makes waves. The word *wave* is treated in English as a noun, a thing. (You will recall that a noun is defined as a person, place, or thing. A wave is not a person or a place; thus ordinary English grants it the status of a thing.) We say, "The wave travels to the shore" or "The wave breaks on the shore." Watts notes, however, that this usage is inaccurate. If we reflect a moment, we can easily appreciate that the wave is not a thing. It is in fact *no*-thing, an organization of water into a temporary form. In like fashion, suggests Watts, the universe produces egos. He converts the nouns to verbs, thus suggesting processes instead of things. It is now possible to say, "As the ocean *waves*, the universe *egos*."

The principle of no-twoness. Zen teaches that most dichotomies are false. They are another aspect of maya. We speak of mind and body, good and bad, tall and short, right and wrong, and so forth. In reality, asserts Zen, members of a duality are aspects of each other. There can be no mind without the body, no good without bad, no tall without short, and no right without wrong. So-called opposites have a complementary relationship, creating each other. They are merely two faces of the same coin. Returning to the subject of the ego or the self, Zen says that it is a mistake to make a subject-object dichotomy between oneself and the world. The Western mind is trained to think in terms of the I "in here" and the world "out there." To illustrate its position, Zen invokes the image of the moon-in-the-lake. Take away the moon, and there is no moon-in-the-lake. Take away the lake, and there is no moon-in-the-lake. The moon-in-the-lake requires the moon and the lake. The phenomenon vanishes if either is removed. Similarly, the person-in-the-world phenomenon requires both the person and the world. The person and the world are aspects of each other. Zen thus sees the division between man and nature as arbitrary.

The words of a Zenlike song by Broadway lyricist Alan Jay Lerner invokes the image of oneness with Nature:

On a clear day
Rise and look around you
And you'll see who you are.

On a clear day
How it will astound you
That the glow of your being
Outshines every star.
You feel part of
*Every mountain, sea and shore . . .**

The principle of no-mind. The principle of no-mind asserts that it is possible to think too much. Again, in Zen we encounter the mistrust of abstract thinking and analytical thought. The Zen goal is to act spontaneously without too much reflection, analysis, and unnecessary cogitation. The psychologically "stuck" person is the person who must overthink everything. Such persons put great faith in their rational faculties. They think if they can gather all the facts, ponder long enough, and be sufficiently logical, they will always make the right decision. Zen says that this is another aspect of maya, the illusion that the conscious mind is sufficient to light the darkness of the maze of existence. Zen, instead, advises us to live with a stronger sense of intuition, to base our decisions at least as much on nonverbal feelings as articulated thoughts.

The principle of no-mind should not be misunderstood as advising rash action. Zen does not see itself as giving license for foolhardy behavior. On the contrary, Zen is simply arguing that some persons are too inhibited. Such persons need to let go of their death grip on their intellects and act more spontaneously. When one is on a mental merry-go-round, Zen advises that one simply jump off! In other words, it says, "Take action! Act now! Even if the decision is the 'wrong' one, it is better than mental paralysis and psychological self-torture."

A bit of perspective can be gained on the principle of no-mind by realizing that Japan is a tradition-oriented culture. The no-mind advice can be of value to persons who are too culture-bound and, in consequence, too inhibited—the kind of person clinical psychology would call "neurotic." In a society that puts out the heavy hand of tradition to keep its members "in line," there may be a high incidence of neurosis. But the principle of no-mind would not be helpful for persons at the opposite end of the pole, persons clinical psychology would place in the category of "character disorders." Such individuals are impulsive, and they do not need no-mind. They need more mind!

In actuality, the Zen principle of no-mind can be correctly understood in terms of the Middle Way of the Four Noble Truths of Buddhism. There is an optimal way of behaving between excessive inhibition and excessive excitation. This optimal way is known as *spontaneity*. Subjectively, spontaneity might be described as the inner feeling that one has the capacity to take right action without undue strain. The spontaneous person trusts himself and his capacity to make decisions.

METHODS OF AWAKENING

It is not enough, according to Zen, to know *about* no-thingness, no-twoness, and no-mind. Intellectual understanding is fine, but the person who has only intellectual understanding is not in fact awakened. He must be "hit" by these ideas like the proverbial ton of bricks. If and when this happens, he experiences *satori*. *Satori* may be thought of as a sudden awakening in which the spell of maya is cast off. One not only realizes intellectually the things we have been talking about in the past few pages; one *directly knows* that they are so. In Western psychology, we would refer to *satori* with the word *insight*. Satori, or insight, suggests an abrupt "seeing into" the heart of a problem. Everything "clicks" into place, and one thinks, "Ah hah! I've got it!"

An analogy may enhance our understanding of *satori*. *Satori* is like a flash of lightning that illuminates a dark landscape. The flash may last for only an instant, but we never forget what we saw during that instant. Similarly, what a person "sees" during *satori* is preserved, brought back to ordinary experience as it were, and may change the person's life forever. Of course, a person may experience *satori* more than once—just as lightning can flash again. But the *satori* experience is not one that can be sustained for long. And an awakened person does not live in a state of constant *satori.*

There are two principal methods of inducing *satori.* The first mode is advocated by the Soto school of Zen, which advocates a gradual approach to *satori. Satori* may be a "flash" in which a person is changed in an instant. But in Soto Zen, there is a slow buildup to the "moment of Truth." Soto Zen places its emphasis on *Za-zen,* which is seated meditation in an approved posture. During *Za-zen,* the novice is instructed to look into his own nature, to meditate upon himself, with no particular goal in mind. It is expected that under such conditions all sorts of thoughts will pass through the mind and that little by little the meditator will come to see that distinctions between the inner and the outer world are like the moon-in-the-lake. He may strive after *satori* in utter frustration for months or for years. But *satori* cannot be willed. Perhaps at a certain point he stops trying to make it happen and just allows matters to take their course. When he least expects it, *satori* may occur. It happens of its own accord, spontaneously, from the depths of his being. About two-thirds of the Zen temples in Japan are Soto temples.

The other principal mode of inducing *satori* is advocated by the Rinzai school of Zen. It emphasizes the *koan,* the paradoxical question, as a means of hastening the arrival of *satori.* (The Soto school also uses the *koan* occasionally. But its principal advocate is the Rinzai school.) The *koan* is a question designed to create a psychological double bind. Hours and hours of meditating on a *koan* "blows the mind" and may result in sudden illumination or *satori.* There are many *koans*; about 1,700 different ones are used. Here are a few examples:

What is the sound of one hand clapping?

What was your original face before you were born?

A girl is crossing the street. Is she the younger or the older sister?

When you are working, where is your true self?

When the student has meditated long enough on *koans,* he sees that they are nothing but tangles of words. He is brought to the realization that words are traps, the agents of maya. Reality itself is beyond words and must be comprehended and acted on at a nonverbal level. In a well-known *koan,* the Zen master shows a student a stick. He says, "If you say this is a stick, I will hit you with it. If you say it is not a stick, I will hit you with it." The master's words seem to create an impossible double bind. The student may say, "It is a staff," thinking he is clever by assigning a different label to the stick. Much to his surprise, the master hits him with the stick! The *koan* is properly understood if the student takes the stick away from the master and simply breaks it. A nonverbal response solves the seemingly impossible paradox.

Rinzai Zen uses the *koan* along with *Za-zen*, seated meditation, to facilitate the internal processes that bring the student to *satori*. When the aspirant really *knows*, as opposed to intellectual understanding, that subject-object dichotomies (dualisms) are false, that they are forms of maya created by the way human beings use words, he is enlightened.

THE ENLIGHTENED LIFE

According to Zen, one does not have to join a religious order to live an enlightened life. Zen beams its message out to the world. Its philosophy is designed to bring enlightenment to persons in all walks of life. This is not to say that most people who read about Zen achieve enlightenment. As we have already seen, there is a vast difference between enlightenment itself and learning about enlightenment on an academic level. Nonetheless, Zen need not be understood as an esoteric practice reserved for a few reclusive monks in Japanese monasteries. As noted previously, it is a "way of liberation" from unnecessary human suffering. As such, it has general value.

Let us set up a hypothetical person, the *enlightened person*, a person who has achieved *satori* in Zen terms. The image is created to get across an idea, the idea of the enlightened life. Actual persons might come close to or depart far from the image; but the image gives us a standard against which to measure behavior. The enlightened person could be almost anybody doing anything. He would not have to have a high-status position, have a profession, make a lot of money, or be highly creative. He would have no exalted goals. He would have only realistic ambitions, not burning ambitions. The enlightened person would have overcome the opposites of success and failure. These too, according to Zen, are aspects of maya.

The enlightened person would be able to cry and to laugh, to play and to work. But he would not get "stuck" in various emotional states and behaviors. He would not, for example, suffer from chronic depression, anger, or anxiety. He would not be addicted to either play or work. He would not worry about what he is getting out of life. As Watts said, "Why worry about what you are getting out of life when you don't get out?" This itself is a sort of *koan* designed to reveal the Zen idea that life is similar to a dance. We dance to dance, not to get to New York from Los Angeles. We cannot get "out" of life. According to Zen, "Life is like a sword that cannot cut itself."

Spontaneity would be another characteristic of the enlightened person. As previously noted, the individual would have the inner feeling that he has the capacity to make correct choices without undue strain. Spontaneity should be understood as an optimal trait between excessive inhibition and excessive excitation. To illustrate, a person who has a problem with alcohol may be straining to resist it. He is on the wagon, he won't touch a drop. This represents the extreme pole of excessive inhibition. He pays a heavy price for not drinking—he is tense and uptight. Then he falls off the wagon. He drinks too much. He has no self-control. This represents the opposite end of the pole, excessive excitation. Contrast the behavior of the problem drinker with the behavior of a person who does not have a problem. His feeling about alcohol is "I can take it or leave it." Sometimes he drinks. Sometimes he refuses a drink. He drinks in moderation spontaneously, without "willpower" or effort. If this second individual could behave with similar spontaneity in all domains of his existence, he would be an enlightened person.

What about the moral and ethical behavior of the enlightened person? Would an enlightened person live what is generally called a "decent" life? The answer is that for the enlightened person the general rules of everyday conduct would remain about the same as for persons in general. He would fit in with his general culture and not fight it. He would not be vigorously pro-Establishment, nor vigorously anti-Establishment. The ideas of the conservatives and radicals, the ideas of all men, are simply more strands of the web of maya. He would not, therefore, be sold on the Absolute Truth of any particular moral-ethical code. He would look upon social conventions as significant local customs, however. As a consequence, he would observe them. He would practice the dictum "When in Rome do as the Romans do." Practical, reality-oriented, interested in surviving, and having a reasonable desire to enjoy life, the enlightened person would spontaneously follow the general behavioral norms of his culture without particular effort.

The picture we have painted of the enlightened person is not in the Western tradition of the hero. The enlightened person would be amused by a character such as Cervantes's Don Quixote, the self-proclaimed rescuer, forever tilting at windmills. The enlightened person does not seek psychological mountains to climb; he is not interested in Great Tasks in life. He is more interested in a plain philosophy, such as "live and let live." He would feel a kinship with the Italian folk saying "*Che sera, sera*," meaning "What will be, will be." He accepts the fact that the Tao, the great river of existence, flows on inexorably and that we can have only a minimal effect on its direction.

Briefly, Zen has its roots in Taoism and Chinese Buddhism. As a Japanese form of meditative Buddhism, it has developed a world view having a color of its own. The Zen world view emphasizes the importance of Nature, the value of being close to the Earth. Piercing the veil of maya brings the person home, to *this* ground he walks on. The enlightened person, the person who has attained *satori*, is not a wonder worker or a wizard. Instead, he is a modest person, living a practical life. His one great achievement, if it can be called that, is that he is liberated from unnecessary suffering. The Western philosopher Ludwig Wittgenstein once wrote, "What is your aim in philosophy?—to show the fly the way out of the fly-bottle." Wittgenstein meant that the person caught in a psychological trap is like the fly in the bottle. The way out is clear, but he cannot see it. In Zen, the bottle would be a part of maya. Our traps in life, our psychological problems, are the products of our own minds. Like Wittgenstein, Zen seeks to show the suffering person the way out of the invisible bottle that keeps him a prisoner. And that is why it is appropriate to speak of Zen as a "way of liberation."

MEDITATION: THE SERENE MIND

In both the Yoga and the Zen traditions, meditation plays a key role. In Yoga, meditation is used to achieve *samadhi*. In Zen, meditation is used to achieve *satori*. In both cases, meditation is used as a tool to break through the veil of maya. Behind maya is presumed to reside the domain of reality itself as opposed to the world of appearances. The goal of meditation is to gain at least temporary entry into the domain of reality itself. In *Meditation*, Watts writes:

The art of meditation is a way of getting into touch with reality. And the reason for meditation is that most civilized people are out of touch with reality. They confuse the world as it is with the world as they think about it, talk about it, and describe it. For on the one hand there is the real world and on the other a whole system of symbols about that world which we have in our minds. These are very, very useful symbols; all civilization depends on them. But like all good things, they have their disadvantages, and the principal disadvantage of symbols is that we confuse them with reality in the same way as we confuse money with actual wealth, and our names, ideas, and images of ourselves with ourselves. (p. 5)

For centuries, human beings have sought ways of finding islands of serenity in the often stormy sea of human existence. Advocates of meditation claim that it can momentarily lift its practitioner out of the mundane world of everyday affairs to a calm place in his own mind, a place that has always been there but has been undiscovered. When the meditator "returns" to the world, he returns with a more serene mind. It is claimed that, as a consequence, he functions more efficiently than the average person.

KINDS OF MEDITATION

There is more than one kind of meditation. I will specify four types. But before I deal with specifics, let me make the general observation that there is a common thread running through all the modes of meditation: *concentration*, the focusing of one's attention on a limited range of stimuli. In *The Psychology of Consciousness*, psychologist Robert Ornstein notes that meditators often refer to the successful achievement of the focusing of attention as "one-pointedness of mind" (p. 125).

The four kinds of meditation that will be reviewed are (1) intellect-oriented meditation, (2) feeling-oriented meditation, (3) body-oriented meditation, and (4) action-oriented meditation. The four types are adapted from *How To Meditate* by psychologist Lawrence LeShan. It should be understood that the four kinds of meditation are not mutually exclusive and that they overlap to a large degree.

Intellect-oriented meditation.   In intellect-oriented meditation, the meditator gives his attention to something that stimulates or challenges his thinking capacities. The Zen *koan* provides a classic example. But isn't this paradoxical? Isn't the aim of Zen meditation to reach a state of *satori,* a no-mind state beyond the intellect and abstract thinking? "Of course," agrees the Zen master. "However, we use thought to annihilate thought. We use concepts to destroy concepts." It is much like fighting fire with fire.

Another example of intellect-oriented meditation is the approach of the Indian sage J. Krishnamurti. In one of his books, *Think on These Things,* Krishnamurti provides a list of more than one hundred thought-provoking questions at the back of the book. Examples are:

It is true that society is based on acquisitiveness and ambition; but if we had no ambition would we not decay?

Discontent prevents clear thinking. How are we to overcome this obstacle?

Why do we want to live in luxury?

It is presumed that by sincerely pondering these and similar questions at length, the meditator will find himself becoming progressively illuminated about his relationship to existence. Again, note that the meditative tradition is based on the assumption that the answers to life's most important questions reside within oneself.

Feeling-oriented meditation.   In feeling-oriented meditation, the meditator gives his attention to an emotion-laden symbol. Traditionally, the symbol has usually been one having religious associations. For example, a Christian might meditate upon the Holy Cross and its meaning for him. A member of an Eastern religion might meditate upon a *mandala*, a venerated circular pattern. Or he might meditate upon a *mantra*, a sacred word or chant. The symbol acts as a focusing device for one's attention. As attention wanders, the meditator brings it back to the symbol. It is this kind of meditation, feeling-oriented meditation, that is the one most usually associated with states of bliss, such as *samadhi*.

Transcendental meditation, discussed later, is derived from the feeling-oriented meditation in which a mantra is used.

Body-oriented meditation.   In body-oriented meditation, the meditator usually gives his attention to an autonomic process. For example, he may count his breaths, focus on his pulse rate, or concentrate on the position of his body. Hatha Yoga is a form of body-oriented meditation. Body-oriented meditation, like any of the varieties of meditation, may lead an individual to an altered state of consciousness. In addition, body-oriented meditation may lead the individual to acquire greater self-control over autonomic processes—the kind of self-control aimed at by biofeedback training.

Action-oriented meditation.   In action-oriented meditation, the meditator concentrates his attention upon a behavior pattern. *Tai Chi Chuan* provides one example of action-oriented meditation. A Chinese art, it requires that the individual perform a habitual movement consciously and deliberately. To illustrate, instead of just lifting one's arms over one's head, the meditator might lift them in slow motion, thus augmenting his sense of behavioral awareness. This is clearly another way of reclaiming for the voluntary domain that which has been "lost" in the involuntary domain.

Another example of action-oriented meditation is provided by the Zen tradition. In *The Method of Zen*, Eugen Herrigel, a European student of Zen, writes:

It is astonishing and, for the European, almost inconceivable how much time the Japanese spend in restraining and controlling gestures which can at most be regarded as aesthetic faults. Say someone slams the door in a temper. In the East this is not taken as the expression of a forceful personality, nor is it regarded as a lapse which should not be taken seriously. Anyone who does such a thing will not, like the European, deem it justified by the situation, or excuse himself by saying that his feelings ran away with him. He will go back to the door, open it, close it softly, and say to it: "I beg your pardon." Thereafter he will take care how he shuts doors. (p. 32)

The theme of concentration on actions is similarly reflected in Zen archery, swordsmanship, flower arranging, painting, and the Japanese tea ceremony. All these represent different aspects of action-oriented meditation.

TRANSCENDENTAL MEDITATION

As already noted, transcendental meditation (TM) is derived from feeling-oriented meditation in which a mantra, a sacred word or chant, is used. TM, a Yogic technique, was brought to the widespread attention of Americans by the Maharishi Mahesh Yogi. Adam Smith, author of *Powers of Mind*, says, "Transcendental Meditation is the McDonald's of the meditation business" (p. 126). It is estimated that about 600,000 people in the United States practice TM with some frequency. There is a Maharishi International University in Iowa. And the Students International Meditation Society (SIMS) is active on college campuses throughout the country.

No less an authority than Hans Selye, a pioneer researcher on stress-induced diseases, wrote an approving foreword to the bestselling *Transcendental Meditation: Discovering Inner Energy and Overcoming Stress* by physician Harold Bloomfield and two coauthors, Michael Cain and

The Yogic technique of Transcendental Meditation was brought to the widespread attention of Americans by the Maharishi Mahesh Yogi.

Dennis Jaffe. Selye concludes his foreword with this enthusiastic endorsement of TM:

In all, I feel that TM will enjoy immediate success and offer the general public a most effective explanation of how pure awareness and creative intelligence, combined with what medical science has taught us about the bodily effects of stress, can help humanity face "the crisis of modern life." . . . (p. xii)

What happens during transcendental meditation? The authors of *Transcendental Meditation* answer the question thus:

A person allows his mind to experience a relaxed and enjoyable state which draws his attention inward. He experiences a state in which the mind becomes very quiet, but extraordinarily alert. Though sense impressions, feelings or thought may be present during TM, meditators report brief or sometimes extended periods of "blank awareness," "being awake inside with nothing going on," "not being asleep, but not being aware of anything in particular." . . . When a meditator allows his attention to shift inward, he experiences quiet levels of the mind in which he becomes increasingly aware of the unbounded nature of his awareness in the absence of objects. This state, which will be termed pure awareness, *consists of nothing more than being wide awake inside without being aware of anything except awareness itself. (p. 11)*

The state referred to as pure awareness is induced by mentally reciting a mantra, usually in rhythm with one's normal breathing. The mantra acts as a focusing device, aiding concentration. As the meditator repeats the mantra, his attention will drift from it. He is instructed to gently bring his wandering attention back to the mantra. An analogy may be made by taking a child for a walk in the park. The child will stray from the main path, running toward the swings, chasing a butterfly, and so forth. The understanding adult will return the child to the main path without anger or force. Similarly, as the attention wanders from the mantra, the meditator, without anger or force, simply returns his attention to the mantra. In anywhere from five to fifteen minutes, the meditator will begin to experience "pure awareness."

TM is usually practiced twice a day for ten to twenty minutes per session almost anywhere; in a bus station, in a waiting room, riding on a train, and so forth. The state described as pure awareness is induced more easily with practice. The experienced meditator slips into it rather easily. Being basically alert and awake, the practitioner of TM can come out of the state easily and at will. TM *is* an altered state of consciousness, but it is not sleep. This point is elaborated later.

Advocates of TM detach it from any philosophical, theological, or religious overtones. The assertion is that one can practice TM whatever one's world view. It does not contradict any dogma or the teachings of any organized religious organization. Thus TM enthusiasts say it can be practiced by anyone and have beneficial results. Members of SIMS see TM as a gift from the East, a gift that can free its recipients from stress-induced diseases. It is also asserted that the beneficial effects of TM will in the long run free many persons from a dependence on such drugs as antihypertensive agents and antianxiety agents.

Teachers of TM associated with the Maharishi's movement warn against learning TM from a book without the assistance of a qualified guide. It is asserted that a suitable mantra cannot be selected by the novice himself. The "vibrations" may not be right for the particular individual and may have an adverse effect on his nervous system. Others argue that this is a dubious contention and that almost any pleasant word or sentence can be used as a mantra. In any case, large numbers of people are practicing some version of TM. It behooves us to ask: To what extent are the TM claims valid? Let us now explore the answer to this question.

THE RELAXATION RESPONSE

The principal value claimed for TM is that it helps to combat stress-induced, or "psychosomatic," diseases. The argument is that the complexities of modern civilization produce psychological conflicts which result in nervous tension, anxiety, chronic anger, and so forth. It is presumed that these primitive reactions often have no adequate outlet. Unreleased, the person suffers. In the following statement taken from Smith's *Powers of Mind*, he speaks of pterodactyls, flying reptiles that existed during the Mesozoic era. He makes the reference as a loose metaphor to suggest that our forebears faced various dangers we do not face. But we are still programmed with their primitive fight-or-flight reactions. In a modern setting, in the absence of a clear physical danger, the primitive internal mechanism can cause trouble:

Minds. The trouble is minds, not organic medicine, not some germ that comes flying through the air looking for a home. This is Dr. Han Selye, sixty-eight years old, the distinguished dean of stress medicine. Stress is "a physiologic response inappropriate to the situation." Misfired signals between mind and body. The physiologic response is the caveman's response when the shadow of a pterodactyl falls over him. Adrenal secretions increase and muscles tense and the coagulation chemistry gets ready to resist wounds. Fight or flight. But what pterodactyl is this? They tell you: the market is down twenty points, or the vice-president wants to see you, or, the whole operation is going to be shut down and moved to Chicago. Blam, pterodactyl time. Gives you, says Dr. Selye, headaches, insomnia, high blood pressure, sinus, ulcers, rheumatism, cardiovascular and kidney disease. And more. (p. 5)

Does TM give relief from the adverse effects of the primitive fight-or-flight reaction? The question has been studied by Herbert Benson, associate professor of medicine at the Harvard Medical School, and his answer is a qualified yes. TM does seem to have beneficial effects. It appears to unlock a mechanism Benson calls the *relaxation response*, an innate pattern that is antagonistic to the fight-or-flight reaction. By calling up the relaxation response, the individual to some degree neutralizes the effects of the primitive fight-or-flight reaction.

Benson's work clearly suggests that TM is not sleep. During sleep, oxygen consumption falls about 8 percent below normal, and it requires about four or five hours to reach this stage. During meditation, oxygen consumption falls from 10 to 20 percent, and this tends to occur within the first three minutes of meditation. Another difference between sleep and meditation noted by Benson is that alpha waves increase during meditation but are not associated with sleep. Alpha waves seem to be associated with alert relaxation. The finding that meditators produce a large percentage of alpha waves lends further credence to the TM claims. Benson also notes that blood lactate decreases during meditation. This is considered significant because it is purported that a high level of blood lactate is associated with anxiety. Sleep, notes Benson, is not meditation; and meditation is not sleep. The one cannot replace the other. Each has a different function and a different value.

Benson is not, however, particularly enchanted with the rituals associated with TM. He has had persons meditate upon the word *one*, selected arbitrarily, and has found the same physiological changes as those produced by persons meditating upon a mantra especially selected for them by a TM trainer. Benson feels that his laboratory research has simply validated age-old wisdom, that it has produced no innovations in and of itself. Stripping the relaxation response of any religious, cultic, or mystical associations, Benson says that four conditions are helpful in bringing forth the relaxation response: (1) a quiet environment; (2) a mental device, used to shift one's attention to a constant stimulus; (3) a passive attitude, an attitude in which one "lets" relaxation happen rather than "makes" it happen; and (4) a comfortable position.

Benson warns that although a little meditation may be beneficial, a lot of meditation may be harmful. Excessive elicitation of the relaxation response for prolonged periods of time may produce hallucinations similar to those experienced during sensory deprivation. Such adverse side effects do not seem to occur, says Benson, among those who meditate for ten or twenty minutes at a time twice a day.

Benson asserts in his book *The Relaxation Response* that the relaxation response is a natural gift, that anyone can turn it on and use it. He concludes, "We could all greatly benefit by the reincorporation of the Relaxation Response into our daily lives. At the present time, most of us are simply not making use of this remarkable, innate, neglected asset" (p. 125).

Briefly, meditation is an ancient technique. Its practitioners have variously claimed that it is a tool for achieving *samadhi, satori*, and serenity. There are several kinds of meditation. All of them, however, require concentration and the focusing of attention on a limited range of stimuli. Transcendental meditation is a Yogic technique that appears to call forth an innate relaxation response. The relaxation response appears to be antagonistic to the fight-or-flight reaction and, as such, may be useful in combating stress-induced diseases.

CRITIQUE

There are few domains of psychological investigation that evoke more passionate claims and counterclaims than transpersonal psychology. Speaking of "Eastern science" in *The Psychology of Consciousness,* Ornstein comments, ". . . there is no other area of human experience, save perhaps sexuality, about which so much garbage has been written" (p. 116). And Ornstein tends to be favorably disposed toward transpersonal psychology! Let us survey a few of the reservations that may be expressed about the field of transpersonal psychology.

1 Faultfinders readily level many put-downs of transpersonal psychology. It is accused of being replete with fuzzy thinking, useless ideas, and idle speculation. It is said that the transpersonal approach is based on personal experience not amenable to the experimental method, that the transpersonal approach is hostile to Western science and its research methods. It is feared by some that transpersonal psychology represents the potential destruction of all that academic psychology has worked so hard for—objectivity in behavioral study.

2 Censurers of the transpersonal approach can become particularly vocal when they speak of the claims made in favor of paranormal phenomena such as extrasensory perception or psychokinesis. These "abilities" are seen as absurd. The censurer claims that there is really no hard evidence in favor of psychic powers. There are only colorful anecdotes and experiments of doubtful validity.

3 The skeptic takes a negative view of the claim made by mystics that their minds penetrate past the world of appearances and arrive at a perception of the True Reality. To the skeptic, mystical experiences are hallucinatory phenomena similar to those experienced during sensory deprivation. The doctrine of *empiricism*, a key doctrine in Western philosophy and science, states that we can know about the world only through our sense organs. The mystical approach and the empirical approach are highly incompatible.

4   The orthodox thinker says that transpersonal psychology tends to take the individual away from involvement with the world. If the view that everything is maya is taken to its logical conclusion, then life as we know it is a mere illusion and, in consequence, rather meaningless. Even loving one's spouse or one's child are maya. For some, the Eastern view would seem to make of life a cruel joke. The view that all experience is maya is said to be reminiscent of the thinking of certain demoralized early existential philosophers who saw everything as absurd and unreal.

5   Looking at the negative side of Yoga, its goal of *samadhi*, the identification of mind with Supreme Consciousness, hardly seems to be a worthwhile end in and of itself. If the person who "trips out" does not bring something back of value for others, it merely seems that superconsciousness is a form of self-indulgence. There are yogis who spend several hours a day in an ecstatic state, and one wonders if they are not "hooked" on *samadhi* somewhat like drug users might be addicted to a particular drug. It is true that the Yoga tradition warns against the misuse of *samadhi.* Nonetheless, it would appear that for some the warning is not enough.

6   Cynics note that much of what esoteric disciplines have to say is known to Western science in different language. They take the attitude that there really isn't much that is new beneath the sun. Students of experimental psychology and perception know the psychological world is our construction. The philosophy of modern science teaches that so-called things or perceptual objects are space-time events. (Recall that this point was also made by Korzybski, as noted in Chapter Four.) Maslow, Rogers, Perls, and others—like Zen—speak in favor of spontaneous behavior. Thus the cynic may yawn upon hearing the ideas of transpersonal psychology and ask, "So what else is new?"

7   Zen says that concepts represent maya. Yet Zen cannot do without concepts itself. Against dualism, it nonetheless sets up its own dualisms, such as the enlightened versus the unenlightened person. If dualisms are arbitrary, then there are just persons—neither enlightened nor unenlightened. If you were to challenge a Zen master with this observation, he might smile and answer, "You are right." But if this is so, there is nothing to seek because the division between the *satori* experience and ordinary perception is also arbitrary. "Quite so," the Zen master might agree. And you are nowhere—like a dog chasing his own tail. This sense-nonsense approach of Zen leaves many an initial enthusiast in a totally baffled state. The critic of Zen feels that a philosophy that purports to be down to Earth and back to Nature should be direct and unequivocal. Zen seems to lack the very attributes it claims to have.

8   Advocates of transpersonal psychology often seem to smugly act as if "we know something you don't know." They frequently appear to be playing the game of "Mine is better than yours." Pretentious posturing plays no role of value in human adjustment and personal growth and reduces transpersonal psychology to a fad. The superficial cultist may use transpersonal psychology as a put-down of the way people in the Western world traditionally think and behave. This is more a criticism of the way some people respond to transpersonal psychology than it is a criticism of transpersonal psychology itself. The venerable traditions of such disciplines as Yoga and Zen would appear to deserve better than the vapid attention of dilettantes.

In brief, at one end of the pole is the tough-minded psychologist with his anti-intuitive and proanalytical stance. At the other end of the pole is the tender-minded thinker with his prointuitive and antianalytical stance, declaiming in favor of transpersonal psychology. It is difficult to reconcile the two stances in a meaningful way. Nonetheless, some sort of meeting of the minds, some sort of compromise is necessary between the two orientations. What is needed is balance, not blind enthusiasm for, or categorical rejection of, transpersonal psychology.

IMPLICATIONS FOR ADJUSTMENT AND GROWTH

A wit once wrote:

What is mind?
No matter.
What is matter?
Never mind.

Transpersonal psychology is in total disagreement with those four lines of doggerel. Transpersonal psychology asserts that mind does matter, that mental science can and does exist, and that this mental science can be used by the individual to transform his life. Yoga is probably the most well-developed example of this point of view, but other esoteric psychologies make the same point to greater and lesser degrees. The following are some of the ways transpersonal psychology may contribute to growth and adjustment.

1   In a broad and general sense, transpersonal psychology enhances our sense of human potential. Like existential-humanistic psychology, with which it has a great kinship, it says that we are unique beings. We have tremendous capacities and unknown powers, and the human spirit may be liberated to soar to untold heights. The book *Jonathan Livingston Seagull* by author-flyer Richard Bach portrays the transpersonal point of view in allegorical form, telling of the seagull Jonathan, who finds that his existence is boundless:

Don't believe what your eyes are telling you. All they show is limitation. Look with your understanding. Find out what you already know, and you'll see the way to fly. (p. 125)

The tremendous success enjoyed by *Jonathan Livingston Seagull* suggests that the transpersonal orientation strikes a common chord in many people.

2   Transpersonal psychology reminds us to not be taken in by superficialities. It directs us to look below the surface of our lives. With maya and similar doctrines, it asserts that we must not be addicted to narrow ambitions, small dreams, and petty emotions. They are unworthy of a whole human being.

3   What transpersonal psychology has to say about finding the Middle Path seems to be of particular importance. This point is not, of course, unique to transpersonal psychology. More than two thousand years ago, the Western philosopher Aristotle spoke of negative excesses of any kind. And Ernest Jones, a psychoanalyst, once commented, ''The art of living is the art of compromise.'' Instead of discrediting the Eastern view of the Middle Path, these observations lend greater credence to it. The wisdom of the ages teaches that effective personalities have the capacity to reconcile opposing demands within themselves.

4   Transpersonal psychology, like speculative philosophy, stimulates us to think profoundly about the nature of human existence. The Zen *koan,* the questions of Krishnamurti, and other problems posed by transpersonal psychology, prod us to reevaluate our assumptions about life. The questions of a naive child frequently help an adult see the world from a fresh perspective. Similarly, the ''absurd'' questions posed by transpersonal psychology can freshen stale perceptions.

5   One of the more valuable aspects of transpersonal psychology is the stress it places on voluntary control. People are not the slaves of habits, desires, or their assumptions about the world. There are, says transpersonal psychology, ways of breaking free from psychological chains. Yoga and Zen, for example, offer explicit techniques for self-liberation.

6   The Yogic techniques seem to be of particular promise in helping to reduce the impact of stress-induced diseases. Internal self-control strategies devised by yogis may be combined with biofeedback training. The two modes are quite compatible. In tandem, Yoga and biofeedback offer hope to sufferers from psychosomatic ailments.

7   Transpersonal psychology gives us a broad view of human existence, placing the individual into a larger space-time perspective. Seeing one's life as if from a great distance helps the person to become more objective about his feelings and his behavior. The transpersonal approach is intended to introduce a certain "psychological distance" between the person and his immediate situation. If the intent meets with success in a particular case, the person in question does not feel so hung up on his problems. Their significance fades when contrasted to the vast panorama of eternity, infinity, and the ever-changing universe. Unwieldy psychological boulders are sometimes reduced to manageable psychological pebbles by the transpersonal approach.

In a hard world of physical danger, disease, war, overpopulation, and other maladies, transpersonal psychology is at once the oldest and the newest star on the psychological horizon. It represents the reappearance, in the Western world, of the star of mental science. In a hard world, perhaps there is a place for unorthodox/subjective "soft" transpersonal psychology.

SUMMARY AND SELF-TEST

1 Transpersonal psychology is sometimes called a "Fourth Force" in psychology.

T   F

2 A mystic is a person who believes that through the use of intuition he can have a direct experience wtih Ultimate Reality.
T   F

3 The doctrine of maya asserts that our perceptions are in fact identical with reality.
T   F

4 The doctrine of maya says that all suffering occurs because the person attaches himself to reality.
T   F

5 No distinction is made in the Castaneda books between ordinary reality and nonordinary reality.
T   F

6 The exercise of what don Juan refers to as "controlled folly" requires that one shift one's attention beyond the immediate event.
T   F

7 The term *phenomenal world* is used to refer to the world as perceived.
T   F

8 The Tanner-Swets theory of visual detection suggests that perception can be altered by motives and expectancies.
T   F

9 The general aim of all of the Yoga techniques is spiritual growth.
T   F

10 Jnana Yoga is "Royal" Yoga, the oldest form of Yoga.
T   F

11 According to Yoga, when the Kundalini reaches the crown *chakra,* the yogi experiences *samadhi.*
T   F

12   In Yoga philosophy it is considered justified to get "hooked" on *samadhi*; the yogi has no responsibility to his fellow human beings.
T   F

13   Yoga rejects the possibility of paranormal phenomena.
T   F

14   The research on parapsychology is easy to evaluate objectively.
T   F

15   Zen holds that we are an indivisible aspect of Nature.
T   F

16   The Fourth Noble Truth proposed by Chinese Buddhism is that there is an Eightfold Middle Path between excessive desire and excessive self-denial.
T   F

17   Zen sets itself against the world we live in.
T   F

18   Suzuki summarizes the world view of Zen with such words as analytical, discriminative, inductive, intellectual, and objective.
T   F

19   The Zen principle of no-thingness teaches that pencils, cups, tables and so forth are not things, but abstractions we have made from the great flow of the Tao.
T   F

20   Zen says that it is a mistake to make a subject-object dichotomy between oneself and the world.
T   F

21   *Satori* is quite different from the Western psychology concept of insight.
T   F

22   The Rinzai school of Zen emphasizes the *koan*, the paradoxical question, as a means of hastening the arrival of *satori*.
T   F

23   Zen teaches that the enlightened person has exalted goals and places his prime interest in success.
T   F

24   According to Zen, spontaneity is a characteristic of the enlightened person.
T   F

25 Advocates of meditation claim that it can lift its practitioners out of the mundane world of everyday affairs to a calm place in their own minds.

T   F

26 Intellect-oriented meditation and feeling-oriented meditation require concentration; body-oriented meditation and action-oriented meditation do not require concentration.

T   F

27 Transcendental meditation (TM) is derived from feeling-oriented meditation in which a mantra, a sacred word or chant, is used.

T   F

28 Hans Selye, a pioneer researcher on stress-induced diseases, is a hostile critic of TM.

T   F

29 According to Herbert Benson, TM appears to unlock a mechanism he calls the "relaxation response."

T   F

30 Benson says that only two conditions are required to bring forth the relaxation response: (1) a quiet environment and (2) a mental device, used to shift one's attention to a constant stimulus.

T   F

ANSWER KEY

1 *True.* Transpersonal psychology is sometimes called a "Fourth Force" in psychology.

2 *True.* A mystic is a person who believes that through the use of intuition he can have a direct experience with Ultimate Reality.

3 *False.* The doctrine of maya asserts that we mistakenly take our perceptions for reality itself.

4 *False.* The doctrine of maya says that all suffering occurs because the person attaches himself to an illusion.

5 *False.* The Castaneda books make a distinction between ordinary reality and nonordinary reality.

6 *True.* The exercise of what don Juan refers to as "controlled folly" requires that one shift one's attention beyond the immediate event.

7 *True.* The term *phenomenal world* is used to refer to the world as perceived.

8 *True.* The Tanner-Swets theory of visual detection suggests that perception can be altered by motives and expectancies.

9 *True.* The general aim of all of the Yoga techniques is spiritual growth.

10 *False.* Raja Yoga is "Royal" Yoga, the oldest form of Yoga.

11 *True.* According to Yoga, when the Kundalini reaches the crown *chakra,* the yogi experiences *samadhi.*

12 *False.* In Yoga philosophy it is considered an error to get "hooked" on *samadhi*; the yogi has a responsibility to his fellow human beings.

13 *False.* Yoga accepts the possibility of paranormal phenomena.

14 *False.* The research on parapsychology is difficult to evaluate objectively.

15 *True.* Zen holds that we are an indivisible aspect of Nature.

16 *True.* The Fourth Noble Truth proposed by Chinese Buddhism is that there is an Eightfold Middle Path between excessive desire and excessive self-denial.

17 *False.* Zen does not set itself against the world we live in; it appreciates the world we live in.

18 *False.* Suzuki summarizes the world view of Zen with such words as synthetic, totalizing, integrative, and subjective.

19 *True.* The Zen principle of no-thingness teaches that pencils, cups, tables, and so forth are not things, but abstractions we have made from the great flow of the Tao.

20 *True.* Zen says that it is a mistake to make a subject-object dichotomy between oneself and the world.

21 *False.* Satori is quite similar to the Western psychology concept of insight.

22 *True.* The Rinzai school of Zen emphasizes the *koan,* the paradoxical question, as a means of hastening the arrival of *satori.*

23 *False.* Zen teaches that the enlightened person does not have exalted goals and that he has overcome the opposites of success and failure.

24 *True.* According to Zen, spontaneity is a characteristic of the enlightened person.

25 *True.* Advocates of meditation claim that it can lift its practitioners out of the mundane world of everyday affairs to a calm place in their own minds.

26 *False.* All four of the types of meditation require concentration.

27 *True.* Transcendental meditation (TM) is derived from feeling-oriented meditation in which a *mantra*, a sacred word or chant, is used.

28 *False.* Hans Selye, a pioneer researcher on stress-induced diseases, has favorable things to say about TM.

29 *True.* According to Herbert Benson, TM appears to unlock a mechanism he calls the "relaxation response."

30 *False.* Benson says that four conditions are helpful in bringing forth the relaxation response: (1) a quiet environment, (2) a mental device, (3) a passive attitude, and (4) a comfortable position.

DISCUSSION QUESTIONS

PERCEPTION: THE SPELL OF MAYA

1 Do you agree with the doctrine of maya that all of us live in a kind of waking dream?

2 Do you accept the distinction made in the Castaneda books between ordinary reality and nonordinary reality?

3 Can you see any practical value to the distinction made by don Juan between merely looking and *seeing*?

4 Can you think of a personal example in which a motive or an expectancy has affected your perception?

YOGA: AN ANCIENT MENTAL SCIENCE

1 If you were to actually be interested in the practice of Yoga, which of the five basic kinds of Yoga would be most compatible with your personality?

2 Do you believe that the "torrential bliss" of *samadhi* does in fact represent identification of the individual consciousness with Cosmic Consciousness? Or are you a skeptic, taking the position that *samadhi* is a kind of delusion?

3 In your opinion, do psi abilities, such as extrasensory perception, psychokinesis, and telepathy, actually exist? What are some of the pros and cons concerning the existence of psi abilities?

ZEN: THE ENLIGHTENED LIFE

1 Zen holds that our true nature is not divided from Nature itself, that we are an indivisible aspect of Nature. What significance do you attach to this point of view?

2 Does it seem plausible that acceptance of the Tao and the Four Noble Truths would in fact free a human being from unnecessary suffering?

3 How does the world view of the Zen poet Basho differ from the world view of the Western poet Tennyson? Is there any way to reconcile these two world views?

4 The Zen principle of no-twoness teaches that most dichotomies are false. What is your reaction to this teaching?

5 Have you ever had anything resembling a *satori* experience?

6 Do you know anyone who seems similar to the Zen description of an enlightened person? How does this person differ from other persons?

MEDITATION: THE SERENE MIND

1 Have you had any direct experience with formal kinds of meditation? If so, what is your evaluation of meditation?

2 Do you view the current interest in transcendental meditation (TM) as a passing fad? Or do you feel that the interest in TM will grow over the years?

3 Advocates of TM assert that its beneficial effects will in the long run free many persons from a dependence on such drugs as antihypertensive agents and antianxiety agents. Does this seem to be a Utopian dream to you? Or do you think that much of the enthusiasm for TM is justified?

4 What is the fight-or-flight reaction? Does it seem credible to you that the relaxation response described by Benson can be used to neutralize the effects of the fight-or-flight reaction?

REFERENCES

Albertson, E. *Spiritual Yoga for the Millions.* Los Angeles: Sherbourne Press, 1969.

Bach, R. *Jonathan Livingston Seagull.* New York: Macmillan Co., 1970.

Benson, H. *The Relaxation Response.* New York: William Morrow & Co., 1975.

Blakney, R. B. *The Way of Life: Lao-tzu.* New York: New American Library, 1955.

Bloomfield, H. H., Cain, M. P., and Jaffe, D. T. *Transcendental Meditation: Discovering Inner Energy and Overcoming Stress.* New York: Delacorte Press, 1975.

Castaneda, C. *A Separate Reality.* New York: Simon & Schuster, 1971.

―――. *The Teachings of don Juan: A Yaqui Way of Knowledge.* New York, Ballantine Books, 1968.

Chance, P. "Telepathy Could Be Real." *Psychology Today* (February 1976), vol. 9, pp. 40–44.

Chaudhuri, H. *Integral Yoga.* Wheaton, Ill.: Theosophical Publishing House, 1965.

Friedman, H. *The Amazing Universe.* Washington, D.C.: National Geographic Society, 1975.

Fromm, E., Suzuki, D. T., and DeMartino, R. *Zen Buddhism and Psychoanalysis.* New York: Harper & Row, 1970.

Henderson, C. W. *Awakening.* Englewood Cliffs, N.J.: Prentice-Hall, 1975.

Herrigel, E. *The Method of Zen.* New York: Random House, 1960.

Hilton, J. *Lost Horizon.* New York: William Morrow & Co., 1933.

Kennett, J. *Selling Water by the River.* New York: Random House, 1972.

Krishnamurti, J. *Think on These Things.* New York: Harper & Row, 1964.

LeShan, L. *How to Meditate.* Boston: Little, Brown & Co., 1974.

Mishra, R. S. *Yoga Sutras.* New York: Julian Press, 1963.

Ornstein, R. E. *The Psychology of Consciousness.* New York: Penguin Books, 1972.

Pearce, J. *The Crack in the Cosmic Egg.* New York: Julian Press, 1971.

Prabhavananda, Swami, and Manchester, F., eds. *The Upanishads.* New York: New American Library, 1957.

Rhine, J. B. *The Reach of the Mind.* New York: William Sloane Associates, 1947.

Smith, A. *Powers of Mind.* New York: Random House, 1975.

Stace, W. *The Teachings of the Mystics.* New York: New American Library of World Literature, 1960.

Suzuki, D. T. *What Is Zen?* New York: Harper & Row, 1972.

Tanner, W. P., Jr., and Swets, J. A. "A Decision-Making Theory of Visual Detection." *Psychological Review*, 61 (1954), 401–409.

Toben, B., Sarfatti, J., and Wolf, F. *Space-Time and Beyond.* New York: E. P. Dutton & Co., 1975.

Vishnudevananda, Swami. *The Complete Illustrated Book of Yoga.* New York: Julian Press, 1960.

Watts, A. *Meditation.* New York: Pyramid Communications, 1974.

———. *The Way of Zen.* New York: Random House, 1957.

Wood, E. *Zen Dictionary.* Rutland, Vt.: Charles E. Tuttle Co., 1957.

Yogananda, P. *Autobiography of a Yogi.* Los Angeles: Self-Realization Fellowship, 1974.

Wittgenstein, L. As quoted in *Change.* Watzlawick, P., Weakland, J., and Fisch, R., authors. New York: W. W. Norton & Co., 1974.

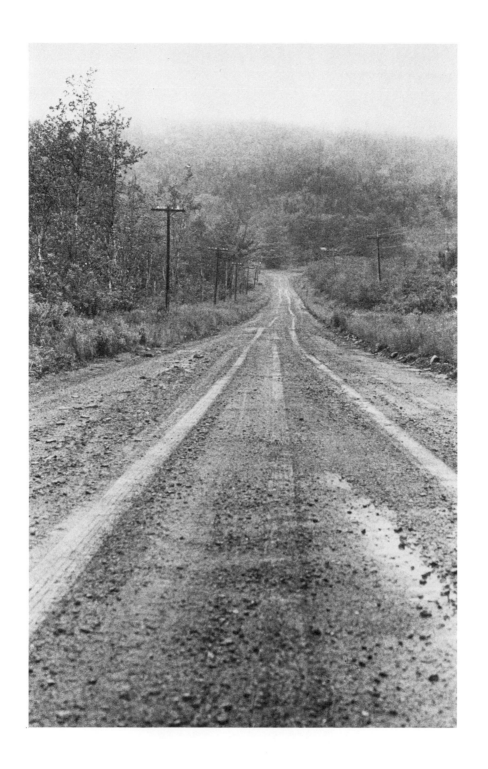

CHAPTER 9
SYNTHESIS:
IS THERE
A PATHWAY
OF PATHWAYS?

Is there a Royal Road to better living?

OVERVIEW

OUTLINE

Is there a pathway of pathways leading to greater adjustment and personal growth? *Systematic thinkers*, advocates of one particular school of thought, answer yes. The Royal Road to better living is the one that they speak and write about. On the other hand, there are *eclectic thinkers*, represented in psychology by those who pick and choose from various schools of thought those conceptions that seem to be of particular value. The eclectic psychologist does not completely reject or embrace any one mode of thinking about adjustment and growth. Although the majority of psychologists are somewhat dissatisfied with eclecticism, they feel that it is the only realistic stance to take toward a field that is as profuse with ideas as psychology. Thus the consensus statement of contemporary psychology is: No, there is no single pathway that is *the* pathway leading toward greater adjustment and personal growth.

Eclecticism has much to recommend it. But it also has its pitfalls. Psychologists Ernest Hilgard and Gordon Bower warn, in *Theories of Learning*, that if opposing points of view are presented as equally plausible, a choice between them may seem to be completely arbitrary (p. 13). They note that a person may fall into a vapid eclecticism, relying on the general formula "There's much to be said on all sides." The warning has merit. On the other hand, the choice is not between being systematic or eclectic. A *dynamic*, as opposed to vapid, eclecticism is possible. The individual may have strong leanings, personal preferences, and biases and still be generally eclectic in his approach to psychology. There is room for passion and conviction within an eclectic position. An illustration of how a psychologist can have a dynamic eclectic orientation is provided in an autobiographical sketch by Paul T. Young, one of the deans of American psychology:

In the current social unrest and turmoil over problems of war and peace, exploding populations, poverty, pollution of the environment, crime and violence, revolution, and others, I am sure that one must view human nature as it actually is—partly rational, partly emotional, partly dominated by habit, partly spiritual. . . . My approach to behavioral problems has been eclectic and multidisciplinary. (p. 352)

Young clearly identifies himself as an eclectic, but he is not bland in his approach to psychology. He was the winner of the Distinguished Scientific Contribution Award of the American Psychological Association in 1965, and he expresses strong biases:

I have never abandoned the concept of consciousness. I continue to believe that the science of psychology has a unique responsibility to analyze and interpret subjective phenomena such as perceptions, mental images, the experiences of memory and thought, the awareness of feelings, and emotions. (p. 339)

Like Young, as you survey the seven pathways toward adjustment and growth discussed in this book, you need not fall into a vapid eclecticism. In terms of you, the individual, all approaches are *not* equally valid. One approach will click for you; another approach will leave you cold. It is natural to have preferences for one way of thinking over another. Only by following the conceptions that directly appeal to you will you be able to usefully employ those conceptions. As already noted, the eclectic position does not completely reject or embrace any one approach. None-theless, differences in emphasis, in which one approach is greatly favored over another, are possible.

RECURRENT ADJUSTMENT-GROWTH ISSUES

Although an eclectic orientation recognizes the valid distinctions among the seven pathways discussed in this book, it should be noted that the pathways crisscross, overlap, and are not totally distinct from each other. Psychologists representing different schools of thought often say similar things with different words. Freud's id, Berne's Child, and Perls's underdog are similar concepts. Assertiveness training in behavioral psychology is similar to the concept of authentic living, or "being real," in existential-humanistic psychology. Korzybski's view of "things" as space-time events is paralleled in the Zen principle of no-thingness. Many other specific parallels could be easily drawn. But let us draw away from specific parallels.

Let us, instead, take a giant step backward so that we can view the pathways as if from a great distance. Details now fade, but broad general patterns emerge. We see that there are certain recurrent adjustment-growth issues, issues that cut across all the pathways. Like two-edged swords, the issues tend to present themselves as pairs of opposites: (1) freedom versus determinism, (2) unconscious versus conscious, (3) motives and habits versus thought and will, and (4) group similarities versus individual differences. The issues will be briefly sketched, and then a unifying statement will be made.

FREEDOM VERSUS DETERMINISM

The philosophy of *determinism* asserts that all behavior is caused. It is caused by genetic factors, motives, learned responses, or some other specifiable source. This orientation does not allow for human freedom. If accepted, determinism relieves the individual of Ultimate Responsibility for his life. He did not choose his genetic structure, his biological drives, his conditioning experiences, his situation in life, and so forth. He is the "victim" of forces beyond his control. In contrast, the opposing orientation, known as *voluntarism*, asserts that free will is a reality, that we can make real choices, and that we are not the pawns of fate.

UNCONSCIOUS VERSUS CONSCIOUS

A powerful and influential contention is that our behavior is determined largely by unconscious mental processes. Psychoanalysis amplified this contention and made it into the keystone of its system. In view of the fact that for a number of years psychoanalysis dominated the psychological landscape along with behaviorism, the significance of unconscious factors cannot be dismissed lightly. The counterorientation is the contention that consciousness is both real and powerful and that its reality and power make a difference. This second view finds its strongest expression in rational analysis and existential-humanistic psychology.

MOTIVES AND HABITS VERSUS THOUGHT AND WILL

The two great "mechanical" forces underlying human behavior are motives and habits. They are mechanical in that they represent both involuntary and automatic action. Our basic drives are said to arise from deep sources within ourselves. These are our primary motives. Our secondary drives, or learned motives, are acquired by conditioning. Many of our behaviors are also acquired by conditioning and are said to be habits. Also, our perceptions of the world are colored by our motives and our habits. We would seem to be "locked in" to a fixed set of behaviors by the two giant processes of motivation and learning.

Although motivation and learning are accepted as significant processes, two opposing conceptions are often brought forth as principal counterprocesses: thinking and willing. It is said that we can think, that we have the capacity to reflect, to analyze, and to solve problems. For example, psychologists favorably disposed to rational analysis assert that thought to some degree can modify the impact of motives and habits. It is also said that we can will; that we are not only driven creatures, but that we can at least sometimes be driving human beings. Existential-humanistic psychologists expound this point of view. (As noted in Chapter Seven, the "driving" example was given by Rollo May.)

GROUP SIMILARITIES VERSUS INDIVIDUAL DIFFERENCES

Systematic thinkers tend to favor the view that the similarities among individuals are more important than the differences among individuals.

This view tends to "swamp out" the particular person. His idiosyncracies, his interests, his specific talents, his unique potentialities are reduced to "error variance" in an experiment. The grand goal is to organize data into parsimonious theoretical statements. The living individual, seeking information about adjustment and growth, often cares little for the elegant theories of the systematist, however. He is looking for practical information that will help him cope with his problems and deal effectively with the challenges of life. Thus he is attracted to views which assert that individual differences are more important than the similarities among individuals. He wants to know what is applicable to his particular life situation, and he tends to be favorably disposed to views that respect his unique personhood.

A UNIFYING STATEMENT

Pairs of opposites such as the ones presented in the previous pages are not easily reconciled. They represent broad points of view, not scientifically testable hypotheses. And because they are recurrent issues, we are probably best off if we learn to live with the tension of their bipolarity. It is an old observation that opposing conceptions define each other. Alan Watts says, in *Meditation*, "I have a friend who was born blind. She has no idea what darkness is" (p. 49).

Ancient Eastern philosophy understands pairs of conceptual opposites in terms of *yin* and *yang*, the negative and positive aspects of the world. Such dualities as right and wrong, light and darkness, and good and bad are not seen as realities in themselves, but as the products of the thinking-perceiving process. Similarly, pairs of opposites, such as determinism versus freedom, can be seen as contrasts instead of mutually exclusive opposites. This is a difficult model to accept. We are well trained in either-or thinking, and it would seem that a choice must be made. But it is well to remind ourselves that we are merely striving to make a choice among *concepts*, ways we imagine reality to be, not reality itself. This point is as ancient as the writings of Lao-tzu and as contemporary as the modern philosophy of science. Let us now elaborate this last point.

FIGURE 9.1 Ancient Eastern philosophy understands pairs of conceptual opposites in terms of yin and yang.

OF TRUTH AND MODELS

The modern philosophy of science teaches that our various scientific theories are not Truth. They could be Truth only if each one was reality itself. They are statements *about* reality. Thus they have the status of conceptions. That is why contradictory conceptions can stand for centuries. It is because they are each a glimpse from a particular angle of whatever reality "is." This last point is implicit in Plato's allegory of the cave (Chapter Eight), in general semantics, in Kantian philosophy, in the doctrine of empiricism, in the yin and yang of Eastern philosophy, in the doctrine of maya, and in the experimental study of perception. This is why, although we may yearn for the one True Pathway toward a better life, we must content ourselves with the lesser achievement of finding incomplete and sometimes contradictory pathways. We grasp reality not directly, but through our conceptions about it. Our conceptions are the building blocks of what philosophers of science call "models."

KINDS OF MODELS

What is a model? A *model* is something that represents the real thing. For example, a model of a jet airliner suggests to us what the actual airplane is like; but it is clearly not the airplane itself. Similarly, psychological models represent real processes, but must not themselves be confused with the actual processes. In the sciences, including psychology,

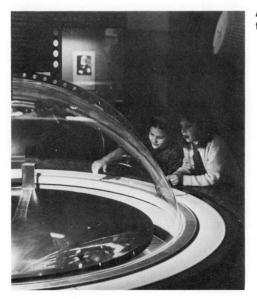

A model is something that represents the real thing.

three kinds of models are used: (1) physical models, (2) ordinary language models, and (3) mathematical models.

Physical models.   A physical model is made out of wood, metal, glass, or some other substance. Say that Professor Jones brings into a psychology class a clear glass bowl. He pours water into the bowl and says, "Let the waterline represent the division between the conscious mind and the unconscious mind. The entire container and its contents represent the mind." Now he drops a few Ping-Pong balls into the container, and they float. "The floating balls are like conscious ideas." He drops some small stones into the water, and they sink. "These are like repressed ideas." The demonstration continues. Professor Jones is using a crude physical model to represent certain aspects of depth psychology. Of course, more sophisticated physical models can be built. An example of advanced physical model-building is provided by using computers to simulate processes of the central nervous system. As we watch the computer mimic nervous-system action, we may acquire new insights about actual biological processes.

Ordinary language models.   An ordinary language model is made out of words, sentences, and concepts. The "substances" that make it up are the symbols by which human communication is possible. The great danger of ordinary language models is that they do not seem to be models at all. They seem to be the Truth itself. Physical models are clearly not the things they represent. But a theory of psychology, such as psychoanalytic theory, can be widely held—by even relatively sophisticated persons—to be a reality. Clear thinking demands that we recognize ordinary language models as symbolic conceptions about behavioral processes, not as the processes themselves.

The bulk of this book has been made up of elaborations on numerous ordinary language models. One of the harshest criticisms we can make of almost all of the models is that they use the language of truth, implicitly suggesting that the model in question is not a model, but "the real thing." The majority of theorists do not say, "Here is a useful conception." Instead, they say, "This is the way it is." This seemingly trivial distinction is the source of endless confusion, making us feel that we have to take sides when none have to be taken.

Mathematical models.   A mathematical model, like an ordinary language model, is made out of symbols. *Numerals*, used to represent quantities, and *operators*, used to manipulate sets of numerals, are the principal symbols used in mathematical models. For example, $2+3=5$ is a mathematical model. The 2, the 3, and the 5 represent quantities. They are not quantities in and of themselves, only symbols. (The underlying quantities represented by symbols are called *numbers* in contrast to the numerals, which are merely marks on paper.) The plus sign and the equals sign are operators. They "operate" on the numerals and transform them into other forms.

Just as ordinary words can be used to represent behavioral processes, mathematical equations can be used to mimic these same processes. A substantial amount of work has been done, for example, on mathematical models for learning. *Stochastic processes*, probability processes in which events are neither wholly dependent on nor wholly independent of past occurrences, can be elegantly represented by mathematical models. *Stochastic Models for Learning* by Robert Bush and Frederick Mosteller provides one example of how it is possible to build a mathematical model that simultaneously incorporates the contrasting concepts of determinism and voluntarism into a single formula.

Mathematical models have not played a large part in the psychology of adjustment and growth. Because they do not communicate their meanings in familiar terms, they are of little direct value to the general reader. Also, mathematical models tend to deal with a limited range of behavioral phenomena. They focus on *molecular*, or "small," behaviors as opposed to *molar*, or "big," behaviors, the wide-ranging response patterns to the problems and challenges of daily living discussed in prior chapters. Of the three kinds of models discussed in this secion—physical, ordinary language, and mathematical—the one that is overwhelmingly favored as the favorite mode of presenting adjustment-growth pathways is the ordinary language model.

ALLEGORIES

Allegories are useful devices for conveying ideas in a richer form. It is all well and good to understand intellectually that ordinary language models are not the Truth, only ways of apprehending it. Nonetheless, this abstract understanding may fail to hit home in any significant way. That is why authors often turn to such devices as allegories to illustrate their meanings in more concrete form.

Perhaps the most famous allegory used to distinguish between the concepts that we have about reality and reality itself is Plato's formulation of the prisoner in the cave. The prisoner sees only shadows and takes these appearances to be the world itself. Plato's allegory was referred to in Chapter Eight. Another well-known allegory used to convey essentially the same point is "The Blind Men and the Elephant" by John Godfrey Saxe:

It was six men of Indostan
To learning much inclined,
Who went to see the elephant
(Though all of them were blind),
That each by observation
Might satisfy his mind.

The First approached the elephant,
And happening to fall
Against his broad and sturdy side,
At once began to bawl:
"God bless me! But the elephant
Is nothing but a wall!"

The Second, feeling of the tusk,
Cried: "Ho! What have we here
So very round and smooth and sharp?
To me 'tis mighty clear
This wonder of an elephant
Is very like a spear!"

The Third approached the animal,
And happening to take
The squirming trunk within his hands,
Thus boldly up and spake:
"I see," quoth he, "The elephant
Is very like a snake!"

The Fourth reached out his eager hand,
And felt about the knee:
"What most this wondrous beast is like
Is mighty plain" quoth he;
" 'Tis clear enough the elephant
Is very like a tree."

The Fifth, who chanced to touch the ear,
Said "E'en the blindest man
Can tell what this resembles most;
Deny the fact who can,
The marvel of an elephant
Is very like a fan!"

The Sixth no sooner had begun
About the beast to grope,
Thus, seizing on the swinging tail
That fell within his scope,
"I see," quoth he, "The elephant
Is very like a rope!"

And so these men of Indostan
Disputed loud and long
Each in his own opinion
Exceeding stiff and strong
Though each was partly in the right,
And all were in the wrong!*

Like the blind men approaching the elephant, each explorer into the domain of psychology comes with a different vision of reality depending on his preconceptions, the quality of his data, and the particular aspect (or aspects) of behavior he chooses to study. That is why there is no single adequate psychology of adjustment and growth, but a set of psychologies. Each psychology has value in its own right, none being completely correct or completely incorrect. Again, an intelligent eclecticism is demanded. The individual must pluck the best from each formulation in terms of his unique interests and needs.

PSYCHOLOGICAL HEALTH

Chapter One had a section titled "Conceptions of Mental Illness." We have come full circle now, and it is fitting for the book to close with a section on psychological health. Let us stop a moment to ponder the fact that we also approach psychological health through concepts, the mental models we construct about it in our minds. Thus one person's idea of psychological health may not square with another person's idea. Forewarned, let us explore some possibilities.

INFORMAL CONCEPTIONS

In a loose sense, almost everybody "knows" what psychological health is. The problem is to articulate it. Many informal expressions exist to describe persons who have psychological health: "He's really got it all together." "She's got a clean act." "Tom is really an OK person." "Mary really understands herself." "Bill knows where he's going in life and how he's going to get there." "I've never met a happier, more optimistic person than Nancy." "Harry is a person with a lot of wisdom."

I asked students in an introductory psychology class to write brief responses to the following question: "What is your conception of psychological health?" Unedited, here are a few of the responses:

Being able to deal with life and the mental problems it can bring. Finding solutions to problems dealing in health. The state of mind can have a psychological effect on your health.

To me this means the state of mind that you're in. How well you deal with people and occurrences in the world around you. Also, how you deal with the worlds other people tend to live in. People that are in good psychological health are able to be at ease and deal well with what goes on or comes along. But those in bad psychological health are kind of lost and confused with what's happening.

How healthy one's mind is in terms of outlook on life, how he views himself and others. Being aware of the natural world and things beyond our reason. Keeping

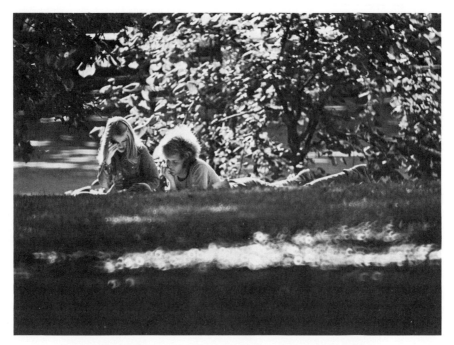

In a loose sense, we all "know" what psychological health is.

an open mind, not closed by fears, mainly of human nature. Realizing our mortality. Always striving for the "Right way to live."

My concept of psychological health is being free from anxiety. In other words, not having so many things to worry about that I can't think about anything else or get my work done.

It is the balance or imbalance of a person's emotional habits—how well they can adjust to certain things that happen in everyday life.

Being able to adapt yourself to life. Adjusting to your social and business pressures, etc. Functioning: no matter what the circumstances or situations.

The students who wrote those responses were not advanced psychology students. Their replies were written during their third week of instruction, and represent commonsense views of psychological health. As such, they are quite congruent with views of psychological health set forth by professional psychologists. Keep the student responses in mind as we turn to a more formalized presentation of the concept of psychological health.

A UNIFYING VIEW

A unifying view of personality appreciates that no one attribute is *the* key attribute of psychological health. The human personality is complex, consisting of a set of attributes. Moreover, the set of attributes tends to take on different patterns in different individuals. It would seem reasonable to assert that there is no one unique pattern that represents psychological health. The concept of psychological health must certainly allow for individual differences in human beings. Having said this, let me—with some trepidation—abstract from the seven pathways, the major psychologies presented in this book, the implicit attributes associated with psychological health. Keep in mind that the statements listed are sweeping abstractions and, as such, will simultaneously have the advantage of great power and the disadvantage of being much too general. Psychologically healthy persons tend to manifest the following characteristics:

1 *Insight.* Healthy persons have a substantial amount of insight into their motivational structures. They are not the slaves of forbidden desires and repressed wishes. A minimum of self-deception is practiced.

2 *Positive habits.* Healthy persons are more or less free of "bad" habits. They have established a set of "good" habits. It might also be argued that healthy persons are able to modify, extinguish, or break habits when they are motivated to do so.

3 *Clear thinking.* Healthy persons have a great capacity for reality-oriented clear thinking. They are more rational than irrational, allowing for the notion that a bit of irrationality can itself be of some value for psychological health. Also, healthy persons can use their capacity for clear thinking to cope constructively with their emotions. Thus they are not at the mercy of chronic anxiety, anger, or depression.

4 *Effective communication.* Healthy persons have the ability to communicate effectively. They are able to state their desires and feelings without putting down another person. It is presumed that the capacity for effective communication is of particular importance in highly significant interpersonal relationships—those involving parents, children, husbands, wives, and close friends. Communication skills enhance the likelihood that intimacy, or emotional closeness, will emerge and endure between two persons.

5 *Physical well-being.* Healthy persons have organic as well as psychological health. The supposition is that we are organisms and that any division we might care to make between mind and body is arbitrary. It takes a well-balanced biochemical state within the brain and nervous system to produce what people call "a healthy mind."

6 *Authentic living.* Healthy persons are, on the whole, able to lead authentic lives. They feel that they are not wasting their lives, that they are making the most of their talents and potentialities. Also, they have a well-defined sense of values. Living in terms of their values, they feel that life is meaningful and worth living. Similarly, they feel that they are in charge of their own existence, that they have the capacity to will their own behavior.

7 *Larger vision.* Healthy persons have what might be called "larger vision." They do not view their lives in small or petty terms. They see themselves as part of the grand sweep of existence. They usually have a strong identification with humankind, feeling an empathy for these famous lines by the English poet John Donne: "No man is an island, entire of himself. Every man is a piece of the continent, a part of the main."

These, then, are the attributes we may associate with psychological health as derived from the seven principal orientations toward human adjustment and personal growth presented in this book. A somewhat longer or shorter list might be presented. No pretense is made that the foregoing list is final or definitive. Indeed, you would do well to turn back to Chapter Seven and reread the list of attributes Maslow gave for self-actualizing persons. His conception of psychological health and the one presented in this chapter are similar.

CONCLUDING REMARKS
We adjust to external demands and may grow as persons throughout our lives. There is no such person as the individual who is well adjusted once and for all. If he existed, he would be a robot or one of Perls's paper persons. There is, similarly, no such human being as the self-actualized person, the person who has fulfilled every talent and potentiality. There are, instead, self-actualizing people, people who keep alive the "growing tip" of their personalities. In short, adjusting and growing are dynamic processes.

A perennial question asked by speculative philosophy is, What is the good life? Obviously, there is no categorical answer to this question. In a sense, this entire book is an attempt to give a partial answer to the question. Certain things are clear. The good life is not rooted to a particular kind of place—such as a commune or a kibbutz or a farm or the Big City. Nor is the good life tied to a particular time—such as the Good Old Days or the Age of Aquarius or the Golden Future. The good life may be found in various times and places because healthy personalities determine the good life.

Also, there are no absolute criteria for the good life. It is not possible to say that personal happiness can be found by having three children or a new car or $100,000 in the bank or a profession or any other explicit symbol of success. The criteria for the good life are largely subjective. They are determined by the individual's unique personality; they depend on what he finds to be rewarding, meaningful, and gratifying. The philosopher Bertrand Russell commented, "The good life is one inspired by love and guided by knowledge" (Egner, p. 17). This was his definition of the good life, and it allows for a broad range of personal interpretation. Perhaps Russell's definition will do. In any event, it is my hope that this book in some way contributes to a good life for you.

SUMMARY AND SELF-TEST

1 Eclectic thinkers say that there is a pathway of pathways leading to greater adjustment and growth.
T   F

2 A dynamic eclecticism is impossible.
T   F

3 Assertiveness training in behavioral psychology is similar to the concept of authentic living, or "being real," in existential-humanistic psychology.
T   F

4 The philosophy of determinism asserts that all behavior is caused.
T   F

5 Voluntarism, like determinism, asserts that all behavior is caused.
T   F

6 The view that consciousness is both real and powerful finds its strongest expression in the writings of the behaviorists.
T   F

7 Our secondary drives, or learned motives, are said to be acquired by conditioning.
T   F

8 Systematic thinkers tend to favor the view that the similarities among individuals are more important than the differences among individuals.
T   F

9 Ancient Eastern philosophy understands pairs of conceptual opposites in terms of *yin* and *yang,* the negative and positive aspects of the world.
T   F

10 The modern philosophy of science teaches that our various scientific theories represent Truth.
T   F

11 In the sciences, including psychology, just two kinds of models are used: (1) physical models and (2) ordinary language models.

T   F

12 Stochastic processes are probability processes in which events are neither wholly dependent on nor wholly independent of past occurrences.

T   F

13 Molecular behaviors are "big" behaviors, wide-ranging response patterns to the problems and challenges of daily living.

T   F

14 Plato's famous allegory concerning the prisoner in the cave was used to indicate that the concepts we have about reality are reality itself.

T   F

15 The text suggests that like the blind men approaching the elephant, each honest explorer into the domain of psychology comes home with the same vision of reality.

T   F

16 A unifying view of personality appreciates that no one attribute is *the* key attribute of psychological health.

T   F

17 Having a substantial amount of insight into their own motivational structures, psychologically healthy persons tend to practice a minimum of self-deception.

T   F

18 The text suggests that psychologically healthy persons have the capacity for clear thinking and that they can use this capacity to cope constructively with their emotions.

T   F

19 The text suggests that communication skills enhance the likelihood that intimacy, or emotional closeness, will emerge and endure between two persons.

T   F

20 The philosopher Bertrand Russell said that the good life is one inspired by love and guided by knowledge.

T   F

ANSWER KEY

1 *False.* Eclectic thinkers say that there is no single pathway that is *the* pathway leading to greater adjustment and personal growth.

2 *False.* A dynamic eclecticism is possible.

3 *True.* Assertiveness training in behavioral psychology is similar to the concept of authentic living, or "being real," in existential-humanistic psychology.

4 *True.* The philosophy of determinism asserts that all behavior is caused.

5 *False.* Voluntarism, unlike determinism, asserts that free will is a reality.

6 *False.* The view that consciousness is both real and powerful finds its strongest expression in the writings of the existential-humanistic psychologists.

7 *True.* Our secondary drives, or learned motives, are said to be acquired by conditioning.

8 *True.* Systematic thinkers tend to favor the view that the similarities among individuals are more important than the differences among individuals.

9 *True.* Ancient Eastern philosophy understands pairs of conceptual opposites in terms of *yin* and *yang*, the negative and positive aspects of the world.

10 *False.* The modern philosophy of science teaches that our various scientific theories are not Truth, but statements *about* reality.

11 *False.* In the sciences, including psychology, three kinds of models are used: (1) physical models, (2) ordinary language models, and (3) mathematical models.

12 *True.* Stochastic processes are probability processes in which events are neither wholly dependent on nor wholly independent of past occurrences.

13 *False.* Molecular behaviors are "small" behaviors. The reflexes discussed in the chapter on behavioral psychology provide examples of molecular behaviors.

14 *False.* Plato's famous allegory concerning the prisoner in the cave was used to indicate that the concepts we have about reality are not reality itself.

15 *False.* The text suggests that like the blind men approaching the elephant, each honest explorer into the domain of psychology comes home with a different vision of reality depending on his preconceptions, the quality of his data, and the particular aspect (or aspects) of behavior he chooses to study.

16 *True.* A unifying view of personality appreciates that no one attribute is *the* key attribute of psychological health.

17 *True.* Having a substantial amount of insight into their own motivational structures, psychologically healthy persons tend to practice a minimum of self-deception.

18 *True.* The text suggests that psychologically healthy persons have the capacity for clear thinking and that they can use this capacity to cope constructively with their emotions.

19 *True.* The text suggests that communication skills enhance the likelihood that intimacy, or emotional closeness, will emerge and endure between two persons.

20 *True.* The philosopher Bertrand Russell said that the good life is one inspired by love and guided by knowledge.

DISCUSSION QUESTIONS

RECURRENT ADJUSTMENT-GROWTH ISSUES

1   Recognizing that an absolute choice is unnecessary, do you nonetheless have a preference for determinism over voluntarism? Or do you prefer voluntarism over determinism?

2   How important is the idea of unconscious mental processes to you? Do you feel that our lives are largely under the control of invisible psychological forces?

3   Are you attracted to views which assert that the similarities among individuals are more important than the differences among individuals? Or are you more favorably disposed to views which assert that individual differences are more important than the similarities among individuals?

4   Do you accept the ancient Eastern philosophy of yin and yang? Or does it seem too glib to you, a philosophical, sugarcoated pill designed to smooth over real differences?

OF TRUTH AND MODELS

1   Can you accept the view that we can know about reality only indirectly through models? Or does this view somehow seem too limiting and confining? Is there any alternative?

2   What kind of impact did the allegory of the blind men and the elephant have on you?

PSYCHOLOGICAL HEALTH

1   What is your conception of psychological health?

2   What do the words "authentic living" mean to you?

3   The text suggests that psychologically healthy persons have what might be called "larger vision." What significance does this concept have in terms of your life?

4   From your point of view, what is the good life?

REFERENCES

Bush, R. R., and Mosteller, F. *Stochastic Models for Learning.* New York: John Wiley & Sons, 1955.

Egner, R. E., Ed. *Bertrand Russell's Best*. New York: New American Library, 1958.

Hilgard, E. R., and Bower, G. H. *Theories of Learning*, 3rd ed. New York: Appleton-Century-Crofts, 1966.

Saxe, J. G. "The Blind Men and the Elephant," in A. L. Alexander, ed., *Poems That Touch the Heart*. New York: Doubleday & Co., 1956.

Watts, A. *Meditation*. New York: Pyramid Communications, 1974.

Young, P. T. "An Eclectic in Psychology," in T. S. Krawiec, ed., *The Psychologists*. New York: Oxford University Press, 1972.

PHOTO CREDITS

Chapter One

Opener, Ray Ellis/Rapho-Photo Researchers. 5, Robert A. Issacs/Photo Researchers. 8, David Strickler/Monkmeyer. 20, Monkmeyer. 25, Sybil Shelton/Monkmeyer. 31, Mimi Forsyth/Monkmeyer.

Chapter Two

Opener, Springer/Bettmann Film Archive. 42, Courtesy GTE Service Corporation. 48, Van Bucher/Photo Researchers. 49 and 54, The Bettmann Archive. 57, from *The Standard Edition of the Complete Psychological Works of Sigmund Freud,* edited by James Strachey in collaboration with Anna Freud, Vol. XIX, 1923-1925, *The Ego and the Id and Other Works,* London, The Hogarth Press. 68, The Bettmann Archive. 77, Paul Conklin/Monkmeyer. 79, 87 and 88, The Bettmann Archive. 89, Hans Namuth/Photo Researchers.

Chapter Three

Opener, Alice Kandell/Rapho-Photo Researchers. 118, Marilyn Silverstone/Magnum. 123, Courtesy Stoelting Company. 127, Yan/Rapho-Photo Researchers. 134, David S. Strickler/Monkmeyer. 138, Sam Flak/Monkmeyer. 141, Suzanne Szasz/Photo Researchers. 150, Paul Conklin/Monkmeyer. 163, Carolyn Watson/Monkmeyer.

Chapter Four

Opener, Mimi Forsyth/Monkmeyer. 186, Les Mahon/Monkmeyer. 192, (left) Springer/Bettmann Film Archive, (right) Wide World Photos. 198, Fujihira/Monkmeyer. 205, UPI. 210, Hugh Rogers/Monkmeyer.

Chapter Five

Opener, Sybil Shelton/Monkmeyer. 229, Wide World Photos. 234, Myron Wood/Photo Researchers. 238, Mimi Forysth/Monkmeyer. 247, Springer/Bettmann Film Archive. 258, Mimi Forsyth/Monkmeyer. 267, Joel Gordon. 269, Bruce Roberts/Rapho-Photo Researchers.

Chapter Six

Opener, Lew Merrim/Monkmeyer. 288, Courtesy Wilder Penfield, M.D., Montreal Neurological Institute. 299, Mimi Forsyth/Monkmeyer. 309, Christa Armstrong/Rapho-Photo Researchers. 317, Robert Doisneau/Rapho-Photo Researchers. 322, Mimi Forsyth/Monkmeyer.

Chapter Seven

Opener, The Bettmann Archive. 344, Richard S. Durrance/Photo Researchers. 350, Jan Lukas/Rapho-Photo Researchers. 355, Lynn McLaren/ Rapho-Photo

Researchers. 357, The Bettmann Archive. 361, Bob Combs/Rapho-Photo Researchers, 368, The Bettmann Archive. 373, Alexander Lowry/Photo Researchers. 381, Springer/Bettmann Film Archive.

Chapter Eight

Opener, Tom Tucker/Photo Researchers. 403, Springer/Bettmann Film Archive. 410, The Bettmann Archive. 412, Wide World Photo. 422, Alexander Lowry/Photo Researchers. 431, Wide World Photos.

Chapter Nine

Opener, Bettye Lane/Photo Researchers. 455, Inger McCabe/Rapho-Photo Researchers. 460, Ed Caram/Photo Researchers.

GLOSSARY

Abreaction. An emotional release involving the "reliving" or vivid recall of painful emotional experiences. (p. 51)

Aboutism. In the context of Gestalt therapy, the tendency to make bland intellectualizations about one's existence. Perls also used the term to mean academic second-hand study as opposed to direct learning and first-hand experience. (p. 382)

Action-oriented meditation. Kind of meditation in which the meditator concentrates his attention upon a behavior pattern. (p. 430)

Active listening. Listening in such a way that one decodes the emotional message behind a set of surface words, and reflects this decoded message back to the speaker. (p. 369)

Activity. In transactional analysis, a form of social interaction in which the transactions are programmed by the nature of the material with which people are working. (p. 258)

Adjustment. Successfully adapting to one's environment; establishing a harmonious relationship with the environment. (p. 29)

Adult ego state. In transactional analysis, that aspect of one's personality capable of making decisions, planning ahead, and taking reality into account. (p. 238)

Affective disorders. Psychotic reactions characterized principally by disturbances of mood. The two principal kinds of affective disorders are involutional melancholia and manic-depressive reactions. (p. 16)

Alienation. The feeling that one is an outsider. A psychological state in which the individual does not feel a sense of belonging or identification with either nature or other human beings. (p. 17)

Alpha rhythm. An electroencephalographic pattern occurring at the rate of about eight to fourteen cycles per second. (p. 317)

Amaroscope. An instrument made up of photoelectric cells capable of transmitting visual patterns through the lower brain to the visual cortex. (p. 298)

Amphetamines. Various kinds of stimulants with a structure closely resembling the brain's own norepinephrine. (p. 309)

Amygdalae. Two almond-shaped brain structures located near the hypothalamus. They appear to play an important role in the experience of pain. (p. 292)

Anal-expulsive character. In Freudian theory, a personality structure underlying such behaviors as being disorderly, defiant, cruel to others, or "making a mess." (p. 64)

Anal-retentive character. In Freudian theory, a personality structure underlying such behaviors as being stingy, excessively orderly, and holding back affection. (p. 64)

Anal stage. In Freudian theory, the second psychosexual stage. This second psychosexual stage is estimated to last from about eighteen months of age to the third year of life. (p. 62)

Analytic therapies. Modes of psychotherapy that employ the concept of the unconscious, making the assumption that an analysis or interpretation of one's motivational structure will bring about insight itno the roots of a psychological-emotional problem. (p. 27)

Angular transaction. A transaction involving a total of three of the ego states of two people. (p. 249)

Anima. In Jungian theory, an archetype of the self representing one's female personality. (p. 84)

Animus. In Jungian theory, an archetype of the self representing one's male personality. (p. 84)

Anorexia nervosa. Chronic lack of appetite without apparent organic basis. A person suffering from anorexia nervosa finds food repugnant, and it is believed that this active rejection of food is associated with emotional conflicts. (p. 296)

Antabuse therapy. A form of aversion therapy in which the mixture of alcohol and antabuse in the body releases a toxin into the blood. (p. 125)

Anthropomorphism. Assigning human qualities to organisms or entities that are not human. (p. 186)

Antianxiety agents. Kinds of sedative-hypnotic agents widely prescribed to treat chronic anxiety associated with neurotic reactions. (p. 308)

Antihypertensive agents. Drugs used to combat chronic high blood pressure. (p. 311)

Antipsychiatry. A counterculture movement opposed to institutional psychiatry. (p. 375)

Antipsychotic agents. Drugs used to combat the effects of psychotic reactions. (p. 306)

Antiscript. In transactional analysis, the mirror image or logical opposite of the script. (p. 268)

Antisocial reaction. A kind of character disorder often characterized by a willingness to manipulate and use others with little regard for their feelings or well-being. (p. 18)

Antivitalism. Doctrine asserting that the existence of life can be explained without such concepts as the soul or a "vital energy." Antivitalism holds that life is explained by the interaction of known electrochemical reactions. (p. 50)

Anxiety reaction. A neurotic reaction characterized by chronic apprehension. (p. 13)

Apperception. Similar to the concept of *subliminal perception,* the ability of an organism to record an event without conscious awareness. (p. 45)

Apperceptive mass. A mental reservoir consisting of all of our ideas and all of our past experiences. (p. 46)

Archetype. In Jungian theory, an enduring pattern in the mind derived from centuries of similar experiences by members of the human race. The equivalent of instincts in animals. (p. 80)

Asanas. Various postures used in Hatha Yoga. (p. 413)

Assertiveness training. A program of learning designed to increase a person's competence in dealing with other human beings. (p. 158)

Astral body. According to Yoga, a "second" body made of finer matter than the ordinary body. Yoga teaches that the astral body can travel in higher dimensional planes. (p. 416)

Attitudinal values. Values that are realized by taking a courageous stance toward limiting conditions. (p. 373)

Attribution. In transactional analysis, a statement to the actual child that he has such-and-such personality characteristics. (p. 252)

Authentic living. Pursuing a life in which one is true to oneself as an individual, not pledging false allegiance to the values and standards arbitrarily imposed by other people or one's culture. (p. 344)

Authoritarian home. A home atmosphere in which the parent is a dictator, treating the children with little respect. (p. 368)

Autogenic training. An autosuggestive method of inducing relaxation developed in Germany in the 1920s. (p. 319)

Autonomic nervous system. The subsystem of the entire nervous system that controls the smooth muscles associated with the body's internal organs and endocrine glands. It is traditionally said to function on an involuntary basis. (p. 315)

Autonomy. Self-directed behavior. In the

context of transactional analysis, game-free and scriptfree living. (p. 268)

Aversion therapy. A form of hehavior therapy in which the cues that trigger an undesirable behavior pattern are paired with some noxious stimulus. (p. 124)

Avoidance conditioning. A form of conditioning in which an organism learns on cue to avoid contact with a particular kind of stimulus. (p. 142)

Banal manifestation. In transactional analysis, a version of one's life script that is nondramatic. (p. 267)

Barbiturate. Kind of sedative-hypnotic agent. A drug that acts as a sedative, depressing the brain's arousal mechanisms. (p. 307)

Basic anxiety. According to Karen Horney, the underlying feeling that one is alone and helpless in a hostile world. (p. 75)

Behavior therapies. Modes of psychotherapy that emphasize the importance of action in contrast to the concept of insight. Behavior therapies stress the extinction and/or modification of conditioned responses and habits. (p. 28)

Being. According to Heidegger, Being is the simple fact that a person or thing exists. He capitalizes Being in order to stress that existence is a concrete reality, not an abstraction. (p. 345)

Being-for-itself. As formulated by Sartre, the right of a human being to exist simply because he exists, not because he serves the purposes of others or of God. (p. 347)

Being-in-itself. According to Sartre, the kind of existence associated with things and animals. Existing without the ability to change given characteristics. (p. 347)

Being-in-the world. As formulated by Heidegger, existing as a person on this planet in a particular place and time. (p. 345)

Being needs. As formulated by Maslow, various aspects of the need for self-actualization. (p. 359)

Being real. In the context of Gestalt therapy, a phrase used by Perls to describe authentic living. (p. 384)

Beta rhythm. An electroencephalographic pattern occurring at the rate of about fourteen cycles per second or more. (p. 318)

Bhakti Yoga. Kind of Yoga in which mystical union with the All is achieved by the means of fervent worship. (p. 413)

Biofeedback training. A procedure by which a subject can learn to bring physiological processes under voluntary control. (p. 313)

Blockage. In transactional analysis, conceptualized as a condition in which there is a psychological barrier between one ego state and the Adult ego state. (p. 240)

Body-oriented meditation. Kind of meditation in which the meditator gives his attention to an autonomic process such as breathing. (p. 430)

Broken record. In assertiveness training, a skill that involves calm repetition of one's position. (p. 164)

Caffeine. An alkaloid substance that stimulates the activity of the central nervous system. (p. 308)

Cardia arrhythmias. Odd patterns in the usual pumping action of the heart. (p. 320)

Catastrophic thinking. As formulated by Ellis, a tendency to over-generalize in which a single negative instance of a phenomenon is used by the subject to predict total disaster. (p. 199)

Chakras. According to Yoga, wheel-like patterns of energy located at various places in the body. (p. 414)

Character disorder. Term used to describe an individual who exhibits irresponsible behavior in conventional terms. Synonymous with the term *personality disorder*. (p. 15)

Chemotherapy. Type of somatic therapy for mental illness. Various kinds of drugs are given to patients with the aim of altering their thought processes, perceptions, and moods. (p. 23)

Child ego state. In transactional analysis, a set of emotional "recordings" carried forward from childhood. (p. 231)

Chlorpromazine. Antipsychotic agent with a great calming effect on agitated mental patients. (p. 306)

Choleric. A temperament that is easily excited to anger. (p. 21)

Clarification. In the context of client-centered therapy, clarification takes place when the therapist abstracts the core or essence of a set of remarks by the clients. (p. 367)

Client-centered counseling. Form of counseling advocated by Rogers in which the person himself is the subject of interest, not his symptoms and problems. (p. 362)

Clinical antidepressants. Various kinds of stimulants that facilitate the production of norepinephrine. (p. 308)

Closure. As formulated by Gestalt psychology, the tendency of an incomplete figure to form an organized whole in perception. (p. 308)

Cocaine. A stimulant obtained from coca leaves. (p. 306)

Collective unconscious. In Jungian theory, an impersonal psychological level made of universal psychological patterns shared by the entire human race. (p. 79)

Compensation. An ego defense mechanism used to defend against feelings of inferiority. Striving to demonstrate that one is competent in areas where there is some question about one's competence. (p. 67)

Complementary transaction. A transaction free of conflict. On a transactional analysis diagram, the lines representing the transactions are parallel. (p. 243)

Concentration. In Gestalt therapy, a technique in which the person focuses on the here-and-now. (p. 383)

Concrete operations. As formulated by Piaget, it refers to a stage of cognitive development lasting from about the age of seven to the age of twelve. An intermediate stage of mental development in which the child elaborates his capacity for symbolic thought and becomes more flexible in his thinking. (p. 187)

Conditioned inhibition. In Hull's learning theory, a learned tendency not to respond to a conditioned stimulus. Conditioned inhibition is antagonistic to the conditioned response. (p. 129)

Conditioned response. A learned response. A response arising from a learned response potential. (p. 120)

Conditioned stimulus. A stimulus to which there exists in the organism a learned response potential. (p. 120)

Conduct disorder. Kind of a character disorder identified principally with alcoholism or drug addiction. (p. 18)

Congruence. As used by Rogers, it refers to the degree of agreement between one's self-concept and one's ideal self. (p. 365)

Conscience. In Freudian theory, a sub-agent of the superego. The conscience sets up inhibitions, restraints within the individual against taking certain kinds of actions. (p. 59)

Contamination. In transactional analysis, encroachment by the Parent or the Child ego states into the psychological territory of the Adult ego state. (p. 239)

Contiguity. In Guthrie's learning theory, the presentation to an organism of two stimuli at the same time. (p. 137)

Continuous reinforcement. Reinforcement in which there is a one-to-one relationship between the instrumental response and the reinforcer. (p. 145)

Contractual psychiatry. As formulated by Szasz, a kind of psychiatry in which the sufferer voluntarily seeks help, feels distressed, and may find relief. (p. 375)

Controlled folly. As taught by don Juan, a technique for dealing with personal disappointments in which one shifts one's attention beyond pain or loss associated with the immediate event. (p. 409)

Counterscript. In transactional analysis, what a child was told to do in words by parental figures as opposed to what he was programmed to do by ulterior psychological messages. (p. 268)

Creative self. According to Adler, the capacity of an individual to shape his own personality and his own destiny. (p. 356)

Creative values. Values that are realized by producitve action. (p. 372)

Crossed transaction. A transaction in which there is conflict between two or more people. On a transactional analysis diagram, the lines representing the transactions cross. (p. 246)

Dasein. According to Heidegger, Being-in-the world. Existing as a person on this planet in a particular place and time. (p. 346)

Daseinanalysis. As formulated by Binswanger, the analysis of Being-in-the-world. (p. 348)

Defense mechanisms. A set of psychological devices by which the ego distorts its perception of reality in favor of the fantasy-oriented wishes of the id. (p. 67)

Deficiency-needs. As formulated by Maslow, basic needs for food, water, safety, belongingness, love, respect, and self-esteem. (p. 359)

Delta rhythm. An electroencephalographic pattern occurring at the rate of about four cycles per second or less. (p. 318)

Delusion. A perception on the part of a given individual that most of us would reject as "untrue." (p. 14)

Democratic household. A home atmosphere in which there is a feeling of mutual respect between a child and his parents. (p. 368)

Depression script. In transactional analysis, a script in which the central theme is lovelessness. (p. 267)

Depressive neurosis. A neurotic reaction in which the person is discouraged, demoralized, and life barely seems worth living. (p. 13)

Depth psychology. The psychology of unconscious mental processes. (p. 42)

Determinism. The doctrine that all behavior is caused. (p. 452)

Dialogue. In Gestalt therapy, a technique used to help an individual deal with splits in the personality. For example, the person might speak first as his topdog and then as his underdog. (p. 382)

Discriminative stimulus. In instrumental learning, a stimulus that provides an organism with information that an operant act is presently paying off or not paying off. (p. 140)

Displacement. An ego defense mechanism in which the ego allows the individual to place upon one stimulus an emotional reaction that properly should be placed upon another stimulus. (p. 69)

Dream work. In Freudian dream theory, the distortion of the latent content into a symbolic manifest content that is relatively innocent to the conscious mind. (p. 52)

Drive. In learning theory, conceptualized as a source that energizes the behavior of an organism. (p. 136)

Drive-reduction theory. The hypothesis that habits are reinforced when they reduce the intensity of drive states within the organism. (p. 136)

Drug addiction script. In transactional analysis, a script in which the central theme is a dependence on a spectrum of drugs ranging from alcohol to caffeine. (p. 267)

Dualism. The philosophical position that the body and the soul (including the mind) are two distinct and different substances. (p. 6)

Duplex transaction. A transaction involving a total of four of the ego states of two people. (p. 250)

Dynamic psychology. Roughly synonymous with depth psychology. Any psychology that assumes there are unconscious psychological forces and that ideas within the mind push and shove each other about. (p. 55)

Dynamism. According to Harry Stack Sullivan, a behavioral pattern similar to a habit or a trait. The concept of dynamism stresses habitual reactions to other people. (p. 76)

Dyssocial reaction. A kind of character disorder in which an individual's behavior is "normal" in terms of the standards of an "abnormal" or antisocial subgroup. (p. 18)

Eclectic. Selecting from a variety of theories, schools, and methods. Seeing value in more than one point of view. (p. 450)

Ego. In Freudian theory, the *I* or the conscious center of the personality. The ego is said to be reality-oriented. (p. 56)

Egocentric. The inability to see any point of view but one's own. Perceiving the world as revolving about one's self. (p. 186)

Ego-ideal. In Freudian theory, a sub-agent of the superego. The ego-ideal sets an individual's level of aspiration, presenting him with a mental picture of what he should do with his life. (p. 59)

Ego state. As formulated by Berne, the actual experience of acting like a child, a parent, or an adult. (p. 231)

Ego strength. Primarily a psychoanalytic concept. A person with a high level of ego strength is well-oriented in time and space, knows the practical limits of his capacities, and in general is able to cope effectively with the challenges of life. (p. 58)

Electra complex. A term sometimes used to suggest the female counterpart of the Oedipus complex in males. (p. 63)

Electrical stimulation of the brain. A form of psychosurgery in which electrode implants are placed deep within the paleocortex ("old brain"), making it possible to apply small amounts of elec-

tric current to selected brain regions. (p. 291)

Electroconvulsive therapy. A kind of shock therapy in which electric current is used to induce a seizure. (p. 289)

Electromyograph. A record of momentary muscle tension. (p. 314)

Electroshock therapy. Type of somatic therapy in which a brief pulse of electricity is sent through the frontal portion of the brain. Used primarily for psychosis and extreme depression. (p. 289)

Elicited behavior. Behavior in which a particular stimulus produces a predictable response. (p. 140)

Emitted behavior. Behavior that does not appear to be a response to a readily identifiable external stimulus. (p. 140)

Emotional trauma. A painful psychological experience. (p. 64)

Empathic understanding. As formulated by Rogers, the capacity of a therapist to sense the client's world as if it were his own. (p. 366)

Empiricism. A philosophical doctrine that asserts that all of human knowledge is based on experience acquired via the sense organs. (p. 90)

Encounter groups. Groups in which people exchange thoughts and feelings for the purpose of maximizing human potentialities. Emphasis is on relatively normal people becoming more authentic and self-actualizing. (p. 379)

Erogenous zones. Sometimes referred to as erotogenic zones. Zones that are particularly rich in nerve endings responsive to touch. These are the oral, anal, and the genital areas. (p. 62)

Exhibitionism. The act of exposing one's body (often the genitals) in public places. (p. 18)

Existential guilt. Kind of guilt one experiences when one does not fulfill one's possibilities in life. (p. 348)

Existential-humanistic psychology. An orientation toward psychology that asserts the importance of human consciousness. The principal underlying assumption of existential-humanistic psychology is that self-awareness can make a crucial difference in the way we behave. (p. 340)

Existential neurosis. As formulated by Frankl, the kind of neurotic reaction experienced by the person who can see no purpose to his life, who can discover no meaning to his existence. (p. 371)

Existential position. A stance we take toward ourselves, our relationships with others, and life itself. (p. 251)

Existential therapies. Modes of psychotherapy that emphasize the importance of making the most of one's life. What is analyzed in the existential approach is the relationship of the person to existence itself. (p. 28)

Existential vacuum. As formulated by Frankl, the feeling that one's life is a ovid, that existence is empty of meaning. (p. 371)

Existentialism. A very general point of view in philosophy that places greater value on subjective experience than upon objective data. (p. 343)

Experiential values. Values that are realized by being open to impressions from the world. (p. 373)

Experimental neurosis. The deviant response pattern of an organism that cannot make an adequate discrimination between two conflicting conditioned stimuli. (p. 124)

Extensional words. Words that refer to direct perceptual objects such as a spoon, a dog, or a salt shaker. (p. 188)

Extinction. In conditioning theory, learning to stop responding to the conditioned stimulus. (p. 120)

Extroverted attitude. In Jungian theory, a tendency to have a dominant interest in the outside world as opposed to the inner world of thought and the mind. (p. 89)

Failure identity. As formulated by Glas-

ser, persons with a failure identity feel that they cannot achieve their goals. (p. 209)

False negative. In the context of the Tanner-Swets theory of visual detection, deciding that no signal is present when in fact a signal is present. (p. 411)

False positive. In the context of the Tanner-Swets theory of visual detection, deciding that a signal is present when in fact no signal is present. (p. 411)

Fantasy. An ego defense mechanism in which the ego allows the individual to indulge in imaginary wish-fulfilling experiences. (p. 68)

Fantasy enhancers. Psychedelic agents that are said to augment imaginative capacities. (p. 312)

Feeling enhancers. Psychedelic agents that are said to augment emotional responses. (p. 312)

Feeling-oriented meditation. Kind of meditation in which the meditator gives his attention to an emotion-laden symbol. (p. 430)

Feeling talk. As formulated by Salter, a systematic assertive skill in which the person more openly expresses feelings. (p. 163)

Fictional finalism. As formulated by Vaihinger and elaborated by Adler, the doctrine that one's imagined future determines one's present actions. (p. 354)

Fixation. In Freudian theory, refers to the libido or part of the libido becoming permanently attached to one of the infantile levels of psychosexual development. (p. 64)

Fogging. In assertiveness training, a skill that teaches acceptance of manipulative criticism by the strategy of superficially agreeing with a critic. (p. 165)

Formal operations. As formulated by Piaget, refers to the last stage of cognitive development. Characterized by the appearance of high-level cognitive capacities. (p. 187)

Free association. Used as a way of probing the unconscious mental processes of a patient in psychoanalysis. The patient is asked to relax and tell the therapist anything that comes to mind. (p. 72)

Frontalis. The forehead muscle. (p. 319)

Functional hypoglycemia. Hypoglycemia without apparent organic basis. (p. 300)

Game. Formulated by Berne, refers to a set of manipulative transactions between at least two people. (p. 261)

General semantics. An approach to adjustment and growth that places great emphasis on the importance of improving our language environment. (p. 187)

Genital stage. In Freudian theory, the final stage of psychosexual development. It is estimated that this stage begins approximately the twelfth or thirteenth year of life, and there is no psychosexual stage beyond it. (p. 63)

Gestalt. A German word with such meanings as pattern, configuration, and organized whole. (p. 380)

Gestalt techniques. In Gestalt therapy, various methods of helping an individual integrate fragmented parts of himself and to recognize the nature of impasses in his own life. (p. 382)

Grand mal seizure. A large convulsion manifested by the epileptic person. (p. 289)

Habit. In learning theory, conceptualized as a learned response pattern. (p. 453)

Hallucinogen. A drug that alters conventional perception and thought. (p. 311)

Hatha Yoga. Kind of Yoga used to help the individual attain better physical health. The most popular form of Yoga in the Western world. (p. 413)

Hedonism. As an explanation of human behavior, the view that pleasure and pain are the main factors in human motivation. (p. 135)

Higher-order conditioning. Learning to respond to a second conditioned stimulus in which the learning is reinforced by a first conditioned stimulus, *not* by an unconditioned stimulus. (p. 122)

Holism. The doctrine that an organism is an organized whole that cannot be meaningfully divided into parts. (p. 326)

Homosexuality. A preference for sexual activity with members of the same sex. (p. 18)

Hyperkinetic child. A child who strongly manifests such behavioral characteristics as impulsivity, distractability, excitability, perceptual problems, and motor coordination problems. Several theories exist to account for the behavior of the hyperkinetic child. (p. 310)

Hypochondriacal reaction. A neurotic reaction characterized by excessive worry over physical health. (p. 13)

Hypoglycemia. A pathological condition in which the individual suffers from chronic low blood sugar. (p. 300)

Hysterical neurosis, conversion type. A neurotic reaction in which anxiety is converted into a bodily symptom such as blindness, deafness, or paralysis. (p. 13)

Hysterical neurosis, dissociative type. A neurotic reaction in which the individual may manifest such symptoms as amnesia or multiple personality. (p. 13)

I-it relationship. A relationship in which the subject reduces the other individual to a thing or an object in the subject's environment. (p. 385)

I-thou relationship. As formulated by Buber, a relationship in which the subject recognized that the other individual is a real person with feelings and a world-view of his own. (p. 385)

Id. In Freudian theory, the primitive and basic portion of the personality. (p. 45)

Ideal self. The self that one feels he would like to be or that he ought to be. (p. 364)

Identification. An ego defense mechanism in which the individual associates his ego with the ego of an admired person. (p. 68)

Identity. A sense of continuity as a person. The feeling that one knows who one really is. Association of the self with one's social roles. (p. 209)

Impasse. In Gestalt therapy, a psychological block that keeps the individual from seeing the true nature of his problem. (p. 380)

Implosive therapy. A form of behavior therapy in which a client adapts to fearful stimuli by experiencing anxiety at very high levels. (p. 131)

Individual psychology. Approach toward psychology formulated by Adler. Individual's capacity to direct his own life. (p. 350)

Individuation process. In Jungian theory, a process of inner psychological growth. A tendency in the direction of self-realization and wholeness. (p. 93)

Inferiority complex. As formulated by Adler, a set of negative beliefs about oneself, all revolving about a central core. (p. 353)

Insight. In psychoanalytic theory, becoming aware of a previously unconscious idea or motive. Also, gaining greater understanding of a personal problem. (p. 73)

Instinctoid. Term used by writers such as Jung and Maslow to suggest inborn behavioral tendencies in human beings that bear distinct similarities to instincts in animals. (p. 359)

Institutional psychiatry. As formulated by Szasz, a kind of psychiatry in which the sufferer has psychiatric treatment imposed upon him. (p. 375)

Instrumental conditioning. Learning that certain actions will produce certain results. Performing in such a way as to obtain reinforcers. (p. 133)

Insulin coma therapy. A kind of shock therapy in which insulin is used to burn up blood sugar at a rapid rate, sending the patient into a coma. (p. 288)

Integral Yoga. As formulated by the Indian sage Aurobindo, a kind of Yoga combining the best elements of the five principal Yoga systems. (p. 414)

Intellect-oriented meditation. Kind of meditation in which the meditator gives his attention to something that stimulates or challenges his thinking capacities. (p. 429)

Intensional words. Words that refer to internal states or subjective evaluations such as anger, love, beauty, hunger, curiosity, frustration, hope, ecstasy, and decency. (p. 188)

Interpersonal processes. The psychological-emotional exchanges we have with other persons. Communication between human beings. (p. 226)

Intimacy. Psychological or emotional closeness. In transactional analysis, refers to gamefree emotional exchanges between people. (p. 269)

Introverted attitude. In Jungian theory, a tendency to have a dominant interest in the inner world of thought and the mind as opposed to the outside world. (p. 90)

Involutional melancholia. A psychotic affective disorder characterized by depression. Associated with the later years of life—the involutional or ''change of life'' portion of the life cycle. (p. 16)

Jnana Yoga. Kind of Yoga in which harmony with the Infinite is acquired through self-knowledge. (p. 413)

Karma Yoga. Kind of Yoga asserting that self-realization can be attained by leading a responsible life.

Knowledge of results. In the psychology of human learning, the principle that learning is facilitated if one knows the results of what one is doing. Similar to the concepts of reinforcement and feedback. (p. 314)

Koan. In Zen, a ''puzzler'' or thought-provoking paradox used to foster enlightenment. (p. 426)

Kundalini. According to Yoga, the name of the female serpent asleep at the base of the spine of the ordinary person. Yoga teaches that the Kundalini can be awakened by special techniques. (p. 415)

Latency stage. In Freudian theory, the fourth stage of psychosexual development. It is estimated that the latency stage lasts from about the sixth year of life to about the twelfth year of life. During the latency stage there is no conscious interest in sexuality. (p. 63)

Latent learning. Learning that takes place without reinforcement and lays dormant until it is ready to be used (p. 137)

Latent level. In Freudian dream interpretation, it refers to what the dream is about, what the dream means. The deep or real layer of the dream. (p. 71)

Law of effect. As formulated by Thorndike, the view that actions leading to a state of satisfaction are learned by the organism. (p. 135)

Libido. In Freudian theory, the energy that makes the mechanisms of personality go. Freud felt that this energy was both psychological and sexual in nature. (p. 61)

Limen. The threshold of consciousness. (p. 45)

Lobotomy. A surgical procedure in which the connections between the frontal lobes of the cortex are severed from the subcortex. (p. 290)

Logotherapy. As formulated by Frankl, a form of psychotherapy in which it is asserted that psychological health is associated with the capacity to express one's inborn will to meaning. (p. 370)

Long-range hedonism. As formulated by such thinkers as Ellis and Mowrer, the view that it is better to maximize one's total happiness over a lifespan than to live only for the pleasure of the moment. (p. 199)

Madness. A nonclinical term for psychotic reactions. (p. 377)

Madness script. In transactional analysis, a script in which the central theme is psychosis or a fear of psychosis. (p. 267)

Major Primal Scene. In Janov's primal theory, a single experience producing in the child a split between his real self and unreal self. (p. 95)

Major tranquilizers. Various kinds of drugs used to combat psychotic reactions. (p. 308)

Mandala. In Eastern religions, a venerated circular pattern. (p. 84)

Manifest level. In Freudian dream interpretation, refers to the surface features of a dream. (p. 71)

Mantra. A sacred word or chant used in meditation for the purpose of facilitating concentration. (p. 430)

Maya. In Eastern philosophy, the doctrine that the perceived world is an illusion veiling reality. (p. 405)

Meditation. Concentration of thought and attention. In Eastern philosophy, meditation is used to achieve mystical union with the All. In the West, meditation may be used with the lesser goal of finding greater serenity and peace of mind. (p. 429)

Megavitamin therapy. Prescribing massive doses of selected vitamins for a sufferer. Megavitamin therapy is applicable to both physical and psychological ailments. (p. 301)

Melancholic. A moody and easily depressed temperament. (p. 21)

Metrazol therapy. A kind of shock therapy in which Metrazol, a drug prepared from camphor, is used to induce convulsions. (p. 288)

Microrevolutions. In the context of antipsychiatry and the thinking of Laing, the making of significant modifications in family patterns and institutional psychiatry. (p. 376)

Minimal brain damage. A condition in which damage to the nervous system is so slight that the individual in question seems to be organically normal. (p. 303)

Minor Primal Scenes. In Janov's primal theory, transient experiences in which the parents fail to meet the child's basic psychological and emotional needs. (p. 95)

Minor tranquilizers. Various kinds of antianxiety agents used to treat neurotic reactions. (p. 308)

Molar behavior. "Big behavior" including such phenomena as how to raise children, communication between people, overcoming personal problems, seeking meaning in life, and so forth. (p. 457)

Molecular behavior. "Little behavior" including such isolated phenomena as reflexes, color perception, sensory thresholds, and the affects of massed practice on learning. (p. 457)

Mysticism. The doctrine that through the use of a power of the mind such as intuition it is possible for a human being to have a direct experience with God or Ultimate Reality. (p. 404)

Mystification of experience. As formulated by Laing, refers to the perceptions of a child in a family that sends to that child confusing and conflicting messages about life and himself. (p. 377)

Narcolepsy. An involuntary tendency to fall asleep at inappropriate times. (p. 294)

Negative reinforcer. A reinforcer that precedes an instrumental action. In such a case the instrumental action is a means of avoiding or escaping from the negative reinforcer. (p. 142)

Neurasthenic reaction. A neurotic reaction involving feelings of fatigue, lack of energy, and general weakness. (p. 13)

Neurosis. An emotional disorder often characterized by anxiety, restlessness, nervous tension, phobias, obsessive-compulsive patterns, and depression. The neurotic person has not broken with conventional perceptions of reality. He is struggling with his life situation. (p. 12)

Nicotine. A stimulant obtained from tobacco leaves. (p. 308)

Nihilism. The view that nothing, including existence, is of any value. A doctrine of scepticism in which the denial of our capacity to know anything for certain is made a central principle. (p. 370)

Nondirective counseling. An older name, no longer in vogue, for client-centered counseling. Suggested that the client-centered therapist does not give explicit advice to his client about how to conduct his life or how to solve a personal problem. (p. 366)

Nonordinary reality. According to don Juan, the world that appears during special states of altered consciousness. (p. 408)

Norepinephrine. A hormone produced by the adrenal glands. When found in the nervous system, it acts as a transmitter substance between neurons. (p. 307)

Nothingness. As formulated by Sartre, the other side of Being. (p. 346)

Noumenon. The thing-in-itself, the reality. (p. 364)

Numinous dream. In Jungian theory, a dream that seems to glow in the mind. A dream that is long-remembered and somehow seems to be of great importance. (p. 92)

Obsessive-compulsive reaction. A neurotic reaction characterized by a constant preoccupation with certain ideas. Partial relief is obtained by performing personal rituals designed to magically counteract the nagging ideas. (p. 113)

Oepidus complex. In Freudian theory, a set of conflicting ideas associated with a core incest fantasy during early childhood toward the parent of the opposite sex. (p. 50)

Operant behavior. Any behavior that produces a change in the external environment. Virtually synonymous with instrumental behavior. (p. 139)

Opiate. A narcotic with the dual actions of sedation and pain relief. In moderate doses, it produces euphoria or a sense of well-being. (p. 311)

Oral character. In Freudian theory, a personality structure underlying such oral gratifications as excessive talking, smoking, and eating. (p. 64)

Oral stage. In Freudian theory the first psychosexual stage, lasting from birth to between twelve and eighteen months of age. (p. 62)

Ordinary reality. According to don Juan, the world as perceived by the average individual, the consensual world. (p. 408)

Orthomolecular psychiatry. Kind of psychiatric practice in which the psychiatrist prescribes that the mental patient follow a sound nutritional regime. Often the psychiatrist prescribes massive doses of selected vitamins. (p. 301)

Oversocialized. As formulated by Eysenck, it refers to a person who is too concerned with the letter of the law, too inhibited, and correct to a fault. (p. 160)

Pantheism. A doctrine that asserts there is no distinction between the universe and God. (p. 404)

Paper people. A metaphor used by Perls to describe people who lack inner vitality, people for whom life is a lackluster affair with little zest, joy, or meaning. (p. 379)

Paranoia. A psychotic reaction characterized by an organized delusional system. (p. 16)

Parent ego state. In transactional analysis, a set of value-oriented "recordings" carried forward from childhood, consisting of a number of "oughts" and "shoulds." (p. 236)

Partial reinforcement. Reinforcement in which the instrumental response is successful in producing the reinforcer only some of the time. (p. 145)

Partial reinforcement effect. A phenomenon in which organisms manifest greater resistance to extinction when trained under conditions of partial reinforcement than when trained under conditions of continuous reinforcement. (p. 145)

Pastime. In transactional analysis, a series of complementary transactions having to do with a particular subject. (p. 258)

Peak experience. As formulated by Maslow, the experience associated with a wonderful moment in one's life—a moment of ecstasy, rapture, or creativity. (p. 361)

Pedophilia. A preoccupation with children as objects of sexual desire. (p. 18)

Perceptions. The organized wholes constructed by the individual out of the raw data of experience. (p. 410)

Perceptual-conscious. In early writings of Freud, the "surface" of the mind; the portion of the mind in moment-to-moment contact with reality. (p. 54)

Permissive home. A home atmosphere in which the child is allowed to be a dictator, often treating the parents with little respect. In the permissive home, freedom is confused with license. (p. 368)

Persona. In Jungian theory, an archetype of the self representing one's public self or social mask. (p. 85)

Personal Growth. As used in this book, synonymous with the concept of self-actualization: Developing one's talents and potentialities. (p. 30)

Personal unconscious. Concept introduced by Carl Jung to distinguish the Freudian unconsciousness from Jung's formulation of a collective unconscious. The personal unconscious consists of an individual's repressed ideas based on his unique personal experiences. (p. 79)

Personality. A more or less stable set of traits, habits, and motivational predispositions characteristic of a particular individual. (p. 26)

Personality disorder. Term used to describe an individual who exhibits irresponsible behavior in conventional terms. Synonymous with the term *character disorder.* (p. 15)

Phallic character. In Freudian theory, a personality structure associated with unresolved conflicts over masturbation and incest wishes. It is asserted that the person with a phallic character structure is unable to give others real love, only synthetic love. (p. 65)

Phallic stage. In Freudian theory, the third psychosexual stage. This third psychosexual stage is estimated to last from about the third year to the sixth year of life. (p. 62)

Phenomenal field. The world as the individual perceives it. (p. 364)

Phenomenology. The study of the way the individual perceives and constructs his own version of reality. (p. 364)

Phenomenon. The appearance of a thing in the mind, things as perceived. (p. 364)

Phlegmatic. An apathetic temperament. (p. 21)

Phobic reaction. A neurotic reaction characterized by irrational fear, a fear that the individual himself recognizes as groundless. (p. 13)

Placebo effect. The capacity of almost any treatment "to please" the patient or client and to elicit a temporary improvement. (p. 11)

Playing the projection. In Gestalt therapy, a technique in which the individual role plays his psychological projection. For example, an individual might role play objects in a dream. (p. 383)

Positive reinforcer. A reinforcer that follows an instrumental action. (p. 141)

Prana. A vital energy believed by yogis to be in the air we breathe. (p. 414)

Pranayama. Controlled kind of breathing used in Hatha Yoga. (p. 414)

Preconscious. In early writings of Freud, the portion of the mind just below the conscious surface; similar to the popular psychology concept of "the subconscious mind." (p. 54)

Pregenital sexuality. In Freudian theory, the sexual life of infants and children. Sensuous gratification received through erogenous zones in the early years, form-ing the foundation for genital or adult sexuality. (p. 61)

Preoperational thought. Thinking that is stimulus-bound, anthropomorphic, and egocentric. (p. 186)

Primary hypertension. High blood pressure of unknown origin. (p. 311)

Primary process. According to Freudian theory, the mental process used by the id; the process by which ideas have nonrational connections. (p. 53)

Principle of no-mind. In Zen, the teaching that too much conscious thought may interfere with spontaneous action. (p. 423)

Principle of no-thingness. In Zen, the teaching that the objects of perception are not things, but abstractions we have made out of the current of existence. (p. 421)

Principle of no-twoness. In Zen, the teaching that most dichotomies are false. (p. 423)

Projection. The tendency to perceive the external world in terms of our personal motivational structure. As an ego defense mechanism, a tendency to see our failures and shortcomings as arising from external sources. (p. 69)

Projective tests. Personality tests based on the assumption that an individual's response to an ambiguous stimulus reveals a great deal about his unconscious mental life. (p. 24)

Protein complementarity. The capacity of one protein to supplement another one. (p. 298)

psi abilites. Mental capacities asserted to transcend the mind's normal limits. Telepathy and extrasensory perception would be examples of psi abilities. (p. 416)

Psyche. Greek word for soul. Also used in psychology to signify the mind and/or the personality. (p. 6)

Psychedelic agents. Synonymous with psychotomimetic agents. Drugs that produce an experience in the taker similar to the experience of a psychotic reaction. (p. 312)

Psychic determinism. The point of view that all mental events have a cause. (p. 44)

Psychoanalysis. Refers to both a theory of personality and a kind of psychotherapy. Based on Freud's thinking with an emphasis on the importance of unconscious aspects of mental life. (p. 47)

Psychological functions. In Jungian theory, the processes by which the consicous mind orients itself toward the outer world and the inner world. Jung designated four psychological functions: thinking, feeling, sensation, and intuition. (p. 90)

Psychological testing. The giving of standardized tests of intelligence, personality, aptitude, or interest. (p. 23)

Psychomotor epilepsy. A form of epilepsy in which the patient is conscious during a seizure, but lacks voluntary control over his actions. (p. 295)

Psychopharmacological agents. Drugs that affect perception, thought, and emotion. (p. 313)

Psychopharmacology. The study of how drugs affect psychological and emotional processes. (p. 305)

Psychosis. The psychiatric term used to denote extreme mental illness. A person who is manifesting a psychotic reaction seems to lose contact with conventional perceptions of reality. Such individuals display poor space-time orientations and disordered thought processes. (p. 14)

Psychosocial development. Development of the human personality based upon a child's relationship with significant other persons in his life. (p. 76)

Psychosomatic illness. An illness that is either caused by psychological-emotional factors or greatly aggravated by them. (p. 311)

Psychosurgery. Type of somatic therapy for mental illness. A broad term that includes lobotomy and electrical stimulation of the brain. (p. 290)

Psychotechnology. In broad general terms, almost any aspect of applied behavioral science. Tends to be associated primarily with such domains of interest as psychosurgery, nutrition and behavior, drugs, and biofeedback. (p. 286)

Psychotherapy. Treatment of emotional and behavioral disorders by psychological methods. (p. 17)

Psychotomimetic agents. Drugs that produce an effect that is said to "mimic" or copy the experience of a psychotic reaction. (p. 312)

Racket. In transactional analysis, a person's unique pattern of cashing in psychological trading stamps for either bad or good feelings. (p. 259)

Radical psychology. A counterculture movement within psychology which asserts that most existential suffering is due to oppressive aspects of familiar social institutions. (p. 374)

Raja Yoga. "Royal" Yoga, the oldest form of Yoga. In Raja Yoga, meditation is used to pierce the veil of maya in order to attain ecstatic union with the All. (p. 413)

Rational-emotive therapy. As formulated by Ellis, an approach to adjustment and growth in which the client is encouraged to replace irrational ideas with rational ones. (p. 197)

Rationalization. An ego defense mechanism in which a cover motive replaces a real motive when the real motive is unacceptable to the ego. (p. 67)

Reaction formation. An ego-defense mechanism in which a repressed thought or feeling is converted into its conscious opposite. (p. 66)

Reactive inhibition. In Hull's learning theory, a temporary fatiguelike process that acts to suppress a conditioned response. (p. 126)

Reality therapy. As formulated by Glasser, an approach to adjustment and growth that emphasizes facing reality and accepting responsibility. (p. 204)

Reciprocal inhibition. In systematic desensitization, the use of relaxation to counteract anxiety. (p. 126)

Recognition hunger. In transactional analysis, the need to have others confirm one's presence and existence. (p. 233)

Refined carbohydrates. Carbohydrates modified from original organic wholes into processed products. Examples are white flour and table sugar. (p. 300)

Reflection. In the context of client-centered therapy, reflection takes place when the therapist repeats fragments of what the client has said with very little change, conveying to the client a non-judgmental understanding of his statements. (p. 367)

Regression. An ego defense mechanism in which the individual exhibits behavior patterns that brought comfort at an earlier age. (p. 66)

Reinforcer. A stimulus that increases the probability of occurrence of a certain class of behavior. (p. 133)

Relaxation response. As formulated by Benson, an innate pattern that is antagonistic to the fight-or-flight reaction. (p. 433)

Repression. A process by which a psychological force opposes certain ideas and shoves them "down" into the nether territory of the unconscious. (p. 55)

Reserpine. A drug extracted from the Rauwolfia serpentina plant. The drug is sometimes used to treat psychotic reactions. (p. 306)

Resistance. A concept used in psychoanalysis to indicate mental blocks that thwart honest self-disclosure. Also used to indicate the unwillingness of a patient to accept a psychoanalytic interpretation. (p. 72)

Respondent behavior. Term used by Skinner to identitfy behavior associated with classical conditioning. Refers to behavior elicited by known stimuli. (p. 140)

Reward. As distinguished from a reinforcer in learning theory, a reward is defined in terms of what the giver of the reward subjectively believes to be of value to another organism. (p. 141)

Rinzai Zen. A school of Zen Buddhism utilizing the *koan* or paradoxical question as a device for hastening the arrival of *satori* or illumination. (p. 425)

Ritual. In transactional analysis, a series of predictable complementary transactions. (p. 257)

Samadhi. The supreme goal of Yogic training. Experience of great bliss associated wtih mystical union with God, the All, or Ultimate Reality. (p. 414)

Sanguine. An optimistic and good-natured temperament. (p. 21)

Satori. In Zen, a sudden awakening in which the spell of maya is cast off. (p. 424)

Schizophrenia, catatonic type. A psychotic reaction characterized by withdrawal, inactivity, and sometimes by odd postures and poses. (p. 16)

Schizophrenia, hebephrenic type. A psychotic reaction characterized by regression to an infantile level of functioning. (p. 16)

Schizophrenia, paranoid type. A psychotic reaction characterized by feelings of grandeur or persecution. (p. 16)

Schizophrenia, simple type. A psychotic reaction characterized by a general disintegration of the personality. (p. 16)

Script protocol. According to transactional analysis, a crude image of how the future will be. The choice of a script protocol is a decision made by the Child ego state. (p. 266)

Scripts. In transactional analysis, an unconscious life plan. (p. 265)

Secondary process. According to Freudian theory, the mental process used by the ego; the process by which we are in contact with reality, think logically, and make rational decisions. (p. 63)

Sedative-hypnotic agents. Chemical substances that depress the action of brain arousal mechanisms. (p. 307)

Self-actualization. As formulated by Goldstein, striving toward becoming a complete person. As elaborated by Maslow, an inborn tendency to make the most of one's possibilities as a person. (p. 30)

Self-alienated. As formulated by Laing, a personality that is torn apart. A psychological situation such that a false outer self represses a real inner self. (p. 377)

Self-concept. The way the individual sees himself, consisting of the attributes he perceives himself as having. (p. 364)

Self-regard. As formulated by Rogers, it refers to the need to have a reasonably positive estimate of one's self. (p. 365)

Semantic reaction. An emotional response to a word. (p. 189)

Sensations. The raw data of experience underlying organized perceptions. For example, patches of color and brightness are some of the sensations making up the organized perception of a landscape. (p. 410)

Sexual deviations. Forms of sexual behavior our society defines as either taboo or criminal. (p. 18)

Shadow. In Jungian theory, an archetype of the self representing the animal side of one's personality. Similar to Freud's concept of the id. (p. 88)

Shock therapies. Therapies in which the treatment involves sending the organism into a state of shock by either electrical or chemical means. (p. 288)

Shooting script. In transactional analysis, an unconscious life plan filled out with a cast of actual characters. The shooting script is associated with adulthood. (p. 266)

Social interest. According to Adler, an inborn drive to be gregarious and also

concerned about the welfare of other human beings. (p. 355)

Somatic nervous system. The subsystem of the nervous system that controls the muscles attached to the skeleton. Traditionally, said to be under one's voluntary control. (p. 315)

Somatic therapies. Therapies applied directly to the body for the purpose of alleviating the effects of mental illness. (p. 22)

Soto Zen. A school of Zen Buddhism advocating a gradual approach to satori. Emphasis is placed on seated meditation. (p. 425)

Spontaneous recovery. The reappearance after a rest period of a conditioned response previously extinguished. (p. 121)

Stimoceiver. An electrode-radio brain implant that can receive activating messages and also transmit information about brain states. (p. 292)

Stimulants. Drugs that tend to increase one's alertness, quickening central nervous system arousal mechanisms. (p. 308)

Stimulus-bound. As formulated by Piaget, refers to a child's thinking when he makes his evaluations on the basis of one and only one outstanding aspect of a stimulus situation. (p. 186)

Stimulus generalization. Progressive decrements in the magnitude of a conditioned response on either side of an original conditioned stimulus value. The capactiy of an organism to detect similarities and differences among a set of conditioned stimuli. (p. 122)

Stimulus hunger. The craving for some kind of sensory input. (p. 256)

Stochastic processes. Probability processes in which events are neither wholly dependent on nor wholly independent of past occurrences. (p. 457)

Stroke. In transactional analysis, any act that recognizes the presence of another person. (p. 233)

Structural analysis. In transactional analysis, structural anaysis is the study of how the three ego states—Parent, Adult, and Child—relate to each other in a single individual. (p. 243)

Structure hunger. The craving for "something to do" or "somewhere to go." (p. 256)

Style of life. According to Adler, the unique set of strategies the individual develops to cope with situations and attain his goals. (p. 353)

Sublimation. In Freudian theory, a process in which direct sexual expression of libido is repressed and reappears in modified form as a general interest in the wider world. (p. 63)

Subliminal perception. The ability of an organism to record an event without conscious awareness. (p. 45)

Success identity. As formulated by Glasser, persons with a success identity feel that they will achieve their goals. (p. 209)

Superego. In Freudian theory, that aspect of the personality that orients itself toward abstract concepts of good and bad, right and wrong, decency and indecency. The superego is said to be morality-oriented. (p. 58)

Superiority striving. According to Adler, a striving to make the most of oneself. (p. 352)

Superman. According to Nietzsche, a person with the strength and the will to rise above the gray existence of the masses. (p. 345)

Survival of the fittest. As formulated by Darwin, only those organisms most suited to their environments live long lives and produce large numbers of offspring. Each organism struggles for its existence in competition with other organisms. (p. 345)

Swami. A Yoga master. (p. 412)

Synapse. The gap between two neurons. (p. 307)

Synergic society. A society in which people cooperate together for mutual advantage. (p. 362)

Systematic desensitization. A learning procedure by which an individual learns to adapt to anxiety-arousing and fear-arousing stimuli. In systematic desensitization, the noxious stimuli are presented in a hierarchy from most noxious to least noxious. (p. 119)

Systematic thinkers. Advocates of one particular school of thought such as psychoanalysis or behaviorism. (p. 451)

Tabula rasa. As formulated by the philosopher John Locke, the view that the mind at birth contains no inborn ideas. (p. 90)

Tai Chi Chuan. A Chinese discipline requiring that the individual perform movements consciously and deliberately. (p. 430)

Tao. In Chinese thought, the fundamental principle of life. The Way, the Master Way, of existence. (p. 418)

Taoism. The ancient religion of China. (p. 418)

Tender-minded. According to William James, it refers to a trait of temperament in which the individual tends to be characterized by the following adjectives: Rationalistic, intellectualistic, idealistic, optimistic, monistic, religious, feeling-oriented, free-willist, and dogmatical. (p. 6)

Theta rhythm. An electroencephalographic pattern occurring at the rate of about four to eight cycles per second. (p. 318)

Topdog. As formulated by Perls, an aspect of the human personality tending to be righteous, authoritarian, and a bully. (p. 379)

Tough-minded. According to William James, it refers to a trait of temperament in which the individual tends to be characterized by the following adjectives: Empiricistic, sensationalistic, materialistic, pessimistic, pluralistic, irreligious, hard-headed, fatalistic, and skeptical. (p. 6)

Trading stamp. In transactional analysis, a psychologcal unit used to "purchase" both bad and good feelings. (p. 259)

Transaction. According to Berne, the

unit of social intercourse in which there is some sort of communicative give and take between at least two persons. (p. 243)

Transactional analysis. As formulated by Berne, an approach to adjustment and growth that emphasizes the positive value of nonmanipulative communication. (p. 226)

Transcendental Meditation. A Yogic technique brought to the widespread attention of Americans by the Maharishi Mahes Yogi. In Transcendental Meditation, the meditator focuses on a *mantra* as a means of attaining a state of pure awareness. (p. 431)

Transference. In psychoanalytic theory, the transfer by patients of feelings held in childhood toward their parents to the therapist. (p. 74)

Transpersonal psychology. An orientation toward psychology representing a blend of Eastern philosophy, esoteric knowledge, and Western psychology. "Mental science" in contrast to tough-minded behavioral science. (p. 402)

Trepanning. Surgery performed upon the skull. (287)

Ulterior transactions. Transactions containing a hidden message. (249)

Unconditional positive regard. As formulated by Rogers, an orientation on the part of the therapist in which the client as a person is not judged by the therapist. (p. 366)

Unconditioned response. A response that is not learned. A response arising from a presumably inborn response potential. (p. 120)

Unconditioned stimulus. A stimulus to which there exists in the organism an unlearned response potential. (p. 120)

Unconscious mind. In early writings of Freud, a domain of the personality not accessible to the conscious ego. (p. 42)

Underdog. As formulated by Perls, an aspect of the human personality that plays the crybaby and tries to "win by losing," employing such strategies as apology,

defensiveness, cussing, whining, and the like. (p. 379)

Undersocialized. As formulated by Eysenck, it refers to a person who is not sufficiently concerned with the law and the rights of others. (p. 160)

Voluntarism. The doctrine that free will is a reality. (p. 453)

Voyeurism. A preoccupation with attaining sexual gratification by looking at arousing stimuli (for example, a nude member of the opposite sex or a couple engaged in coitus). (p. 18)

Will to meaning. As formulated by Frankl, an inborn impulse that motivates us to do things that make sense to us in terms of our place in the larger scheme of things. (p. 370)

Will to power. As formulated by Nietzsche and elaborated by Adler, the contention that there is an inborn tendency in all of us to gain ascendency over others. (p. 345)

Yang. In Eastern philosophy, the name given to positive aspects of the world. (p. 454)

Yin. In Eastern philosophy, the name given to negative aspects of the world. (p. 454)

Yoga. A world-view associated with East Indian philosophy. Yoga teaches that it is possible for the person to go beyond maya or perceptual reality and achieve perfect union with God or Ultimate Reality. (p. 403)

Yogi. One who practices Yoga. The term suggests that the practitioner has attained a certain level of expertise. (p. 313)

Za-zen. As advocated by Soto Zen, seated meditation in an approved posture. (p. 425)

Zeitgeist. A German word referring to the dominant mood or way of thinking typical of a particular culture or time period. (p. 47)

Zen Buddhism. A meditative approach to Buddhism in which a prime goal is to see into one's own true nature. (p. 318)

INDEX